Media and the Well-Being of Children and Adolescents

Media and the Well-Being of Children and Adolescents

EDITED BY
AMY B. JORDAN

and

DANIEL ROMER

OXFORD
UNIVERSITY PRESS

OXFORD
UNIVERSITY PRESS

Oxford University Press is a department of the University of Oxford.
It furthers the University's objective of excellence in research, scholarship,
and education by publishing worldwide.

Oxford   New York
Auckland   Cape Town   Dar es Salaam   Hong Kong   Karachi
Kuala Lumpur   Madrid   Melbourne   Mexico City   Nairobi
New Delhi   Shanghai   Taipei   Toronto

With offices in
Argentina   Austria   Brazil   Chile   Czech Republic   France   Greece
Guatemala   Hungary   Italy   Japan   Poland   Portugal   Singapore
South Korea   Switzerland   Thailand   Turkey   Ukraine   Vietnam

Oxford is a registered trademark of Oxford University Press
in the UK and certain other countries.

Published in the United States of America by
Oxford University Press
198 Madison Avenue, New York, NY 10016

© Oxford University Press 2014

Library of Congress Cataloging-in-Publication Data
Media and the well-being of children and adolescents / edited by Amy B. Jordan & Daniel Romer.
pages cm
Includes bibliographical references and index.
ISBN 978-0-19-998746-7
1. Mass media and children—United States.   2. Mass media and teenagers—United States.
3. Child welfare—United States.   I. Jordan, Amy B. (Amy Beth) editor of compilation.
HQ784.M3M4193 2014
302.23083—dc23
2013039920

9 8 7 6 5 4 3 2 1
Printed in the United States of America
on acid-free paper

CONTENTS

CONTRIBUTORS

Craig A. Anderson, PhD, is Distinguished Professor of Liberal Arts and Sciences and director of the Center for the Study of Violence in the Department of Psychology at Iowa State University.

Jeanette Betancourt, EdD, is senior vice president for Community and Family Engagement at Sesame Workshop.

Amy Bleakley, PhD, MPH, is a senior research scientist at the Annenberg Public Policy Center of the University of Pennsylvania.

Dina L. G. Borzekowski, EdD, is a professor at the University of Maryland, School of Public Health in College Park, Maryland.

Jane D. Brown, PhD, is professor emeritus of journalism and mass communication at the University of North Carolina at Chapel Hill.

Stephanie C. Brown is a graduate student in the Department of Psychology at Iowa State University.

Sandra L. Calvert, PhD, is a professor of psychology and director of the Children's Digital Media Center at Georgetown University.

David Cohen is director for Research and Evaluation at Sesame Workshop.

Anne Collier is founder and executive director of Net Family News, Inc., and co-director of ConnectSafely.org.

Sherine El-Toukhy, PhD, is a postdoctoral research associate at the Gillings School of Global Public Health at the University of North Carolina at Chapel Hill.

Douglas A. Gentile, PhD, is an associate professor of psychology at Iowa State University.

Jennifer L. Harris, PhD, MBA, is a senior research scientist and director of marketing initiatives at the Rudd Center for Food Policy & Obesity at Yale University.

Amy B. Jordan, PhD, is director of the Media and the Developing Child sector of the Annenberg Public Policy Center at the University of Pennsylvania.

Jennifer Kotler, PhD, is vice president of Research and Evaluation at Sesame Workshop.

Alexis R. Lauricella, PhD, MPP, is a research associate at the Center on Media and Human Development at Northwestern University.

Dafna Lemish, PhD, is interim dean and a professor in the College of Mass Communication & Media Arts at Southern Illinois University and founder and co-editor of the *Journal of Children and Media*.

Michael H. Levine, PhD, is executive director of the Joan Ganz Cooney Center.

Sonia Livingstone, PhD, is a professor of social psychology in the Department of Media and Communications at the London School of Economics and Political Science.

Marisa Nightingale is senior media advisor for the National Campaign to Prevent Teen and Unplanned Pregnancy.

Rebecca Ortiz, PhD, is an assistant professor of advertising in the College of Media & Communication at Texas Tech University.

Sara Prot is a graduate student in the Department of Psychology at Iowa State University.

Michael Rich, MD, MPH, is an associate professor of pediatrics at Harvard Medical School, and director of the Center on Media and Child Health.

Melissa N. Richards, MPP, is a graduate student in the Department of Psychology at Georgetown University.

Daniel Romer, PhD, is associate director of research at the Annenberg Public Policy Center of the University of Pennsylvania.

Victor C. Strasburger, MD, is Distinguished Professor of Pediatrics and Family & Community Medicine at the University of New Mexico School of Medicine.

Edward L. Swing, PhD, is director of research at the Arizona Pain Specialists. and a graduate student in the Department of Psychology at Iowa State University.

Lori M. Takeuchi, PhD, is director of research at the Joan Ganz Cooney Center.

Sarah Vaala, PhD, is a postdoctoral research fellow at the Annenberg Public Policy Center of the University of Pennsylvania.

Ellen Wartella, PhD, is Al-Thani Professor of Communication, a professor of psychology, a professor of human development and social policy, a professor of medical social sciences, and director of the Center on Media and Human Development at Northwestern University.

Michele Ybarra, PhD, is president and research director of the Center for Innovative Public Health Research.

PREFACE

Amy B. Jordan and Daniel Romer

Media and the Well-Being of Children and Adolescents is a book born from a conference of the same name held at the Annenberg Public Policy Center of the University of Pennsylvania in April 2012. More than 100 students, scholars, researchers, media industry professionals, advocates, and funders spent a beautiful spring day in Philadelphia discussing the ways in which media technologies have changed the experience of childhood. Our focus was not solely on media's harmful effects, nor were we Pollyannaish about media's benefits for the developing child. Instead, we approached the topic of youth and media with an eye toward balance and the need to consider the three C's of media research: content, context, and child characteristics (Guernsey, 2007; Linebarger & Vaala, 2010).

Content

Dan Anderson and colleagues offer a compelling statement in their 2001 monograph, in which they describe the findings of their longitudinal study on the effects of television on children's academic achievement. They write, "Marshall McLuhan appears to have been wrong. The *medium* is not the message. The *message* is the message" (p. 134). This research team found that preschoolers' viewing of educational television was associated with greater reading, higher grades, and greater creativity in high school, even while taking into account all the variables we know would affect school performance, such as family SES and child IQ. Viewing the same amount of entertainment media, such as superhero cartoons, was associated with lower grades in girls and higher aggression in boys. As this and many other studies have shown, media are not monolithic and content matters. Even video games, which are often written off as innocuous time wasters at best and violence-inducing at worst, can foster prosocial skills, are effective teaching aids, and can encourage healthier lifestyles. As Sara Prot and colleagues write in chapter 7, media, including video games, "are better understood in terms of multiple dimensions than a 'good or bad' dichotomy." Similarly, as noted by Jane Brown, Sherine El-Toukhy and Rebecca Ortiz in chapter 6, though media provide many problematic portrayals of sexual behavior, adolescents' exposure to safe sex behaviors in entertainment-education programming can lead to greater self efficacy to engage in safe sex.

Context

So much of what children learn from the content of media is interpreted through the lens of the important people (such as parents) and settings (such as schools) that guide their development. As Amy Bleakley and colleagues illustrate in chapter 1, children grow up immersed in media technologies. According to the Annenberg Media Environment Survey, conducted with a national sample of more than 1,500 parents, children and adolescents spend nearly 3 hours a day watching television, 1½ hours using the computer, and just over 1 hour playing video games. Their bedrooms are often multimedia centers – nearly half have a TV, one third have a DVD player, and nearly a quarter have a desktop or laptop computer. Add to this the video game consoles, iPads, and e-readers that are widely available in the home, particularly to teens, and one imagines that the context of childhood has become centered around screens. But this is only part of the story of what it means to grow up in the twenty-first century. The "digital generation" still has parents, teachers, peers, and other important people who exist in "real life" settings and who shape how they think about and what they do with media. As Lori Takeuchi and Michael Levine write in chapter 2, "Too often, research on media effects and/or learning with media focuses on the human-computer interaction to the exclusion of what surrounds these interactions, including the human-human, human-environment, even environment-environment interactions that simultaneously shape the mediated experience" (p. 37).

Research often overlooks vulnerable children who grow up in contexts in which media can actually help prepare them for the challenges they face, whether it is dealing with devastating natural disasters (chapter 10) or having a parent deployed in war (chapter 14). As Dafna Lemish writes in chapter 10, we need to ask ourselves, "How can we use different means of communication to make a difference, most specifically to vulnerable and disadvantaged children, in ways that build their resiliency to survive, thrive and set them off on a trajectory of a better life?" (p. 170).

Child Characteristics

Just as we cannot treat media content as though it were monolithic, we cannot treat children as though they respond to media in exactly the same way. Children's developmental trajectories are shaped by a variety of factors, including their familial characteristics, their personality traits, their cognitive capacities, and, of course, their age. As Jennifer Harris writes in chapter 4, younger children are more susceptible to advertising because it is not until about the age of 7 or 8 that they begin to understand the persuasive intent of the ads they see (until then, children see ads as a source of information). As children grow, so too does their interest in the larger world—and their opportunities for risk taking. We observe, for example, that teenagers who are exposed to alcohol advertising and portrayals of characters using alcohol in the media are more at risk for underage drinking (see Victor Strasburger, chapter 5). However, understanding the unique characteristics of youth audiences can allow producers to craft messages that resonate with their developmental ages and stages. Ellen Wartella and Alexis Lauricella write in chapter 11 that when media are created with a clear curriculum that acknowledges how young children learn, this can enhance early learning. And as Marisa Nightingale describes in chapter 13, it is possible to work with media producers to create messages that correct the myths and misperceptions that teens have about sex and sexuality to reduce the likelihood of teen pregnancy. But this can only happen if we acknowledge and account for the unique characteristics of children's and adolescents' views of the world and their place in it.

The Organization of This Volume

This volume brings together some of the best and brightest media scholars and practitioners to reflect on the role of media in the well-being of children and adolescents. We have identified salient issues, both in terms of new media platforms and effects outcomes, and have considered what is known and what still needs to be more thoroughly investigated. The book unfolds in four parts.

We begin by offering a "big picture" perspective on media in the lives of young people. Amy Bleakley, Sarah Vaala, Amy Jordan, and Dan Romer (chapter 1) present data that show the ubiquity of traditional and new media in American homes, as well as the amount of time children and adolescents spend engaged with screens. By exploring age-based differences in media access and time, we see how media use varies across the stages of childhood. In chapter 2, Lori Takeuchi and Michael Levine use Urie Bronfenbrenner's ecological systems theory to highlight how media use both reflects and shapes the various contexts of children's lives, for better or for worse. The authors point out, for example, that while Voice over Internet Protocol (VoIP) connections forge deeper relationships between people regardless of distance (for example, schoolchildren in Osaka can now connect with schoolchildren in San Francisco via Skype), personal devices such as smartphones are also blamed for disrupting interactions among individuals living beneath the same roof: they spend more time looking at screens than at each other.

Next we examine the concerns we have about the ways in which media can interfere with healthy development or encourage risk taking among children. In chapter 3, Dina Borzekowski examines the evidence for the impact of media on children's weight. She writes that media contribute to childhood obesity through increasing children's sedentary behavior and promoting the consumption of unhealthy foods and beverages. What's more, she argues, the media create unrealistic expectations about body image because they portray uncharacteristically thin characters as having ideal body types, and at the same time they show no consequences of these characters' poor nutritional practices. Children and adolescents who are exposed to these images develop poor body self-image, which can lead to extreme dieting and a generally unhealthy relationship with food. Jennifer Harris, in chapter 4, develops the argument that food and beverage marketing to children is a major factor in the rise of pediatric obesity, and she cites research that shows that most parents do not understand the impact that food advertising has on their children's food preferences and diet.

We also examine the negative effects of media on issues that are particularly salient for adolescents. In chapter 5, Victor Strasburger explores how media may implicitly and explicitly encourage smoking, illicit drug use, and underage alcohol consumption. And in chapter 6, Jane Brown, Sherine El-Toukhy, and Rebecca Ortiz lay out the evidence for the ways in which exposure to sexual media content affects relationship beliefs, sexual initiation, and sexual risk taking. In the final two chapters of this section, authors examine the effects of particular media platforms. Sara Prot and colleagues synthesize the evidence of the effects of video game playing in chapter 7, focusing on violent video games and their effect on aggressive behavior. In chapter 8, Sonia Livingstone reviews research from the EU Kids Online project, which investigated the risks and harms of Internet use by 9- to 16-year-olds in 25 different countries.

This section explores the ways in which opportunities for positive youth development are enhanced by the media. It begins with Michele Ybarra's synthesis of how digital media technology has been used to affect youth behavior change. In chapter 9, Ybarra also highlights the ways that she and her colleagues have been able to use Internet and text-message-based programs to promote HIV prevention in Uganda and encourage smoking cessation in Turkey. As Dafna Lemish describes in chapter 10, media can also be effective aids for children in vulnerable circumstances, such as war or natural disaster. Her work on UNICEF's resource package entitled *Communicating with Children: Principles and Practices to Nurture, Inspire, Excite, Educate and Heal* also includes a checklist of principles that can be used to produce children's media and also to evaluate existing materials. The final two chapters of this section focus on the potential of educational media to advance young children's learning. Ellen Wartella and Alexis Lauricella (chapter 11) consider whether and how newer digital technologies can enhance academic readiness, while Sandra Calvert and Melissa Richards (chapter 12) find that the parasocial relationships that children form with media characters function much like "real life" friendships. In both chapters, we see that early experiences with media can and should be optimized to afford the best possible social, cognitive, and physical outcomes.

This section also offers a trio of chapters that look at how research on the effects of media on children and adolescents can inform the efforts of those who work within the media industry. In chapter 13, Marisa Nightingale takes readers behind the scenes as she describes the ways in which The Campaign to Prevent Teen and Unplanned Pregnancy works with Hollywood to create more realistic and prosocial messages about sex. David Cohen, Jeanette Betancourt, and Jennifer Kotler (chapter 14) describe the development, reach, and effectiveness of a preschool series from Sesame Workshop to help the children of military families as they prepare for deployment or deal with injury and loss. The last chapter of this section (chapter 15) comes from Anne Collier, who offers an overview of the evolving media-related concerns that we have had as a society and that are often overblown by the news media. She offers an important reality check on what we really need to worry about, as well as sage advice for parents and child advocates who seek to maximize the benefits and minimize the risks of growing up in a digital age.

We conclude *Media and the Well-Being of Children and Adolescents* with a chapter that considers what we have not covered in this volume as well as opportunities for future research. Dr. Michael Rich, who was at our 2012 conference on Media and the Well-Being of Children and Adolescents, joins us in considering the future of the field. Despite the challenges of rapid change and limited research funds, scholars have made incredible progress in illuminating the ever-increasing role of media technology in children's development. Our hope and expectation is that the reflections of the authors contained within this volume serve to advance the conversation.

References

Anderson, D., Huston, A., Schmitt, K., Linebarger, D., & Wright, J. (2001). Early childhood television viewing and adolescent behavior: The recontact study. *Monographs of the Society for Research in Child Development*, 66(1), i–vii, 1–147.

Guernsey, L. (2007). Into the minds of babes: How screen time affects children from birth to age five. New York, NY: Basic Books.

Linebarger, D. L. & Vaala, S. E. (2010). Screen media and language development in infants and toddlers: An ecological perspective. *Developmental Review*, 30(2), 176–202.

CHAPTER 1

The Annenberg Media Environment Survey

MEDIA ACCESS AND USE IN U.S. HOMES WITH CHILDREN AND ADOLESCENTS

Amy Bleakley, Sarah Vaala, Amy B. Jordan, and Daniel Romer

In April 1962, months before their city was to host the World's Fair, third-graders from a Seattle elementary school were asked what predictions they had for the twenty-first century (Broom, 2012). Their expectations included personal rockets for space travel, flying cars, and new, futuristic food products. Though one young student did foresee that "you will be able to have a telephone in your pocket" in the new millennium, developments in media technology were largely not considered by these young visionaries. Fifty years later their children and grandchildren likely have much difficulty imagining life in a home with only one television set and four channels, let alone a childhood devoid of computers, tablets, video games, cell phones, MP3 players, and other near-ubiquitous modern technologies.

As media technologies and content have proliferated and evolved over the years, so too have their potential—and the potential pitfalls—with regard to family life and children's development. Decades of research on television, for example, have identified numerous favorable outcomes associated with viewing quality, age-appropriate programming, including improved academic achievement and school readiness skills (e.g., Anderson, Huston, Schmitt, Linebarger, & Wright, 2001; Rice, Huston, Truglio, & Wright, 1990) and positive social-emotional development (Mares & Woodard, 2012). However, the same body of literature also suggests a host of unfavorable consequences of television viewing, such as increased aggression (Huesmann, Moise-Titus, Podolski, & Eron, 2003; Paik & Comstock, 1994); overweight and obesity (Gortmaker et al., 1996; Robinson,

1999); decreased academic performance (Borzekowski & Robinson, 2005; Shin, 2004), and materialism (Buijzen & Valkenburg, 2003). Overall, existing literature indicates that the extent and nature of influence depends on characteristics of the combination of media content, child viewer, and media use context.

Increasingly, scholars perceive the value in understanding the home media context (Clark, 2012). Mapping the landscape of families' home media access and use is critical not only for its own sake, but also to better understand the patterns of use and influence of media among youth. A number of prior studies have shown that the nature of children's home access to media, such as the number and placement of televisions, is related to the amount of time they spend consuming media (e.g., Cillero & Jago, 2010; Jackson, Brown, & Pardun, 2008; Jordan et al., 2010; Saelens et al., 2002). The rules parents set about the amount and types of media content their children are allowed to consume also predicts the extent of children's exposure (Barradas, Fulton, Blanck, & Huhman, 2007; Cillero & Jago, 2010), and are influenced in turn by the benefits and drawbacks parents perceive with regard to children's media use (Valkenburg, Krcmar, Peeters, & Marseille, 1999; Warren, Gerke, & Kelly, 2002). Research indicates that patterns in parents' media use are consistently related to their children's media consumption as well (e.g., Bleakley, Jordan, & Hennessy, 2013; Davison, Francis, & Birch, 2005).

Ecological systems (Bronfenbrenner, 1979) and social cognitive theories (Bandura, 1986) offer insight into these and other observed relationships between structural and relational home environments and youth media use. Ecological systems theory contends that children's lives and development unfold within the "nested environments" in which youth are embedded (Bronfenbrenner, 1979; Jordan, 2004; Takeuchi & Levine, this volume). These environments include children's immediate contexts, such as home and school, as well as broader contexts that may have more indirect influence, such as cultural norms and institutions. Media can influence children's lives and development directly as youth consume and interact with various platforms in their everyday lives. Media can also affect children through more indirect pathways. For example, parents' use of digital technologies in the workplace could influence their use of and attitudes toward media, which could affect the atmosphere of the home as well. Additionally, the surrounding culture relays messages to youth about the value and normative use of media technologies, which can influence their own patterns of use in turn (see Takeuchi & Levine, this volume).

Based on social cognitive theory, youth observe the actions of others around them—in person or via media—as well as the consequences of those actions (Bandura, 1986). The likelihood that a child will imitate the behavior they view depends on various factors including the attractiveness or perceived similarity of the model and the nature of consequences of the behavior to the model and others around him/her. Considering media use as one such behavior, then, youth may pattern their own media use after the media use they observe among their parents and siblings (see Notten, Kraaykamp, & Konig, 2012). Together, these two theories shed light on the means through which the home environment can socialize children into various patterns of media consumption.

Children and adolescents in the U.S are living in media-saturated homes (Rideout, 2011; Rideout, Foehr, & Roberts, 2010). Parent surveys conducted by the Kaiser Family Foundation (Rideout et al., 2010) and Common Sense Media (Rideout, 2011) indicate that the number of technologies to which youth have access, as well as the amount of time they spend consuming media, increased during the first decade of the new millennium. The present chapter offers an updated snapshot of the media environment and consumption patterns among a national sample of parents with children ages 17 and under. We conducted the Annenberg Media Environment Study (AMES) to update our knowledge of media trends in U.S. households with children since the earlier surveys. AMES was conducted in March 2012 with a national sample of 1,550 parents (54% female) who had children 17 years old or younger. We examined the media technologies available in the home, patterns of media use by parents and their children, and parents' practices and concerns regarding their children's media use in households with children in three age groups: 5 years and younger, 6–11 years, and 12–17 years.[1] Survey questions asked specifically about a "target child" in one of the above age groups (St. Peters, Fitch, Huston, Wright, & Eakins, 1991) because media behaviors and parents' attitudes would most likely vary by child age. Unless otherwise noted, the results we present were weighted to match national household demographics for each age group.

The average age of the parents in the survey was 38.8 years old. The racial/ethnic breakdown of parents in the sample matched U.S. demographic profiles: 64% white, 12% African-American, 17% Hispanic, and 6.5% other. Nearly one-third of parents had a bachelor's degree or more education (32%), 28.9% attended some college, and 39.2% received less than high school or a high school education. The median income level was $60,000. Forty percent of the households had just one child between birth and age 17 in the home, 39% had two children, and the rest (21%) reported having three or more children living in the home. The majority of respondents were married or living with a partner (86%), and 68% reported being currently employed.

Media Access in the Home

Parents were asked about media that were accessible in different rooms of their homes. Nearly all households had at least one TV in the household (98%), as well as a DVD player (91%). On average, the households in the sample reported three televisions and two DVD players in the home. Present in 76% of homes, video game consoles were limited to approximately 1 per home (1.2). Most homes also contained a desktop or laptop computer (89%), with families having one or two computers (1.6) on average. Internet access was present in multiple (2.7) rooms. Cable/satellite access, present in 77% of homes, could also be found in multiple rooms of the house on average (2.3).

We were particularly interested in the media available in the target child's bedroom. Access to television in the child's bedroom is associated with heavier television use (Jordan et al., 2010) and the initiation of health risk behaviors in adolescents (Jackson et al., 2008), as well as less physical activity, poor dietary habits, and poorer school performance (Barr-Anderson, van den Berg, Neumark-Sztainer, & Story, 2008). The effects of access to other media in the bedroom are less well studied, but equally important now that television content is available on multiple platforms (e.g., computers). For example, about one-quarter (27.3%) of the teens in this survey who *did not* have a television in their bedroom had a computer there, and 89% of those with bedroom computers had internet access in their bedroom as well.

As shown in Figure 1.1, bedroom media access was highest among 12- to 17-year-olds for every medium. Bedroom television reached 63% of adolescents, with internet access being almost as common (54%). Not surprisingly, internet access was heavily tied to having a computer in the bedroom. For 6- to 11-year-olds and 12- to 17-year-olds, of those with a computer in their rooms, 91% and 92% respectively had access to the internet. Similarly, 85% of those children ages 5 and younger with a computer in their bedroom had internet access in their bedroom as well. Since more youth have internet access than have a computer, it is likely that youth are accessing the web through their smartphones, tablets, or other portable devices (Madden, Lenhart, Duggan, Cortesi, & Gasser,

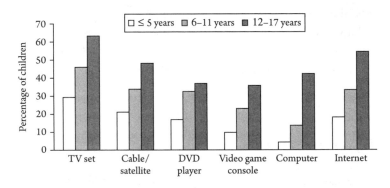

Figure 1.1 Media in Children's Bedrooms.

2013). Notably, although bedroom television sets were less prevalent than in previous surveys, bedroom internet access was higher than in earlier reports (Rideout et al., 2010). For example, in the 2009 Kaiser Family Foundation survey, Rideout and colleagues (2010) found that 76% of 11- to 18-year-olds had a television set in their bedrooms and only 33% of 8- to 18-year olds had bedroom internet access.

The media environment in parents' bedrooms seemed to largely revolve around television sets. Figure 1.2 shows the different media available, with 70% of parents reporting that they have a television in their bedroom. Cable/satellite access and DVD players accompany television access in most cases. And while slightly more than one-quarter of parents had a desktop or laptop computer in their bedroom (27%), 88% of that group also had internet access in their bedroom. Particularly rare were video game consoles, present in less than 10% of parents' bedrooms (8.4%).

In addition to the bedrooms of target children and parents, TV sets and their associated cable access and DVD players were common in the social spaces of the home. Table 1.1 presents data on the media available in different rooms in the home. The distribution of internet access across various rooms of the home is also notable, due likely to wireless internet capabilities and portable media technologies. Just as in the child's bedroom, internet access exceeds the presence of computers, suggesting that many children and adolescents can access online media content throughout their homes (Madden et al., 2013).

Use of new media technologies is also growing in U.S. households with children. Comparisons with prior surveys suggest rates of mobile device ownership are rising, at least among homes with very young children. The Common Sense Media report in 2011 indicated that 21% of children under age 8 had access to a video iPod or similar device, 9% had an e-reader, and 8% had a tablet device such as an iPad in the home (Rideout, 2011). Within the AMES sample, 28% of

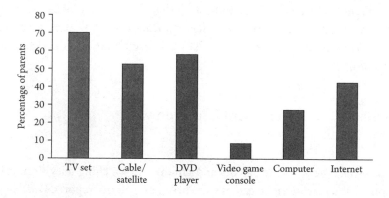

Figure 1.2 Media in Parents' Bedrooms.

Table 1.1 **Weighted Percentage of Households with Access to Media, by Room**

	Television	DVD Player	Video Game Console	Desktop or Laptop	Internet Access	Cable or Satellite Access
Child's bedroom	48.0	35.7	29.4	23.9	22.4	37.2
Other bedrooms	36.5	20.0	12.3	14.6	28.5	24.2
Family room/den	54.2	46.3	31.1	29.3	42.5	42.3
Living room	62.8	51.7	33.0	28.7	45.8	48.4
Kitchen	8.3	1.6	0.5	5.7	21.8	6.1
Dining room	1.9	0.8	0.7	4.7	20.2	1.8
Other room (home office, garage, bathroom, basement)	19.1	11.0	9.0	24.0	33.4	17.3

children 5 and younger had access to a video iPod or similar device within the home, 20% had an e-reader, and 25% had an iPad or other tablet.

In comparison, 44% of children 8 and younger in the Common Sense Media study owned handheld video game consoles. Similarly, the most common portable media in our survey were handheld video game players, with 72.4% of households with 6- to 11-year-olds and 66.4% of households with 12- to 17-year-olds reporting that they are available in their homes. Thirty-five percent of parents of children 5 or younger also reported owning a video game player, which in households of that age group is as common as a portable DVD player (35.6%) and a DVR (35.5%). Figure 1.3 shows the availability of other new media technologies in households by age group of the target child. Having a DVR, e-reader, and tablet did not vary by child age, indicating that those technologies are perhaps driven by parent use, in contrast to video game players, DVD players, and video iPods or related devices which are most likely used by the (older) children in the homes.

Time Spent by Parents and Children with Major Media Devices

Estimates of time spent by parents and children in watching television, using a computer, and playing video games were based on parents' reports. *Watching television* was defined by the following statement: "When we say TV, we mean TV

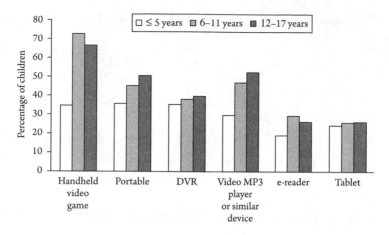

Figure 1.3 New Media Technologies in Children's Homes.

shows, DVDs, or movies that you watch on a television set or a computer." *Using a computer* was defined as using a desktop, laptop, or tablet, when not at work or working (for parents) and when not in school (for the target child). Finally, for *playing video games,* we told parents that "we mean those games that are played on a gaming console like PlayStation, Xbox, or Wii or a handheld device like Nintendo DS or PSP." Parents reported time spent with each device in 30-minute increments in the morning, afternoon, and evening, on a typical weekday (i.e., last Tuesday) and a typical weekend day (i.e., last Saturday). While it is common to use parental reports of their children's media time, studies have shown that parents tend to underestimate their children's screen time (Bryant, Lucove, Evenson, & Marshall, 2007; Gortmaker et al., 1999; Jordan, Hersey, McDivitt, & Heitlzer, 2006).

Tables 1.2a and 1.2b provide average daily time spent with television, computers, and video games for parents and their children, respectively. Children's time spent with these devices increased with age, with rates tending to converge with that of their parents for TV and computers. Increased media use

Table 1.2a **Parent Average Daily Time (in Hours) Spent with Media**

Media	Parents' Time Overall Mean [CI]	Parents of 5-Year-Olds and Younger Mean [CI]	Parents of 6- to 11-Year-Olds Mean [CI]	Parents of 12- to 17-Year-Olds Mean [CI]
Television	4.07 [3.86, 4.28]	4.19 [3.82, 4.56]	4.21 [3.73, 4.68]	3.91 [3.58, 4.24]
Computer use	2.69 [2.50, 2.88]	2.60 [2.27, 2.92]	2.79 [2.38, 3.19]	2.76 [2.48, 3.04]
Video games	0.71 [0.55, 0.87]	0.67 [0.48, 0.85]	1.24 [0.69, 1.79]	0.47 [0.30, 0.64]

Table 1.2b **Parent Estimates of Children's Average Daily Time (in Hours) Spent with Media**

Media	Child Time Overall Mean [CI]	Ages 5 and Under Mean [CI]	Ages 6–11 Mean [CI]	Ages 12–17 Mean [CI]
Television	2.81 [2.66, 2.97]	2.34 [2.08, 2.59]	2.83 [2.52, 3.15]	3.31 [3.05, 3.56]
Computer use	1.40 [1.27, 1.53]	0.36 [0.26, 0.46]	1.14 [0.94, 1.34]	2.56 [2.31, 2.82]
Video games	1.12 [0.94, 1.30]	0.43 [0.29, 0.57]	1.44 [0.99, 1.88]	1.60 [1.30, 1.90]

throughout early and middle childhood has generally been found in earlier surveys of youth media use as well (Rideout, 2011; Rideout, Foehr, & Roberts, 2010). The largest difference between age groups was in time spent using a computer, with adolescents spending approximately 3 hours per day, compared to 6- to 11-year-olds, who spent 1 hour and 8 minutes. This difference is consistent with greater reported access to computers in bedrooms among adolescents, as has been found with television (Jordan, et al., 2010). As discussed earlier, 42.3% of adolescents had a computer in the bedroom compared to 13.8% of 6- to 11-year-olds and 4.0% of children 5 and younger.

Parents only played video games at the same rate as their children in the 6- to 11-year-old age range: almost 1 hour and 15 minutes per day. However, parents of adolescents only played about 28 minutes a day, while their adolescents played at about the same rate as the 6- to 11-year-olds. It could be that video game playing is a more social, family-centered activity among families with 6- to 11-year-olds, and becomes more of a socially isolated activity in adolescence. This pattern may also reflect parents' greater concerns about possible harmful effects of video games on younger children compared to older adolescents, which may lead them to engage in more mediation of content when their children are younger.

Home Media Practices

The survey examined media practices in the home with regard to background television and screen time before bed. Background television, or having the television on when the child is not directly watching, is associated with several adverse outcomes in younger children, such as reduced social interaction and play behavior (Kirkorian, Pempek, Murphy, Schmidt, & Anderson, 2009; Schmidt, Pempek, Kirkorian, Lund, & Anderson, 2008), reduced executive function (Barr, Lauricella, Zack, & Calvert, 2010), and disrupted cognitive skill development (Barr et al., 2010). It is hypothesized that background television acts as a distraction from focused play by creating background noise and also may draw parents' attention away from their children (Kirkorian et al., 2009).

Another media practice is eating meals with the television on, which has been linked to unhealthy eating behaviors (Bellissimo, Pencharz, Thomas, & Anderson, 2007; Coon, Goldberg, Rogers, & Tucker, 2001; Fitzpatrick, Edmunds, & Dennison, 2007). Studies suggest that television interrupts individuals from recognizing physiologic cues about their satiety (Bellissimo et al., 2007). The relationship between eating with the television on and unhealthy eating could also be the result of exposure to television content that discourages the consumption of healthy foods; it may also indicate a larger family dynamic that could explain the association (Coon et al., 2001). Additionally, screen media before bedtime has been linked to poor sleep outcomes (Eggermont & Van den Bulck, 2006; Zimmerman, 2008). It is hypothesized that the brightness of the screen, whether it be a screen from a television, computer, or some portable device, suppresses melatonin production, a hormone that aids in bringing about sleep (Zimmerman, 2008).

To measure background television, parents were asked how often a TV was on in their home even if no one was watching (Vandewater et al., 2005), and how often TV was on in their home during meals. Response options for both items were as follows: never, a little of the time, some of the time, and most of the time. Figure 1.4 shows, by child age, the percent of parents who answered "most of the time." Approximately one-quarter of households across all child age groups reported the television being on in the background most of the time. Notably,

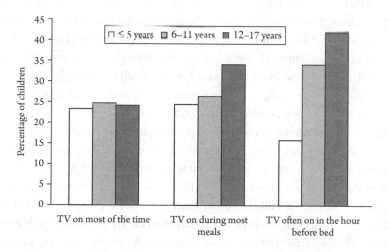

Figure 1.4 Household Media Habits.

this incidence is lower than the most recent prior surveys, which indicated that 39% of homes with children whose ages range from newborn to 8 years old (Rideout, 2011) and 45% of homes with children between the ages of 8 and 18 have the television on at least most of the time even when no one is watching it (Rideout et al., 2010). The television being on at mealtimes, also shown in Figure 1.4, is higher for families with adolescents than for families with younger children. However, given that only 8% and 2% parents report having a television in the kitchen or dining room, respectively, it seems likely that eating might be happening in other areas, or that the television is simply on in another room while the family eats in the kitchen or dining room.

We also asked about the use of any screen media (i.e., watching television or a movie; playing a video game; going on a computer; reading a book on an e-reader; or talking, texting, or going online with a cell phone) in the hour before bedtime. Parents reported that their adolescent children were more likely to use screen media "often" (compared to never, rarely, or sometimes) in the hour before bedtime than parents with younger children (see Figure 1.4). In other words, children's bedtime screen media use increased with age: from 15.8% among children 5 and younger, to 34% of 6- to 11-year-olds, and 41.8% of adolescents. This trend suggests that adolescents may be more at risk of sleep disruption due to screen exposure prior to bedtime.

Parental Concern about Media

We were interested to learn more about how concerned parents were about their children's media use. In addition, beliefs about media held by their parents are an important part of a child's media socialization. As one aspect of the home media ecology, parents' beliefs about children's media may affect their behavior with regard to children's media consumption (e.g., restricting children's viewing of certain types of content). We asked parents about how concerned they were (not at all, not really, somewhat, or very)—specifically with regard to their (target) child's exposure—about media content from various sources, issues specific to internet use (e.g., online bullying), and the use of mobile devices.

Table 1.3 displays the percentage of parents, by their child's age group, who reported that they were "very concerned" about each of these domains. In general, the extent of parents' concern about what their children are exposed to and the time they spend with media was less for adolescents than for younger groups. In addition, parents of children older than age 5 were more concerned about what their children may see on the internet than on TV or in movies. Moreover, concern about internet issues such as seeing inappropriate content, experiencing online bullying, being exposed to a predator, or receiving sexually explicit

Table 1.3 **Weighted Percentage of Parents "Very Concerned" about Media Content, Internet, and Mobile Use**

	Parents of 5-Year-Olds and Younger %	Parents of 6- to 11-Year-Olds %	Parents of 12- to 17-Year-Olds %
Media Content Concerns			
What child sees on television	34.5	34.6	19.2
What child sees at movies	25.3	31.8	19.0
Video games child plays	20.5	20.8	12.0
Computer games child plays	21.2	25.3	13.3
Magazines child reads	19.1	21.0	12.4
Content of books child reads	19.5	20.9	13.4
Music lyrics child listens to	23.9	28.2	19.4
Internet Concerns			
What child can see on internet	28.4	47.8	31.2
Child could be target of online bullying	19.5	31.1	21.4
Child could be exposed to predator	26.1	45.5	37.6
Child could receive sexually explicit pictures	24.4	37.0	31.4
Mobile Use Concern			
Time child spends talking and texting on phone	13.3	16.2	15.5

pictures was highest among parents of 6- to 11-year-olds. This pattern in parents' concerns according to their children's age is counter to the trend reported in a 2007 Kaiser Family survey of parents with children from 2 to 17 years old, which found that parents' concerns about the negative influence of media rose as children grew older (Rideout, 2007). Again, this divergence may reflect methodological differences or changes in parents' concerns about media.

Another common concern among parents is that media use may decrease the time their child spends reading. Fifty-three percent of parents with a 6- to 11-year-old and 50% of parents with an adolescent agreed that television viewing would decrease reading time. The concern was not limited to television, however. Among parents of 6- to 11-year-old children, 41.6% agreed that internet use would decrease the time their child spent reading, and 45.6% thought the same of video game playing. Adolescents' parents had similar levels of concern: 48.8% and 41.6% thought that internet use and video game playing, respectively, would displace reading.

There has been increasing concern about adolescents' exposure to video games, because many of these games involve violent content (see Chapter 7 by Prot and colleagues, this volume). Age- and content-based media ratings exist in part to help allay parental concern, and to help parents make informed choices about their children's media exposure. However, the different rating systems that exist for television shows, movies, music lyrics, and videos games have often been a source of confusion, about both the application of the ratings and whether or not parents find them helpful (Strasburger, Wilson, & Jordan, 2009). Indeed, violent content has been increasing in popular movies, with little difference between films rated as appropriate for children ages 17 and older (R) and those rated as appropriate for children 13 and older (PG-13) (Nalkur et al., 2010).

We asked parents in our sample how useful (not at all, not too, somewhat, very) the different rating systems were in helping to guide their family's choices. As shown in Table 1.4, less than 40% of parents overall found any of the rating systems "very useful." The percent of parents overall who found the ratings systems "very useful" was less than what has been reported in previous studies (Rideout, 2007). In analyses of a 2006 survey, Rideout (2007) found that 49% of parents with children ages 2 to 17 years found television ratings to be "very useful." For ratings of movies, video games, and music, the percentages of parents who felt the same were 53%, 58%, and 56%, respectively. Compared to other parents, more parents of 6- to 11-year-olds found the ratings to be "very useful."

Table 1.4 **Weighted Percentage of Parents Who Find Ratings for Media "Very Useful" by Age of Child**

	All Parents %	Parents of 5-Year-Olds and Younger %	Parents of 6- to 11-Year-Olds %	Parents of 12- to 17-Year-Olds %
Television ratings	27.4	27.8	35.8	22.0
Movie ratings	39.2	37.2	51.7	33.2
Music advisories	27.8	25.9	38.8	22.5
Video game ratings	34.3	32.2	47.9	26.5

Discussion

At a time of emerging new technologies and shifting media landscapes, AMES survey is a unique and up-to-date snapshot of the home media environments of children and adolescents. By providing data on the time youth spend with media in the context of household access, family practices, and parental media habits, we highlight key points from our findings on the various influences that shape media use among children and adolescents.

Youth of all ages are growing up in homes containing many and diverse media technologies. Our data confirm what may seem obvious: most households offer youth access to a range of traditional and new media. Interestingly, the average number of traditional media technologies, such as television sets, computers, and video game consoles, were slightly lower in the homes of the families that comprise our sample compared to national estimates from 2009 (Rideout et al., 2010). This may be due to increasing rates of ownership of mobile digital technologies, such as tablets, e-readers, handheld video game devices, and smartphones. Our analyses also suggest changes in youth bedroom media. Compared to reports from several years ago (Rideout, 2011; Rideout et al., 2010), our study finds fewer children and adolescents have a bedroom TV. However, the rates of bedroom computer and internet access seem to be increasing. As discussed by Sonia Livingstone (Chapter 8, this volume), this growth is noteworthy as internet-capable technologies provide youth with access to unique activities, such as social networking and instant messaging, while also serving as an alternative means for viewing television and video content.

Children's age is an important factor in their access to and time spent with media. Based on parents' estimates, both access to and time spent with television, computers, and video games increase as children get older. The role of age could be attributed to developmental differences, demands on their free time, or parents' ideas about the vulnerability of younger versus older children to potential adverse outcomes associated with media use. The higher rates of bedroom media and mobile media access in adolescence suggest that older children have more access to independent, unsupervised media use. Though television viewing still dominates their time spent using media, there are increasingly diverse ways in which teens access the internet, both at home and elsewhere. While the present study combines viewing of television content across platforms, research suggests that as much as 20% of media use among 8- to 18-year-olds occurs on mobile devices, with an additional 11% consisting of traditional media (e.g., television content, music videos) viewed on computers (Rideout et al., 2010). The development of media use habits during these years is particularly informative given that media use in adolescence is predictive of media use in adulthood (Hancox, Milne, & Poulton, 2004; Rideout et al., 2010).

Parents' concern about media content and it effects on their children is highest for parents of youth in middle childhood. Although adolescents have the most access to media and spend the most time with media, concern about media content and other issues is greatest among parents of 6- to 11-year-olds. Perceived usefulness of the ratings systems is also highest among parents of this age group, and supports the notion that parents may perceive youth at this age as more vulnerable and more impressionable than older children, or children under 5 whose media exposure is largely under parental control. Nevertheless, current ratings systems do not appear to be very helpful to most parents and, given their variation across media, they may be a source of confusion. Follow-up research is needed to determine whether parents would use more helpful ratings systems and how parents mediate their children's media use across age groups.

Youth spend many hours of their time outside of school with media. The American Academy of Pediatrics recommends that children over the age of 2 spend no more than two hours per day with noneducational or entertainment screen media (AAP, 2013). The results from this study indicate that only 34% of children older than 2 years are using screen media less than 2 hours per day. While the time estimates from AMES presented here do not take into account the *content* of the media (i.e., educational versus entertainment), other surveys have found that children's time with media consists primarily of entertainment media consumption (Anderson et al., 2001; Bickham et al., 2003; Rideout, 2011). As noted by Borzekowski (Chapter 3, this volume) and Harris (Chapter 4), the amount of time youth spend with media can have consequences for their physical well-being, for example. However, media content is a key determinant of numerous learning and behavioral outcomes (e.g., Anderson et al., 2001; Gottfried, Vaala, Bleakley, Hennessy, & Jordan, 2013; Romer, Bagdasarov, & More, 2013). Elsewhere in this volume authors consider the nature of the content with which children engage when examining specific outcomes such as sexual initiation (see Brown, El-Toukhy & Ortiz, Chapter 6, and Nightingale, Chapter 13) and academic learning (see Wartella & Lauricella, Chapter 11, and Calvert & Richards, Chapter 12).

The estimates of media use presented in this chapter do not account for the simultaneous use of multiple media, or media multitasking. Studies have reported that, on an average day, most youth (upwards of 80%) engage in multiple media use. Moreover, their media use is often in addition to another non-media activity, such as homework (Foehr, 2006; Roberts & Foehr, 2008). A substantial percentage (24–39%) of youth report that they engage in media multitasking "most of the time" that they use media, depending on the specific media in question (Foehr, 2006). The measurement implications of multiple media use present many challenges to researchers, and are often not carefully considered. Furthermore, the effects of using multiple media simultaneously on physical and behavioral outcomes are not yet well understood. Some studies suggest that media multitasking is associated with reduced attention and ability to filter distractions (Ophir, Nass, & Wagner, 2009) as well as a higher incidence of depression and social anxiety (Becker, Alzahabi, & Hopwood, 2013).

Parents spend a lot of time with media, regardless of their child's age. Some of the most interesting findings from AMES concern parental time spent with media, the inclusion of which is a unique feature of this survey data. Parent time with television is the same regardless of their child's age, but video game playing has a different pattern. Understanding parents' time with media is imperative because we know that parents' time with media is related to children's time, both among younger children (Bleakley, Jordan, & Hennessy, 2013; Davison et al., 2005; Hardy et al., 2006; Jago, Fox, Page, Brockman, & Thompson, 2010; Jago et al., 2008) and adolescents (Barradas et al., 2007). As social cognitive theory suggests, parents may model media behavior that their children begin to imitate over time (Bandura, 1986). Additionally, an ecological perspective of media use highlights the importance of household media use in the fabric of everyday family life (Bronfenbrenner, 1979).

Conclusion

As media technologies continue to evolve and youth continue to adopt them into their daily lives, it will be critical for researchers to develop innovative ways to capture an accurate picture of their daily media use. Such media use includes unprecedented use of cell phones and smartphones, which are replacing desktops and laptops as adolescents' primary devices to access the internet (Madden et al., 2013). As youth incorporate new platforms, devices, and technologies into their lives, one of the many challenges facing researchers is to understand the nature of and implications of such use in a timely way. However, understanding the environments and family dynamics that pertain to youth media use in its various forms helps to create the knowledge base necessary to realize the intervention potential of media in its various forms.

In addition to the role they play in the lives of youth, new technologies allow researchers to track the internet sites youth visit, the amount of time they spend on each site, and where they click on the screen (Vandewater & Lee, 2009). Modern study participants can also wear digital technologies that track and translate the video media they are exposed to throughout the day. Smartphone apps could be designed to enable more accurate experience-sampling methodologies; for example, because cell phones typically travel everywhere with their owners, an alarm in the phone could cue respondents to record and describe their current media use using the app. A limitation of traditional surveys such as AMES lies in the fact that parents often underestimate reports of their children's time spent with media (Bryant et al., 2007; Christakis & Garrison, 2009; Gortmaker et al., 1999; Jordan, Hersey, McDivitt, & Heitzler, 2006). Moving forward, alternatives to self- or parental reports need to be explored.

Although the results presented here are descriptive, they offer a foundation for pursuing richer, more detailed inquiries on the relationships among these structural and relational aspects of the home media environment. There is no question that media have become prominent in children's lives; as such, media use constitutes a prime context, much like home or school, through which youth learn, play, and develop. Understanding how the rapidly evolving media landscape affect children's development will require continued effort and innovative approaches from researchers, as well as clinicians, policy-makers, and child advocates.

Notes

1. Respondents were selected from an online probability panel (KnowledgePanel) recruited by GfK. The panel is designed to be representative of adults (ages 18+) in the United States. GfK relies on probability-based sampling to recruit households to the panel. Households are provided with access to the Internet and hardware if needed. Panel members are recruited through national random samples, originally by telephone and now almost entirely by postal mail. KnowledgePanel recruitment uses dual sampling frames that include both listed and unlisted telephone numbers, telephone and non-telephone households, and cell-phone-only households, as well as households with and without Internet access. Thus, KnowledgePanel members could have been recruited by either the former random digit dialing sampling or the current address-based sampling methodologies. AMES respondents were randomly selected from three separate population groups from the KnowledgePanel (parents of children 5 years or younger, parents of children 6-11, and parents of adolescents 12-17). The survey response rate was 50% for the main sample. Separate post-stratification weights were applied when analyzing all parents as a group and when analyzing parents by their child's age group. The respondents were weighted to be representative of the U.S. population for their particular group based on the demographic and geographic data from the Current Population Survey (CPS). The data were weighted based on the following variables from (CPS): gender, age, race/Hispanic ethnicity, education level, census region, metropolitan area, and household income. The survey took approximately 17 minutes to complete.

References

American Academy of Pediatrics, Council on Communications and Media. (2013). Children, adolescents, and media. *Pediatrics, 132*(5), 958–961.

Anderson, D. R., Huston, A. C., Schmitt, K. L., Linebarger, D. L., & Wright, J. C. (2001). Early childhood television viewing and adolescent behavior: The recontact study. *Monographs of the Society for Research in Child Development, Serial 264, 66*(1), i–154.

Bandura, A. (1986). *Social foundations of thought and actions: A social cognitive theory.* Englewood Cliffs, NJ: Prentice Hall.

Barr, R., Lauricella, A., Zack, E., & Calvert, S. L. (2010). Infant and early childhood exposure to adult-directed and child-directed television programming. *Merrill-Palmer Quarterly, 56*(1), 21–48.

Barr-Anderson, D. J., van den Berg, P., Neumark-Sztainer, D., & Story, M. (2008). Characteristics associated with older adolescents who have a television in their bedrooms. *Pediatrics, 121,* 718–724. doi:10.1542/peds.2007-1546

Barradas, D. T., Fulton, J. E., Blanck, H. M., & Huhman, M. (2007). Parental influences on youth television viewing. *The Journal of Pediatrics, 151*(4), 369–373.

Becker, M. W., Alzahabi, B. S., & Hopwood, C. J. (2013). Media multitasking is associated with symptoms of depression and social anxiety. *Cyberpsychology, Behavior, and Social Networking, 16*(2), 132–135. doi:10.1089/cyber.2012.0291

Bellissimo, N., Pencharz, P. B., Thomas, S. G., & Anderson, G. H. (2007). Effect of television viewing at mealtime on food intake after a glucose preload in boys. *Pediatric Research, 6*(6), 745–749.

Bickham, D. S., Vandewater, E. A., Huston, A. C., Lee, J. H., Caplovitz, A. G., & Wright, J. C. (2003). Predictors of children's electronic media use: An examination of three ethnic groups. *Media Psychology, 5,* 107–137.

Bleakley, A., Jordan, A., & Hennessy, M. (2013). The relationship between parents' and children's television viewing. *Pediatrics, 132,* e364–e371.

Borzekowski, D. L., & Robinson, T. N. (2005). The remote, the mouse, and the No. 2 pencil: the household media environment and academic achievement among third grade students. *Archives of Pediatrics & Adolescent Medicine, 159*(7), 607.

Bronfenbrenner, U. (1979). *The ecology of human development.* Cambridge, MA: Harvard University Press.

Broom, J. (2012, April 14). In 1962, third-graders predicted pocket phones, flying cars. *The Seattle Times.* Retrieved from http://seattletimes.com/html/localnews/2017984268_thirdgrader-list15m.html

Bryant, M., Lucove, J., Evenson, K., & Marshall, S. (2007). Measurement of television viewing in children and adolescents: a systematic review. *Obesity Reviews, 8,* 197–209.

Buijzen, M., & Valkenburg, P. M. (2003). The effects of television advertising on materialism, parent-child conflict, and unhappiness: A review of research. *Applied Developmental Psychology, 24,* 437–456.

Christakis, D. A., & Garrison, M. M. (2009). Preschool-aged children's television viewing in child care settings. *Pediatrics, 124,* 1627–1632. doi:10.1542/peds.2009-0862

Cillero, I. H., & Jago, R. (2010). Systemic review of correlates of screen-viewing among young children. *Preventative Medicine, 51,* 3–10.

Clark, L. S. (2012) *The Parent APP: Understanding Families in the Digital Age.* New York, NY: Oxford University Press.

Coon, K. A., Goldberg, J., Rogers, B. L., & Tucker, K. L. (2001). Relationships between use of television during meals on children's food consumption patterns. *Pediatrics, 107,* 7–15.

Davison, K. K., Francis, L. A., & Birch, L. L. (2005). Links between parents' and girls' television viewing behaviors: A longitudinal examination. *Journal of Pediatrics, 147,* 436–442.

Eggermont, S., & Van den Bulck, J. (2006). Nodding off or switching off? The use of popular media as a sleep aid in secondary-school children. *Journal of Paediatrics and Child Health, 42,* 428–433.

Fitzpatrick, E., Edmunds, L. S., & Dennison, B. A. (2007). Positive effects of family dinner are undone by television viewing. *Journal of the American Dietetic Association, 107,* 666–671.

Foehr, U. G. (2006). Media multitasking among American youth: Prevalence, predictors and pairings. Menlo Park, CA: Kaiser Family Foundation.

Gortmaker, S., Must, A., Sobol, A., Peterson, K., Colditz, G., & Dietz, W. (1996). Television viewing as a cause of increasing obesity among children in the United States, 1986–1990. *Archives of Pediatrics & Adolescent Medicine, 150,* 356–362.

Gortmaker, S., Peterson, K., Wiecha, J., Sobol, A., Dixit, S., & Fox, M. (1999). Reducing obesity via a school-based interdisciplinary intervention among youth. *Archives of Pediatrics & Adolescent Medicine, 153,* 409–418.

Gottfried, J. A., Vaala, S. E., Bleakley, A., Hennessy, M., & Jordan, A. (2013). Does the effect of exposure to TV sex on adolescent sexual behavior vary by genre? *Communication Research, 40*(1), 73–95.

Hancox, R. J., Milne, B. J., & Poulton, R. (2004). Association between child and adolescent television viewing and adult health: a longitudinal birth cohort study. *The Lancet, 364*(9430), 257–262.

Hardy, L. L., Baur, L. A., Garnett, S. P., Crawford, D., Campbell, K. J., Shrewsbury, V. A. (2006). Family and home correlates of television viewing in 12–13 year old adolescents: The Nepean Study. *International Journal of Behavioral Nutrition and Physical Activity, 3,* 24–32.

Huesmann, L. R., Moise-Titus, J., Podolski, C., & Eron, L. D. (2003). Longitudinal relations between children's exposure to TV violence and their aggressive and violence bahvior in young adulthood: 1977–1992. *Developmental Psychology, 39,* 201–221.

Jackson, C., Brown, J. D., & Pardun, C. J. (2008). A TV in the bedroom: Implications for viewing habits and risk behaviors during early adolescence. *Journal of Broadcasting & Electronic Media, 52,* 349–367.

Jago, R., Fox, K., Page, A., Brockman, R., & Thompson, J. (2010). Parent and child physical activity and sedentary time: Do active parents foster active children? *BMC Public Health, 10*(1), 194.

Jago, R., Page, A., Froberg, K., Sardinha, L. B., Klassen-Heggebo, L., & Andersen, L. B. (2008). Screen-viewing and the home TV environment: The European youth heart study. *Preventative Medicine, 47,* 525–529.

Jordan, A. (2004). The role of media in children's development: An ecological perspective. *Developmental and Behavioral Pediatrics, 25,* 196–206.

Jordan, A., Bleakley, A., Manganello, J., Hennessy, M., Stevens, R., & Fishbein, M. (2010). The role of television access in the viewing time of US adolescents. *Journal of Children and Media, 4,* 355–370.

Jordan, A., Hersey, J., McDivitt, J., & Heitzler, C. (2006). Reducing children's television-viewing time: A qualitative study of parents and their children. *Pediatrics, 118,* e1303–e1310.

Kirkorian, H. L., Pempek, T. A., Murphy, L. A., Schmidt, M. E., & Anderson, D. R. (2009). The impact of background television on parent-child interaction. *Child Development, 80,* 1350–1359.

Madden, M., Lenhart, A., Duggan, M., Cortesi, S., & Gasser, U. (2013). Teens and technology 2013. Retrieved from http://www.pewInternet.org/Reports/2013/Teens-and-Tech.aspx

Mares, M. L., & Woodard, E. H. (2012). Effects of prosocial media content on children's social interactions. In D. G. Singer & J. L. Singer (Eds.), *Handbook of children and the media* (2nd ed.) (pp. 197–214). Thousand Oaks, CA: Sage Publications, Inc.

Nalkur, P. G., Jamieson, P. E., & Romer, D. (2010). The effectiveness of the motion picture association of America's rating system in screening explicit violence and sex in top-ranked movies from 1950 to 2006. *Journal of Adolescent Health, 47*(5), 440–447.

Notten, N., Kraaykamp, G., & Konig, R. P. (2012). Family media matters: Unraveling the intergenerational transmission of reading and television tastes. *Sociological Perspectives, 55,* 683–706.

Ophir, E., Nass, C., & Wagner, W. D. (2009). Cognitive control in media multitaskers. *Proceedings of the National Academy of Sciences, 106,* 15583–15587.

Paik, H., & Comstock, G. (1994). The effects of television violence on antisocial behavior: a meta-analysis. *Communication Research, 21,* 516–546. doi:10.1177/009365094021004004

Rice, M. L., Huston, A. C., Truglio, R., & Wright, J. C. (1990). Words from "Sesame Street": Learning vocabulary while viewing. *Developmental Psychology, 26,* 421–428.

Rideout, V. (2007). Parents, children & media: A Kaiser Family Foundation survey. Menlo Park, CA: Kaiser Family Foundation.

Rideout, V. (2011). Zero to eight: Children's media use in America. San Francisco, CA: CommonSense Media.

Rideout, V., Foehr, U., & Roberts, D. (2010). Generation M2: Media in the Lives of 8 to 18 Year Olds. Retrieved from http://kaiserfamilyfoundation.files.wordpress.com/2013/01/8010.pdf

Roberts, D. F., & Foehr, U. G. (2008). Trends in media use. *The Future of Children, 18*(1), 11–37.

Robinson, T. (1999). Reducing children's television viewing to prevent obesity: A randomized controlled trial. *Journal of the American Medical Association, 282,* 1561–1567.

Romer, D., Bagdasarov, Z., & More, E. (2013). Older versus newer media and the well-being of United States youth: Results From a national longitudinal panel. *Journal of Adolescent Health, 52,* 613–619.

Saelens, B. E., Sallis, J. F., Nader, P. R., Broyles, S. L., Berry, C. C., & Taras, H. L. (2002). Home environmental influences on children's television watching from early to middle childhood. *Developmental and Behavioral Pediatrics, 23*(3), 127–132.

Schmidt, M. E., Pempek, T. A., Kirkorian, H. L., Lund, A. F., & Anderson, D. R. (2008). The effects of background television on the toy play behavior of very young children. *Child Development, 79,* 1137–1151.

Shin, N. (2004). Exploring pathways from television viewing to academic achievements in school age children. *Journal of Genetic Psychology: Research and Theory on Human Development, 165,* 367–382.

St. Peters, M., Fitch, M., Huston, A. C., Wright, J. C., & Eakins, D. J. (1991). Television and families: What do young children watch with their parents? *Child Development, 62,* 1409–1423. doi: 10.1111/J.1467-8624.1991.tb01614.x

Strasburger, V. C., Wilson, B. J., & Jordan, A. B. (2009). The family and media. In V. C. Strasburger, B. J. Wilson, & A. B. Jordan (Eds.), *Children, Adolescents, and Media* (2nd ed.) (pp. 499–518). Los Angeles, CA: Sage.

Valkenburg, P. M., Krcmar, M., Peeters, A. L., & Marseille, N. M. (1999). Developing a scale to assess three styles of television mediation: "Instructive mediation," "restrictive mediation," and "social coviewing." *Journal of Broadcasting & Electronic Media, 43*(1), 52–66.

Vandewater, E. A., Bickham, D. S., Lee, J. H., Cummings, H. M., Wartella, E. A., & Rideout, V. J. (2005). When the television is always on: Heavy television exposure and young children's development. *American Behavioral Scientist, 48,* 562–577.

Vandewater, E. A., & Lee, S. J. (2009). Measuring children's media use in the digital age: Issues and challenges. *American Behavioral Scientist, 52,* 1152–1176.

Warren, R., Gerke, P., & Kelly, M. A. (2002). Is there enough time on the clock? Parental involvement and mediation of children's television viewing. *Journal of Broadcasting & Electronic Media, 46*(1), 87–111.

Zimmerman, F. (2008). Children's media use and sleep problems: Issues and unanswered questions. Research brief. Retrieved from http://kaiserfamilyfoundation.files.wordpress.com/2013/01/7671.pdf

CHAPTER 2

Learning in a Digital Age

TOWARD A NEW ECOLOGY OF HUMAN DEVELOPMENT

Lori M. Takeuchi and Michael H. Levine

Since its inception in the 1970s, Urie Bronfenbrenner's *ecological systems theory* (EST) has provided a generation of scholars and practitioners a powerful tool for understanding human development. Conceived during a period of increasing economic disparity, EST provided a strong argument for the design and establishment of key family support programs that remain pillars of the modern welfare system, including Head Start, Nurse-Family Partnerships Home Visitation, and California Proposition 10. According to this theory, children grow and learn within a set of nested and interrelated environments—the microsystem, mesosystem, exosystem, and macrosystem, each to be described in detail below (Bronfenbrenner, 1977, 1979). The chronosystem, conceived a bit later in Bronfenbrenner's writing, represents temporal changes in terms of the developing individual's lifespan as well as the broader socio-historical context (Bronfenbrenner, 1986). Factors in each system either directly or indirectly shape the routines and interactions a child has with the people and objects in her immediate environments. These interactions, in turn, further alter these settings such that the relationship between child and environment is reciprocal in nature.

Bronfenbrenner once cited the television show as a particular threat to family routines "not so much in the behavior it produces as the behavior it prevents—the talks, the games, the family festivities and arguments through which much of the child's learning takes place and his character is formed" (1974, p. 170). Television and other forms of media (e.g., books, radio, movies) were entrenched in family routines by the 1970s, but Bronfenbrenner wrote surprisingly little about the role media play in shaping the contexts of childhood (Jordan, 2004). Since the 1970s, however, these contexts have been wholly transformed by the infiltration of digital media platforms. Perhaps now he would find much more to write about!

This chapter is organized into four sections. First we report on the events that brought about these transformations, and then provide a brief and selective review of how children today may be developing differently as a consequence—socio-emotionally, cognitively, and physically. We then don our ecological lenses to bring into focus influences at each level of the system that are shaping the settings in which children interact with digital media today. In taking a systems view of their development in relation to the tools that now surround them, we manage to demonstrate the enduring relevance and utility of the ecological framework. To end, we offer advice to those who both directly and indirectly influence the experiences children have with digital media today to ensure that these experiences are most beneficial to their learning and healthy growth.

Impact of the ICT Revolution on Children's Microsystems

In the four decades that have passed since Bronfenbrenner first introduced EST, we have moved out of the Industrial and into the Information Age. Most of us living in the United States have had our work and personal lives transformed by two developments in the information and communications technology (ICT) sector. First, advancements in microprocessor technology have rendered computing technologies faster, more powerful, more affordable, and more mobile at an exponential rate.[1] Second, the advent of the internet (c. 1969) has opened up multiple channels for communication and information sharing that are remarkably cost-effective and flexible compared to older systems (i.e., telephone and print). Together, these events have led to a burgeoning consumer electronic marketplace and revolutionary changes in how business gets done across all sectors of the U.S. workforce, and set the historical context—what Bronfenbrenner called the *chronosystem*—for kids growing up today.

The consumer electronics sector and the parental workplace, in turn, are elements of the *exosystem*, settings that a child does not directly participate in, but that influence what occurs in her immediate environments, or *microsystem*. As such, the exosystem indirectly shapes a child's development. Consider, for example, how the electronics industry's ever-accelerating output of personal communication and entertainment innovations only seems to fuel the public's desire to purchase next new thing. In 2012, U.S. sales of consumer electronics were expected to exceed $206 billion, up from $94.2 billion in 2002 (Consumer Electronics Association, 2012). Families with young children are major contributors to this trend: in 2009, the NPD Group (2009a), a global market research company, reported that households with 4- to 14-year-old kids owned an average of 11 electronic devices. As the prices of devices continue to drop, parents are increasingly inclined to purchase TV sets, cell phones, and laptops for their kids' individual use, too. In 2011, 42% of children under the age of 8 had a TV in their bedroom and 24% had their own handheld gaming device (Common Sense Media, 2011).

Content geared toward children helps drive sales of these platforms, and represents billion-dollar industries. Annual video game revenues in the U.S. ($25 billion; Entertainment Software Association (ESA), 2011) currently surpass those of the film and music industries, and families with children under the age of 12 account for 45% of these sales (NPD, 2009b). Although for the most part websites aimed at children remain free, many are adopting subscription models (e.g., Club Penguin, Webkinz World), which minimize the junk food and toy ads that tend to plaster the free online hangouts, as a way of appealing to concerned parents (Tuten, 2008). But children aren't the only ones susceptible to advertising. Media promoted as educational or enriching—whether evidence exists to back these claims—entice parents in search of quality content for their kids, as evidenced by the millions of dollars spent on Baby Einstein videos whose claims of being beneficial for babies' development were later revealed as unfounded (DeLoache et al., 2010).

In effect, digital media are invading children's microsystems—their homes, classrooms, day care facilities, and other settings they frequent—and altering communication, learning, and entertainment routines therein. Although children still watch a lot of TV—in 2011, children 8-years-old and younger spent, on average, an hour and 40 minutes viewing video content per day—they're doing so via the internet, mobile devices, and other digital delivery systems. In general, kids' digital consumption is on the rise: 60% of 5- to 8-year-olds have played a handheld game, 81% have played a console game, and 90% have used a computer. Book reading, regrettably, is on the decline: in 2011, children between the ages of 6 months and 6 years spent 29 minutes per day reading or being read to, compared to 40 minutes per day in 2005 (Common Sense Media, 2011). And while most kids start using first cell phones by age 12 or 13 (46%), a fifth of them own one by age 11 (Lenhart, Ling, Campbell, & Purcell, 2009).

The ICT revolution is both the product of and driving force behind the knowledge economy, whose outputs are innovations and information; hence it demands a differently skilled workforce than economies past (Drucker, 1969). The rise of positions requiring high levels of education has led to the dramatic rise of women earning post-secondary degrees since the 1970s, which in large part explains the increase of mothers in the workforce, from 47% in 1975 to 71% in 2011 (U.S. Department of Labor, 2009). The simultaneous decline and foreign outsourcing of manufacturing and service-sector jobs have resulted in underemployment across the U.S. population, especially among lower-income families. For these parents, increased shift work and multiple jobs have become necessary to make ends meet, placing strains on child care arrangements, family functioning, and the well-being of their children (Council of Economic Advisors, 2010; National Research Council, 2003; Strazdins, Korda, Lim, Broom, & D'Souza, 2004).

In the white-collar world, tools such as email, productivity software, and smartphones have revised the ethos of the American office such that employees are expected to accomplish far more in a day than ever before, and be available even when not physically at the office. In fact, the workday is no longer confined to time spent on site (Derks & Bakker, 2010; Towers, Duxbury, Higgins, & Thomas, 2006). Work time spills over into people's cars and homes, and into the hours parents might otherwise devote exclusively to their spouses and children (Scelfo, 2010). In what time both blue- and white-collar parents have to spend with their children, they may be exhausted and consequently less engaged and more willing to let their child spend that extra hour online, watching TV, or playing video games (Takeuchi, 2011).

Second only to home, kids spend most of their waking hours at school. Schools are on a less aggressive track toward technological transformation as they struggle to integrate cell phones, social networking tools, and video games into campus culture and instructional practices. While 44% of U.S. public elementary school teachers in 2009 reported using computers during instructional time often, the remaining 56% reported using computers only sometimes (31%) or less frequently (17% rarely; 8% never; 1% not available; Gray, Thomas, & Lewis, 2010). Furthermore, as families steadily increase annual spending on home technologies (Consumer Electronics Association, 2012), PBS's 2010 survey on school media and technology use found that 54% of K–12 schools *decreased* their budgets for media spending over the past year. Elementary school teachers in particular reported time constraints and a paucity of age-appropriate content as being key barriers to using digital resources in their instruction (PBS & Grunwald Associates LLC, 2010). Still, 98% of U.S. schools reported broadband connections to the internet in 2006 (National Center for Education Statistics, 2006), and some students (e.g., African-American students) are more likely to have access to the internet and high-quality media at school than they are at home (Warschauer & Matuchniak, 2010).

Digital Media in Children's Microsystems Shape Development

As children's microsystems evolve, so do the way families communicate, play, and learn. For instance, whereas families once owned a single TV set placed in a central location in the home, watching TV together is no longer as common in the age of YouTube, tablets, and bedroom TV sets (Barkhuus & Brown, 2009; Courtois & D'heer, 2012). When our media-based activities give in to new form factors and take up a growing proportion of our waking hours, what happens to the ways in which children think, interact with people, and approach the world? How are children today developing—cognitively, socio-emotionally, and physically—as a result of their interactions with and around the media that fill their lives? Following is a sampling of empirical research and journalistic accounts that delve into these questions, and together they reveal how digital media both directly and indirectly shape the development and learning of young children.

COGNITIVE DEVELOPMENT

Consider what children today have gained cognitively as a result of the changes wrought by the ICT revolution. A recent randomized controlled trial involving 398 preschool children in 80 classrooms around the Unites States demonstrated that preschool teachers who implement a curriculum that integrates public television video content with teacher-led activities can improve their students' early literacy skills (Penuel et al., 2009). Children assigned to the literacy curriculum, which featured video and interactive games from *Super Why!*, *Between the Lions*, and *Sesame Street*, outscored children in the comparison group (which instead received a media-based science curriculum) on four of five literacy measures. Key to the success of this intervention, according to researchers, were the training and coaching provided to teachers that helped them effectively implement the curriculum. Though studies of this size are rare, this study follows a long line of smaller-scale research showing that technology, when properly deployed in instruction, may facilitate, deepen, and inspire young people's learning in ways that textbooks and more traditional forms of media may not (Brown, Collins, & Duguid, 1989; Kozma, 1991; Roschelle, Pea, Hoadley, Gordin, & Means, 2000). Mapping applications, simulations, digital cameras, spreadsheets, sensors, and probeware adapted for use in K–12 science classrooms, for instance, allow students to collect, manage, and analyze their own data in the context of the current lesson (Krajcik, 2001) and, in doing so, participate in authentic scientific practices and ways of thinking (Edelson, 1998; Linn, 2003; National Research Council, 2006).

For reasons ranging from inadequate teacher training to constraints imposed by standardized testing, however, not all students have access to these tools at school (Warschauer & Matuchniak, 2010). Fortunately, the advent of the internet has made out-of-school, self-directed learning more common and convenient than ever before. Kids today can Google answers to questions and YouTube how-to advice on just about any topic that piques their curiosity. Online they have the opportunity to develop deep expertise, connect to peers who share similar interests, and distribute their work to gain status within networked communities (Ito et al., 2009). The social and technical skills they pick up along the way, experts argue, will prepare them for productive participation in contemporary society (Ito et al., 2009; Jenkins, Clinton, Purushotma, Robison, & Weigel, 2006).

Of course, children aren't just surfing the internet in the name of learning. Video games, music, and social networking sites compete with homework and other academic activities for time they spend outside of school and sleep. This may prove especially consequential for lower-income children, who are more likely to use computers for fun than for learning (Vigdor & Ladd, 2010). Cummings and Vandewater (2007) discovered that adolescents who play video games spend 30% less time reading and 34% less time doing homework than nongamers do. As younger children increasingly participate in digital pastimes, more research is needed to determine how their time-use patterns may also be shifting.

SOCIO-EMOTIONAL DEVELOPMENT

The media-saturated microsystem may have socio-emotional consequences for the developing child as well. Voice over internet protocol (VoIP) applications like Facetime and Skype allow children to videoconference with grandparents living clear across the country, if not the world, without charging for airtime,[2] which has increased the presence of distant relatives in their lives (Ames, Go, Kaye, & Spasojevic, 2010; Scelfo, 2011). Today, children's microsystems are no longer as bound by the physical demarcations of home, school, and neighborhood and, as such, children have access to a broader set of perspectives than ever before. Classrooms of kindergarteners in San Francisco can Skype with their counterparts in Osaka, Japan, and not only see and hear what the other looks and sounds like—as television and movies first made possible—but actually get to know them as individuals. Research in elementary schools has found that these interactions can deepen multicultural understanding across international borders (Cifuentes & Murphy, 2000; Gerstein, 2000; Thurston, 2004), a key competency in an increasingly global society (Jenkins et al., 2006).

As VoIP connections forge deeper relationships across distances, personal devices are blamed for disrupting interactions among individuals living beneath the same roof. A mother, father, and child may each engage more with their smartphone, laptop, or Nintendo DS than the person sitting beside them at the dinner table (Ito & Okabe, 2005; Turkle, 2011). As younger children go online to socialize—forsaking old-fashioned in-person play dates—they may be deprived of experiences to read facial expressions and body language, which help them develop empathy and understand emotional nuance (Small & Vorgan, 2009). In Pea and colleagues' (2012) survey of 3,461 8- to 12-year-old girls, those who spent more time in face-to-face interactions were more likely to report social success, greater feelings of normalcy, more sleep, and fewer friends whom parents judged to be bad influences than girls who spent a lot of time watching videos and media multitasking. But Grimes and Fields (2012) urge caution here: with the rise of social networking sites, online games, and virtual worlds aimed at the under-8 set, we cannot assume the research on adolescent online socialization applies to younger kids. New research is needed to understand how children's developmental stages intersect with their online socialization activities.

PHYSICAL DEVELOPMENT

Recent technological shifts may also have implications for how children develop *physically*. Exergames such as *Dance Dance Revolution* have rejuvenated the formerly dreaded PE period at some schools (Lanningham-Foster et al., 2006), giving students a fun way to move around indoors, especially when it's too hot, too cold, or too dangerous outside (Weir, Etelson, & Brand, 2006). Marketing campaigns for physical gaming consoles such as the Nintendo Wii target parents concerned about the sedentary nature of sit-down forms of video game play, and apparently to great effect; many attribute the commercial success of the Wii to its messaging on fitness and family time (Rusetski, 2012; Ulicsak, Wright, & Cranmer, 2009). Biddiss and Irwin's (2010) systematic review of published studies examining the physical benefits of active video game (AVG) play (1998 through 2009) found that while AVGs enable light to moderate physical activity, more research is needed to understand how sustainable AVG play may be for longer-term health maintenance.

Although 59% of U.S. parents of 3- to 10-year-olds worry that digital media can prevent children from getting exercise (Takeuchi, 2011), research has failed to produce uniform evidence that the time children spend with digital media displaces time spent participating in physical activities (Attewell, Suazo-Garcia, & Battle, 2003; Hofferth, 2010). Hofferth (2010), for example, found no relationship between minutes logged on the computer or playing video games versus time spent playing sports in her analysis of the Children Development Supplement of the Panel Study of Income Dynamics (PSID), a 30-year longitudinal survey of a representative sample of U.S. 6- to 12-year-olds (i.e., Child Development Supplement data, 1997–2003). Video game play, however, was associated with less time spent in outdoor activities such as walking, pleasure drives, gardening, or camping. Another possible threat digital media may pose to children are the ads for unhealthy foods now seen in online games, search engines, social networking sites, and virtual worlds. Research has established a relationship between unhealthy eating habits and exposure to commercials for nutritionally poor foods on TV (Birch, Parker, & Burns, 2011; Taras et al., 1989), but more research is needed to determine whether online ads have a similar effect.

MEDIA MULTITASKING IN CHILDREN'S MICROSYSTEMS

Technological progress has made it a lot easier for people to accomplish several things at once by converging multiple media into common interfaces. Whereas personal computers once served a few primary purposes—word processing and email, perhaps—today one can almost simultaneously Google a factoid, listen to an album on iTunes, and instant-message a friend or coworker. Media convergence has made multitasking common not only when operating multiple technologies, but when doing other things too, such as checking a work email account while keeping an eye on one's child (Good, 2006). Today, we juggle activities as though it's fashionable (Turkle, 2011), despite the research telling us that we perform poorer at tasks we do simultaneously than those to which we devote our full attention (Rubinstein & Meyer, 2001; Ophir, Nass, & Wagner, 2009).

Media multitasking may be the norm in the work world (Wallis, 2006), but how is it affecting family interactions at home? In their ethnographic study of 30 dual-income families with children, Campos, Graesch, Repetti, Bradbury, and Ochs (2009) found that because the kids were often so immersed in the TV, video games, or phone by the time their later-working fathers arrived home, many failed to greet them or even acknowledge their return. According to Common Sense Media (2011), 23% of 5- to 8-year-olds use more than one medium simultaneously, and of the 79% who have homework, 21% report doing so with the TV on. If a child is watching *SpongeBob* while reading for homework and instant-messaging a friend on the side, it's easy to guess which task will suffer most.

Beyond diminished family interaction and poorer task performance, multitasking may have consequences for early brain development. For instance, young children may become more habituated to constant task switching and less able to sustain attention when it's called for (Posner & Rothbart, 2000). And when kids have an array of entertainment and communication options at their fingertips on a 24/7 basis, what becomes of downtime, the chance the brain has to rest, imagine, and reflect (Richtel, 2010; Turkle, 2011)? Executive function skills—the set of cognitive controls that manage other cognitive processes, including inhibition, attention, working memory, and planning—are no less important now than they were before the technology revolution and, in fact, have been associated with higher academic achievement (Blair & Razza, 2007; Zimmerman, 1990).

NEW CHALLENGES FOR A DIGITAL AGE

As this brief and selective review[3] illustrates, technological progress doesn't always result in what's best for kids. Historically speaking, technological progress has always involved a set of losses that we eventually remedy, adapt to, or just get over. With the invention of the printing press in the 14th century, people feared the demise of the oral tradition and our capacity to memorize lengthy narratives verbatim. And while we did lose these cherished practices and skills, books helped to draw Western civilization out of the Middle Ages and set the stage for the scientific revolution. Computers, word processors, and calculators were met with similar resistance in their early years, and serve as recent reminders that the gains we make as a result of technological progress usually make up for any losses or added challenges this progress imposes as these changes transition into mainstream routines. It is through the creation of new technologies that we manage to distribute work across an even wider set of tools and resources outside of the human mind, thereby freeing it up to contemplate and conjure greater ideas and inventions than ever before (Pea, 1993).

What sets the current era of technological upheaval apart from earlier ones is the rate at which these tools are invading family life and transforming daily routines. Whereas decades elapsed between the introduction of the telephone, the radio, and television—leaving time for parents, educators, and researchers to see what effect each had on family interactions and then figure out how to effectively counteract these effects—the most recent technology trends (e.g., e-readers, texting, YouTube, Twitter) are being widely adopted by consumers within a matter of months, and by younger and younger consumers. Given this rapid penetration rate, children born just years apart are demonstrating distinct patterns of media consumption, communication, and levels of multitasking (Rosen, 2010).

System Factors Mediating Children's Technology Use

Technological progress will steam ahead regardless of what impact it may be having on how our children grow and learn. But the fate of their healthy development is by no means out of our hands. An ecological perspective reminds us that the video games kids play and the tablets they've become so enamored with aren't solely responsible for the behavioral metamorphoses we are now witnessing. It is the *what, how,* and *with whom* children use these media that lead to these changes, and it is well within our ability to exert some influence over the circumstances of their use. We have argued so far that the historical circumstances (chronosystem) and subsequent outputs of the technology sector (exosystem) have provided children with direct access to tools that are rapidly transforming

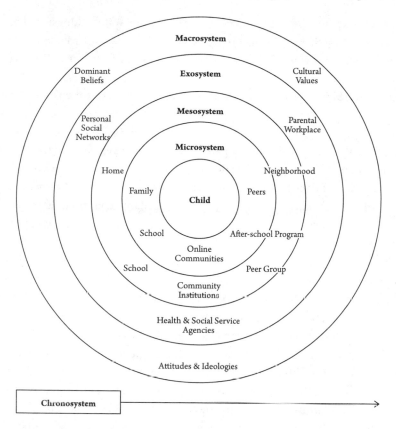

Figure 2.1 The Nested Spheres of Influence around the Developing Child (Bronfenbrenner, 1979). Diagram adapted from Weiss, Kreider, Lopez, & Chatman-Nelson (2010).

how they learn, play, and communicate and, consequently, how they are developing cognitively, socio-emotionally, and physically. Now let us turn to the factors in the micro-, meso-, exo-, and macrosystems that are *mediating*—in other words, directly or indirectly shaping or exerting some influence over—children's interactions with these tools (see Figure 2.1).

MICROSYSTEM FACTORS

Since the predigital era, parents have been managing and regulating their children's experiences with media, from imposing telephone time limits to denying permission to see anything but G-rated movies. Back when families owned just one television—centrally placed in the home—parents could keep tabs on how much TV their kids were watching since programs aired at regularly scheduled 30- or 60-minute timeslots. This setup also made it fairly easy for parents to see what shows their kids were watching—if not watch alongside them on the sofa—a practice that Valkenburg, Krcmar, Peeters, and Marseille (1999) termed "social coviewing." The other two forms of *parental mediation*, according to Valkenburg and colleagues' taxonomy, include "instructive mediation" or parents' efforts to explain television content, and "restrictive mediation," which includes using media to reward or punish, and setting time or content limits on kids' viewing.

In a 2010 survey of American parents of 3- to 10-year-olds, 64% said they limit children's media use on a case by case basis, versus just 22% who said they set strict rules (Takeuchi, 2011). Modern circumstances make it difficult, if not unrealistic, to set hard-and-fast rules (Evans, Jordan, & Horner, 2011; Jordan, 2005). Beyond limits on "screen time" and keeping media out of children's bedrooms (American Academy of Pediatrics Council on Communications and Media, 2010), professional guidelines around specific varieties of digital media still don't exist. As noted above, these things take time—the American Academy of Pediatrics, in fact, issued its first policy statement regarding limits on children's TV exposure in 2001, four decades after TV sets had become ubiquitous in U.S. homes (c. 1960). Even with respect to time limits—the AAP (2013) recommends a daily dose of no more than two hours of entertainment screen media for 2- to 18-year-old children—it's harder for middle-class parents today to *see* how much screen time their kids are getting, given the mobile and connected nature of new platforms. These qualities make it possible for kids to log unseen hours on the school bus, at a friend's house, or in their own bedrooms. There are other reasons why certain parents can't easily enforce the AAP's two-hour limit with their kids despite philosophical support for these guidelines. Evans, Jordan, and Horner (2011) found in interviews with 180 families that television has come to play essential roles as a (a) conflict mitigator; (b) economical and low-hassle activity for families; and (c) source of babysitting, entertainment, and educational content. Reducing TV time in these families would simply disrupt established routines and efficiencies, especially for those with fewer monetary and community resources.

Research in the 1970s and '80s found that children who watch educational TV with their parents learn more from the show than children who watch alone (e.g., Ball & Bogatz, 1970; Reiser, Tessmer, & Phelps, 1984; Salomon, 1977). While coviewing and instructive mediation may be more awkward around today's smaller screens designed for individual use (Livingstone & Helsper, 2008), video games, social networking sites, and authoring tools offer new opportunities for families to converse, cooperate, compete, create, and critique. Clark (2011) argues that "participatory learning" be added as a fourth parental mediation strategy that recognizes the potential of newer media to engage interpersonal relationships and collaborative creativity. There has been a general resurgence of interest among researchers to investigate intergenerational and sibling engagement with media (e.g., Barron, Martin, Takeuchi, & Fithian, 2009; Clark, 2011; Raffle et al., 2011; Stevens, Satwicz, & McCarthy, 2008). According to Takeuchi and Stevens (2011),

> The vast landscape of media use…calls for new focus on the ways that people engage with media together. The stereotype of singular engagement in media has influenced how media are designed—as if all users are isolated individuals. It is time for that to change. We need to better understand how people use media together and how individuals interact with and around all forms of media, especially those that dominate young people's time and experience. As we come to better understand *joint media engagement*, our methods of designing will undoubtedly change so that we may better take advantage of the unique capacity of human beings to work, learn, think, and make things together. (p. 5)

EXOSYSTEM FACTORS

A major challenge for both researchers and media producers interested in fostering joint media engagement is how to think about families that don't spend a lot of time together. When parents work all day, not only do they spend less time consuming media with their children; they exert less control over the media their kids consume without them, because day care centers, babysitters, grandparents, older siblings, and other caretakers set after-school agendas.

Parental income largely determines what media children have access to at home. For example, nearly 72% of children age 8 and younger have computers at home, but ownership ranges from 48% among families with incomes of less than $30,000/year to 91% among families with incomes of more than $75,000/ year. The figures for internet access in these same households are 42% and 92%, respectively (Common Sense Media, 2011). Parenting styles have been found to differ along class lines, such that working-class parents grant their children more freedom to decide what they do during the nonschool hours of their days, including the amounts of media they consume. Middle-income parents, on the other hand, practice the "concerted cultivation" of their children, filling their schedules with sports, arts, and other enrichment activities (Lareau, 2003), leaving precious little time for media (Jordan, 1992; Kohn, 1995). In effect, children 8-years-old and younger from higher-income families (>$75,000/year) spend 2 hours and 47 minutes per day with media, compared to the 3 hours and 34 minutes that children from low-income families (<$30,000/year) log on a daily basis (Common Sense Media, 2011).

Other issues from the parent work world shape children's media practices. As described above, the internet and mobile technologies have blurred the boundaries between work and our personal lives such that the home becomes a virtual extension of the office. Would it come as any surprise for a child who grows up in a home around parents who text at the dinner table to exhibit similar behaviors when she gets her own cell phone? Young children imitate their parents' behaviors around media (Plowman, McPake, & Stephen, 2008; Woodward, 2000) and attitudes toward media (McPake & Plowman, 2009; Takeuchi, 2011), just as they pick up any other range of behaviors and attitudes their parents intentionally or inadvertently model. In our case studies of the digital media practices of four families, children as young as age 7 echoed their parents' positions on the benefits and harms of various forms of media (Takeuchi, 2011). For instance, when we asked 8-year-old Gabriela how often she plays with her Nintendo DS, she answered, "Not every day where I would get addicted to it," and "I don't like sleep with my DS close because I don't want to start playing it because I know that I have to get a good night's sleep." These responses reflect the sentiments expressed by her father Hector in a separate set of interviews, in which he retold the alarming stories his coworker shared about her son being "sucked into the video games" and "sucked into the computer."

MACROSYSTEM FACTORS

Hector also mentioned wanting to protect Gabriela from the online predators he's seen in the news, a powerful vehicle through which public opinion is both shaped and reflected. In 2011, the FrameWorks Institute conducted a content analysis of the mainstream news on issues related to digital media and learning. They found that stories tend to emphasize the perceived risks of digital media— namely, cyberbullying, privacy concerns, and distractions from quality social time—and basically ignore the potential of these tools for learning (Arvizu, Simon, Lindland, & O'Neil, 2011). These findings aligned with the Institute's 2010 analysis of U.S. public opinion on the same issues, which revealed cultural orientations toward digital media as entertainment-focused (inessential), automatic, passive, and dangerous (Kendall-Taylor, Lindland, & Mikulak, 2010). Together,

> public thinking and media coverage are likely to coalesce and contribute to a powerfully co-constructed and mutually reinforcing narrative about digital media as dangerous and distracting. This association both explains current skepticism about, and predicts further public resistance to, increased use of digital media in classrooms and communities. (Arvizu et al., 2011, p. 5)

These analyses also explain how the mainstream news may shape parenting practices around digital media. As Hector clarified, "If we allowed [Gabriela] to access the internet or go onto certain websites, she could get into some kind of trouble or people talking to her, you see those photos on television. So, we limit her as much as possible."

The FrameWorks Institute's 2010 analysis of public opinion also revealed the cultural models, or shared understandings, that Americans use to think about how people learn: specifically, that in-school learning is distinct from real-world learning; that school learning is led by a teacher, involves books and facts, requires minimal distraction, and is hard; and that students must be safe to learn. Current educational policy in many ways instantiates these beliefs about learning, as evidenced by the No Child Left Behind (NCLB) Act, which aimed to improve the achievement of all students—especially the underserved—by focusing schools' attention on raising standardized test scores and holding teachers accountable for their students' performance on these tests. In turn, these policies serve to further reinforce the public's beliefs about the teacher-centric, fact-based, hard-work model of learning, which also happens to oppose the cultural models about digital media (i.e., that it's entertainment-focused, automatic, passive, and dangerous; Kendall-Taylor et al., 2010). NCLB has, in effect, misaligned K–12 classrooms with the modes of learning that digital media best support: deeply engaging (versus rote-oriented); student-centered and driven; and hands-on and situated in real-world contexts (Kendall-Taylor et al., 2010).

The macrosystem, the outermost sphere of Bronfenbrenner's nested systems, can influence activity in the microsystem via the intermediary exosystem. Case in point: NCLB has also been in part blamed for the shift that occurred in the educational software industry between the 1990s and 2000s, from the production of innovative titles that engaged students in constructivist-based investigations toward drill-and-practice titles aimed at raising students' test scores (Molenda & Bichelmeyer, 2005). In hopes of doing just this, school districts nationwide invested millions of dollars in such software (Paley, 2007). Tragically, research suggests that the drill-and-practice titles favored in lower-income school districts tend to be ineffective—if not detrimental—to student achievement. Wenglinsky (2005), for example, found a negative relationship between the frequency of drill-and-practice software use and fourth grade math test scores, as well as eighth grade science and reading test scores. Conversely, simulations, games, data analysis, and the constructivist educational software titles that higher-income schools more often use with their students were associated with higher test performance (Wenglinsky, 2005).

Subcultural values may also shape how and whether parents restrict their children's media use. Leonardi (2003), for example, discovered in focus groups comprising 78 working-class Latino immigrants how cultural orientations guide perceptions and uses of cell phones, computers, and the internet. All participants identified cell phones as supporting their values around communication, while computers and internet promoted individualism, a threat to values held around community. While the limitations of this study must be considered (participants lived from the same community in the western U.S. and are therefore not representative of all Latino immigrants in the U.S.), it may shed some light on Latino technology consumption patterns across both immigrant and native populations. According to Pew Hispanic Center data, in 2010, 45% of Hispanic households had broadband internet access, compared to 65% of white and 52% of black homes (Livingston, 2011). By contrast, in 2012, 49% of Hispanic adults reported owning smartphones, as did 49% of black adults, both surpassing smartphone ownership among white adults at 45% (Smith, 2012). Katz's (2010) interviews with 22 Latino immigrant families also revealed how they value various media through their purchases. Most of the families owned computers—17 of the 22—but only a few had internet access. All families subscribed to cable television, which parents and children often watched together. As seen in both the Katz and Leonardi studies, the prioritization and subsequent purchase of media that support family communication, togetherness, and entertainment— as opposed to access to information, as afforded by the internet—may pose constraints to their children's learning.

THE MESOSYSTEM: CONNECTIONS BETWEEN SETTINGS

The *mesosystem* comprises the interactions that take place in one setting that shape interactions in another (Bronfenbrenner, 1979). For example, what happens at home influences how children behave at school and with their peers, and vice versa. Some children's mesosystems may also include church, after-school centers, or extracurricular activities (sports, music). When it comes to learning, the mesosystem is often overlooked in both research and practice circles. As the 2011 FrameWorks Institute analysis revealed, Americans view school learning as distinct and disconnected from out-of-school learning, which for many children is not so far from the truth. These students may find the fact-based, linearly designed content they encounter at school to be far less compelling—if not simply irrelevant—compared to the dynamic, hyperlinked, narrative-embedded content they actively seek outside of school (Prensky, 2001). Given the contrast, some students may have difficulty staying engaged with their schoolwork, while others may channel their energies outside of school, setting aggressive learning agendas in their home-based hobbies, online communities, sports teams, and so on (Ito et al., 2009).

Barron (2004) has proposed a *learning ecologies* framework—which extends Bronfenbrenner's thinking on the mesosystem—to better understand how learning at home relates to learning at school and the other settings a child lives in, and how school learning in turn relates to learning outside of school. Parents of young children play particularly influential roles in these connective activities by instigating or supporting their interest in a given topic to the point that the child independently seeks opportunities in each setting to further deepen his expertise on that topic. Parental supports come in the form of reading books to their child; providing learning resources and tools (e.g., books, a computer); making trips to the library, museum, and other community spaces; paying for extracurricular classes or camps; making things together (e.g., cooking, building models); teaching and explaining; and doing other, familiar parent-child activities (Barron, Martin, Takeuchi, & Fithian, 2009).

The connectivity and portability of cell phones, tablet computers, and other handheld devices have opened up new pathways for communicating and learning across settings, and may further enable children to carry their interests with them wherever they go, breaking down currently conceived divides between in- and out-of-school learning. These technologies may also facilitate parental support of their children's learning, especially parents who may not have the time, financial means, or confidence to otherwise do so. Cell phones were found to be an effective medium for delivering PBS *Ready to Learn* literacy content to middle- and low-income parents, who in turn were able to help teach this content to their preschool children (Revelle, Reardon, Green, Betancourt, & Kotler, 2007). Parents appreciated getting text-message tips on how to incorporate letter recognition and letter sound activities into everyday family routines, and the children enjoyed watching letter video clips hosted by their beloved friend Elmo. This intervention acknowledged the potential of the mesosystem in two ways. First, it set up a technical infrastructure to support anytime-anywhere learning—at home, at the supermarket, at the doctor's office, and so on. Second, it not only prepared the children to make the *ecological transition* from "child at home to pupil at school" (Bronfenbrenner, 1977, p. 525), it also prepared the parents with skills to better support their children once they are in school.

Unfortunately, extended channels of cross-setting interaction are also being used for dysfunctional purposes. Kids today are being bullied not only on the school playground, but online and on their cell phones too, where messages may reach them at home and other locales once considered safe. According to a 2011 survey of 12- to 17-year-olds, 15% of teens who use social media have been the target of online meanness in the past 12 months; data on younger children are called for as their presence on social media rapidly rises (Grimes & Fields, 2012). Turkle (2011) has documented the role that cell phones are playing in delaying the parent-child separation: whereas there used to be a moment in a child's life when he took that first unaccompanied step into the world beyond home and school (e.g., navigating the city alone for urban kids), it is not uncommon for college students to still text their parents at least a dozen of times a day on even the most trivial topics, just as they might have when they were in elementary school. With cell phones, writes Turkle, "Everyone important is on speed dial. In this sense, the generations sail down the river together and adolescents don't face the same pressure to develop the independence we have associated with moving forward into adulthood" (2011, p. 173).

Opportunities across the System

In a 1979 interview with Ron Brandt for *Educational Leadership*, Urie Bronfenbrenner lamented,

> We are busy doing other things. We just don't have time for children. Kids used to work alongside adults, helping to raise food and do other important chores. As we developed sophisticated technology and greater mobility, joint activity between the older and younger generations began to disappear. That doesn't mean that technology is bad; if we put our minds to it we can use technology to build an environment even more effective than the ones that used to occur naturally. But we haven't had that in mind. Nowadays the important thing is for all adults to work fulltime if they possibly can. (p. 459)

Bronfenbrenner hearkens back to an agrarian ideal that is, for many families, impossible to reclaim. Today, parents do in fact need to work full time to make ends meet, and simply cannot spend as many hours with their children as their own parents probably spent with them. And as much as adults appreciate the technological advancements made in the scientific, medical, transportation, communication, and entertainment sectors, many simultaneously wish things would slow down a bit when it comes to their kids. Childhood, as many parents view it, is not what their children have today, but what they remember having back when they were young (McPake & Plowman, 2009). But childhood *isn't* what it used to be. Families have evolved and so too must the ideals we hold family life to. In the past 40 years, technological tools and media have become so entrenched in our daily routines that even when parents admit their kids could do with less TV, video games, and the internet, they can't fathom how life would function without media (Evans, Jordan, & Horner, 2011). Screens fill nearly every room of our homes and come with us wherever we go—in the car, on the bus, in our purses, in our back pockets. We adults, after all, have become just as hooked on the digital as our children have.

Unless we are willing to forfeit the innovations and luxuries that techno-logical progress has brought us, we need to look forward rather than back to raise healthy children in this day and age. And, as Bronfenbrenner noted, "If we put our minds to it we can use technology to build an environment even more effective than the ones that used to occur naturally" (Brandt, 1979, p. 459). In other words, we can leverage technology to help counter the effects of too much technology. If humans possess the imagination and technical know-how to create irresistibly addictive digital games, phones that function as personal computers, and websites that get us to publicly reveal our deepest feelings, it is certainly within our capacity to fix what negative effects these products are having on our lives.

To do so, however, we must better understand how the contexts children live in influence their digital media choices, experiences, and subsequent develop-ment. Too often, research on media effects or on learning with media focuses on the human-computer interactions to the exclusion of what surrounds these interactions, including the human-human, human-environment, even environment-environment interactions that simultaneously shape the mediated experience. Bronfenbrenner's ecological systems theory—originally offered to child development researchers to bring a balance of rigor and relevance to their "experiments" (1977)—forces us to consider the above-described contex-tual factors, which according to Jordan (2004), "are often 'controlled for' rather than integral components of research models" (p. 196). "What is useful about the ecological perspective," Jordan continues, "is that it allows for a simultane-ous focus on the characteristics of the individual child, the critical setting of the home, and the ubiquitous cultural environment" (p. 196). What is challenging about the ecological perspective, on the other hand, is that by acknowledging the inextricability of "environmental structures and the processes taking place within and between them" (Bronfenbrenner, 1977, p. 84), it is difficult to isolate "causes" or the directionality of observed effects.

This chapter presents just a snapshot in time, as seen through the lens of a theory generated more than 30 years ago. We hope this chapter has made clear that digital media alone do not determine how children behave, how they think, what they eat, or the ways in which they interact (or do not interact) with other people. In fact, the point of our analyses has been to illustrate how factors in the micro-, meso-, exo-, and macrosystems work in inextricable concert to shape children's settings, which in turn shape and are shaped by their interactions with digital media. We believe that an ecological perspective reveals that, across these nested spheres of influence, there are plenty of opportunities to guide children toward the positive and away from the negative experiences with digital media. Capitalizing on these opportunities, however, will require coordination across all levels of the broader system.

If every system player encircling the developing child—parents, teachers, technology manufacturers, media producers, journalists, policymakers, and so on—can commit to understanding their role in influencing the new ecology of human development, children will have a better chance of realizing the promises, rather than the pitfalls, of digital media. In the *microsystem*, for instance, parents can simply be more attuned to the ways in which their actions as purchasers, role models, playmates, and monitors influence what their children do with digital media (Barron et al., 2009; Takeuchi, 2011). By better understanding dynamics of the *mesosystem*, practitioners (e g, educators, media producers) can take fuller advantage of cross-system interactions to deepen learning. In the *exosystem*, producers of digital media and tools for children may wish to pay closer attention to the ways in which their products shape "in-room" interactions among family members, in addition to the "in-game" interactions they typically design for (Stevens et al., 2008). Finally, at the level of the *macrosystem*, the press may aim to tell a more balanced story about the risks and benefits of digital media use by seeking the expertise of researchers from a range of fields, including education, cognitive science, neuroscience, computer science, and child development. By donning an ecological perspective, each of us can better understand the distinct but connected role we play in raising healthy, productive children in the twenty-first century.

Notes

1. According to Moore's Law, over the history of computing hardware, the number of transistors on integrated circuits doubles about every two years (Moore, 1965).
2. This, of course, requires access to or ownership of an internet-connected computer, which is not free.
3. See Jordan (2004) for a more comprehensive review of the role of media in children's development, also from an ecological perspective.

References

American Academy of Pediatrics Council on Communications and Media. (2010). Policy statement—media education. *Pediatrics, 126*(5), 1–6.

American Academy of Pediatrics Council on Communications and Media. (2011). Policy statement—children, adolescents, obesity, and the media. *Pediatrics, 128*(1), 201–208.

American Academy of Pediatrics Council on Communications and Media. (2013). Policy statement: Children, adolescents, and the media. *Pediatrics, 132,* 958–961.

Ames, M., Go, J., Kaye, J., & Spasojevic, M. (2010). Making love in the network closet: The benefits and work of family videochat. In *Proceedings of the 2010 ACM conference on computer supported cooperative work* (pp. 145–154). New York, NY: ACM.

Arvizu, S., Simon, A., Lindland, E., & O'Neil, M. (2011). Where's the learning? An analysis of media stories of digital media and learning. Retrieved from http://www.frameworksinstitute.org/assets/files/PDF_dml/dmlmediacontentanalysis.pdf

Attewell, P., Suazo-Garcia, B., & Battle, J. (2003). Computers and young children: Social benefit or social problem? *Social Forces, 82*, 277–296.

Ball, S., & Bogatz, G. A. (1970). A summary of the major findings in "The first year of Sesame Street: An evaluation." Retrieved from http://files.eric.ed.gov/fulltext/ED122799.pdf

Barkhuus, L., & Brown, B. (2009). Unpacking the television: User practices around a changing technology. *ACM Transactions on Computer-Human Interaction (TOCHI), 16*(3), 15.

Barron, B. (2004). Learning ecologies for technological fluency: Gender and experience differences. *Journal of Educational Computing Research, 31*(1), 1–36.

Barron, B., Martin, C. K., Takeuchi, L., & Fithian, R. (2009). Parents as learning partners in the development of technological fluency. *International Journal of Learning and Media, 1*(2), 55–77.

Biddiss, E., & Irwin, J. (2010). Active video games to promote physical activity in children and youth: A systematic review. *Archives of Pediatric & Adolescent Medicine, 164*(7), 664–672.

Birch, L. L., Parker, L., & Burns, A. (2011). *Early childhood obesity prevention policies*. Washington, DC: National Academies Press.

Blair, C., & Razza, R. P. (2007). Relating effortful control, executive function, and false belief understanding to emerging math and literacy ability in kindergarten. *Child Development, 78*(2), 647–663.

Brandt, R. (1979). On families and schools: A conversation with Urie Bronfenbrenner. *Educational Leadership, 36*(7), 459–463

Bronfenbrenner, U. (1974). Developmental research, public policy, and the ecology of childhood. *Child Development, 45*(1), 1–5.

Bronfenbrenner, U. (1977). Toward an experimental ecology of human development. *American Psychologist, 32*(7), 513–530.

Bronfenbrenner, U. (1979). *The ecology of human development: Experiments by nature and design*. Cambridge, MA: Harvard University Press.

Bronfenbrenner, U. (1986). Ecology of the family as a context for human development: Research perspectives. *Developmental Psychology, 22*(6), 723–742.

Brown, J. S., Collins, A., & Duguid, P. (1989). Situated cognition and the culture of learning. *Educational Researcher, 18*(1), 32–42.

Campos, B., Graesch, A. P., Repetti, R., Bradbury, T., & Ochs, E. (2009). Opportunity for interaction? A naturalistic observation study of dual-earner families after work and school. *Journal of Family Psychology, 23*(6), 798–807.

Cifuentes, L., & Murphy, K. L. (2000). Promoting multicultural understanding and positive self-concept through a distance learning community: Cultural connections. *Educational Technology Research & Development, 48*(1), 69–83.

Clark, L. S. (2011). Parental mediation theory for the digital age. *Communication Theory, 21*(4), 323–343.

Common Sense Media. (2011). Zero to eight: Children's media use in America. Retrieved from http://www.commonsensemedia.org/sites/default/files/research/zerotoeightfinal2011.pdf

Consumer Electronics Association. (2012). CE industry to reach record-high revenues in 2012, according to CEA. Retrieved from http://www.ce.org/News/News-Releases/Press-Release s/2012-Press-Releases/CE-Industry-to-Reach-Record-High-Revenues-in-2012,.aspx

Council of Economic Advisers. (2010). Work-life balance and the economics of workplace flexibility. Retrieved from http://www.whitehouse.gov/files/documents/100331-cea-econ omics-workplace-flexibility.pdf

Courtois, C., & D'heer, E. (2012). Second screen applications and tablet users: Constellation, awareness, experience, and interest. Paper presented at the 10th European Conference on Interactive TV and Video, Berlin, Germany.

Cummings, H. M., & Vandewater, E. A. (2007). Relation of adolescent video game play to time spent in other activities. *Archives of Pediatric & Adolescent Medicine, 161*, 684–689.

DeLoache, J. S., Chiong, C., Sherman, K., Islam, N., Vanderborght, M., Troseth, G. L., ... O'Doherty, K. (2010). Do babies learn from baby media? *Psychological Science, 21*(11), 1570–1574.

Derks, D., & Bakker, A. B. (2010). The impact of email communication on organizational life. *Journal of Psychosocial Research on Cyberspace*, 4(1).

Drucker, P. (1969). *The age of discontinuity: Guidelines to our changing society*. New York: Harper and Row.

Edelson, D. C. (1998). Realising authentic science learning through the adaptation of scientific practice. In K. G. Tobin & B. J. Fraser (Eds.), *International handbook of science education* (pp. 317–332). Dordrecht, Netherlands: Kluwer Academic Publishers.

Entertainment Software Association. (2011). Essential facts about the computer and video game industry. Retrieved from http://www.theesa.com/facts/pdfs/ESA_EF_2011.pdf

Evans, C. A., Jordan, A. B., & Horner, J. (2011). Only two hours? A qualitative study of the challenges parents perceive in restricting television time. *Journal of Family Issues*, 32(9), 1223–1244.

Gerstein, R. (2000). Videoconferencing in the classroom: Special projects toward cultural understanding. *Computers in the Schools*, 16(3/4), 177–186.

Good, J. (2006). Negotiating an interactive web of activities: A critical look at working parents' multitasking (Working Paper No. 48). Los Angeles, CA: UCLA Sloan Center on Everyday Lives of Families.

Gray, L., Thomas, N., & Lewis, L. (2010). Teachers' use of educational technology in US public schools: 2009 (NCES 2010-040). Retrieved from http://nces.ed.gov/pubs2010/2010040.pdf

Grimes, S. M., & Fields, D. A. (2012). Kids online: A new research agenda for understanding social networking forums. New York, NY: The Joan Ganz Cooney Center at Sesame Workshop.

Hofferth, S. L. (2010). Home media and children's achievement and behavior. *Child Development*, 81(5), 1598–1619.

Ito, M., Baumer, S., Bittanti, M., boyd, d., Cody, R., Herr-Stephenson, R.,…Tripp, L. (2009). *Hanging out, messing around, geeking out: Living and learning with new media*. Cambridge, CA: MIT Press.

Ito, M., & Okabe, D. (2005). Technosocial situations: Emergent structuring of mobile email use. In M. Ito, D. Okabe, & M. Matsuda (Eds.), *Personal, portable, pedestrian: Mobile phones in Japanese life* (pp. 257–275). Cambridge, MA: MIT Press.

Jenkins, H., Clinton, K., Purushotma, R., Robison, A. J., & Weigel, M. (2006). Confronting the challenges of participatory culture: Media education for the 21st century. Retrieved from http://www.macfound.org/media/article_pdfs/JENKINS_WHITE_PAPER.PDF

Jordan, A. B. (1992). Social class, temporal orientation, and mass media use within the family system. *Critical Studies in Mass Communication*, 9(4), 374–386.

Jordan, A. B. (2004). The role of media in children's development: An ecological perspective. *Developmental and Behavioral Pediatrics*, 25(3), 196–206.

Jordan, A. B. (2005). Learning to use books and television: An exploratory study in the ecological perspective. *American Behavioral Scientist*, 48(5), 523–538.

Katz, V. (2010). How children of immigrants use media to connect their families to the community. *Journal of Children and Media*, 4(3), 298–315.

Kendall-Taylor, N., Lindland, E., & Mikulak, A. (2010). "Faster and fancier books": Mapping the gaps between expert and public understandings of digital media and learning. Retrieved from http://www.frameworksinstitute.org/assets/files/PDF_dml/dmlmapthegaps.pdf

Kohn, M. L. (1995). Social structure and personality through time and space. In P. Moen, G. H. Elder, & K. Lüscher (Eds.), *Examining lives in context: Perspectives on the ecology of human development* (pp. 141–168). Washington, DC: American Psychological Association.

Kozma, R. B. (1991). Learning with media. *Review of Educational Research*, 61(2), 179–211.

Krajcik, J. (2001). Supporting science learning in context: Project-based science. In J. Krajcik & R. F. Tinker (Eds.), *Portable technologies: Science learning in context* (pp. 7–28). New York, NY: Kluwer Academic/Plenum Publishers.

Lanningham-Foster, L., Jansen, T. B., Foster, R. C., Redmond, A. B., Walker, B. A., Heinze, D., & Levine, J. (2006). Energy expenditure of sedentary screen time compared with active screen time for children. *Pediatrics*, 118, e1831–e1835.

Lareau, A. (2003). *Unequal childhoods: Class, race, and family life*. Berkeley, CA: University of California Press.

Lenhart, A., Madden, M., McGill, A. R., & Smith, A. (2007). Teens and social media. Retrieved from   http://www.pewinternet.org/~/media/Files/Reports/2007/PIP_Teens_Social_Media_Final.pdf.pdf

Leonardi, P. M. (2003). Problematizing "new media": Culturally based perceptions of cell phones, computers, and the Internet among United States Latinos. *Critical Studies in Media Communication, 20*(2), 160–179.

Linn, M. C. (2003). Technology and science education: Starting points, research programs, and trends. *International Journal of Science Education, 25*(6), 727–758.

Livingston, G. (2011). Latinos and digital technology, 2010. Washington, DC: Pew Hispanic Center.

Livingstone, S., & Helsper, E. J. (2008). Parental mediation of children's Internet use. *Journal of Broadcasting and Electronic Media, 524*, 581–599.

McPake, J., & Plowman, L. (2009). At home with the future: Influences on young children's early experiences with digital technologies. In N. Yelland (Ed.), *Contemporary perspectives on early childhood education*. Berkshire, UK: Open University Press.

Molenda, M. & Bichelmeyer, B. (2005). Issues and trends in instructional technology: Slow growth as economy recovers. In M. Orey, J. McClendon, & R. M. Branch (Eds.), *Educational media and technology yearbook 2005* (Vol. 30). Englewood, CO: Libraries Unlimited.

Moore, G. E. (1965). Cramming more components onto integrated circuits. *Electronics, 38*(8). Retrieved from http://www.computerhistory.org/semiconductor/assets/media/classic-papers-pdfs/Moore_1965_Article.pdf

National Center for Education Statistics. (2006). Internet access in US public schools and classrooms: 1994–2005. Retrieved from http://nces.ed.gov/pubs2007/2007020.pdf

National Research Council. (2003). *Working families and growing kids: Caring for children and adolescents*. Washington, DC: The National Academics Press.

National Research Council. (2006). *Learning to think spatially: GIS as a support system in the K–12 curriculum*. Washington, DC: National Academy Press.

NPD Group. (2009a). Households with kids up to 12 years of age account for 45 percent of video game industry revenue. Retrieved from http://www.npd.com/press/releases/press_090910.html

NPD Group. (2009b). *Kids' use of consumer electronics devices such as cell phones, personal computers and video game platforms continue to rise* (Vol. 2009). Port Washington, NY: NPD.

Ophir, E., Nass, C., & Wagner, A. D. (2009). Cognitive control in media multitaskers. *Proceedings of the National Academy of Sciences, 106*(37), 5583–15587.

Paley, A. R. (2007, April 5). Software's benefits on tests in doubt. *The Washington Post*. Retrieved from http://www.washingtonpost.com/wp-dyn/content/article/2007/04/04/AR2007040402715.html

PBS & Grunwald Associates LLC. (2010). Deepening connections: Teachers increasingly rely on media and technology. Retrieved from http://www-tc.pbs.org/about/media/about/cms_page_media/182/PBS-Grunwald-2011e.pdf

Pea, R. (1993). Practices of distributed intelligence and designs for education. In G. Salomon (Ed.), *Distributed cognitions: Psychological and educational considerations* (pp. 47–87). Cambridge, UK: Cambridge University Press.

Pea, R. D., Nass, C., Meheula, L., Rance, M., Kumar, A., Bamford, H.,…Zhou, M. (2012). Media use, face-to-face communication, media multitasking, and social well-being among 8- to 12-year-old girls. *Developmental Psychology, 48*(2), 327–336.

Penuel, W. R., Pasnik, S., Bates, L., Townsend, E., Gallagher, L. P., Llorente, C., & Hupert, N. (2009). Preschool teachers can use a media-rich curriculum to prepare low-income children for school success: Results of a randomized controlled trial. Retrieved from http://rtl.cct.edc.org/pdf/RTLEvalReport.pdf

Plowman, L., McPake, J., & Stephen, C. (2008). Just picking it up? Young children learning with technology at home. *Cambridge Journal of Education, 38*(3), 303–319.

Posner, M., & Rothbart, M. K. (2000). Developing mechanisms of self-regulation. *Development and Psychopathology, 12*, 427–441.

Prensky, M. (2001). Digital natives, digital immigrants. Part 2: Do they really think differently? *On the Horizon, 9*(6), 1–6.

Raffle, H., Revelle, G., Mori, K., Ballagas, R., Buza, K., Horii, H., . . . Spasojevic, M. (2011). *Hello, is Grandma there? Let's read! StoryVisit: Family video chat and connected e-books*. Paper presented at the 29th International Conference on Human Factors in Computing Systems, Vancouver, British Columbia, Canada.

Reiser, R. A., Tessmer, M. A., & Phelps, P. C. (1984). Adult-child interaction in children's learning from *Sesame Street*. *Educational Technology Research & Development, 32*(4), 217–223.

Revelle, G., Reardon, E., Green, M. M., Betancourt, J., & Kotler, J. (2007). The use of mobile phones to support children's literacy learning. *Persuasive Technology, 4744*, 253–258.

Richtel, M. (2010, November 21). Growing up digital, wired for distraction. *The New York Times*. Retrieved from http://www.nytimes.com/2010/11/21/technology/21brain.html

Roschelle, J. M., Pea, R. D., Hoadley, C. M., Gordin, D. N., & Means, B. M. (2000). Changing how and what children learn in school with computer-based technologies. *The Future of Children, 10*(2), 76–101.

Rosen, L. D. (2010). *Rewired: Understanding the iGeneration and the way they learn*. New York, NY: Palgrave Macmillan.

Rubinstein, J. S., & Meyer, D. E. (2001). Executive control of cognitive processes in task switching. *Journal of Experimental Psychology, 27*(4), 763–797.

Rusetski, A. (2012). The whole new world: Nintendo's targeting choice. *Journal of Business Case Studies, 8*(2), 197–212.

Salomon, G. (1977). Effects of encouraging Israeli mothers to co-observe *Sesame Street* with their five-year-olds. *Child Development, 48*(3), 1146–1151.

Scelfo, J. (2010, June 9). The risks of parenting while plugged in. *The New York Times*. Retrieved from http://www.nytimes.com/2010/06/10/garden/10childtech.html

Scelfo, J. (2011, December 22). Video chat reshapes domestic rituals. *The New York Times*. Retrieved from http://www.nytimes.com/2011/12/22/garden/video-chat-reshapes-domestic-rituals.html

Small, G., & Vorgan, G. (2009). *iBrain: Surviving the technological alteration of the modern mind*. New York, NY: Harper Collins.

Smith, A. (2012). 46% of American adults are smartphone owners. Retrieved from http://pewinternet.org/~/media/Files/Reports/2012/Smartphone%20ownership%202012.pdf

Stevens, R., Satwicz, T., & McCarthy, L. (2008). In-game, in-room, in-world: Reconnecting video game play to the rest of kids' lives. In K. Salen (Ed.), *The ecology of games: Connecting youth, games, and learning* (pp. 41–66). Cambridge, MA: MIT Press.

Strazdins, L., Korda, R. J., Lim, L. L., Broom, D. H., & D'Souza, R. M. (2004). Around-the-clock: Parent work schedules and children's well-being in a 24-hour economy. *Social Science & Medicine, 59*(7), 1517–1527.

Takeuchi, L. (2011). Families matter: Designing media for a digital age. Retrieved from http://www.joanganzcooneycenter.org/wp-content/uploads/2011/06/jgcc_familiesmatter.pdf

Takeuchi, L., & Stevens, R. (Eds.). (2011). The new coviewing: Designing for learning through joint media engagement. Retrieved from http://www.joanganzcooneycenter.org/wp-content/uploads/2011/12/jgc_coviewing_desktop.pdf

Taras, H. L., Sallis, J. F., Patterson, T. L., Nader, P. R., & Nelson, J. A. (1989). Television's influence on children's diet and physical inactivity. *Journal of Development and Behavioral Pediatrics, 10*, 176–180.

Thurston, A. (2004). Promoting multicultural education in the primary classroom: Broadband videoconferencing facilities and digital video. *Computers & Education, 43*(1/2), 165–177.

Towers, I., Duxbury, L., Higgins, C., & Thomas, J. (2006). Time thieves and space invaders: Technology, work and the organization. *Journal of Organizational Change Management, 19*(5), 593–618.

Turkle, S. (2011). *Alone together: Why we expect more from technology and less from each other.* New York, NY: Basic Books.

Tuten, T. L. (2008). *Advertising 2.0: Social media marketing in a Web 2.0 world.* Westport, CT: Greenwood Publishing Group.

Ulicsak, M., Wright, M., & Cranmer, S. (2009). Gaming in families: A literature review. Bristol, UK: Futurelab.

US Department of Labor. (2009). Women in the labor force: A databook. Retrieved from http://www.bls.gov/cps/wlf-databook-2009.pdf

Valkenburg, P. M., Krcmar, M., Peeters, A. L., & Marseille, N. M. (1999). Developing a scale to assess three styles of television mediation: "Instructive mediation," "restrictive mediation," and "social coviewing." *Journal of Broadcasting and Electronic Media, 43*(1), 52–66.

Vigdor, J. L., & Ladd. (2010). Scaling the digital divide: Home computer technology and student achievement. Retrieved from http://www.nber.org/papers/w16078.pdf?new_window=1

Wallis, C. (2006). The multitasking generation. *Time*(167), 48–55.

Warschauer, M., & Matuchniak, T. (2010). New technology and digital worlds: Analyzing evidence of equity in access, use, and outcomes. *Review of Research in Education, 34*(179), 179–225.

Weir, L. A., Etelson, D., & Brand, D. A. (2006). Parents' perceptions of neighborhood safety and children's PA. *Preventative Medicine, 43*, 212–217.

Weiss, H., Kreider, H., Lopez, M. E., & Chatman-Nelson, C. (2010). *Preparing educators to engage families: Case studies using an ecological systems framework* (2nd ed.). Thousand Oaks, CA: Sage Publications.

Wenglinsky, H. (2005). *Using technology wisely: The keys to success in schools.* New York, NY: Teachers College Press.

Woodward, E. (2000). Media in the home, 2000. Retrieved from http://www.annenbergpublicpolicycenter.org/downloads/media_and_developing_child/mediasurvey/survey7.pdf

Zimmerman, B. J. (1990). Self-regulated learning and academic achievement: An overview. *Educational Psychologist, 25*(1), 3–17.

CHAPTER 3

Examining Media's Impact on Children's Weight

AMOUNT, CONTENT, AND CONTEXT

Dina L. G. Borzekowski

Media messages and the technology through which they are delivered greatly affect the health and well-being of message receivers and technology users. Children and adolescents seem to be shaped especially by their use of both older and newer media. For decades, researchers have been trying to understand whether and to what extent media affect youth; in this chapter, we offer a framework to use in thinking about and considering media's specific influence on children's weight and body size. While the focus is on weight, the thoughts we provide can be used to study media's effect on a range of health outcomes.

To examine media's impact on various health outcomes and interventions, one must consider three factors: the amount of time children spend with media, the content of the media, and the context in which this occurs. These factors can help us consider media's influence on disordered eating among children and adolescents, from the growing obesity problem to the alarming rates of anorexia and bulimia.

Amount

Children and adolescents spend an alarming amount of time with media. Total media time for the youngest infants, from birth to 12 months, is around 1 hour and 55 minutes daily; by age 8, it is 3 hours and 46 minutes (Common Sense, 2011). A 5- to 8-year-old American child may spend around 2 hours watching TV, DVDs or videos, 40 minutes playing media games, and another 7 minutes with other computer activities (Common Sense, 2011). But what is the influence of all this time spent with media?

Considering 20 years of research, the Institute of Medicine of the National Academies (2006) found that there was a small but statistically significant relationship between time spent with media and childhood obesity. A meta-analysis of 52 independent samples found the sample-weighted fully corrected effect size to be 0.084 (Marshall, Biddle, Gorely, Cameron, & Murdey, 2004). Furthermore, weekly hours of screen time (more so than patterns of physical activity) in childhood predict obesity in adolescence and adulthood (Boone, Gordon-Larsen, Adair, & Popkin, 2007; Hancox, Milne, & Poulton, 2004). Video game play time is the only amount that is questionable. Neither correlational nor longitudinal studies show consistent relationships between hours spent playing and weight, perhaps because the content and physical requirements of video games vary tremendously.

Besides studies of overweight and obesity, research also shows problems on the other end of the continuum. Interestingly, time with media is associated with body dissatisfaction. Three years after the introduction of broadcast television to rural regions of the Pacific Island of Fiji, researchers found that Fijian adolescent girls who spent more time with media exhibited the beginnings of weight and body shape preoccupation, purging behavior to control weight, and body disparagement (Becker, 2004). Repeated and frequent exposure to beauty ideals and characters seemed to alter individuals' sense of self and sometimes their behaviors. This relationship is not exclusive to television. A large longitudinal study of more than 2,500 middle and high school girls from Minnesota found that heavy readers of magazines were twice as likely to engage in disordered weight-control behaviors (Van der Berg, Neumark-Sztainer, Hannan, & Haines, 2007). On the internet, a recent phenomenon has emerged where images and websites describe, endorse, and support eating disorders (Borzekowski, Schenk, Wilson, & Peebles, 2010). Those who reported more hours on these pro-anorexia and pro-bulimia websites (commonly known as "pro-ana" and "pro-mia" sites) had more severe eating disorder behaviors and poorer quality of life (Peebles et al., 2012).

The scientific interventions ($N = 47$) that have tried to lessen children's time spent with media offer some promising results (Schmidt et al., 2012). Nearly two-thirds of the interventions (29 out of 47) were successful in reducing media use; the most effective ones used electronic monitoring devices, contingent feedback systems, and clinic-based counseling (Schmidt et al., 2012). Of the effective interventions that measured BMI as an outcome ($N = 18$), half reported reductions. None of these media reduction interventions explored attitudes about body size and beauty; it would be fascinating to see if a pure decrease in time could alter one's perceptions around self-esteem and ideals with regard to body size and beauty.

Content

Rather than espouse the simple "couch-potato explanation," —the idea that children who spend time with media are not active enough to control their weight—researchers are currently exploring the hypothesis that constant exposure to food and beverage advertising underlies the relationship between media exposure time and children's growing weight problems (Hingle & Kunkel, 2012; Zimmerman & Bell, 2010). Content analyses consistently find that on television, the majority of food advertisements (>79%) are for high-calorie and low-nutrient foods (Kunkel, McKinley, & Wright, 2009). While several media and entertainment companies have put forth new policies to limit child-directed marketing to products that meet certain (higher) nutritional standards, these pledges do not cover new media (Kraak, Story, Wartella, & Ginter, 2011). Foods and beverages of low nutritional value are being advertised through new online technology and many of the same promotional techniques (e.g., attention-getting productions features, branded characters, and repetition) are being employed (Alvy & Calvert, 2008).

Repeated and ubiquitous exposure to messages promoting unhealthy foods and beverages can shape children's dietary preferences, food and drink requests, dietary intake, and weight (Institute of Medicine of the National Academies, 2006). But the messages don't need to be frequent—experimental research has shown that even exposure to a 10-second commercial is associated with a shift in preschool children's choices about food products (Borzekowski & Robinson, 2001). Other studies examining children's viewing of programming with and without advertisements has found that children watching educational television, videos, and DVDs do not exhibit concurrent or subsequent obesity (Zimmerman & Bell, 2010).

What food messages do children see? A recent content analysis found that in the last decade or so, although there has been a decrease in the rate of food and beverage messages in children's programming, the majority (86%) of featured food messages promote products high in fat, sugar, or sodium (Powell, Schermbeck, Szczypka, Chaloupka, & Braunschweig, 2011). A clever classification scheme known as "Whoa, Slow, and Go," developed by Kunkel and colleagues (2010), shows that in children's programming from 2009, 72.5% of the food advertisements are for items that are only good to eat on special occasions, 26.6% are for items that are good to eat a few times a week, and only 1% are for foods that are good to eat every day.

Typically, the actors promoting these unhealthy foods do not look like the (literally) growing consumers of these products. Popular programs on the Disney and Nickelodeon channels present images and dialogue that suggest that white, thin girls represent the ideal of beauty (Northup & Liebler, 2010).

Exposure to such actors can make the child or adolescent who differs from this ideal suffer from body dissatisfaction. A meta-analysis of 25 experimental studies reports that especially for adolescent girls, greater exposure to thin models is associated with a more negative body self-image (Groesz, Levine, & Murnen, 2002). Unpacking the research on how and why the introduction of broadcast television in Fiji altered young girls' perceptions of self, researchers found many of the changes had to do with the type of content being watched through this new media. Fascinating quantitative and qualitative papers described that these Fijian girls were paying particularly close attention to the female models and actors in the Western shows (Becker, Burwell, Herzog, Hamburg, & Gilman, 2002; Becker, 2004).

Besides television, the pattern of greater exposure to unrealistic body ideals, extreme dieting, and lower body satisfaction has been observed with other media. Van der Berg and colleagues (2007) found that reading magazine articles about diet trends and the importance of weight loss strongly predicted, among girls but not boys, unhealthy weight control behaviors (such as vomiting or using laxatives) five years later. Boys' personal body images decreased following the playing of video games, which can depict males as muscular superheroes and females as sexualized curvy vixens (Barlett & Harris, 2008).

Context

The context in which children are exposed to and use media can affect the influence of these media messages. Context involves with whom and where a child receives media. It also involves the background of the receiver and the framing of the message.

A child's household environment and the behaviors his or her parents engage in are associated with the amount and effect of screen media on children and adolescent health behaviors (Pearson, Salmon, Crawford, Campbell, & Timperio, 2011). A significant contextual variable is access to media technology. A 2011 survey found that among a nationally representative sample of U.S. children who ranged in age from 6 months to 6 years, around 42% had a TV in the bedroom, up from 36% in 2003 (Common Sense Media 2011). Another survey of 781 adolescents found that nearly two-thirds (62%) had a bedroom TV (Barr-Anderson, van den Berg, Neumark-Sztainer, & Story, 2008). Children and adolescents also have access to and are watching media on mobile devices. From 2004 to 2009, cell phone and iPod ownership among 8- to 18-year-olds increased from 39% to 66% (Kaiser Family Foundation, 2010).

When content is delivered through a bedroom TV or through a mobile device, a parent is less able to monitor either the amount or content of media consumed by a child. Research shows that boys and girls who have a bedroom TV are more likely than other kids to report more TV viewing time, less physical activity, poorer dietary habits, and fewer family meals (Barr-Anderson et al., 2008). Around 40% of young people say their parents have some rules about media content and time spent with media, but they say those rules aren't always enforced (Kaiser Family Foundation, 2010).

While the majority of parents indicate that they mediate screen media use by their children (watching television alongside their children, overseeing the video games and websites they use), fewer children agree with these parental reports. Parental mediation can affect media's effect on children and adolescents. In the children and media literature, three mediation styles have emerged: (1) instructive mediation, guidance, and explanation of the formal and informal features of technology and content; (2) restrictive mediation, rule-making, and the use of devices to control what media children access and when; and (3) social coviewing, when parents and children use media together. In this last and most commonly used style, comments are subtle and less purposeful but still have immediate and long-term effects with regard to shaping media's influence on children (Borzekowski & Robinson, 2007).

All types of mediation styles seem to influence children's attitudes toward food and beverage advertising. Parents can shape children's understanding of how commercials play a role in developing food preferences by overtly discussing the advertising's intent and the quality of the presented products (Oates, Blades, Gunter, & Don, 2003; Hoffner & Buchanan, 2002). Yu (2011) recently showed with a sample of 7- to 12-year-old children that the level of verbal interaction between parent and child while using media, the parents' level of control over media, and the overall amount of time parents spent watching TV with their children were all significantly and negatively related to the child's attitudes toward snack and fast food advertising. Furthermore, this study found that all three of these factors were independently associated with children's BMI (Yu, 2011).

While many offer it as an option, there are mixed findings with regard to whether media literacy interventions for children and adolescents can alter the impact of media on food and weight (Rozendaal, Lapierre, van Reijmersdal, & Buijzen, 2011; Livingstone & Helsper, 2006). One issue might be that proper defenses against media messages require more sophisticated cognitive development and functioning than most children have (Rozendaal et al., 2011). Perhaps it might be more useful to work with parents and caregivers. A successful intervention was done with a small group of Head Start parents; after completing the curriculum, parents had more sophisticated understanding and more critical attitudes about television advertisements. These parents also had greater self-efficacy regarding TV mediation behaviors and saying no to children's requests for unhealthy products (Hindin, Contento, & Gussow, 2004).

Conclusion

Despite recent attention by public health officials and the mass media, childhood obesity prevalence rates remain high, at 16.9% of the U.S. child and adolescent population (birth through 19 years of age) (Ogden, Carroll, Kit, & Flegal, 2012). Without effective changes, some predict this rate could increase to 30% by 2030 (Wang, Beydoun, Liang, Cabellero, & Kumanyika, 2008).

Unless something equally attractive comes along, it is unlikely that the amount of time children and adolescents spend with media screens will decrease any time soon. New technologies enter the market, and often the youngest citizens are the early adopters. The likelihood of altering content also seems doubtful. In the United States, at least, efforts to change content or even provide content labels are obstructed by fierce supporters of the First Amendment. Even when hundreds of studies show the negative impact of media content on children and adolescents, free-speech advocates and multinational corporations that align with them, block regulations of digital content. Given that content is extremely difficult to control, altering context may serve as the most feasible option to reduce media's impact on childhood obesity.

References

Alvy, L. M., & Calvert, S. L. (2008). Food marketing on popular children's web sites: A content analysis. *Journal of the American Dietetic Association, 108*, 710–713.

Barr-Anderson, D. J., van den Berg, P., Neumark-Sztainer, D., & Story, M. (2008). Characteristics associated with older adolescents who have a television in their bedrooms. *Pediatrics, 121*, 718–724.

Barlett C., & Harris, R. (2008). The impact of body emphasizing video games on body image concerns on men and women. *Sex Roles, 59*, 586–601.

Becker, A. E., Burwell, R. A., Herzog, D. B., Hamburg, P., & Gilman, S. E. (2002). Eating behaviours and attitudes following prolonged exposure to television among ethnic Fijian adolescent girls. *The British Journal of Psychiatry, 180*, 509–514.

Becker, A. E. (2004). Television, disordered eating, and young women in Fiji: Negotiating body image and identity during rapid social change. *Culture, Medicine and Psychiatry, 28*, 533–559.

Boone, J. E., Gordon-Larsen, P., Adair, L. S., & Popkin, B. M. (2007). Screen time and physical activity during adolescence: Longitudinal effects on obesity in young adulthood. *International Journal of Behavioral Nutrition and Physical Activity, 4*, 26. doi:10.1186/1470-5868-4-26.

Borzekowski, D. L. G., & Robinson, T. N. (2001). The 30-second effect: An experiment revealing the impact of television commercials on food preferences of preschoolers. *Journal of the American Dietetic Association, 101*, 42–46.

Borzekowski, D. L. G., & Robinson, T. N. (2007). Conversations, control, and couch-time: The assessment and stability of parental mediation styles and children's TV and video viewing. *Journal of Children and Media, 1*, 162–176.

Borzekowski, D. L. G., Schenk, S., Wilson, J. L., & Peebles, R. (2010). E-Ana and e-Mia: A content analysis of pro-eating disorder web sites. *American Journal of Public Health, 100*, 1526–1534.

Common Sense Media (2011). Zero to eight: Children's media use in America. Retrieved from http://www.commonsensemedia.org/sites/default/files/research/zerotoeightfinal2011.pdf

Groesz, L. M., Levine, M. P., & Murnen, S. K. (2002). The effect of experimental presentation of thin media images on body satisfaction: a meta-analytic review. *International Journal of Eating Disorders, 31*, 1–16.

Hancox, R. J., Milne, B. J., & Poulton, R. (2004). Association between child and adolescent television viewing and adult health: A longitudinal birth cohort study. *The Lancet, 364*, 257–262.

Hindin, T. J., Contento, I. R., & Gussow, J. D. (2004). A media literacy nutrition education curriculum for Head Start parents about the effects of television food advertising on their children's food requests. *Journal of the American Dietetic Association, 104*, 192–198.

Hingle, M., & Kunkel, D. (2012). Childhood obesity and the media. *Pediatric Clinics of North America, 59*, 677–692.

Hoffner, C., & Buchanan, M. (2002). Parents' responses to television violence: The third person perception, parental mediation, and support for censorship. *Media Psychology, 4*, 231–252.

Institute of Medicine of the National Academies (2006). *Food marketing to children and youth: Threat or Opportunity?* Washington, DC: National Academies Press.

Kaiser Family Foundation (2010). Generation M2: Media in the lives of 8- to 18-year olds. Retrieved from http://kaiserfamilyfoundation.files.wordpress.com/2013/04/8010.pdf

Kunkel, D., McKinley, C., & Wright, P. (2010). *The impact of industry self-regulation on the nutritional quality of foods advertised on television to children.* Oakland, CA: Children Now.

Kraak, V. I., Story, M., Wartella, E., & Ginter, J. (2011). Industry progress to market a healthful diet to American children and adolescents. *American Journal of Preventive Medicine, 41*, 322–333.

Livingstone, S., & Helsper, E. J. (2006). Does advertising literacy mediate the effects of advertising on children? A critical examination of two linked research literatures in relation to obesity and food choice. *Journal of Communication, 56*, 560–584.

Marshall, S. J., Biddle, S. J. H., Gorely, T., Cameron, N., & Murdey, I. (2004). Relationships between media use, body fatness, and physical activity in children and youth: A meta-analysis. *International Journal of Obesity, 28*, 1238–1246.

Northup, T., & Liebler, C. M. (2010). The good, the bad, and the beautiful. *Journal of Children and Media, 4*, 265–282.

Oates, C., Blades, M., Gunter, B., & Don, J. (2003). Understanding of television advertising: A qualitative approach. *Journal of Marketing Communications, 9*, 59–72.

Ogden, C. L., Carroll, M. D., Kit, B. K., & Flegal, K. M. (2012). Prevalence of obesity and trends in body mass index among US children and adolescents, 1999-2010. *Journal of the American Medical Association, 307*, 483–490.

Pearson, N., Salmon, J., Crawford, D., Campbell, K., & Timperio, A. (2011). Are parental concerns for child TV viewing associated with child TV viewing and home sedentary environment? *International Journal of Behavioral Nutrition and Physical Activity, 8*, 102. doi:10.1186/1470-5868-8-102.

Peebles, R., Wilson, J. L., Borzekowski, D. L. G., Hardy, K. K., Lock, J. D., Mann, J. R., & Litt, I. F. (2012). Disordered eating in a digital age: Eating behaviors, health, and quality of life in users of websites with pro-eating disorder content. *Journal of Medical Internet Research, 14*(5), e148.

Powell, L. M., Schermbeck, R. M., Szczypka, G., Chaloupka, F. J., & Braunschweig, C. L. (2011). Trends in the nutritional content of television food advertisements seen by children in the United States. *Archives of Pediatric and Adolescent Medicine, 165*, 1078–1086.

Rozendaal, E., Lapierre, M. A., van Reijmersdal, E. A., & Buijzen, M. (2011). Reconsidering advertising literacy as a defense against advertising effects. *Media Psychology, 14*, 333–354.

Schmidt, M. E., Haines, J., O'Brien, A., McDonald, J., Price, S., Sherry, B., & Taveras, E. M. (2012). Systematic review of effective strategies for reducing screen time among young children. *Obesity, 20*, 1338–1354.

Van der Berg, P., Neumark-Sztainer, D., Hannan, P. J., & Haines, J. (2007). Is dieting advice from magazines helpful or harmful? Five-year associations with weight-control behaviors and psychological outcomes in adolescents. *Pediatrics, 119,* e30–e37.

Wang, Y., Beydoun, M. A., Liang, L., Caballero, B., & Kumanyika, S. K. (2008). Will all Americans become overweight or obese? Estimating the progression and cost of the U.S. obesity epidemic. *Obesity, 16,* 2323–2330.

Yu, H. (2011). Parental communication style's impact on children's attitudes toward obesity and food advertising. *Journal of Consumer Affairs, 45,* 87–107.

Zimmerman, F. J., & Bell, J. F. (2010). Associations of television content type and obesity in children. *American Journal of Public Health, 100,* 334–340.

CHAPTER 4

Demonstrating the Harmful Effects of Food Advertising on Children and Adolescents

OPPORTUNITIES FOR RESEARCH TO INFORM POLICY

Jennifer L. Harris

Key actors—from food and beverage companies, to restaurants, food retailers, trade associations, the media, government and others—all have an important role to play in creating a food marketing environment that supports, rather than undermines, the efforts of parents and other caregivers to encourage healthy eating among children and prevent obesity. (White House Task Force on Childhood Obesity [White House], 2010, p. 28)

In 2009–2010, 30% of children and adolescents in the United States were overweight or obese, and obesity rates have more than tripled since the 1970s (Ogden, Carroll, Kit, & Flegal, 2012). The economic and social costs of this crisis are staggering. Overweight children are tormented by weight-based bullying (Puhl, 2011) and face a lifetime of chronic health issues, including type 2 diabetes and heart disease (White House, 2010). As a result of obesity-related disease, this generation may be the first to live shorter lives than their parents (Olshansky et al., 2005). Although the dramatic rise in childhood obesity has been fueled by numerous environmental factors that negatively affect both diet and physical activity, public health experts argue that the overwhelmingly unhealthy food-marketing environment that surrounds young people is a significant contributor (Institute of Medicine [IOM], 2006; White House, 2010; World Health Organization [WHO], 2010).

To address this crisis, the White House (2010) has called on industry and the government to create a food marketing environment that supports parents' efforts to raise healthy children. I will argue that the research community also plays an essential role. Empirical evidence has established that children and adolescents view thousands of advertising messages every year for foods and beverages that do not contribute to a healthful diet. Research also shows that young children are not equipped to view any form of advertising critically. However, academic research is just beginning to examine key issues regarding food advertising effects, including young people's understanding of newer forms of advertising, such as marketing messages disguised as entertainment or delivered virally through peers; how food advertising affects food preferences and other predictors of eating behaviors; and whether it is even possible to defend against the implicit unhealthy messages conveyed in most food advertising or to use media to encourage healthy eating behaviors. This research—together with communication of the findings to parents, advocacy organizations, policymakers, and the food and media industries—is necessary to identify effective solutions and create the political will to resolve this crisis.

The Food Advertising Environment

Young people are surrounded by food and beverage advertising—on television, radio, the internet, and increasingly on mobile devices—that almost exclusively promotes calorie-dense, nutrient-poor products. In 2006, food companies spent $1.6 billion in marketing directly targeted to children and adolescents, with the largest expenditures for carbonated beverages ($492 million), restaurant foods ($294 million), and breakfast cereals ($237 million) (Federal Trade Commission [FTC], 2008). On television alone, 2- to 11-year-olds viewed 12.8 food and beverage ads every day on average in 2011, while 12- to 17-year olds viewed 16.2 ads (Yale Rudd Center, 2012). In 2009, 86% of TV food ads seen by children were for products high in saturated fat, sugar, or sodium (Powell, Schermbeck, Szczypka, Chaloupka, & Braunschweig, 2011). In 2010, candy products overtook prepared foods as the third most frequently viewed category of food advertising by youth, behind sugary cereals and fast food (Yale Rudd Center, 2012).

The messages presented in food advertising viewed by children raise additional concerns. Most child-targeted food advertising portrays unhealthy eating behaviors. For example, 58% modeled snacking between meals (Harrison & Marske, 2005), while just 11% showed eating in a kitchen, dining room or restaurant (Reece, Rifon, & Rodriguez, 1999). In addition, these ads often imply positive emotional benefits, such as fun, happiness, and being "cool," from consuming nutrient-poor foods (Folta, Goldberg, Economos, Bell, & Meltzer, 2006; Schor & Ford, 2007). An analysis of sugary cereal ads found predominantly unrealistic and contradictory messages about product attributes and healthy eating (Weinberg, Harris, & Schwartz, 2013). For example, 91% of ads viewed by children ascribed extraordinary powers to these products and 67% portrayed both healthy and unhealthy eating messages in the same ad.

Although food companies spent nearly half (46%) of their youth-targeted marketing budgets on television (FTC, 2008), food companies also extensively advertise to young people in other media. Children viewed on average 281 brand appearances (i.e., product placements) for foods and beverages during prime-time programming in 2008, and adolescents viewed 444 (Speers, Harris, & Schwartz, 2011). Just one company sponsored 60% to 70% of appearances viewed by youth—Coca-Cola—and children viewed more product placements than traditional television commercials for Coke. Similarly, of the 200 movies that were top-20 U.S. box office hits from 1996 through 2005, more than two-thirds contained at least one food brand, primarily sugar-sweetened beverages and fast food (Sutherland, MacKenzie, Purvis & Dalton, 2010). Most food brands that advertise directly to children also maintain child-targeted websites that contain branded games (i.e., advergames) and other engaging activities to encourage children to "play" with these foods (Moore & Rideout, 2007). These websites are very popular. Approximately 1.2 million children (6–11 years old) visited food company-sponsored advergame sites every month in 2009 (Harris, Speers, Schwartz, & Brownell, 2012). Child visitors spent 63 minutes per month on the most popular site (Millsberry.com) and visited 101 pages. As in television advertising, child-targeted food-company websites promote calorie-dense, nutrient-poor foods, featuring sugary cereals, fast food, and candy on the most popular sites (Harris, Speers, et al., 2012; Moore & Rideout, 2007). Food and beverage companies also advertise their products to young people on other (i.e., third-party) websites (Alvy & Calvert, 2008; Lingas, Dorfman, & Bukofzer, 2009). On average, 208 million banner ads for foods and beverages appear each month on children's websites, such as Nick.com, Neopets. com, and CartoonNetwork.com (Ustjanauskas, Harris, & Schwartz, 2012). As with television advertising, 84% of child-targeted banner ads promote products high in calories, sugar, saturated fat, or sodium. Banner advertisements for child-targeted products typically feature highly engaging content within the ads, including advergames, and direct links to food company–sponsored websites (Harris, Schwartz, et al., 2009, 2010, 2011).

Food and beverage companies also have quickly adopted social media to advertise their products. As of 2010, 11 of the 12 largest fast food restaurants had Facebook pages and YouTube channels, and all maintained Twitter accounts (Harris, Schwartz, et al., 2010). Similarly, 33 sugary drink brands had Facebook pages, 25 had YouTube channels, and 23 had Twitter accounts (Harris, Schwartz, et al., 2011). Recently, these companies have begun to advertise extensively in mobile media, through banner advertising and mobile applications (Harris, Schwartz, et al., 2010, 2011). Although academic researchers have not examined these newest advertising media in depth, numerous market research studies document that social and mobile media disproportionately appeal to adolescents (see Richardson & Harris, 2011).

Impact of Food Advertising to Youth

In a comprehensive review of the literature on food marketing to children and adolescents, the IOM (2006) concluded that food marketing increases children's preferences and requests to parents for advertised products, likely contributes to less healthful diets, and may increase negative diet-related health outcomes and risks. A separate review for the UK Food Standards Agency reached similar conclusions, but went further to state that the research shows that food advertising also likely contributes to increased consumption of categories of foods, not just switching between brands (Hastings et al., 2003). Both reports also stressed the need for more research to examine direct causal effects of food marketing on preferences and consumption of food categories (vs. specific brands) and broader nutrition-related beliefs and behaviors; effects of advertising in other media (i.e., not television); effects on adolescents; and potential positive effects of advertising that promotes healthy products and behaviors.

Since 2006, researchers have begun to address these gaps in the literature. For example, recent studies demonstrate that exposure to television food advertising increases children's consumption of any available snack food (Halford, Gillespie, Brown, Pontin, & Dovey, 2004; Halford, Boyland, Hughes, Oliveria, & Dovey, 2007; Harris, Bargh, & Brownell, 2009); prior exposure to soft drink and fast food advertising is associated with greater consumption of these product categories (Andreyeva, Kelly, & Harris, 2011); and viewing of commercial television, but not other forms (i.e., public television, videos, and DVDs), is related to higher childhood obesity (Zimmerman & Bell, 2010). Examinations of additional advertising techniques show that product placements (Auty & Lewis, 2004), advergames (Mallinckrodt & Mizerski, 2007), and radio (Bao & Shao, 2002) also affect young people's brand preferences. In addition, playing advergames for unhealthy foods increases children's consumption of nutrient-poor snack foods and decreases fruits and vegetables consumed, whereas playing games that promote healthy foods increases fruit and vegetable consumption (Harris, Speers, et al., 2012).

Understanding How Food Advertising Affects Young People

In recent years, the public debate has shifted: the question is no longer whether food advertising to children causes harm, but rather how to protect children and adolescents from its negative influence (Robinson & Sirard, 2005; Swinburn et al., 2008; White House, 2010). Suggested solutions range from educating young people about media literacy and nutrition education to inoculate them from exposure to unhealthy advertising; to promoting healthy diets and physical activity through advertising and social media; to enacting industry self-regulation or government regulation that restricts the types of food advertising targeted to young people (Harris, Pomeranz, Lobstein, & Brownell, 2009). However, additional research is essential to better understand all the ways that food advertising affects young people in order to identify interventions that will be effective at protecting them from its negative influence.

Models of Consumer Development

Beginning in the 1970s, research on how advertising affects young people primarily incorporated a stage model of consumer development focusing on understanding and processing of advertising information (see John, 1999; Wilcox et al., 2004; Ward, Wackman, & Wartella, 1977). This research examined advertising for all children's products and clearly demonstrated that before age 4 or 5 children have difficulty discriminating between commercials and television programs. In addition, until they reach 7 or 8 years old, children do not understand the persuasive intent of advertising; they simply view it as another source of information. As a result of these findings, psychologists and legal scholars argue that any advertising directed to young children is inherently unfair and potentially misleading and warrants significant protections (Wilcox et al., 2004; Pomeranz, 2010).

This early research on children's development as consumers presumed that the ability to recognize advertising and understand its intent produces a "cognitive filter" that enables young people to disregard the biased information presented (Ward et al., 1977). However, more recent research demonstrates additional requirements to effectively resist advertising influence. These newer findings suggest that older children and early adolescents also face substantial obastacles to defend against advertising influence. For example, Kunkel (2010) posits that children also must possess a more nuanced understanding of source bias, which may not occur until age 12. Similarly, John (1999) argues that children require cues to access their understanding of persuasive intent at the time of exposure to advertising, and this ability may not fully develop until 14 years or later.

In addition, as skepticism about advertising has increased among all age groups, marketers have found new ways to persuade while circumventing active processing of advertising information. New forms of advertising, such as advergames, product placements, and social media, are designed specifically to blur entertainment and promotional content and thus deactivate skeptical responses (Boush, Friestad, & Wright, 2009; Petty & Andrews, 2008). Similarly, advertisers attempt to bypass rational processing of advertising and establish brand inferences through positive implicit (i.e., nonconscious) associations using such means as sponsorships, celebrity endorsements, attractive models and settings, and "feel good" advertising (Keller, 2003). Fast food advertising to children, in particular, often is designed to simply create these positive associations with the restaurant (e.g., the Happy Meal box) while providing little or no information about specific food items (Harris, Schwartz, et al., 2010).

These nontraditional forms of advertising are more difficult for young people to recognize. For example, one large study demonstrated that even 12-year-olds could not identify approximately one-quarter of advertisements on web pages (Ali, Blades, Oates, & Blumberg, 2009). In addition, marketers increasingly use emotional marketing, or messages designed simply to create positive feelings about the product, without providing rational benefits or reasons to consume it (Advertising Research Foundation [ARF], 2008). These emotional messages and advertising disguised as entertainment distract the viewer from consciously considering the intent of the ads, which makes understanding of persuasive intent insufficient to counteract their effects (Boush et al., 2009; Petty & Andrews, 2008). This strategy is highly effective, even for adults. An analysis of 880 different advertising campaigns concluded that emotional advertising with "little or no rational content" consistently outperforms advertising with rational messaging (Binet & Field, 2009). Further research is necessary to understand young people's recognition and understanding of newer forms of advertising that disguise its persuasive intent or are designed to circumvent skeptical responses. Such research could be used by public health advocates to argue that it is unfair to target these forms of advertising to older children and early adolescents (Graff, Kunkel, & Mermin, 2012).

HARMFUL EFFECTS OF UNHEALTHY FOOD ADVERTISING

Psychological models predict that frequent exposure to food advertising, especially for the highly palatable products most commonly advertised, can have even more detrimental consequences (see Harris, Brownell, & Bargh, 2009). For example, repeated exposure to food advertising is related to children's normative beliefs about eating, such as "fast food is as nutritious as home-made meals" (Signiorelli & Lears, 1992; Signorielli & Staples, 1997). Research based on expectancy theory demonstrates that pre-existing beliefs about a food, including expectancies established through advertising exposure, affect perceived taste of that food (see Lee, Frederick, & Ariely, 2006). One study with children showed that prior exposure to enjoyable food advertising increased favorable impressions of the novel foods advertised (Moore & Lutz, 2000). Similarly, children liked the taste of foods in McDonald's wrappers more than the same food in a plain wrapper (Robinson, Borzekowski, Matheson, & Kraemer, 2007), as well as foods in packages with popular cartoon characters (Roberto, Baik, Harris, & Brownell, 2010).

Emerging research on the biological bases of food consumption suggests that advertising for calorie-dense, nutrient-poor foods can have highly damaging effects on young people's still-developing brains. For example, neuroimaging studies demonstrate that exposure to high-calorie food images elicits greater activation in reward regions of the brain than exposure to low-calorie food images (Killgore et al., 2003; O'Doherty, Rolls, Francis, Bowtell, & McGlone, 2001). Activation of these reward regions while viewing food advertisements predicted subsequent greater consumption of high-calorie foods and beverages among adolescents (Gearhardt, Yokum, Stice, Harris, & Brownell, 2012). Even adults can recall food advertisements that triggered cravings for tempting foods they knew they should resist (Harris, 2008). Research on the addictive properties of some foods, especially those with added sugar, is likely to provide further evidence of negative consequences of food advertising that encourages young people to consume these products from a very early age (Gearhardt, Grilo, DiLeone, Brownell, & Potenza, 2011; Harris, 2012).

Nonetheless, significantly more research is needed to understand why young people eat what they do, including how advertising affects their food preferences, normative beliefs about diet, biological responses to food, and other predictors of consumption behaviors. In addition, research to evaluate the effects of food advertising on adolescents is essential. Most research has focused on children, but adolescents are also more susceptible to advertising influence compared with adults (Brownell, Schwartz, Puhl, Henderson, & Harris, 2009; Livingstone & Helsper, 2006). Adolescents' ability to inhibit impulsive behaviors and resist immediate gratification for longer-term rewards are not well developed, making them more susceptible to the effects of exposure to unhealthy food advertising compared with adults (Pechmann, Levine, Loughlin, & Leslie, 2005). The effects of advertising designed to appeal specifically to adolescents' unique developmental needs to fit in with peers and actively search for information to shape their own identities (e.g., social media) also has not been studied. In addition, longitudinal evaluations of advertising exposure and health outcomes are required to effectively counter a common food industry argument that there is no causal link between food advertising and healthy diet or BMI (Young, 2002). Finally, the paucity of advertising that promotes healthy products, such as fruits and vegetables, has limited researchers' ability to measure potentially positive effects of exposure to food advertising.

IMPLICATIONS FOR PROTECTING YOUNG PEOPLE FROM UNHEALTHY FOOD ADVERTISING

Researchers argue that protecting young people from negative advertising influence may require new models to understand how advertising affects young people today (Harris, Brownell, & Bargh, 2009; Livingstone & Helsper, 2006). In addition to the ability to recognize advertising and understand its persuasive intent—as proposed by consumer development models—defending against the influence of unhealthy food advertising requires numerous conditions that even adults may find difficult to achieve (Harris, Brownell, & Bargh, 2009). For example, when an individual encounters an unhealthy advertising message, he or she must attend to the message, understand the nature of its effects, know how to effectively counteract those effects, possess the cognitive maturity to effectively resist, and have the necessary cognitive resources available at the time. Research on advertising to children also has largely ignored another critical factor in effectively counteracting the effects of advertising: the motivation to resist (Harris, Brownell, & Bargh, 2009). Advertising to children and adolescents often is informed by developmental psychology and designed specifically to counteract this motivation. Messages from peers (through social and viral media), beloved cartoon characters, and revered celebrities, together with implied emotional benefits from consuming the foods (i.e., having fun, being cool), all appeal to young people's unique developmental needs. Youth-targeted advertising is fun, engaging, and socially rewarding; why would young people want to resist?

Although further research is needed to understand how food marketing affects young people and to identify successful interventions to counteract its influence, empirical evidence does suggest that some approaches are unlikely to succeed. For example, media literacy has been shown to increase children's skepticism about food advertising (Bickham & Slaby, 2012), but a few studies demonstrate that understanding of persuasive intent and skepticism do not moderate food advertising effects (e.g., Ross et al., 1984; Chernin, 2008; Mallinckrodt & Mizerski, 2007). Similarly, nutrition education can teach children that advertised foods are unhealthy and the importance of healthy eating, but young people's food preferences and diet are determined primarily by perceived taste, not nutritional quality (Glanz, Basil, Maibach, Goldberg, & Snyder, 1998; Harris & Bargh, 2009; Neumark-Sztainer, Wall, Perry, & Story, 2003). Even adults have difficulty resisting the appeal of advertising that promotes tempting foods they know they should not consume (Harris, 2008). Social marketing that borrows successful techniques from advertisers, such as emotional messaging, adver-games and viral messages, to encourage reduced consumption of unhealthy foods could be more effective. However, it is unlikely that such efforts could counteract the $1.6 billion the food industry spends every year promoting primarily unhealthy foods to children and adolescents (FTC, 2008), and it is unclear who would fund such a campaign.

As a whole, research suggests that it is extraordinarily difficult for anyone to consistently resist the influence of advertising for highly palatable foods (Harris, Brownell, & Bargh, 2009). Given that there are no known options to protect children and adolescents from the effects of this advertising, and the urgency of the childhood obesity crisis, public health advocates increasingly call for policies to substantially reduce young people's exposure to unhealthy food marketing (WHO, 2010).

Policy Options to Reduce Unhealthy Food Advertising to Youth

A variety of policy options have been proposed to reduce unhealthy food advertising to young people, including industry self-regulation and government-sponsored policies such as expert guidelines, legislation, and regulation (Harris, Pomeranz, et al., 2009; Hawkes, 2007).

INDUSTRY SELF-REGULATION

In most countries, government has ceded the responsibility for advertising to children to the food and media industries through self-regulation (Hawkes, 2007). In the United States, these industries do recognize that advertising to children calls for additional protections. The Children's Advertising Review Unit (CARU) (2008) has established guidelines to protect "the uniquely impressionable and vulnerable child audience" from unfair advertising. In addition, the food industry responded to the IOM's (2006) call to use its "creativity and resources" to promote products that support healthful diets for children and youth by launching the Children's Food and Beverage Advertising Initiative (CFBAI) in 2007 (Kolish, Hernandez, & Blanchard, 2011). CFBAI participating companies have pledged to "shift the mix of foods advertised to children under 12 to encourage healthier dietary choices and healthy lifestyles."

However, limitations of industry self-regulatory programs continue to allow companies to advertise unhealthy products to young people in potentially misleading ways. For example, CARU (2008) prohibits the incorporation of advertising messages within children's television programming, recognizing that young children do not have the cognitive ability to identify advertising that is embedded within entertainment content. Yet there are no self-imposed restrictions on advertising embedded within digital content, such as advergames or child-targeted YouTube videos. In addition, CARU guidelines often leave considerable room for interpretation. For example, CARU requires that advertising "should not mislead children about benefits from use of the product" and "claims should not unduly exploit a child's imagination." However, child-targeted cereal advertising often attributes magical powers to sugary cereals and children who consume them (Weinberg et al., 2013). Apparently, CARU does not consider these messages to be misleading or unduly exploit a child's imagination.

Limitations in the scope of food advertising covered by the Children's Food and Beverage Advertising Initiative (CFBAI) also have been widely criticized. For example, the CFBAI allows participating companies to create their own definitions of "healthier dietary choices"; these criteria vary widely and appear to be designed to allow advertising for as many of each company's own products as possible (Interagency Working Group on Food Marketed to Children [IWG], 2011; Kunkel et al., 2009; Powell et al., 2011). The CFBAI has announced new category-specific uniform nutrition standards to be implemented by 2013 (CFBAI, 2011). However, these new standards will continue to allow companies to advertise products of poor nutritional quality, such as Popsicles and cereals consisting of one-third added sugar. There also are numerous limitations in the types of marketing covered by the CFBAI (IWG, 2011). Companies' nutrition standards apply only to advertising in child-directed media, which participating companies commonly define as media with an audience of 35% or more children (CFBAI, 2012). As a result, companies place no restrictions on advertising during programming viewed by large numbers of children but also viewed by older individuals, such as "tween" and prime-time programming. In addition, many forms of child-targeted marketing are not covered by the CFBAI because they do not appear in children's media, including product packaging, in-store promotions, premium offers, and event and athletic sponsorships (IWG, 2011). Finally, the CFBAI does not apply to advertising to children over age 11 (Kolish et al., 2011). The initiative considers 12- to 14-year-olds to be mature consumers, without the need for protections from unhealthy influence.

A review of the literature since the IOM (2006) report was issued concludes that the food and beverage industry has made moderate progress by instituting the CFBAI, but that the majority of food marketing to youth continues to promote primarily unhealthy products (Kraak, Story, Wartella, & Ginter, 2011). For example, from 2008 to 2012, companies reduced the sugar content of 13 of 16 cereals advertised to children by 1 or 2 g per serving, but they still contained significantly more sugar and sodium and less fiber than adult-targeted cereals and advertising spending for children's cereals increased by 34% during the same period (Harris, Schwartz, et al., 2012). Similarly, Powell and colleagues (2011) found that 86% of food products in TV ads seen by children in 2009 were high in fat, sugar, or sodium compared with 94% in 2003. An analysis of food advertising during children's programming in 2008 found that 73% of ads continued to promote high-calorie nutrient-poor products (Kunkel et al., 2009). In addition, children in the United States saw 5% more television advertisements for foods and beverages in 2011 than they had seen in 2007, the year prior to implementation of the CFBAI (Yale Rudd Center, 2012). The food industry also has failed to launch child-targeted advertising campaigns that promote a healthy eating environment (Kraak et al., 2011).

GOVERNMENT-SPONSORED POLICY OPTIONS

As a result of the limitations of industry self-regulation, government-sponsored policies are likely to be most effective at reducing young people's exposure to food advertising (Koplan & Brownell, 2010; Sharma, Teret, & Brownell, 2010), and a few countries have adopted legislation to limit advertising to children. Based on the early research showing children's greater vulnerability to advertising influence, Norway, Sweden, and Quebec ban all advertising to children under age 13 (WHO, 2012). In Quebec, this ban has resulted in an estimated 13% reduction in fast-food expenditures for French-speaking households and 2.2 to 4.4 billion fewer calories consumed by children annually (Dhar & Baylis, 2011). More recently, in 2007 the United Kingdom banned advertising for foods that do not meet government-defined healthful standards during children's programming and other programming widely viewed by children (Adams, Tyrrell, Adamson, & White, 2012). Malaysia and Thailand also restrict the advertising of some types of foods during children's programming (WHO, 2012).

However, establishment of federal-level policies in the United States appears unlikely in the near future. One often-cited barrier is the First Amendment that protects corporations' rights to "commercial speech;" although legal experts argue that these protections may not apply to food advertising to children (Harris & Graff, 2012; Pomeranz, 2010). As research has shown that children are not capable of understanding the persuasive intent of advertising, it can be argued than any advertising to children is inherently misleading and deceptive, which would not protected by the First Amendment (Pomeranz, 2010). In addition, most food advertisements do not provide consumers with rational benefits and reasons to purchase the product and thus do not assist consumers in rational decision making, the stated rationale for commercial speech protections (Harris & Graff, 2012). Therefore, the U.S. Congress may have the authority to pass laws restricting food advertising to children, and these laws could be upheld by the courts.

The greatest barrier to government policies to regulate food marketing to children in the United States may be the lack of political will to initiate what is sure to be a difficult battle. In 1978, the FTC proposed a ban on advertising to children as unfair under its rule-making authority, but fierce lobbying by advertisers and media companies resulted in Congress removing the agency's authority to limit unfair advertising to children (Kunkel & Wilcox, 2012). A recent attempt by four government agencies, including the FTC, to address the limitations of the CFBAI by establishing a set of voluntary guidelines on nutrition standards and marketing to children and adolescents resulted in a similar strong response from industry (IWG, 2011). Despite strong support from the public health community and 28,000 positive write-in comments (out of 29,000 in total) (FTC, 2011), the commissioner of the FTC reported in March 2012 that the proposed standards were no longer an agency priority (Wilson & Roberts, 2012). The estimated $175 million in federal lobbying spent by food and beverage groups since 2009 likely had some influence on the outcome (Wilson & Roberts, 2012).

PARENTS' ROLE

The most common argument against regulating food advertising to children is that parents are responsible for protecting their children from unwanted influence. According to this argument, parents should say "no" to requests for advertised foods, turn off the television and computer, and tell their children to go out and play. However, inciting children to ask their parents for advertised products is another key objective for marketers who target children, and this "pester power" is highly effective (Henry & Borzekowski, 2011; IOM, 2006). For example, 40% of parents report that their children (6–11 years) ask to go to McDonald's at least once per week, and 15% report that their preschoolers ask to go every day (Harris, Schwartz, et al., 2010). In a study with children (3–8 years), participants were significantly more likely to choose a fast-food item after seeing a television ad for it, including both unhealthy and relatively healthy items (Ferguson, Munoz, & Medrano, 2012). Parental encouragement to choose the healthier item had only a slight moderating effect; the advertising was significantly more influential. Research with parents demonstrates that they also are influenced by advertising for child-targeted products. Parents' exposure to fast-food advertising predicted the belief that others often eat fast food, which mediated how often they took their own children to fast-food restaurants (Grier, Mensinger, Huang, Kumanyika, & Stettler, 2007).

In addition, most parents do not understand the impact that food advertising has on their children's food preferences and diet. Focus groups with parents revealed that many believe child-targeted food advertising is annoying, but harmless (Ustjanauskas et al., 2010). The strongest predictor of parents' support for restrictions on food marketing to children is agreement with statements about the harmful effects of food marketing, and these attitudes mediated the relationship between awareness of food marketing to children and support for restrictions (Goren, Harris, Schwartz, & Brownell, 2010). Media attention to the results of research on food advertising to children and advocacy efforts designed to communicate these findings to a wider audience is essential to increasing parents' awareness of food advertising to their children, understanding of its impact, and support for policies to reduce unhealthy child-targeted food advertising.

The Role of Research in Improving Food Advertising to Children

Significant improvements are required to reach the goal of creating a healthy food marketing environment for children. However, largely due to research documenting food advertising to youth and its effects, some progress has been achieved. Empirical evidence has been essential for policymakers to demonstrate the need for regulation and to garner public support. For example, seminal research on consumer development in the 1970s provided necessary support for government restrictions on advertising to children in Norway, Sweden, and Quebec (WHO, 2012), and the U.S. FTC's attempt to restrict children's advertising in 1978 (Kunkel & Wilcox, 2012). The 2006 IOM report encouraged the food industry to address unhealthy food advertising to children in the United States and led to the establishment of the CFBAI. Around the same time, the Hastings and colleagues (2003) report enabled the United Kingdom to enact restrictions of television food advertising to children. Negative attention from media coverage of research findings also places pressure on the food industry to change its practices. Negative media resulting from research on cereal companies' child-targeted marketing practices likely contributed to recent nutritional improvements in child-targeted cereals and the discontinuation of popular advergame websites (Millsberry.com and Postopia.com) (Harris, Schwartz, et al., 2012).

Additional research is required to further demonstrate long-term effects of continual exposure to food marketing on young people's nutrition-related beliefs and behaviors. A better understanding of how food marketing affects young people also is necessary to identify whether it is possible to offset this influence, such as through social marketing to promote healthy eating or other interventions, or whether restrictions on children's exposure to food advertising are required. In addition, research on communications strategies to increase parents' awareness and concern about the impact of food marketing on their children would inform grassroots campaigns to improve child-targeted marketing practices and help increase public support for government policies. Creating a healthy food marketing environment for children and adolescents is an urgent public health priority, and research is essential for determining how to achieve that goal.

References

Adams, J., Tyrrell, R., Adamson, A. J., & White, M. (2012). Effect of restrictions on television food advertising to children on exposure to advertisements for "less healthy" foods: Repeat cross-sectional study. *PLOS One, 7*(2), e31578.

Advertising Research Foundation [ARF] (2008). Innerscope research: A revolution in audience research. Retrieved from http://s3.amazonaws.com/thearf-org-aux-assets/downloads/cnc/engagement/2008-11-19_ARF_Engagement_Innerscope.pdf on 1/7/2013

Ali, M., Blades, M., Oates, C., & Blumberg, F. (2009). Young children's ability to recognize advertisements in web page designs. *British Journal of Developmental Psychology, 27*(1), 71–83.

Alvy, L. M., & Calvert, S. L. (2008). Food marketing on popular children's web sites: A content analysis. *Journal of the American Dietetic Association, 108,* 710–713.

Andreyeva, T., Kelly, I. R., & Harris, J. L. (2011). Exposure to food advertising on television: Associations with children's fast food and soft drink consumption and obesity. *Economics and Human Biology, 9,* 221–233.

Auty, S., & Lewis, C. (2004). Exploring children's choice: The reminder effect of product placement. *Psychology and Marketing, 21,* 697–713.

Bao, Y., & Shao, A. T. (2002). Nonconformity advertising to teens. *Journal of Advertising Research, 42*(3), 56–65.

Bickham, D. S., & Slaby, R. G. (2012). Effects of a media literacy program in the U.S. on children's critical evaluation of unhealthy media messages about violence, smoking, and food. *Journal of Children and Media, 6,* 255–271.

Binet, L., & Field, P. (2009). Empirical generalizations about advertising campaign success. *Journal of Advertising Research, 49*(2), 130–133.

Boush, D. M., Friestad, M., & Wright, P. (2009). *Deception in the marketplace.* New York, NY: Routledge.

Brownell, K. D., Schwartz, M. B., Puhl, R. M., Henderson, K. E., & Harris, J. L. (2009). The need for bold action to prevent adolescent obesity. *Journal of Adolescent Health, 45,* S8–S17.

Chernin, A. (2008). The effects of food marketing on children's preference: Testing the moderating roles of age and gender. *Annals of the Academy of Political Social Science, 615,* 102–118.

Children's Advertising Review Unit (2008). About the Children's Advertising Review Unit (CARU). Retrieved from http://www.caru.org/about.index.aspx

Children's Food and Beverage Advertising Initiative (2011). Category-specific uniform nutrition criteria. Retrieved from http://www.bbb.org/us/storage/16/documents/cfbai/CFBAI-Category-Specific-Uniform-Nutrition-Criteria.pdf

Children's Food and Beverage Advertising Initiative (2012). Summary of participants' definitions of advertising primarily directed to children under 12 and policies on not directing advertising to children under 6. Retrieved from http://www.bbb.org/us/storage/16/documents/cfbai/CFBAI%20Audience%20Definitions%20March%202012.pdf

Dhar, T., & Baylis, K. (2011). Fast-food consumption and the ban on advertising targeting children: The Quebec experience. *Journal of Marketing Research, 48,* 799–813.

Lingas, E. O., Dorfman, L., & Bukofzer, E. (2009). Nutrition content of food and beverage products on websites popular with children. *American Journal of Public Health, 99,* S587.

Federal Trade Commission (2008). Marketing food to children and adolescents. A review of industry expenditures, activities, and self-regulation. A report to Congress. Retrieved from http://ftc.gov/os/2008/07/P064504foodmktingreport.pdf

Federal Trade Commission (2011). Prepared statement by the Federal Trade Commission on the Interagency Working Group on Food Marketed to Children. Retrieved from http://www.ftc.gov/os/testimony/111012foodmarketing.pdf

Ferguson, C. J., Munoz, M. E., & Medrano, M. R. (2012). Advertising influences on young children's food choices and parental influence. *Journal of Pediatrics, 160*, 452–455.

Folta, S. C., Goldberg, J. P., Economos, C., Bell, R., & Meltzer, R. (2006). Food advertising targeted at school-age children: A content analysis. *Journal of Nutrition Education and Behavior, 38*, 244–248.

Gearhardt, A. N., Grilo, C. M., DiLeone, R. J., Brownell, K. D., & Potenza, M. N. (2011). Can food be addictive? Public health and policy implications. *Addiction, 106*, 1208–1212.

Gearhardt, A. N., Yokum, S., Stice, E., Harris, J. L., & Brownell, K. D. (2012). Elevated reward-region responsivity to food commercials predicts calorie-dense food intake. *Social Cognitive and Affective Neuroscience*, in press.

Glanz, K., Basil, M., Maibach, E., Goldberg, J., & Snyder, D. (1998). Why Americans eat what they do: Taste, nutrition, cost, convenience and weight control concerns as influences on food consumption. *Journal of American Dietetic Association, 98*, 1118–1126.

Goren, A., Harris, J. L., Schwartz, M. B., & Brownell, K. D. (2010). Predicting support for restricting food marketing to youth. *Health Affairs, 29*, 419–424.

Graff, S. K., Kunkel, D., & Mermin, S. E. (2012). Government can regulate food advertising to children because cognitive research shows that it is inherently misleading. *Health Affairs, 31*, 392–398.

Grier, S. A., Mensinger, J., Huang, S. H., Kumanyika, S. K., & Stettler, N. (2007). Fast-food marketing and children's fast-food consumption: Exploring parents' influences on an ethnically diverse sample. *Journal of Public Policy and Marketing, 26*, 221–235.

Halford, J. C. G., Boyland, M. J., Hughes, G., Oliveira, L. P., & Dovey, T. M. (2007). Beyond-brand effect of television (TV) food advertisement/commercials on caloric intake and food choice of 5–7-year-old children. *Appetite, 49*, 263–267.

Halford, J. C. G., Gillespie, J., Brown, V., Pontin, E. E., & Dovey, T. M. (2004). Effect of television advertisements for foods on food consumption in children. *Appetite, 42*, 221–225.

Harris, J. L. (2008). Priming obesity: Direct effects of television food advertising on eating behavior and food preferences. (Unpublished doctoral dissertation). Yale University, New Haven, CT.

Harris, J. L. (2012). Is food advertising feeding Americans' sugar habit? An analysis of exposure to television advertising for high-sugar foods. In K. D. Brownell & M. Gold (Eds.), *Food and addiction: A comprehensive handbook* (pp. 382–387). New York, NY: Oxford University Press.

Harris, J. L., & Bargh, J. A. (2009). Television viewing and unhealthy diet: Implications for children and media interventions. *Health Communication, 24*, 660–673.

Harris, J. L., Bargh, J. A., & Brownell, K. D. (2009). Priming effects of television food advertising on eating behavior. *Health Psychology, 28*, 404–413.

Harris, J. L., Brownell, K. D., & Bargh, J. A. (2009). The food marketing defense model: Integrating psychological research to protect youth and inform public policy. *Social Issues and Policy Review, 3*, 211–271.

Harris, J. L., & Graff, S. K. (2012). Protecting young people from junk food advertising: Implications of psychological research for First Amendment law. *American Journal of Public Health, 102*, 214–222.

Harris, J. L., Pomeranz, J. L., Lobstein, T., & Brownell, K. D. (2009). A crisis in the marketplace: How food marketing contributes to childhood obesity and what can be done. *Annual Review of Public Health, 30*, 211–225.

Harris, J. L., Schwartz, M., Brownell, K., Javadizadeh, J., Weinberg, M. E., Sarda, V.,..., Meija, P. (2011). Sugary drink FACTS: Evaluating sugary drink nutrition and marketing to youth. Retrieved from http://www.sugarydrinkfacts.org

Harris, J. L., Schwartz, M. B., Brownell, K. D., Sarda, V., Dembek, C., Munsell, C.,..., Weinberg, M. (2012). Cereal FACTS 2012: Limited progress in the nutrition quality and marketing of children's cereals. Retrieved from http://www.cerealfacts.org/media/Cereal_FACTS_Report_2012_7.12.pdf

Harris, J. L., Schwartz, M. B., Brownell, K. D., Sarda, V., Ustjanauskus, A., Javadizadeh, J.,..., Ohri-Vachaspati, P. (2010). Fast food FACTS: Evaluation of the nutritional quality and marketing of fast food to youth. Retrieved from http://www.fastfoodmarketing.org

Harris, J. L., Schwartz, M. B., Brownell, K. D., Sarda, V., Weinberg, M. E., Speers, S.,..., Byrnes-Enoch, H. (2009). Cereal FACTS: Evaluating the nutrition quality and marketing of children's cereals. Retrieved from http://cerealfacts.org/media/Cereal_FACTS_Report_2009.pdf

Harris, J. L., Speers, S. E., Schwartz, M. B., & Brownell, K. D. (2012). U.S. food company branded advergames on the Internet: Children's exposure and effects on snack consumption. *Journal of Children and Media, 6*(1), 51–68.

Harrison, K., & Marske, A. L. (2005). Nutritional content of foods advertised during the television programs children watch most. *Am. J. Public Health, 95*, 1568–1574.

Hastings, G., Stead, M., McDermott, L., Forsyth, A., MacKintosh, A., Rayner, M.,..., Angus, K. (2003). Review of research on the effects of food promotion to children. Retrieved from http://www.foodstandards.gov.uk/multimedia/pdfs/foodpromotiontochildren1.pdf

Hawkes, D. (2007). Regulating food marketing to young people worldwide: Trends and policy drivers. *American Journal of Public Health, 97*, 1962–1973.

Henry, H. K. M., & Borzekowski, D. L. G. (2011). The nag factor: A mixed-methodology study in the U.S. of young children's requests for advertised products. *Journal of Children and Media, 5*, 298–317.

Institute of Medicine, Committee on Food Marketing and the Diets of Children and Youth (2006). *Food marketing to children and youth: Threat or opportunity?* Washington, DC: National Academies Press.

Interagency Working Group on Food Marketed to Children (2011). Preliminary proposed nutrition principles to guide industry self-regulatory efforts. Request for Comments. Retrieved from http://www.ftc.gov/os/2011/04/110428foodmarketproposedguide.pdf

John, D. R. (1999). Consumer socialization of children: A retrospective look at twenty-five years of research. *Journal of Consumer Research, 26*, 183–213.

Keller, K. L. (2003). Brand synthesis. The multidimensionality of brand knowledge *Journal of Consumer Research, 29*, 595–600.

Killgore, W. D. S., Young, A. D., Femia, L. A., Bogorodzi, P., Rogowska, J., & Yurgelun-Todd, D. A. (2003). Cortical and limbic activation during viewing of high- versus low-calorie foods. *Neuroimage, 19*, 1381–1394.

Kolish, E. D., Hernandez, M., & Blanchard, K. (2011). The Children's Food and Beverage Advertising Initiative: A report on compliance and implementation during 2010 and a five-year retrospective: 2006–2011. Retrieved from http://www.bbb.org/us/storage/16/documents/cfbai/cfbai-2010-progress-report.pdf

Koplan, J. P., & Brownell, K. D. (2010). Response of the food and beverage industry to the obesity threat. *Journal of the American Medical Association, 304*, 1487–1488.

Kraak, V. I., Story, M., Wartella, E. A., & Ginter, J. (2011). Industry progress to market a healthful diet to American children and adolescents. *American Journal of Preventive Medicine, 41*, 322–333.

Kunkel, D. (2010). Mismeasurement of children's understanding of the persuasive intent of advertising. *Journal of Children and Media, 4*, 109–117.

Kunkel, D., McKinley, C., & Wright, P. (2009). The impact of industry self-regulation on the nutritional quality of foods advertised on television to children. Retrieved from http://www.childrennow.org/uploads/documents/adstudy_2009.pdf

Kunkel, D., & Wilcox, B. L. (2012). Children and media policy: Historical perspectives and current practices. In D. G. Singer & J. L. Singer (Eds.), *Handbook of children and the media* (pp. 569–593). Thousand Oaks, CA: Sage Publications.

Lee, L., Frederick, S., & Ariely, D. (2006). Try it, you'll like it: The influence of expectation, consumption, and revelation on preferences for beer. *Psychological Science, 17*, 1054–1058.

Lingas, E. O., Dorfman, L., & Bukofzer, E. (2009). Nutrition content of food and beverage products on Web sites popular with children. S587–S592.

Livingstone, S., & Helsper, E. J. (2006). Does advertising literacy mediate the effects of advertising on children? A critical examination of two linked research literatures in relation to obesity and food choice. *Journal of Communication, 56*, 560–584.

Mallinckrodt, V., & Mizerski, D. (2007). The effects of playing an advergame on young children's perceptions, preferences, and request. *Journal of Advertising, 36*, 87–100.

Moore, E. S., & Lutz, R. L. (2000). Children, advertising and product experiences: A multimethod inquiry. *Journal of Consumer Research, 27*, 31–48.

Moore, E. S., & Rideout, V. J. (2007). The online marketing of food to children: Is it just fun and games? *Journal of Public Policy and Marketing, 26*, 202–220.

Neumark-Sztainer, D., Wall, M., Perry, C., & Story, M. (2003). Correlates of fruit and vegetable intake among adolescents: Findings from Project EAT. *Preventive Medicine, 37*, 198–208.

O'Doherty, J., Rolls, E. T., Francis, S., Bowtell, R., & McGlone, F. (2001). Representation of pleasant and aversive taste in the human brain. *Journal of Neurophysiology, 85*, 1315–1321.

Ogden, C. I., Carroll, M. D., Kit, B. K., & Flegal, K. M. (2012). Prevalence of obesity and trends in body mass index among U.S. children and adolescents: 1999–2012. *Journal of the American Medical Association, 307*, 483–490.

Olshansky, S. J., Passaro, D. J., Hershow, R. C., Layden, J., Carnes, B. A., Brody, J., . . . Ludwig, D. S. (2005). A potential decline in the life expectancy in the United States in the 21st century. *The New England Journal of Medicine, 352*, 1138–1145.

Pechmann, C., Levine, L., Loughlin, S., & Leslie, F. (2005). Impulsive and self-conscious: Adolescents' vulnerability to advertising and promotion. *Journal of Public Policy and Marketing, 24*, 202–221.

Petty, R. D., & Andrews, J. C. (2008). Covert marketing unmasked: A legal and regulatory guide for practices that mask marketing messages. *Journal of Public Policy and Marketing, 27*(1), 7–18.

Pomeranz, J. L. (2010). Television food marketing to children revisited: The Federal Trade Commission has the constitutional and statutory authority to regulate. *Journal of Law, Medicine and Ethics, 38*(1), 98–116.

Powell, L. M., Schermbeck, R. M., Szczypka, G., Chaloupka, F. J., & Braunschweig, C. L. (2011). Trends in the nutritional content of television food advertisements seen by children in the United States. *Archives of Pediatric and Adolescent Medicine, 165*, 1078–1086.

Puhl, R. M. (2011). Weight stigmatization toward youth: A significant problem in need of societal solutions. *Childhood Obesity, 7*, 359–363.

Reece, B. B., Rifon, N. J., & Rodriguez, K. (1999). Selling food to children. Is fun part of a balanced breakfast? In L. C. Machlin & L. Carlson (Eds.), *Advertising to children: Concepts and controversies* (pp. 189–208). Thousand Oaks, CA: Sage Publications.

Richardson, J., & Harris, J. L. (2011). Food marketing and social media: Findings from Fast Food FACTS and Sugary Drink FACTS. Retrieved from http://www.yaleruddcenter.org/resources/upload/docs/what/reports/FoodMarketingSocialMedia_AmericanUniversity_11.11.pdf

Roberto, C., Baik, J., Harris, J. L., & Brownell, K. D. (2010). The influence of licensed characters on children's taste and snack preferences. *Pediatrics, 126*(1), 88–93.

Robinson, T. N., Borzekowski, D. L., Matheson, D. M., & Kraemer, H. C. (2007). Effects of fast food branding on young children's taste preferences. *Archives of Pediatric and Adolescent Medicine, 161*, 792–797.

Robinson, T. N., & Sirard, J. R. (2005). Preventing childhood obesity: A solution-oriented research paradigm. *American Journal of Preventive Medicine, 28*, 194–201.

Ross, R. P., Campbell, T., Wright, J. D., Huston, A. C., Rice, M. L., & Turk, P. (1984). When celebrities talk, children listen: An experimental analysis of children's responses to TV ads with celebrity endorsement. *Journal of Applied Developmental Psychology, 5*, 185–202.

Schor, J. B., & Ford, M. (2007). From tastes great to cool: Children's food marketing and the rise of the symbolic. *Journal of Law and Medical Ethics, 35*(1), 10–21.

Sharma, L. L., Teret, S. P., & Brownell, K. D. (2010). The food industry and self-regulation: Standards to promote success and to avoid public health failures. *American Journal of Public Health, 100*, 240–246.

Signorielli, N., & Lears, M. (1992). Television and children's conceptions of nutrition: Unhealthy messages. *Health Communication, 4*, 245–257.

Signorielli, N., & Staples, J. (1997). Television and children's conceptions of nutrition. *Health Communication, 9*, 289–301.

Speers, S. E., Harris, J. L., & Schwartz, M. B. (2011). Child and adolescent exposure to food and beverage brand appearances during prime-time television programming. *American Journal of Preventive Medicine, 41*, 291–296.

Sutherland, L. A., MacKenzie, T., Purvis, L. A., & Dalton, M. (2010). Prevalence of food and beverage brands in movies: 1996–2005. *Pediatrics, 125*, 468–474.

Swinburn, B. S., Sacks, G., Lobstein, T., Rigby, N., Baur, L. A., Brownell, K. D., ... & Kumanyika, S. (2008). The "Sydney Principles" for reducing the commercial promotion of foods and beverages to children. *Public Health Nutrition, 11*, 881–886.

Ustjanauskas, A., Eckman, B., Harris, J. L., Goren, A., Schwartz, M. B., & Brownell, K. D. (2010). Focus groups with parents: What do they think about food marketing to their kids? Retrieved from http://www.yaleruddcenter.org/resources/upload/docs/what/reports/RuddReport_FocusGroupsParents_5.10.pdf

Ustjanauskas, A., Harris, J. L., & Schwartz, M. B. (2012). The prevalence and nutritional content of banner advertising for foods and beverages on children's websites. Unpublished manuscript.

Ward, S., Wackman, D. B., & Wartella, E. (1977). *How children learn to buy*. Beverly Hills, CA: Sage Publications.

Weinberg, M. E., Harris, J. L., & Schwartz, M. B. (2013). Sugar as part of a balanced breakfast? What cereal advertisements teach children about healthy eating. *Journal of Health Communication, 18*, 1293–1309.

White House Task Force on Childhood Obesity (2010). Solving the problem of childhood obesity within a generation. Retrieved from http://www.letsmove.gov/tfco_fullreport_may2010.pdf

Wilcox, B. L., Kunkel, D., Cantor, J., Dowrick, P., Linn, S., & Palmer, E. (2004). Report of the APA task force on advertising and children. Retrieved from http://www.apa.org/pi/families/resources/advertising-children.pdf

Wilson, D., & Roberts, J. (2012, April 27). Special report: How Washington went soft on childhood obesity. *Reuters.* Retrieved from http://www.reuters.com/article/2012/04/27/us-usa-foodlobby-idUSBRE83Q0ED20120427

World Health Organization (2010). Set of recommendations on the marketing of foods and non-alcoholic beverages to children. Retrieved from http://whqlibdoc.who.int/publications/2010/9789241500210_eng.pdf

World Health Organization (2012). A framework for implementing the set of recommendations on the marketing of foods and non-alcoholic beverages to children. Retrieved from http://www.who.int/dietphysicalactivity/MarketingFramework2012.pdf

Yale Rudd Center for Food Policy & Obesity (2012). Trends in television food advertising to young people. Retrieved from http://www.yaleruddcenter.org/resources/upload/docs/what/reports/RuddReport_TVFoodAdvertising_5.12.pdf

Young, B. (2002). Does food advertising make children obese? *International Journal of Advertising and Marketing to Children, 4*, 19–26.

Zimmerman, F. J., & Bell, J. F. (2010). Associations of television content type and obesity in children. *American Journal of Public Health, 100*, 334–340.

CHAPTER 5

Wassssup? Adolescents, Drugs, and the Media

◼

Victor C. Strasburger

A cigarette in the hands of a Hollywood star onscreen is a gun aimed at a 12- or 14-year-old.
—Screenwriter Joe Eszterhas (2004)

Our national drug is alcohol. We tend to regard the use [of] any other drug with special horror.
—William S. Burroughs (http://thinkexist.com)

The sixties were when hallucinogenic drugs were really, really big. And I don't think it's a coincidence that we had the type of shows we had then, like *The Flying Nun*.
—Ellen DeGeneres (http://thinkexist.com)

Cigarettes, alcohol, and illicit drugs represent one of the biggest threats to the health of American teenagers, and one of their biggest concerns as well (Figure 5.1). Although levels of drug use have decreased dramatically since the 1960s and 1970s, they are still worrisome. In particular, tobacco and alcohol represent the two most significant health threats to the average teenager, although parents and school seem to worry far more about illicit drugs. This is where the media come in—illicit drugs are obviously not (legally) advertised, nor are they commonly portrayed on TV, in movies, or even on the internet. By contrast, more than $20 billion a year is spent advertising cigarettes, tobacco, and prescription drugs (Strasburger and Council on Communications and Media, 2010). In addition, new research on the impact of smoking and drinking in movie scenes is pointing to movies as a powerful influence on whether teenagers will engage in

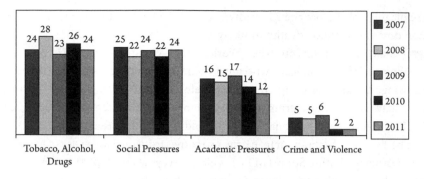

Figure 5.1 Percent of Teens Reporting Different Concerns from 2007 to 2011.
Source: National Center on Addiction and Substance Abuse (2011a). Reprinted with permission.

those activities (Strasburger, Jordan, & Donnerstein, 2013). Finally, social networking sites and YouTube are providing a rich source of drug imagery, with as yet unknown behavioral effects.

Adolescent Drug Use

Tobacco takes the greatest toll on society. More than 400,000 Americans die from tobacco-related causes every year—more than from AIDS, car crashes, murder, and suicide combined (Campaign for Tobacco-Free Kids, 2011). Although the Federal Food and Drug Administration (FDA) has tightened restrictions on tobacco sales to youth, cigarette exports to Third World countries are increasing, and concern is mounting there as well. More than 1.1 billion people currently smoke worldwide, resulting in 4 million deaths per year (Prokhorov et al., 2006). According to the World Health Organization (2008), if this trend continues, more than 1 billion people will die in this century of smoking-related causes.

Unlike tobacco—which when used as directed is intrinsically harmful—alcohol in moderation is thought to have some health benefits. However, it is the most commonly used and abused drug by 12- to 17-year-olds (Committee on Substance Abuse, 2010) and may account for as many as 100,000 deaths per year, including 5,000 people under the age of 21 (U.S. Department of Health and Human Services, 2007). Underage drinkers actually account for about 20% of all alcohol consumption (Foster, Vaughan, Foster, & Califano, 2003) and for one-third of all alcohol industry revenues (Foster, Vaughan, Foster, & Califano, 2006). Alcohol use among young people may also contribute to other risky behaviors, particularly unprotected sexual intercourse (Rehm, Shield, Joharchi, & Shuper, 2012). Alcoholism begins young: nearly half of all alcoholics are diagnosable before age 21 (Brown et al., 2008). Globally, alcohol consumption causes 1.8 million deaths annually and is the leading risk factor for morbidity in many developing countries (World Health Organization, 2002).

Nine out of 10 Americans who meet the medical criteria for addiction started smoking, drinking, or using other drugs before the age of 18. Total costs to federal, state, and local governments of substance use are estimated to be at least $468 billion per year (National Center on Addiction and Substance Abuse,2011a). The best source of data about teen drug use comes from the University of Michigan Monitoring the Future Study (MTF), which surveys nearly 15,000 students annually in the 8th, 10th, and 12th grades at more than 430 public and private schools around the country (www.monitoringthefuture.org). The study began in the mid-1970s and therefore provides unique tracking data for trends in drugs use. But no data set is perfect, and the MTF does not capture high school dropouts and relies on teens' self-reports of drug use. According to the most recent MTF survey (Johnston, O'Malley, Bachman, & Schulenberg, 2012),

- Significant decreases in smoking have occurred. In 1997, 37% of 12th graders reported smoking in the past month; by 2011, that figure had decreased to 19%.
- Nearly three-fourths of 12th graders have tried alcohol at least once, down from a peak of 88% in 1991. However, half of all 12th graders still report ever being drunk; and nearly one-fourth had engaged in binge-drinking (5 or more drinks in a row) in the 2 weeks prior to being surveyed.
- Currently, nearly half of all seniors report having used an illicit drug (Figure 5.2). Most of this is marijuana use, with just over 45% of seniors saying that they have tried marijuana.

What the Research Says about Advertising's Contribution to Adolescent Drug Use

For many years, the contribution of advertising to adolescent drug use was arguable. It no longer is. Dozens of correlational and longitudinal studies now attest to the ability of advertising to influence not only teenagers' use of cigarettes (Tables 5.1 and 5.2) and alcohol but their brand preferences as well (Borzekowski & Strasburger, 2008; DiFranza et al., 2006). Tobacco manufacturers spent more than $13 billion in 2006 (the most recent data available) on marketing and promotion (National Cancer Institute, 2008). Alcohol manufacturers spend more than $5 billion per year (Strasburger & Council on Communications and Media, 2010). Even if there weren't abundant studies to show the impact of advertising, the expenditures alone seem to tell the tale.

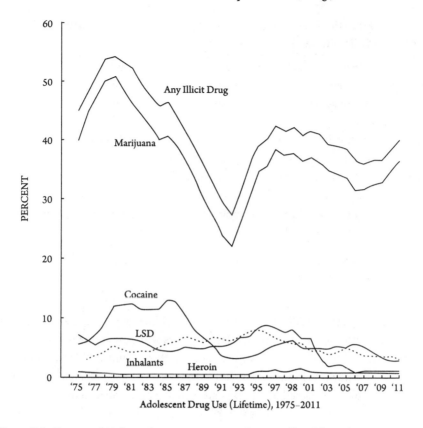

PERCENT

'75 '77 '79 '81 '83 '85 '87 '89 '91 '93 '95 '97 '98 '01 '03 '05 '07 '09 '11

Adolescent Drug Use (Lifetime), 1975–2011

Figure 5.2 Percent of 12th-graders reporting use of various illegal drugs by year.
Source: Monitoring the Future (2012). Reprinted with permission.

Table 5.1 **Numerous Studies Find That Tobacco Advertising Causes Teenagers to Smoke**

Research Question	# of Studies	# of Subjects Studied
Are nonsmoking children exposed to and more aware of tobacco promotion?	4 prospective 12 cross-sectional	37,649
Does exposure to promotions increase the risk of initiation?	12 prospective 14 cross-sectional 2 time-series	349,306
Does a dose-response relationship exist?	2 prospective 7 cross-sectional	25,180

Source: Adapted from DiFranza et al., 2006.
Reprinted from Strasburger (2012). With permission. How Good Is the Research Linking Tobacco Marketing to Onset of Adolescent Smoking?

Table 5.2 **Does the Research on Tobacco Marketing and Onset of Smoking Fulfill the Hill Criteria for Causality[a]?**

1. Children are exposed to tobacco marketing before they begin smoking.
2. Exposure to marketing increases the risk for initiation of smoking.
3. A dose-response relationship does exist: increased exposure results in higher risk.
4. The association between exposure and increased risk is well substantiated with a variety of research methodologies and populations.
5. Cohesive theories can explain the relationship.
6. No other explanation other than causality can explain the relationship.

Source: Reprinted from Strasburger (2012), with permission, Adapted from DiFranza et al., 2006.

[a] Hill, A. B. (1965). The environment and disease: Association or causality? *Proceedings of the Royal Society of Medicine, 58,* 295–300.

The quality of the studies is now quite good, with controls for all known factors associated with cigarette use (particularly parents who smoke) or alcohol use. For example, the National Cancer Institute (2008, p. 3) concludes, "Media communications play a key role in shaping attitudes toward tobacco, and current evidence shows that tobacco-related media exposure affects both tobacco use and prevention." The U.S. Surgeon General's report on alcohol abuse in the U.S. observes,

> Alcohol, in its many forms, is familiar to children and adolescents and often appears relatively benign, if not openly enticing.... Reducing cultural forces that encourage or support underage alcohol consumption lessens both the attraction of alcohol and the likelihood that it will be consumed by youth. (U.S. Department of Health and Human Services, 2007, p. 39)

The research on tobacco advertising and promotion is clear and convincing (Hanewinkel, Isensee, Sargent, & Morgenstern, 2010, 2011), although the size of the effect remains arguable (Lovato, Watts, & Stead, 2011). The research on alcohol advertising is increasingly cogent but shows more modest effects (Smith & Foxcroft, 2009), perhaps because exposure to alcohol comes in so many forms in society (parents, peers, TV, movies, social networking sites, etc.).

What the Research Says about Programming's Contribution to Adolescent Drug Use

Of most concern from newer research is the impact of smoking in movies on the initiation of teen smoking. A report from the National Cancer Institute in

2008 concluded that "the total weight of evidence from cross-sectional, longitudinal, and experimental studies indicates a causal relationship between exposure to depictions of smoking in movies and youth smoking initiation" (National Cancer Institute, 2008, p. 12). In 2011, the World Health Organization issued a report seconding this conclusion and calling not only for a comprehensive ban on tobacco advertising, promotion, and sponsorship but also substantial reductions in smoking imagery in all film media (World Health Organization, 2011). Although the amount of smoking in movies is now decreasing, recent research has shown that it may be one of the leading factors in adolescents' decision whether to smoke or not—perhaps even more important than whether parents smoke (Dalton et al., 2009; de Leeuw et al., 2011; Heatherton & Sargent, 2009; Morgenstern et al., 2011; National Cancer Institute, 2008; Sargent, Gibson, & Heatherton, 2009; Titus-Ernstoff, Dalton, Adachi-Mejia, Longacre, & Beach, 2008).

Movie smoking peaked in the early years of the 21st century and is now decreasing. Four analyses of the top-grossing movies in recent years have found significant decreases (Centers for Disease Control and Prevention, 2011; Glantz, Iaccopucci, Titus, & Polansky, 2012; Jamieson & Romer, 2010; Sargent & Heatherton, 2009). Interestingly, as smoking in movies has decreased, so has the prevalence of smoking among adolescents (Figure 5.3). Tobacco imagery in Europe, however, has not decreased: a study of the most commercially successful films in six European countries between 2004 and 2009 found that 87% of youth-rated films contained smoking (Hanewinkel et al., 2013). According to several researchers who have done large longitudinal studies, movie smoking may account for up to one-third of smoking initiation among young teenagers (Dalton et al., 2002; Titus-Ernstoff et al., 2008).

Other media also contain images of smoking but do not appear to be as powerful in their behavioral impact as movies, although one longitudinal study did find a sixfold increase in the risk of smoking in youth who watch 5 or more hours of TV per day (Gidwani, Sobol, DeJong, Perrin, & Gortmaker, 2002). A study of the top-rated TV series for 12- to 17-year-olds found that 40% of episodes had at least one depiction of tobacco use, and shows rated TV-PG actually had more smoking incidents (50%) than those rated TV-14 (26%) (Cullen et al., 2011). Only a single study has examined the impact of TV on adult smoking—a unique 26-year longitudinal study in New Zealand that followed an unselected cohort of 1000 individuals from birth. Researchers found that heavy TV viewing in childhood correlated with smoking at age 26 and that 17% of adult smoking might be attributable to the influence of excessive TV viewing during childhood (Hancox, Milne, & Poulton, 2004).

Online, tobacco is not as problematic currently, but that could change. Less than 1% of web pages contain tobacco content, and much of that is antitobacco;

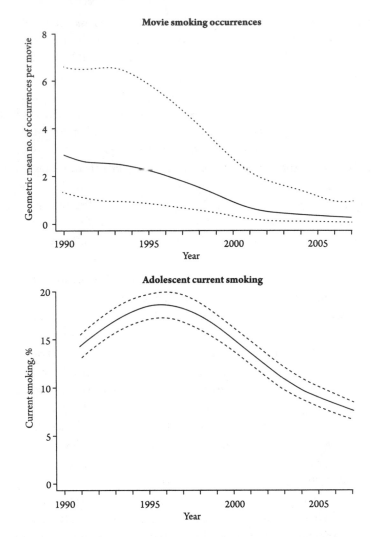

Figure 5.3 Smoking Occurrences in Highest Grossing Movies and Adolescent Smoking in the United States, 1990–2007: Upper and Lower Confidence Intervals Are Shown in Each Case. Source: Sargent et al. (2009). Copyright © JAMA. Reprinted with permission.

however, more than half of the content was from social networking sites (Jenssen, Klein, Salazar, Daluga, & DiClemente, 2009). For many years teenagers could purchase cigarettes easily online, but the recent FDA Tobacco Law now prevents this (Table 5.3).

Generally, tobacco portrayals on TV and online are outnumbered by alcohol and illicit drugs: on primetime TV, 16% of all episodes studied in one analysis featured smoking, 29% featured illicit drug use, but fully one-third featured alcohol (Murphy, Hether, & Rideout, 2008). In films, an analysis of the 100

Table 5.3 **Some Provisions of the New FDA Tobacco Law, Signed into Law by the President on June 22, 2009**

- All advertising for cigarettes and smokeless tobacco must be black text on white background only (effective 6/22/10)

- No advertising in magazines with > 15% or 2 million youth readers (effective 6/22/10)

- No outdoor advertising within 1,000 feet of schools, parks, or playgrounds (effective 6/22/10)

- No branded sponsorships of athletic or cultural events by cigarette manufacturers (effective 6/22/10)

- FDA must issue regulations to prevent the sale of tobacco products to youth via the internet or mail-order (effective 10/1/12)

- FDA must issue regulations addressing the marketing and promotion of tobacco products on the internet (effective 4/1/13)

Source: American Academy of Pediatrics, Office of Government Affairs, Washington, DC. Reprinted from Strasburger, Wilson, & Jordan (2013), with permission.

top-grossing movies from 1996 through 2004 found that half of all R and PG-13 rated movies and one-fourth of PG movies contained alcohol use (Tickle, Beach, & Dalton, 2009). A 2006 study found that 92% of a random sample of 601 contemporary movies contained alcohol use (Sargent, Wills, Stoolmiller, Gibson, & Gibbons, 2006). Several recent longitudinal studies have found that exposure to scenes of drinking alcohol in movies is independently associated with alcohol use (Hanewinkel et al., 2013; Hanewinkel & Sargent, 2009; Primack, Kraemer, Fine, & Dalton, 2009; Stoolmiller et al., 2012; Tanski, Dal Cin, Stoolmiller, & Sargent, 2010). Several large reviews of studies have found modest but significant effect sizes:

- A review of seven cohort studies involved more than 13,000 young people (Smith & Foxcroft, 2009).
- An even larger study—of 13 longitudinal studies involved more than 38,000 young people. The researchers concluded that exposure to media depictions involving alcohol is associated with an increased likelihood of starting to drink and increased alcohol consumption among teens already drinking (Anderson, de Bruijn, Angus, Gordon, & Hastings, 2009).
- A recent cross-sectional survey of more than 16,000 students in six European countries found a robust association between exposure to alcohol use in movies and binge drinking (Hanewinkel et al., 2013).

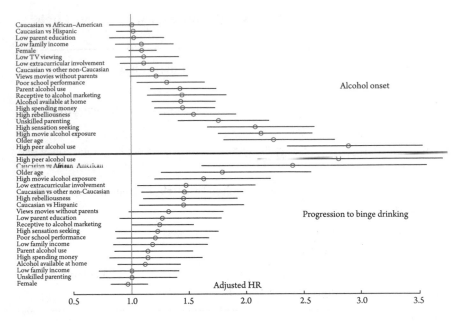

Figure 5.4 A Compendium of the Most Powerful Influences on Teenagers' Alcohol Use. Top panel shows adjusted hazard ratios (AHRs) for time to alcohol onset among alcohol never users; bottom panel shows AHRs for progression to binge drinking among alcohol experimenters. Each panel sorts the AHRs by size, allowing comparison of media, family, and other risk factors. Error bars represent 95% confidence intervals. Circles represent midpoints. Source: Stoolmiller et al. (2012). Copyright © BMJ Open. Reprinted with permission.

- Another recent longitudinal study of more than 6,500 American 10- to 14-year-olds compared all known factors leading to early alcohol use among teens and found that exposure to scenes of alcohol use in movies was one of the leading factors in both onset of alcohol use and binge drinking (Figure 5.4) (Stoolmiller et al., 2012).

Social networking sites represent new ways of reaching teenagers with depictions of substance use. Such depictions may reinforce the notion of the "super-peer theory"—that the media function to exert even greater pressure on teens than their peers do, since the media make certain risky activities (e.g., smoking, drinking, sex) seem like normative behavior (Strasburger, 1995). Two studies of online profiles of older teens have found that 41–56% contain references to alcohol or other drugs (Moreno et al., 2010; Moreno, Parks, Zimmerman, Brito, & Christakis, 2009). Those who reference alcohol on their profiles are more likely to engage in problem drinking (Moreno, Christakis, Egan, Brockman, & Becker, 2012). Another large national survey of more than 1,000 12- to 17-year-olds found that 40% had seen pictures on Facebook or other

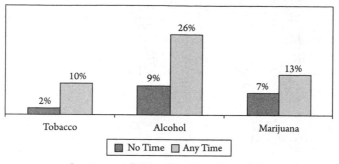

Spent on social Networking Site in Typical Day

Figure 5.5 Does Social Networking Contribute to Substance Use? A study of more than 1,000 12- to 17-year-olds found that there is a correlation between increased levels of ever using tobacco, alcohol, or marijuana with time spent on a social networking site. Source: National Center on Addiction and Substance Abuse (2011). Reprinted with permission.

social networking sites of kids getting drunk or passed out. Often, these pictures are seen at a young (and therefore impressionable) age. Compared with teens who do not access social networking sites in a typical day, teens who do were three times likelier to use alcohol (Figure 5.5) (National Center on Addiction and Substance Abuse, 2011b).

Illicit Drugs on TV; in Music and Music Videos; in Movies; and Online

Illicit drugs are rarely seen on TV, with the exception of programs like Showtime's *Weeds* and *Shameless*, HBO's *Entourage*, and FOX's *That 70s Show*. Marijuana is the most frequent drug seen in movies and has been featured in recent R-rated movies like the *Harold and Kumar* series, *Totally Baked* (2008), *The Pineapple Express* (2008), *The Hangover Part II* (2011), and *Bad Teacher* (2011) (Halperin, 2008). A Columbia University study found that viewing R-rated movies was associated with a sixfold increase in the risk of a teen trying marijuana (Figure 5.6) (National Center on Addiction and Substance Abuse, 2005). Increased consumption of popular music is also associated with marijuana use (Primack, Kraemer, Fine, & Dalton, 2009; Primack, Douglas, & Kraemer, 2010). So, too, are social networking sites: teens who spend time daily on social networking sites were found to be twice as likely to use marijuana in a survey of more than 1,000 12- to 17-year-olds (Figure 5.5) (National Center on Addiction and Substance Abuse, 2011b).

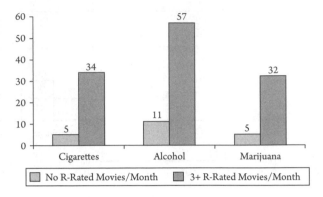

Figure 5.6 Relationship between viewing R-rated movies and adolescent drug use.
Source: National Center on Addiction and Substance Abuse (2005). Reprinted with permission.

Gaps in the Research: Unanswered Questions

No social science research is perfect, and media research is no exception. It is difficult to do and difficult to get funded—and finding even small positive effects may be highly significant given that the media now permeate virtually every corner of people's lives (Comstock & Strasburger, 1993). Tobacco research is stronger, and since nicotine is a highly addictive drug and there are no health benefits from smoking cigarettes, there seems to be little need for more research—other than perhaps to continue to document the many devious ways that the tobacco industry tries to circumvent laws and regulations (Glantz, Slade, Bero, Hanauer, & Barnes, 1998; Kessler, 2001). One gap in the tobacco research is a full understanding of why African Americans seem far more resistant to tobacco advertising than others are (Centers for Disease Control and Prevention, 2006).

For alcohol, new technology seems to be the most fertile area for exploration: do drinking in YouTube videos and alcohol referenced on social networking profiles actually influence young teenagers' behavior and beliefs about alcohol? A study that examines the total influence of media on alcohol attitudes and behavior—summing up exposure to alcohol ads in a variety of media, TV and movie drinking scenes, YouTube videos, and social networking profiles—would also be extremely valuable, particularly if it could be conducted longitudinally during the formative years (e.g., beginning at age 10 and carrying through to age 15 or 17). And, to date, there have been no studies of the impact of illicit drug portrayals in movies or video games on adolescents' substance use and abuse.

Solutions

A COMPLETE BAN ON TOBACCO ADVERTISING IN ALL MEDIA

Many countries have already done this, with inevitable decreases in smoking rates. One study of 30 developing countries found that partial bans reduced consumption 13.6% and complete bans reduced it by 23.5% (Blecher, 2008). All tobacco advertising and sponsorship on television has been banned within the European Union since 1991, and in 2005 the ban was extended to cover other forms of media, such as the internet, print media, radio, and sports events. In the United States, cigarette ads on TV have been banned since 1971 (but the untold story is that Congress passed the Public Health Act of 1971 only because of the acquiescence of the tobacco industry, which then used their TV advertising expenditures for marketing and promotions in other forums; see Fritschler & Hoefler, 2006). Australia and New Zealand have also banned all forms of tobacco advertising for decades.

RESTRICTIONS ON ALCOHOL ADVERTISING

The research is clear that the funny talking animals and sexy beach babes are incredibly effective in interesting children and teens in alcohol (Borzckowski & Strasburger, 2008). So-called tombstone advertising—the industry's own unfortunate but apt term for ads that simply show the product—would eliminate this aspect completely (Figure 5.7); but Congressional attempts to curtail alcohol ads have traditionally been met with an outpouring of campaign contributions from the alcohol industry and subsequently have failed. Alcohol ads could easily be restricted to programming for which less than 15% of the audience are youth: this would decrease alcohol manufacturers' costs by 8%, decrease teens' exposure by 20%, and could reduce teens' alcohol consumption by as much as 25% (Center on Alcohol Marketing and Youth, 2007; Jernigan, 2009; Saffer & Dave, 2006). This idea has been supported by both the U.S. surgeon general and 24 state attorneys general (Join Together Staff, 2011).

MORE AGGRESSIVE AND BETTER COUNTERADVERTISING

Counteradvertising *can* be effective, but it has to be creative, targeted, and reach the airtime density of regular advertising—criteria that are rarely met. In addition, while the "frying egg" ad from the Partnership for a Drug Free America (PDFA) was almost universally recognized by teenagers, the effectiveness of a more recent PDFA campaign has been questioned (Hornik, Jacobsohn, Orwin,

Figure 5.7 Example of Tombstone Advertising for an Alcoholic Beverage.

Piesse, & Kalton, 2008); and the PDFA would never take on cigarettes or alcohol, since those industries contribute to the advertising industry. There have been some notable successes, however:

• A four-year, $50 million campaign in Massachusetts resulted in a 50% reduction in new smoking by young teens (Siegel & Biener, 2000).

• The White House Office of National Drug Control Policy's Above the Influence campaign began in 2005 and has shown some efficacy—exposure to the ads predicted reduced marijuana use among both eighth-grade girls and boys in one study (Slater, Kelly, Lawrence, Stanley, & Comello, 2011) but only among eighth-grade girls in a study of eighth-, tenth-, and twelfth-grade boys and girls (Carpenter & Pechmann, 2011).

• The best known and most creative advertisements have come from the Truth campaign. Funded by as part of the tobacco industry's $246 billion Tobacco Master Settlement Agreement, the nonprofit American Legacy Foundation was established, which produces the Truth ads. Such ads often try to expose the tobacco industry as being manipulative and deceptive and therefore have incurred the wrath of the tobacco industry, which has filed lawsuits to try to have them withdrawn. In one ad, two teenagers carry a lie detector into Philip

Morris's New York headquarters and announce that they want to deliver it to the marketing department. In another, a group of teens in a large delivery truck pulls up in front of the headquarters and begins unloading body bags. A study in Florida found that the campaign accounted for one-fourth of the decline in the prevalence of teen smoking, which decreased from 25% in 1999 to 18% in 2002 (Farrelly, Davis, Haviland, Messeri, & Healton, 2005).

GREATER PUBLIC HEALTH AWARENESS AND RESPONSIBILITY FROM THE ENTERTAINMENT INDUSTRY

Hollywood studios have agreed to put antismoking ads on all new DVDs (Serjeant, 2008), but airing antismoking ads just before movies in theaters would potentially be far more effective (Edwards, Oakes, & Bull, 2007). Hollywood filmmakers need to stop using smoking as signifying an evil or conflicted character (Chapman, 2008), and TV and movie producers need to end the portrayal of getting drunk as being humorous. The group Smoke-Free Movies has called repeatedly for an R-rating to be given to any movie that contains smoking incidents, unless the smoking is portrayed in an unhealthy light or is historically necessary (see http://smokefreemovies.ucsf.edu/). Alternatively, the state of California could pass legislation mandating that movie sets be declared smoke-free so that actors would not be exposed to secondhand smoke.

INCREASED MEDIA LITERACY PROGRAMS IN SCHOOLS

A century ago, to be "literate" meant that you could read and write. In the new millennium, to be literate means that you can read and write, text, download, and tweet. Schools have not kept up with new technology in general (Strasburger, 2012), but their drug education programs usually consist of DARE (Drug Abuse Resistance Education), which is in 75% of public schools in the U.S. but which uses simplistic scare tactics that have been shown to be ineffective (U.S. Department of Health and Human Services, 2007) and that may actually boomerang and increase drug use (Lilienfeld, 2007). A meta-analysis of 20 different studies and a 10-year follow-up study of 1,002 individuals who received the training in sixth grade both found the program lacking (Lynam et al., 1999; Pan & Bai, 2009). Other, effective drug prevention programs, such as Life Skills Training (LST), have been developed (Figure 5.8) but are more time-consuming and expensive (Botvin & Griffin, 2005). Nevertheless, some of the principles of LST have been incorporated into the DARE program.

The United States is unique among Western nations in not requiring some form of media literacy for its students (Brown, 2007). Several studies now indicate that successful drug prevention may be possible through this unique

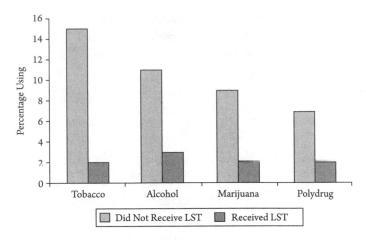

Figure 5.8 Drug Use Following Life Skills Training.

route (Austin & Johnson, 1997; Austin, Pinkleton, Hust, & Cohen, 2005; Kupersmidt, Scull, & Austin, 2010; McCannon, 2013; Potter, 2010; Primack, Fine, Yang, Wickett, & Zickmund, 2009; Primack, Gold, Land, & Fine, 2006; Primack, Sidani, Carroll, & Fine, 2009; Slater et al., 2006). In addition, there are now media education programs that can reduce adolescents' displays of risky behaviors on social networking websites (Moreno, VanderStoep, et al., 2009).

MORE RESEARCH

Considering how significant the impact of the media is on young people, it seems astounding that more financial resources are not being devoted to media research (Christakis & Zimmerman 2006; Strasburger, Jordan, & Donnerstein, 2013). According to the most recent Kaiser report, children and teens spend more than seven hours per day with a variety of different media (Rideout, 2010), yet the Federal government funds only a handful of studies. Currently no foundation funds any media research (the Kaiser Family Foundation announced in February 2010 that it was discontinuing its Program for the Study of Media and Health, which has produced some of the best media research in the past 15 years). New studies of how different teens process drug content in different media are needed, as are continuing studies of the impact of the internet and of social networking sites. Existing research needs to be more widely disseminated as well. A new surgeon general's report or National Institute of Mental Health (NIMH) report on the influence of media on child and adolescent health might prove to be extremely useful to researchers, health professionals, parents, and policymakers and could provide the impetus for increasing funding of research.

The last NIMH report on children and media was in 1982, well before the internet, DVRs, cell phones, digital advertising, and social networking sites.

References

Anderson, P., de Bruijn, A., Angus, K., Gordon, R., & Hastings, G. (2009). Impact of alcohol advertising and media exposure on adolescent alcohol use: a systematic review of longitudinal studies. *Alcohol and Alcoholism, 44,* 229–243.

Austin, E. W., & Hust, S. J. T. (2005). Targeting adolescents? The content and frequency of alcoholic and nonalcoholic beverage ads in magazine and video formats November 1999–April 2000. *Journal of Health Communication, 10,* 769–785.

Austin, E. W., Pinkleton, B. E., Hust, S. J. T., & Cohen, M. (2005). Evaluation of an American Legacy Foundation/Washington State Department of Health Media Literacy Study. *Health Communication, 18,* 75–95.

Austin E. W., & Johnson, K. K. (1997). Effects of general and alcohol-specific media literacy training on children's decision making about alcohol. *Journal of Health Communication, 2,* 17–42.

Blecher, E. (2008). The impact of tobacco advertising bans on consumption in developing countries. *Journal of Health Economics, 27,* 930–942.

Borzekowski, D. L. G., & Strasburger, V. C. (2008). Tobacco, alcohol, and drug exposure. In S. Calvert, B.J. Wilson (Eds.), *Handbook of children and the media* (pp. 432–452). Boston, MA: Blackwell.

Botvin, G. J., & Griffin, K. W. (2005). Models of prevention: School-based programs. In J. H. Lowinson, P. Ruiz, R. B. Millman, & J. G. Langrod (Eds.), *Substance abuse: a comprehensive textbook* (4th ed.) (pp. 1211–1229). Philadelphia, PA: Lippincott.

Brown, J. D. (2007). Media literacy has potential to improve adolescents' health. *Journal of Adolescent Health, 39,* 459–460.

Brown, S. A., McGue, M., Maggs, J., Schulenberg, J., Hingson, R., Swartzwelder, S., . . . & Murphy, S. (2008). A developmental perspective on alcohol and youths 16 to 20 years of age. *Pediatrics, 121*(Suppl. 4), S290–S310.

Campaign for Tobacco-Free Kids (2011). Toll of tobacco in the United States. Retrieved from http://www.tobaccofreekids.org/research/factsheets/pdf/0072.pdf

Carpenter, C. S., & Pechmann, C. (2011). Exposure to the Above the Influence antidrug advertisements and adolescent marijuana use in the United States, 2006–2008. *American Journal of Public Health, 101,* 948–954.

Center on Alcohol Marketing and Youth (CAMY). (2007). *Alcohol advertising and youth.* Washington, DC: CAMY.

Centers for Disease Control and Prevention. (2006). Racial/ethnic differences among youths in cigarette smoking and susceptibility to start smoking—United States, 2002–2004. *Morbidity and Mortality Weekly Reports. 55,* 1275–1277.

Centers for Disease Control and Prevention. (2011). Smoking in top-grossing movies—United States, 2010. *Morbidity and Mortality Weekly Reports, 60,* 910–913.

Chapman S. (2008). What should be done about smoking in movies? *Tobacco Control, 17,* 363–367.

Christakis, D. A., & Zimmerman, F. J. (2006). Media as a public health issue. *Archives of Pediatrics & Adolescent Medicine, 160,* 446–447.

Committee on Substance Abuse, American Academy of Pediatrics. (2010). Alcohol use by youth and adolescents: a pediatric concern. *Pediatrics, 125,* 1078–1087.

Comstock, G. C., & Strasburger, V. C. (1993). Media violence: Q & A. *Adolescent Medicine: State of the Art Reviews, 4,* 495–509.

Cullen, J., Sokol, N. A., Slawek, D., Allen J. A., Vallone, D., & Healton, C. (2011). Depictions of tobacco use in 2007 broadcast television programming popular among US youth. *Archives of Pediatrics and Adolescent Medicine, 165*, 147–151.

Dalton, M. A., Ahrens, M. B., Sargent, J. D., Mott, L. A., Beach, M. L., Tickle, J. J., & Heatherton, T. F. (2002). Correlation between use of tobacco and alcohol in adolescents and parental restrictions on movies. *Effective Clinical Practice, 1*, 1–10.

Dalton, M. A., Beach, M. L., Adachi-Mejia, A. M., Longacre, M. R., Matzkin, A. L., Sargent, J. D., Heatherton, T. F., & Titus-Ernstoff, L. (2009). Early exposure to movie smoking predicts established smoking by older teens and young adults. *Pediatrics, 123*, e551–e558.

de Leeuw, R. N. H., Sargent, J. D., Stoolmiller, M., Scholte, R. H. J., Engels, R. C. M. E., & Tanski, S. E. (2011). Association of smoking onset with R-rated movie restrictions and adolescent sensation-seeking. *Pediatrics, 127*, e96–e105.

DiFranza, J. R., Wellman, R. J., Sargent, J. D., Weitzman, M., Hipple, B. J., & Winickoff, J. P. (2006). Tobacco promotion and the initiation of tobacco use: Assessing the evidence for causality. *Pediatrics, 117*, e1237–e1248.

Edwards, C., Oakes, W., & Bull, D. (2007). Out of the smokescreen II: Will an advertisement targeting the tobacco industry affect young people's perception of smoking in movies and their intention to smoke? *Tobacco Control, 16*, 177–181.

Esterhaus, J. (2004). *Hollywood Animal*. New York: Knopf.

Farrelly, M. C., Davis, K. C., Haviland, M. L., Messeri, P., & Healton, C. G. (2005). Evidence of a dose-response relationship between "Truth" antismoking ads and youth smoking prevalence. *American Journal of Public Health, 95*, 425–431.

Foster, S. E., Vaughan, R. D., Foster, W. H., & Califano, J. A. Jr. (2003). Alcohol consumption and expenditures for underage drinking and adult excessive drinking. *Journal of the American Medical Association, 289*, 989–995.

Foster, S. E., Vaughan, R. D., Foster, W. H., & Califano, J. A. (2006). Estimate of the commercial value of underage drinking and adult abusive and dependent drinking to the alcohol industry. *Archives of Pediatrics & Adolescent Medicine, 160*, 473–478.

Fritschler, A. L., & Hoefler, J. M. (2006). *Smoking & politics: Policy making and the federal bureaucracy* (6th ed.). Upper Saddle River, NJ: Prentice Hall.

Gidwani, P. P., Sobol, A., DeJong, W., Perrin, J. M., & Gortmaker, S. L. (2002). Television viewing and initiation of smoking among youth. *Pediatrics, 110*, 505–508.

Glantz, S. A., Iaccopucci, A., Titus, K., & Polansky, J. R. (2012). Smoking in top-grossing US movies, 2011. *Preventing Chronic Disease, 9*, 120170. doi: 10.5888/pcd9.120170

Glantz, S. A., Slade, J., Bero, L. A., Hanauer, P., & Barnes, D. (1998). *The cigarette papers*. Berkeley, CA: University of California Press.

Halperin, S. (2008, April 18). Going to pot. *Entertainment Weekly*, pp. 38–41.

Hancox, R. J., Milne, B. J., & Poulton, R. (2004). Association between child and adolescent television viewing and adult health: A longitudinal birth cohort study. *Lancet, 364*, 257–262.

Hanewinkel, R., Isensee, B., Sargent, J. D., & Morgenstern, M. (2010). Cigarette advertising and adolescent smoking. *American Journal of Preventive Medicine, 38*, 359–366.

Hanewinkel, R., Isensee, B., Sargent, J. D., & Morgenstern, M. (2011). Cigarette advertising and teen smoking initiation. *Pediatrics, 127*, e271–e278.

Hanewinkel, R., & Sargent, J. D. (2009). Longitudinal study of exposure to entertainment media and alcohol use among German adolescents. *Pediatrics, 123*, 989–995.

Hanewinkel, R., Sargent, J. D., Karlsdottir, S., Jonsson, S. H., Mathis, F., Faggiano, F.,...& Morgenstern, M. (2013). High youth access to movies that contain smoking in Europe compared with the USA. *Tobacco Control, 22*, 241–244.

Hanewinkel, R., Sargent, J. D., Poelen, E. A. P., Scholte, R., Florek, E., Sweeting, H.,...& Morgenstern, M. (2012). Alcohol consumption in movies and adolescent binge drinking in 6 European countries. *Pediatrics, 129*, 1–12.

Heatherton, T. F., & Sargent, J. D. (2009). Does watching smoking in movies promote teenage smoking? *Current Directions in Psychological Science, 18*, 63–67.

Hill, A. B. (1965). The environment and disease: Association or causality? *Proceedings of the Royal Society of Medicine, 58*, 295–300.

Hornik, R., Jacobsohn, L., Orwin, R., Piesse, A. N., & Kalton, G. (2008). Effects of the National Youth Anti-Drug Media Campaign on youths. *American Journal of Public Health, 98*, 2229–2236.

Jamieson, P. E., & Romer, D. (2010). Trends in US movie tobacco portrayal since 1950: A historical analysis. *Tobacco Control, 19*, 179–184.

Jenssen, B. P., Klein, J. D., Salazar, L. R., Daluge, N. A., & DiClemente, R. J. (2009). Exposure to tobacco on the Internet: content analysis of adolescents' Internet use. *Pediatrics, 124*, e180–e186.

Jernigan, D. H. (2009). Alcohol-branded merchandise: The need for action. *Archives of Pediatrics & Adolescent Medicine, 163*, 278–279.

Johnston, L. D., O'Malley, P. M., Bachman, J. G., & Schulenberg, J. E. (2012). *Monitoring the Future: National results on adolescent drug use: Overview of key findings, 2011*. Retrieved from http://www.monitoringthefuture.org/pubs/monographs/mtf-overview2011.pdf

Join Together Staff. (2011, April 29). 24 attorneys general ask FTC to do more to keep alcohol advertising from teens. Retrieved from http://www.drugfree.org/join-together/alcohol/24-attorneys-general-ask-ftc-to-do-more-to-keep-alcohol-advertising-from-teens

Kessler, D. (2001). *A question of intent: a great American battle with a deadly industry*. New York, NY: PublicAffairs.

Kupersmidt, J. B., Scull, T. M., & Austin, E. W. (2010). Media literacy education for elementary school substance use prevention: study of Media Detective. *Pediatrics, 126*, 525–531.

Lilienfeld, S. O. (2007). Psychological treatments that cause harm. *Perspectives on Psychological Science, 2*, 53–70.

Lovato, C., Watts, A., & Stead, L. F. (2011). Impact of tobacco advertising and promotion on increasing adolescent smoking behaviours. *Cochrane Database System Reviews, 10*, CD003439. doi: 10.1002/14651858.CD003439.pub2

Lynam, D. R., Milich R., Zimmerman, R., Novak, S. P., Logan, T. K., Martin, C., … & Clayton, R. (1999). Project DARE: no effects at 10-year follow-up. *Journal of Consulting and Clinical Psychology, 67*, 590–593.

McCannon B. (2013). Media literacy/media education: Solution to Big Media? A review of the literature. In V. C. Strasburger, B. J. Wilson, & A. B. Jordan (Eds.), *Children, adolescents, and the media* (3rd ed.) (pp. 507–558). Thousand Oaks, CA: Sage.

Moreno, M. A., Briner, L. R., Williams, A., Brockman, L., Walker, L., & Christakis, D. A. (2010). A content analysis of displayed alcohol references on a social networking web site. *Journal of Adolescent Health, 47*, 168–175.

Moreno, M. A., Christakis, D. A., Egan, K. G., Brockman, L. N., & Becker, T. (2012). Associations between displayed alcohol references on Facebook and problem drinking among college students. *Archives of Pediatrics & Adolescent Medicine, 166*, 157–163.

Moreno, M. A., Parks, M. R., Zimmerman, F. J., Brito, T. E., & Christakis, D. A. (2009a). Display of health risk behaviors on MySpace by adolescents. *Archives of Pediatrics & Adolescent Medicine, 163*, 27–34.

Moreno, M. A., VanderStoep, A., Parks, M. R., Zimmerman, F. J., Kurth, A., & Christakis, D. A. (2009b). Reducing at-risk adolescents' display of risk behavior on a social networking web site. *Archives of Pediatrics & Adolescent Medicine, 163*, 35–41.

Morgenstern, M., Poelen, E. A. P., Scholte, R., Karlsdottir, S., Jonsson, S. H., Mathis, F., … & Hanewinkel, R. (2011). Smoking in movies and adolescent smoking: cross-cultural study in six European countries. *Thorax, 66*, 875–883.

Murphy, S. T., Hether, H. J., & Rideout, V. (2008). How healthy is prime time? An analysis of health content in popular prime time television programs. Retrieved from http://kaiserfamilyfoundation.files.wordpress.com/2013/01/7764.pdf

National Cancer Institute. (2008). The role of the media in promoting and reducing tobacco use, smoking and tobacco control. Retrieved from http://cancercontrol.cancer.gov/tcrb/monographs/19/m19_complete.pdf

National Center on Addiction and Substance Abuse (NCASA). (2005). National survey of American attitudes on substance abuse IX: Teens and parents. New York, NY: NCASA.

National Center on Addiction and Substance Abuse (NCASA). (2011a). Adolescent substance use: America's #1 public health problem. New York, NY: NCASA.

National Center on Addiction and Substance Abuse (NCASA). (2011b). National survey of American attitudes on substance abuse XVI: Teens and parents. New York, NY: NCASA.

Pan, W., & Bai, H. (2009). A multivariate approach to a meta-analytic review of the effectiveness of the D.A.R.E. program. *International Journal of Environmental Research and Public Health, 6*, 267–277.

Potter, W. J. (2010). *Media literacy*, 5th ed. Thousand Oaks, CA: Sage.

Primack, B. A., Douglas, E., & Kraemer, K. (2010). Exposure to cannabis in popular music and cannabis use among adolescents. *Addiction, 105*, 515–523.

Primack, B. A., Fine, D., Yang, C. K., Wickett, D., & Zickmund, S. (2009). Adolescents' impressions of antismoking media literacy education: qualitative results from a randomized controlled trial. *Health Education Research, 24*, 608–621.

Primack, B. A., Gold, M. A., Land, S. R., & Fine, M. J. (2006). Association of cigarette smoking and media literacy about smoking among adolescents. *Journal of Adolescent Health, 39*, 465–472.

Primack, B. A., Kraemer, K. L., Fine, M. J., & Dalton, M. A. (2009). Media exposure and marijuana and alcohol use among adolescents. *Substance Use and Misuse, 44*, 722–739.

Primack, B. A., Sidani, J., Carroll, M. V., & Fine, M. J. (2009). Associations between smoking and media literacy in college students. *Journal of Health Communication, 14*, 541–555.

Prokhorov, A. V., Winickoff, J. P., Ahluwalia, J. S., Ossip-Klein, D., Tanski S., Lando, H. A.,... & Ford, K. H. (2006). Youth tobacco use: a global perspective for child health care clinicians. *Pediatrics, 118*, e890–e902.

Rehm, J., Shield, K. D., Joharchi, N., & Shuper, P. A. (2012). Alcohol consumption and the intention to engage in unprotected sex: Systematic review and meta-analysis of experimental studies. *Addiction, 107*, 51–59.

Rideout V. (2010). Generation M2: Media in the lives of 8- to 18-year-olds. Retrieved from http://kff.org/other/event/generation-m2-media-in-the-lives-of/

Saffer, H., & Dave, D. (2006). Alcohol advertising and alcohol consumption by adolescents. *Health Economics, 15*, 617–637.

Sargent J. D., Gibson J., & Heatherton, T. (2009). Comparing the effects of entertainment media and tobacco marketing on youth smoking. *Tobacco Control, 18*, 47–53.

Sargent, J. D. & Heatherton, T. F. (2009). Comparison of trends for adolescent smoking and smoking in movies, 1990–2007. *Journal of the American Medical Association, 301*, 2211–2213.

Sargent, J. D., Wills, T. A., Stoolmiller, M., Gibson, J., & Gibbons, F. X. (2006). Alcohol use in motion pictures and its relation with early onset teen drinking. *Journal of Studies of Alcohol, 67*, 54–65.

Serjeant, J. (2008, July 11). Some U.S. DVDs to carry anti-smoking ads. Reuters. Retrieved from http://www.reuters.com/article/entertainmentNews/idUSN1134673320080711

Siegel, M., & Biener, L. (2000). The impact of an antismoking media campaign on progression to established smoking: results of a longitudinal youth study. *American Journal of Public Health, 90*, 380–386.

Slater, M. D., Kelly, K. J., Edwards, R. W., Plested, B. A., Keefe, T. J., Lawrence, F. R., & Henry, K. L. (2006). Combining in-school and community-based media efforts: reducing marijuana and alcohol uptake among younger adolescents. *Health Education Research, 21*, 157–167.

Slater, M. D., Kelly, K. J., Lawrence, F. R., Stanley, L. R., & Comello, M. L. G. (2011). Assessing media campaigns linking marijuana non-use with autonomy and aspirations: "Be Under Your Own Influence" and ONDCP's "Above the Influence." *Preventive Science, 12*, 12–22.

Smith, L. A., & Foxcroft, D. R. (2009). The effect of alcohol advertising, marketing and portrayal on drinking behaviour in young people: systematic review of prospective cohort studies. *BMC Public Health, 9*. doi:10.1186/1471-2458-9-51

Stoolmiller, M., Wills, T. A., McClure, A. C., Tanski, S. E., Worth, K. A., Gerrard, M., & Sargent, J. D. (2012). Comparing media and family predictors of alcohol use: a cohort study of US adolescents. *BMJ Open, 2*, e000543. doi:10.1136/bmjopen-2011-000543

Strasburger, V. C. (1995). *Adolescents and the media: Medical and psychological impact.* Newbury Park, CA, Sage.

Strasburger, V. C. (2012). Adolescents, drugs, and the media. In D. G. Singer, J. L. Singer (Eds). *Handbook of children and media* (2nd ed.) (pp. 419–454). Los Angeles, CA: Sage.

Strasburger, V. C., and Council on Communications and Media. (2010). Children, adolescents, substance abuse, and the media. *Pediatrics, 126,* 791–799.

Strasburger, V. C., Jordan, A. B., & Donnerstein, E. (2013). Children, adolescents, and the media: health effects. *Pediatric Clinics of North America, 59,* 533–587.

Tanski, S. E., Dal Cin, S., Stoolmiller, M., & Sargent, J. D. (2010). Parental R-rated movie restriction and early onset alcohol use. *Journal of Studies of Alcohol and Drugs, 71,* 452–459.

Tickle, J. J., Beach, M. L., & Dalton, M. A. (2009). Tobacco, alcohol, and other risk behaviors in film: how well do MPAA ratings distinguish content? *Journal of Health Communication, 14,* 756–767.

Titus-Ernstoff, L., Dalton, M. A., Adachi-Mejia, A. M., Longacre, M. R., & Beach, M. L. (2008). Longitudinal study of viewing smoking in movies and initiation of smoking by children. *Pediatrics, 121,* 15–21.

U.S. Department of Health and Human Services. (2007). *The surgeon general's call to action to prevent and reduce underage drinking.* Rockville, MD: U.S. Department of Health and Human Services.

World Health Organization. (2002). *World health report.* Geneva, Switzerland: World Health Organization. Retrieved from http://www.who.int/whr/2002/chapter4/en/index6.html

World Health Organization. (2008). *WHO report on the global tobacco epidemic, 2008.* Geneva, Switzerland: World Health Organization.

World Health Organization. (2011). *Smoke-free movies: From evidence to action.* Geneva: Switzerland: World Health Organization.

CHAPTER 6

Growing Up Sexually in a Digital World

THE RISKS AND BENEFITS OF YOUTHS' SEXUAL MEDIA USE

Jane D. Brown, Sherine El-Toukhy, and Rebecca Ortiz

Sexual Identity Development in Adolescence

Adolescence (10- to 19-years-old, according to the World Health Organization, 2012) is a unique developmental stage during which young people experience biological, psychological, and social changes. A primary challenge confronting adolescents is identity formation (Christie & Viner, 2011). Identity has been defined "as a self-structure—an internal self-constructed, dynamic organization of drives, abilities, beliefs, and individual history" (Marcia, 1980, p. 159). As adolescents develop their personal identities, they strive to establish independence, autonomy, and individuation (Christie & Viner, 2011), which typically include some parent-adolescent conflict (Silverberg & Steinberg, 1987) and a transfer of attachment from parents to peers and romantic partners (Fraley & Davis, 1997).

Sexual maturation is integral to adolescents' evolving identities. Adolescents go through three main stages of sexual maturation. The increase in sex hormones (estrogen and testosterone) in the pubertal transition in early adolescence (10–13 years) translates into sexual curiosity and exploration (e.g., masturbation, crushes). Middle adolescence (14–17 years) is characterized by full physical maturation. In many cultures, courting and dating are hallmarks of this stage. Older adolescents (17–19 years) typically are more sexually expressive and develop intimate relationships as they enter into adulthood (Sharpe, 2003).

How young people identify and perceive themselves as sexual beings—their sexual self-concepts—also play a major role in the development of sexual identity. The sexual self-concept of an individual is often related to his or her sexual behaviors and attitudes and includes multiple dimensions, such as cognitive structures associated with sexual aspects of the self derived from previous experiences and sexual motivations for engaging in certain behaviors (Snell, Fisher, & Schuh, 1992; Snell, 2001). Dimensions such as sexual openness, sexual esteem, and sexual anxiety can evolve throughout adolescence and regulate future behavior (Hensel, Fortenberry, O'Sullivan, & Orr, 2011).

Some adolescents engage in risky sexual behaviors as they explore new identities. Sexual intercourse can be a risky behavior for young people if they do not practice safe sex and develop healthy sexual self-concepts. Chlamydia and gonorrhea infection rates, for example, continue to rise among 15- to 19-year-olds (Centers for Disease Control and Prevention, 2011) and despite declines in the 2000s, teen pregnancy is a major issue. Birth rates to teen mothers in the United States remain the highest in the developed world (Martin et al., 2010a, 2010b). These trends are of significant public health concern because risky sexual behaviors, such as having multiple sexual partners and using drugs or alcohol before sexual intercourse (Centers for Disease Control and Prevention, 2008, 2010; Eaton et al., 2006), can result in short- and long-term economic and social costs. The annual cost of teenage pregnancy in the United States, for example, is estimated at $9.1 billion (Hoffman, 2006) and many teen mothers and their children suffer adverse outcomes compared to those who postpone childbearing until adulthood (Coley & Chase-Lansdale, 1998).

Adolescents acquire knowledge, attitudes, and values about sexuality and sexual health from a variety of socialization agents (i.e., family, peers, media, school, work, community, the legal system, and cultural belief systems such as those articulated by religions) (Ward, 2003). The media are especially influential self–sexual socialization agents when other sources of sexual values are reticent or restrictive (Arnett, 1995).

The focus of this chapter is the role the media play in the sexual socialization of adolescents. Media is broadly defined as any mediated form of communication received by an audience (even if the audience is one person), such as television, magazines, movies, music, video games, cellular devices, and the internet. Although an ever-growing body of research provides perspective into how media play a role in youth sexual socialization, a number of questions remain, especially as more interactive, portable media, such as smartphones and tablets, increase accessibility of sexual content for young consumers all over the world.

What We Currently Know

The media make a difference in young people's sexual lives. Based on a review of cross-sectional, longitudinal, and experimental studies, Wright (2011) concluded that, given the substantial evidence to date, exposure to sexual media does affect adolescents' sexual behavior. Greater exposure to sexual media content is associated with physiological outcomes (e.g., sexual arousal), attitudinal outcomes (e.g., stronger endorsement of traditional gender roles, sexual relationship stereotypes, recreational attitudes toward sex), and behavioral outcomes (e.g., increased intentions to have sex, earlier sexual initiation, increased likelihood of adolescent pregnancy) (Arnett, 1992; Brown et al., 2006; Bryant & Rockwell, 1994; Chandra et al., 2008; Collins et al., 2004; Escobar-Chaves et al., 2005; Eyal & Kunkel, 2008; Farrar, 2006; Kim & Ward, 2004; Murnen & Stockton, 1997; Nabi & Clark, 2008; O'Hara, Gibbons, Gerrard, Li, & Sargent, 2012; Pardun, L'Engle, & Brown, 2005; Ward & Friedman, 2006).

Young people often turn to the media for information about sexuality. In a national survey of more than 500 teens and young adults, the media far outranked parents or schools as a source of information about sex (Kaiser Family Foundation/*Seventeen* Magazine, 2004). Television remains the medium youth use most often (Nielsen, 2009; Rideout, Foehr, & Roberts, 2010), as television content is easily accessible on portable devices and personal computers. The internet allows anonymous sexual exploration, including information seeking about sexual health (Valkenburg & Peter, 2011).

The media most popular with adolescents are saturated with sexual content including television (Hetsroni, 2007; Kunkel et al., 2007), magazines (Joshi, Peter, & Valkenburg, 2011), movies (Callister, Stern, & Coyne, 2011), music (Turner, 2011; Wallis, 2011), and video games (Haninger & Thompson, 2004). Many adolescents see teen and young adult characters engage in casual sex with multiple partners on popular television shows and listen to music lyrics such as "I want to f*ck you right now" and "That magic in your pants, it's making me blush." They can also get sex advice from popular magazines and various sites online. Explicit pornography is also readily available on the internet.

At least two three-wave longitudinal analyses suggest a reciprocal pattern of media effects for early adolescents—as adolescents enter puberty, sexual content in the media is more relevant, is paid more attention to, and sometimes sought out (Bleakley, Hennessy, Fishbein, & Jordan, 2008; Kim et al., 2006). The sexual media content adolescents see or listen to increases the saliency of this content and primes sexual scripts or ideas about how sexual encounters unfold (Roskos-Ewoldsen, Roskos-Ewoldsen, & Carpentier, 2002). Some of what adolescents see may shift perceptions of norms. Heavier users may begin to think that early and unprotected sexual intercourse is more typical for young people than it actually is (Gerbner, Gross, Morgan, Signorielli, & Shanahan, 2002). The sexual media practice model (Steele, 1999; Shafer, Bobkowski, & Brown, 2013) also posits reciprocity between sexual media effects and use, such that media users are active in selecting, interpreting, applying, and sharing sexual media content. The model suggests that young people's media use is motivated by their developing sexual self-concepts and identities and their patterns of use, in turn, affect how they think and act as sexual human beings.

Although the portrayal of sexual risks and responsibilities in popular teen media increased in the early 2000s, such portrayals remained infrequent (Kunkel et al., 2007). Most consequences of sexual behavior, nearly equally positive and negative, were transient and emotionally insignificant (Eyal & Finnerty, 2007). Rare sexual health messages in the media (television, magazines, music, and movies) were ambiguous and inaccurate, reinforcing traditional gender stereotypes (e.g., males seek sex, females are responsible for contraception) (Hust, Brown, & L'Engle, 2008). One content analysis of television dramas popular with teens, for example, found that negative consequences were more common in scenes in which female characters initiated sexual activities than in scenes in which male characters initiated sexual activities (Aubrey, 2004).

The lack of discussion or depiction of negative consequences in media content may increase adolescent media users' positive perceptions of sexual behavior and stimulate earlier sexual behavior (Wright, 2011). The positive or negative reinforcement of sexual behaviors may lead to the modeling of relevant behaviors or adoption of certain beliefs (Bandura, 1977, 2009). If a female viewer observes a character engaging in a sexual behavior that is rewarded, for example, she may be more likely to model that behavior in the future. Or if female characters are consistently chastised for their sexual behavior while male characters are rewarded, young female viewers may begin to believe that they should be cautious in expressing their sexuality. One study found that young adults reported more negative attitudes toward premarital intercourse and negative moral judgments of characters after exposure to television shows that portrayed negative consequences of sexual intercourse than did young adults who viewed positive portrayals (Eyal & Kunkel, 2008).

Viewers' orientations, including viewing motivations and perceived reality of the media portrayals, can make a difference in what viewers take away from the experience (Ward & Rivadeneyra, 1999). Also, the more engaged viewers are in the portrayal, either through identification with characters or being transported into a story, the more they will be affected by the portrayal (e.g., Moyer-Guse & Nabi, 2011; Zurbriggen & Morgan, 2006). One study found that after exposure to a character in a television narrative who was depicted discussing his or her sexual history with a new sexual partner, a viewer's stronger identification with the character was positively associated with the viewer's increased self-efficacy to engage in such a discussion in the future (Moyer-Guse, Chung, & Jain, 2011).

Some survey evidence suggests that television and other media may provide "sexual super peers" for female teens, educating them and pushing them into engaging in sex earlier than if they had not been paying attention to such content

(Brown, Halpern, & L'Engle, 2005; Strasburger & Wilson, 2002; Strasburger, Wilson, & Jordan, 2009).

Sexual behavior is also influenced by sociocultural factors (e.g., family, friendships, religious backgrounds and beliefs) and individual differences (e.g., gender). Research suggests, for example, that parental control and parent-child communication may reduce adolescents' susceptibility to peer influence and restrict opportunities for sexual activity (Fisher et al., 2009). Religiosity is also related to later initiation of sex (Crockett, Raffaelli, & Moilanen, 2003). Gender roles are important in how individuals express and experience themselves sexually. Current cultural standards allow males to actively seek sexual partners and endorse sexual exploits by peers, while females are encouraged to wait for a male to approach and to desire affection or love over sex. Such gender differences have been called the sexual double standard in that men and women are subject to different "rules" of sexual behavior (Crawford & Popp, 2003).

Unanswered Questions

A number of unanswered questions about the role of the media in adolescents' sexual socialization remain. Five broad domains of questions were identified based on our review of existing research.

HOW DO SEXUAL MEDIA EFFECTS FIT IN THE BROADER CONTEXT OF ROMANTIC RELATIONSHIPS AND ADOLESCENT DEVELOPMENT?

Romantic relationships, in which "the individual perceives an ongoing, reciprocated, emotional, erotically charged connection with a partner," are the traditional context in which sexual behavior occurs (Karney, Beckett, Collins, & Shaw, 2007, p. xv). Even before young people engage in real-life romantic experiences, they have developed cultural templates—perceptions, expectations, and scripts about romantic love and sexuality (Bachen & Illouz, 1996). Romantic and sexual scripts are cognitive models that people use to guide their interactions, learned from culturally available messages such as those provided in the media (Frith & Kitzinger, 2001). Common scripts to which we are exposed will influence our perceptions of how certain situations are most likely to happen to ourselves and to others (Gagnon & Simon, 2005).

Romantic love is a universal phenomenon (Jankowiak & Fischer, 1992) that typically is first experienced during adolescence (Montgomery & Sorell, 1998). Expectations about love, romance, and marriage may be affected especially by media genres in which love is an "an obsessive theme" (Bachen & Illouz, 1996,

p. 279). Reality dating shows and romantic comedies provide scripts about desirable characteristics of partners and when sex should occur (Johnson & Holmes, 2009). The few empirical studies in this domain have found that frequent exposure to "romance media" is related to dysfunctional beliefs about relationships (e.g., "fate brings soul mates together," "disagreement is destructive to a relationship," "partners should be able to sense each other's thoughts and feelings") (Holmes, 2007; Segrin & Nabi, 2002). Failure to satisfy these ideals and popular myths (e.g., "love at first sight") might result in disillusionment and dissatisfaction with real-life romantic relationships (Galician, 2004).

Most previous research has focused on the physical outcomes of exposure to sexual content in the media. Content analyses have counted the frequency of sexual intercourse (Kunkel, et al., 2007; Pardun et al., 2005) and the primary dependent variable of the major longitudinal studies was initiation of sexual intercourse (e.g., Brown et al., 2006; Collins et al., 2004). We know much less about the precursors to coitus that typically occur in romantic relationships, such as the beliefs, expectations, and even ideal scripts about how such interactions should occur. Further, research is inconsistent on the practice of safe sex at different stages in romantic relationships of different duration (e.g., monogamous relationships vs. one-night stands) (Karney et al., 2007).

Given increased access and exposure to sexually explicit content (pornography, X-rated content) on the internet (Ybarra & Mitchell, 2005), it is especially important to assess the extent to which early exposure to such depictions affects young people's romantic relationship ideals, norms, and sexual scripts. Sexually explicit media content tends to focus on unaffectionate, recreational, and violent sexual activities (Gossett & Byrne, 2002). The little existing research on the effects of exposure to sexually explicit content on the internet among older adolescents suggests that exposure does increase endorsement of recreational and gender stereotypical attitudes toward sex, uncommitted sexual exploration (i.e., one-night stands, hooking up) (Peter & Valkenburg, 2010), and earlier sexual initiation (Braun-Courville & Rojas, 2009; Brown & L'Engle, 2009; Peter & Valkenburg, 2008). We know little, however, about how the early exposure to such content now possible via the internet affects early adolescents' sexual beliefs and sexual self-concepts.

Exposure to sexually explicit media may also contribute to sexual aggression (Allen, D'Alessio, & Brezgel, 1995), acceptance of rape myths (Allen, Emmers, Gebhardt, & Giery, 1995), and risky behaviors (e.g., having unprotected sex, extramarital sex, paid sex, multiple partners) (Wright & Randall, 2012). One longitudinal study found that early adolescent boys who had seen pornography by age 14 were more likely than those who had not to report committing sexual harassment at school (Brown & L'Engle, 2009). Ybarra, Mitchell, Hamburger, Diener-West, and Leaf (2010) found in a nationally representative survey of U.S.

10- to 17-year-olds that those who had seen violent X-rated media were six times more likely than those who had not to report forcing someone "to do something sexual" online or in person. A CDC surveillance study showed that about 8% of high school students (grades 9–12) have been physically forced to have sex and 10% have been subject to dating violence (e.g., hit, slapped) (Centers for Disease Control and Prevention, 2008). It is important to learn more about how early exposure to sexually explicit content affects pre- and post-pubertal adolescents' romantic and sexual expectations and behaviors.

It is also important to incorporate biological, cognitive, and social development into future research (Chapin, 2000). Current theoretical perspectives explain media effects on adolescents' romantic and sexual attitudes and behaviors based primarily on amount of exposure to sexual media content. Various other attributes of the young media consumer should now be integrated into media effects models. For example, pubertal timing and hormone levels might cause earlier initiation of sex as well as more interest in sexual media content (Brown et al., 2005; Chapin, 2000).

Adolescents' developing brains contribute to their risk-taking behaviors. Adolescents face many challenges at a developmental stage in which their brain's self-regulation system is not fully developed but the brain's socio-emotional system, which is associated with reward seeking and susceptibility to peer pressure, is in high gear. These developmental processes push adolescents to engage in risk-taking and risk-seeking behaviors (Casey, Getz, & Galvan, 2008; Fischhoff, 2008; Steinberg, 2008). Thus, individual differences in decision-making competence (Parker & Fischhoff, 2005), reward sensitivity (Bechara, Damasio, Damasio, & Anderson, 1994), and preference for delayed versus immediate rewards (Green, Myerson, & Ostaszewski, 1999) should be taken into account in future studies of the effects of sexual media.

Methodologically, behavioral willingness measures should be prioritized over behavioral intentions measures because adolescents' engagement in risky behaviors is not always deliberative or thoughtful. Adolescents are prone to engage in behaviors they do not intend or expect to do, so measures of "willingness" rather than "intention" may be more appropriate (Gibbons, Gerrard, Blanton, & Russell, 1998; Reyna & Farley, 2006).

HOW EARLY DO MEDIA EFFECTS ON SEXUALITY OCCUR AND HOW LONG DO THEY LAST?

Most existing studies of media sexual socialization were conducted with older adolescents and emerging adults (i.e., college undergraduates). The process by which children and younger adolescents engage with the media and are subsequently affected is still largely unknown. We also know little about the extent to which scripts learned in adolescence persist into adulthood as more permanent relationships are established.

The longitudinal studies conducted in the first decade of the twenty-first century focused on adolescents (usually 14 to 17 years old). Boys and girls now experience puberty at younger ages than in previous generations. In general, girls enter puberty between ages 8 and 13 and reach menarche (first menstruation) several years later, while boys enter puberty between ages 9 and 14 (Kaplowitz, Slora, Wasserman, Pedlow, & Herman-Giddens, 2001). Although we know much about early acquisition of gender role stereotypes (e.g., Hust & Brown, 2008; Ward, Hansbrough, & Walker, 2005) and body image expectations (e.g., Harrison & Hefner, 2006) from the media, we know less about how early exposure to sexual relationships in the media affects children's developing beliefs about and expectations of romantic and sexual relationships.

On the other end of the developmental spectrum, most studies of sexual effects of the media halt after media consumers are in their late teens or early 20s. Given that many young adults, especially those in developed countries, do not marry until their mid- to late 20s, the media may continue to be an important source of sexual norms. Romantic and sexual expectations formed in adolescence may influence a wide range of experiences and decisions, such as marriage expectations and mate selection (Karney et al., 2007), emotional health (Monroe, Rhode, Seeley, & Lewinsohn, 1999), and even academic and job success (Neemann, Hubbard, & Masten, 1995). Longitudinal studies that follow young people into their second and third decades would help track the media's role in relationship development.

HOW DOES ONLINE SEXUAL SELF-DISCLOSURE AND PEER FEEDBACK AFFECT SEXUAL SELF-CONCEPTS AND BEHAVIORS?

Peer influence on adolescents' sexual attitudes and behaviors is well established (e.g., Chia, 2006). In the world of interactive and ubiquitous portable media such as cell phones and tablets, peers may be even more important in adolescents' lives. The social and immersive nature of digital media has important implications for how and what adolescents might learn from sexual content that is often endorsed by peers and sometimes produced by adolescents themselves. With a click of a button, an adolescent can "like" a sexy song or movie or disclose something sexual about herself on Facebook or other social networking site (Bobkowski, Brown, & Neffa, 2012; Moreno, Brockman, & Christakis, 2009). A new boyfriend might encourage an adolescent girl to send him a sexy picture of herself that may go viral.

In the United States, some 4–12% of adolescents have sent sexually suggestive pictures of themselves ("sexts") to others via their cell phones or have had unwanted sexual images sent to them (Ybarra, Mitchell, & Korchmaros, 2011). Some teens even view sexting as a safer alternative to real-life sexual activity (Lenhart, 2009), although one study found that teens who sexted were more likely to be sexually active, and some were more likely to engage in risky sex (Rice et al., 2012).

Sexy media content endorsed or produced by a close friend may be more compelling than traditional media such as television that does not typically include an interpersonal component or feedback from peers. Bandura (2004) suggested that the media might influence behavior both directly and through social mediation. Peer endorsement of specific kinds of content could be incentive enough to model or imitate what is seen. An adolescent's perceived self-efficacy, the belief that she or he can perform or produce a desired result, is also an important motivator of behavior and peers can contribute to a sense of self-efficacy. In their three-wave survey of adolescents, Bleakley, Hennessy, Fishbein, and Jordan (2009) found, for example, that self-efficacy with regard to having sex was strongest among youth who used friends and media as sexual information sources.

Studies of online self-disclosure have found that some adolescents are more likely to disclose their sexual beliefs and behaviors than others, but little is known about the effects of such disclosures. One experiment found that girls who chose sexualized avatars in a virtual environment (e.g., "Second Life") were more likely to be approached in sexual ways by other characters (Noll, Shenk, Barnes, & Putnam, 2009).

Sexual self-disclosure online may also affect the adolescent's sexual self-concept by reaffirming the centrality or salience of sexual components in his or her developing sense of self. Studies of enactment of nonsexual personality characteristics, such as introversion and extroversion, have identified an "identity-shift" dynamic in which the public display of a particular way of being shifts the person toward further similar behavior (e.g., acting in a more extroverted way than they would have otherwise) (Kelly & Rodriguez, 2006). Thus, we might expect that adolescents who engage in online sexual self-disclosures may begin to think and act in more sexual ways in real life, to be consistent with how they are presenting themselves online.

HOW ARE THE SEXUAL SCRIPTS AND MODELS FOUND IN WESTERN MEDIA INTERPRETED AND APPLIED IN NON-WESTERN CULTURES?

Most of what we currently know about media effects on romantic and sexual attitudes and behaviors among young people is based on studies conducted in Western cultures, such as the United States and Europe. As Western media are increasingly accessible all over the world, we need to learn whether and how exposure to the sexual scripts found in Western media may contribute to shifts in cultural norms in non-Western cultures.

Quinn and Holland (1987) describe cultural models as "presupposed, taken-for-granted models of the world that are widely shared...by the members of a society and that play an enormous role in their understanding of that world and their behavior in it" (p. 4). Economic and technological forces of globalization have challenged such cultural models since the 1980s and 1990s. The widespread capitalist model transformed media, especially television, into commercial vehicles heavily saturated with entertainment. Satellite, cable, and internet technologies allow greater flow of content across national borders challenging the dominance of national media. Further, many countries import genre ideas (e.g., American soap operas transformed into *telenovelas* in South American countries) and rely on licensed programming from other countries (e.g., the reality show *Big Brother* originally produced in the United Kingdom has been produced with local contestants in many other countries). Even though this content is adapted to the local culture in a process called glocalization (local plus global), these imports are laden with the cultural imprints of their origins (Straubhaar, 2007).

Evidence suggests that sexual and romantic scripts and models differ by culture and subcultures even within the same country (Simon & Gagnon, 1987). For example, in the United States, Mexican Americans and African Americans adhere to different models of romantic love (Milbrath, Ohlson, & Eyre, 2009). Hollywood-produced television shows and movies that depict permissive sexual behaviors are hard to reconcile in cultures that hold less permissive religious and cultural values. Cultural patterns of sex-segregation, appropriate dress, and the family's role in mate selection and marriage may be challenged (Munshi, 2001). Durham (2004) documented the struggle of South Asian adolescent immigrants as they negotiate the American media narrative around sexuality in light of their Indian and American identities. Similar studies are needed to understand how audiences in foreign countries negotiate, choose, and interpret foreign sexual and romantic media content.

In some more sexually restrictive cultures, television, movies, and music may be especially compelling because they are more engaging than other socializing agents, such as parents and religious institutions that are intent on educating their children to accept mainstream norms and values in an attempt to preserve the social order (Rohn, 2010). On the other hand, family and religiosity may remain important moderators of the influence of the media on sexual behavior in other cultures (El-Toukhy & Brown, 2010).

Some countries apparently have assumed the negative influence of Western values promulgated by the media and have banned some kinds of programs and products. Since 1996, Iran has banned the sale of Barbie dolls. One children's agency in Iran called Barbie a "Trojan horse" that was sneaking in Western influences such as makeup and revealing clothes. In 2012, dozens of toy shops were closed for selling the doll (Karmi, 2012). In Middle Eastern and Muslim countries, a culturally appropriate Barbie doll, named Fulla, was introduced, which embraces Islamic values (http://fulla.com).

In February 2012, the Chinese government issued regulations that banned all imported programs during prime time. Earlier, the State Administration of Radio, Film, and Television had cut many entertainment and reality TV programs, including the popular talent show, *Super Girl*. The ministry said the measures were aimed at rooting out "excessive entertainment and vulgar tendencies" (Lafraniere, Wines, & Wong, 2011).

A few studies in countries other than the United States have found similar patterns of media use and effects on adolescents' sexual and romantic attitudes and behaviors (e.g., Lo, Wei, & Wu, 2010; Peter & Valkenburg, 2008; Regmi, van Teijlingen, Simkhada, & Acharya, 2011) with equally alarming antecedents and consequences (e.g., Bott, Jejeebhoy, Shah, & Puri, 2003; Silva, Karunathilake, & Perera, 2009; Uddin & Choudhury, 2008). It is difficult, however, to discern between influences of Western media and domestic media content. It also remains unclear whether the introduction of Western media content shifted the content of national programming toward more permissive romantic and sexual models and away from traditional values or whether the media were reflecting social trends already under way.

Since both domestic, regional, and international programming are usually available in most countries, it is essential that we know the extent and nature of the sexual and romantic content available to adolescents before any associations between media exposure and sexual socialization can be assumed. It is possible that a wide variety of messages are available to adolescents that portray healthy and unhealthy, traditional and contemporary depictions of sex and romance. Systematic, quantitative media content analyses would be a good first step, and then surveys that focus on the correlation between adolescents' patterns of media exposure and their sexual attitudes and behavior could follow.

CAN MEDIA BE HEALTHY SEXUAL SOCIALIZATION AGENTS?

Media provide information about sexual health and sexuality to children and adolescents and may be especially influential for those youth who have limited access to such information elsewhere. Models of healthy sexual behaviors are important to include in media popular with children and adolescents to provide positive examples on which they may base their own sexual behaviors and scripts. Just as negative, unhealthy sexual media portrayals may encourage risky sexual behaviors, positive media portrayals can encourage healthy sexual behaviors.

Studies have found that exposure to media examples of safe sex behaviors through mass media campaigns, interactive media interventions, and entertainment-education programming often lead to stronger safe sex intentions, greater self-efficacy with regard to engaging in safe sex, and more positive attitudes about engaging in safe sex (e.g., Collins, Martino, & Shaw, 2011; Farrar, 2006; Keller & Brown, 2002; Moyer-Guse et al., 2011; Moyer-Guse & Nabi, 2011; Noar, Pierce, & Black, 2010; Zimmerman et al., 2007). Using a variety of strategies, ranging from short public service announcements to dramatic miniseries, international organizations including the World Health Organization, the UNFPA, and USAID increasingly rely on media such as television to promote family planning and population health (Brown, 2008; Singhal & Rogers, 2001).

As long as much of mainstream entertainment media continues to encourage unhealthy sexual attitudes and behaviors, children and adolescents should be taught how to be intelligent media consumers. Media literacy education can teach young people to become active media consumers and producers and develop the ability to critically analyze media messages. An increasing number of studies suggest that media literacy education can increase adolescents' resistance to media influences on sexual health decision making (e.g., Ito, Kalyanaraman, Ford, Brown, & Miller, 2008; Pinkleton, Austin, Cohen, Chen, & Fitzgerald, 2008). Effective media literacy curricula and evaluation research are needed as young people become increasingly in control of their media use and have greater access to adult-targeted media materials.

Conclusion

Youth today grow up with sexual information and images at their fingertips. An expanding body of research suggests that the media can be powerful, but often unhealthy, sexual socialization agents. The media provide compelling, attractive depictions of romantic and sexual scripts and models. A growing body of research suggests these scripts and models affect young media consumers' beliefs, attitudes, and behaviors (e.g., reinforcing stereotypical gender roles, accelerating sexual initiation) through various mechanisms. A few longitudinal studies reveal a reciprocal process in which sexually curious youth seek out sexual media content, which, in turn, affects sexual attitudes and behaviors. Such attitudes and behaviors formed during adolescence have significant short- and long-term effects.

Much is still unknown about the processes of media effects on youth sexuality, especially in light of more accessible and interactive media, and in countries and cultures other than the United States. Some of the important questions left to answer include the timing and longevity of media effects, the extent to which romantic relationships moderate or mediate sexual media effects, the role of peers in reinforcing online media effects, the effects of online sexual self-disclosure on sexual and romantic attitudes and behaviors, the shift in local media content and cultural norms regarding sex and romance in non-Western cultures, and the extent to which young people can become more literate media consumers.

A fresh research agenda should take into account interactive media as well as media globalization; expand longitudinal and cross-cultural studies; incorporate biological, social, and cognitive development perspectives in media effects theory and research; and translate the fruits of this agenda into more effective risk-reduction interventions.

References

Allen, M., D'Alessio, D., & Brezgel, K. (1995). A meta-analysis summarizing the effects of pornography II: Aggression after exposure. *Human Communication Research, 22,* 258–283.

Allen, M., Emmers, T., Gebhardt, L., & Giery, M. A. (1995). Exposure to pornography and acceptance of rape myths. *Journal of Communication, 45*(1), 5–26.

Arnett, J. (1992). The soundtrack of recklessness: Music preferences and reckless behavior among adolescents. *Journal of Adolescent Research, 7,* 313–331.

Arnett, J. (1995). Adolescents' uses of media for self socialization. *Journal of Youth and Adolescence, 24,* 519–533.

Aubrey, J. S. (2004). Sex and punishment: An examination of sexual consequences and the sexual double standard in teen programming. *Sex Roles, 50,* 505–514.

Bachen, C. M., & Illouz, E. (1996). Imagining romance: Young people's cultural models of romance and love. *Critical Studies in Mass Communication, 13*(4), 179–308.

Bandura, A. (1977). *Social learning theory.* Englewood Cliffs, NJ: Prentice Hall.

Bandura, A. (2004). Social cognitive theory for personal and social change by enabling media. In A. Singhal, M. J. Cody, E. M. Rogers, & M. Sabido (Eds.), *Entertainment-education and social change: History, research, and practice* (pp. 75–96). Mahwah, NJ: Lawrence Erlbaum.

Bandura, A. (2009). Social cognitive theory of mass communication. In J. Bryant & M. B. Oliver (Eds.), *Media effects: Advances in theory and research* (pp. 94–124). New York, NY: Routledge.

Bechara, A., Damasio, A., Damasio, H., & Anderson, S. (1994). Insensitivity to future consequences following damage to human prefrontal cortex. *Cognition, 50,* 7–15.

Bleakley, A., Hennessy, M., Fishbein, M., & Jordan, A. (2008). It works both ways: The relationship between exposure to sexual content in the media and adolescent sexual behavior. *Media Psychology, 11,* 443–461.

Bleakley, A., Hennessy, M., Fishbein, M., & Jordan, A. (2009). How sources of sexual information relate to adolescents' beliefs about sex. *American Journal of Health Behavior, 33*(1), 37–48.

Bobkowski, P. S., Brown, J. D., & Neffa, D. R. (2012). "Hit me up and we can get down:" U.S. youths' risk behaviors and sexual self-disclosure in MySpace profiles. *Journal of Children and Media, 6,* 119–134.

Bott, S., Jejeebhoy, S., Shah, I., & Puri, C. (Eds.). (2003). *Towards adulthood: Exploring the sexual and reproductive health of adolescents in South Asia.* Retrieved from http://whqlibdoc.who.int/publications/2003/9241562501.pdf

Braun-Courville, D., & Rojas, M. (2009). Exposure to sexually explicit web sites and adolescent sexual attitudes and behaviors. *Journal of Adolescent Health, 45*(2), 156–162.

Brown, J. D. (Ed.). (2008). *Managing the media monster: The influence of media (from television to text messages) on teen sexual behavior and attitudes.* Washington, DC: The National Campaign to Prevent Teen and Unplanned Pregnancy.

Brown, J. D., & L'Engle, K. L. (2009). X-rated: Sexual attitudes and behaviors associated with U.S. early adolescents' exposure to sexually explicit media. *Communication Research, 36*(1), 129–151.

Brown, J. D., L'Engle, K. L., Pardun, C. J., Guo, G., Kenneavy, K., & Jackson, C. (2006). Sexy media matter: Exposure to sexual content in music, movies, television, and magazines predicts black and white adolescents' sexual behavior. *Pediatrics, 117*, 1018–1027.

Brown, J. D., Halpern, C. T., & L'Engle, K. L. (2005). Mass media as a sexual super peer for early maturing girls. *Journal of Adolescent Health, 36*, 420–427.

Bryant, J., & Rockwell, S. C. (1994). Effects of massive exposure to sexually oriented prime-time television programming on adolescents' moral judgment. In D. Zillmann, J. Bryant, & A. C. Huston (Eds.), *Media, children and the family: Social scientific, psychodynamic, and clinical perspectives* (pp. 183–195). Hillsdale, NJ: Lawrence Erlbaum Associates.

Callister, M., Stern, L. A., & Coyne, S. M. (2011). Evaluation of sexual content in teen-centered films from 1980 to 2007. *Mass Communication and Society, 14*, 454–474.

Casey, B. J., Getz, S., & Galvan, A. (2008). The adolescent brain. *Developmental Review, 28*, 62–77.

Centers for Disease Control and Prevention. (2008). Youth risk behavior surveillance—United States, 2007. Surveillance Summaries (June 6). *Morbidity and Mortality Weekly Report 57*(SS-4). Atlanta, GA: U.S. Department of Health and Human Services.

Centers for Disease Control and Prevention. (2010). Youth risk behavior surveillance—United States, 2009. Surveillance Summaries (June 4). *Morbidity and Mortality Weekly Report 59*(SS-5). Atlanta, GA: U.S. Department of Health and Human Services.

Centers for Disease Control and Prevention. (2011). *Sexually Transmitted Disease Surveillance 2010.* Atlanta, GA: U.S. Department of Health and Human Services.

Chandra, A., Martino, S. C., Collins, R. L., Elliott, M. N., Berry, S. H., Kanouse, D. E., & Miu, A. (2008). Does watching sex on television predict teen pregnancy? Findings from a national longitudinal survey of youth. *Pediatrics, 122*, 1047–1054.

Chapin, J. R. (2000). Adolescent sex and mass media: A developmental approach. *Adolescence, 35*, 799–811.

Chia, S. C. (2006). How peers mediate media influence on adolescents' sexual attitudes and sexual behavior. *Journal of Communication, 56*, 585–606.

Christie, D., & Viner, R. (2011). ABC of adolescence: Adolescent development. *British Medical Journal, 330*, 301–304.

Coley, R. L., & Chase-Lansdale, P. L. (1998). Adolescent pregnancy and parenthood: Recent evidence and future directions. *American Psychologist, 53*(2), 152–166.

Collins, R. L., Elliott, M. N., Berry, S. H., Kanouse, D. E., Kunkel, D., Hunter, S. B., & Miu, A. (2004). Watching sex on television predicts adolescent initiation of sexual behavior. *Pediatrics, 114*, e280–e289.

Collins, R. L., Martino, S., & Shaw, R. (2011). *Influence of new media on adolescent sexual health: Evidence and opportunities.* Retrieved from http://www.rand.org/pubs/working_papers/WR761.html

Crawford, M., & Popp, D. (2003). Sexual double standards: A review and methodological critique of two decades of research. *Journal of Sex Research, 40*, 13–26.

Crockett, L. J., Raffaelli, M., & Moilanen, K. L. (2003). Adolescent sexuality: Behavior and meaning. In G. R. Adams & M. D. Berzonsky (Eds.), *Blackwell handbook of adolescence* (pp. 371–392). Malden, MA: Blackwell Publishing Ltd.

Durham, M. G. (2004). Constructing the "new ethnicities": Media, sexuality, and diaspora identity in the lives of South Asian immigrant girls. *Critical Studies in Media Communication*, 21(2), 140–161.

Eaton, D. K., Kann, L., Kinchen, S., Ross, J., Hawkins, J., Harris, W. A., . . . & Wechsler, H. (2006). Youth risk behavior surveillance—United States, 2005. *Journal of School Health*, 76, 353–372.

El-Toukhy, S., & Brown, J. (2010). Exposure to Western television and perceptions of romantic relationships in Egypt. Paper presented at the Annual Convention of the International Communication Association, Singapore.

Escobar-Chaves, S. L., Tortolero, S. R., Markham, C. M., Low, B. J., Eitel, P., & Thickstun, P. (2005). Impact of the media on adolescent sexual attitudes and behaviors. *Pediatrics*, 116(1), 303–326.

Eyal, K., & Finnerty, K. (2007). The portrayal of sexual intercourse on prime-time programming. *Communication Research Reports*, 24(3), 225–233.

Eyal, K., & Kunkel, D. (2008). The effects of sex in television drama shows on emerging adults' sexual attitudes and moral judgments. *Journal of Broadcasting & Electronic Media*, 52(2), 161–181.

Farrar, K. M. (2006). Sexual intercourse on television: Do safe sex messages matter? *Journal of Broadcasting & Electronic Media*, 50, 635–650.

Fischhoff, B. (2008). Assessing adolescent decision-making competence. *Developmental Review*, 28, 12–28.

Fisher, D. A., Hill, D. L., Grube, J. W., Bersamin, M. M., Walker, S., & Gruber, E. L. (2009). Televised sexual content and parental mediation: Influences on adolescent sexuality. *Media Psychology*, 12, 121–147.

Fraley, R. C., & Davis, K. (1997). Attachment formation and transfer in young adults' close friendship and romantic relationships. *Personal Relationships*, 4(2), 131–144.

Frith, H., & Kitzinger, C. (2001). Reformulating sexual script theory: Developing a discursive psychology of sexual negotiation. *Theory & Psychology*, 11(2), 209–232.

Gagnon, J. H., & Simon, W. (2005). *Sexual conduct: The social sources of human sexuality* (2nd ed.). Piscataway, NJ: Transaction Publishers.

Galician, M. (2004). *Sex, love, and romance in the mass media: Analysis and criticism of unrealistic portrayals and their influence*. Mahwah, NJ: Lawrence Erlbaum Associates.

Gerbner, G., Gross, L., Morgan, M., Signorielli, N., & Shanahan, J. (2002). Growing up with television: Cultivation processes. In J. Bryant & D. Zillmann (Eds.), *Media effects: Advances in theory and research* (2nd ed.) (pp. 43–67). Mahwah, NJ: Lawrence Erlbaum Associates.

Gibbons, F. X., Gerrard, M., Blanton, H., & Russell, D. W. (1998). Reasoned action and social reaction: Willingness and intention as independent predictors of health risk. *Journal of Personality and Social Psychology*, 74, 1164–1180.

Gossett, J. L., & Byrne, S. (2002). "Click here:" A content analysis of internet rape sites. *Gender and Society*, 16, 689–709.

Green, L., Myerson, J., & Ostaszewski, P. (1999). Discounting of delayed rewards across the life span: Age differences in individual discounting functions. *Behavioral Processes*, 46, 89–96.

Haninger, K., & Thompson, K. M. (2004). Content and ratings of teen-rated video games. *Journal of the American Medical Association*, 291, 856–865.

Harrison, K., & Hefner, V. (2006). Media exposure, current and future body ideals, and disordered eating among preadolescent girls: A longitudinal panel study. *Journal of Youth and Adolescence*, 35, 153–163.

Hensel, D. J., Fortenberry, J. D., O'Sullivan, L. F., & Orr, D. P. (2011). The developmental association of sexual self-concept with sexual behavior among adolescent women. *Journal of Adolescence*, 34, 675–684.

Hetsroni, A. (2007). Three decades of sexual content on prime-time network programming: A longitudinal meta-analytic review. *Journal of Communication*, 57, 318–348.

Hoffman, S. D. (2006). *By the numbers: The public costs of teen childbearing*. Washington, DC: National Campaign to Prevent Teen Pregnancy.

Holmes, B. M. (2007). In search of my "one-and-only:" Romance-related media and beliefs in romantic relationship destiny. *The Electronic Journal of Communication, 17*(3&4). Retrieved from http://www.cios.org/EJCPUBLIC/017/3/01735.HTML

Hust, S. J. T., & Brown, J. D. (2008). Gender, media use, and effects. In S. L. Calvert & B. J. Wilson (Eds.), *The handbook of children, media, and development* (pp. 98–120). Malden, MA: Wiley-Blackwell.

Hust, S. J. T., Brown, J. D., & L'Engle, K. L. (2008). Boys will be boys and girls better be prepared: An analysis of the rare sexual health messages in young adolescents' media. *Mass Communication & Society, 11*(1), 3–23.

Ito, K. E., Kalyanaraman, S., Ford, C. A., Brown, J. D., & Miller, W. C. (2008). "Let's talk about sex": Pilot study of an interactive CD-ROM to prevent HIV/STIs in female adolescents. *AIDS Education and Prevention, 20*(1), 78–89.

Jankowiak, W. R., & Fischer, E. F. (1992). A cross-cultural perspective on romantic love. *Ethnology, 31*(2), 149–155.

Johnson, K. R., & Holmes, B. M. (2009). Contradictory messages: A content analysis of Hollywood-produced romantic comedy features. *Communication Quarterly, 57*(3), 352–373.

Joshi, S. P., Peter, J., & Valkenburg, P. M. (2011). Scripts of sexual desire and danger in US and Dutch teen girl magazines: A cross-national content analysis. *Sex Roles, 64*, 463–474.

Kaiser Family Foundation/*Seventeen* Magazine. (2004). *Sex smarts: Birth control and protection.* Menlo Park, CA: Kaiser Family Foundation.

Kaplowitz, P. B., Slora, E. J., Wasserman, R. C., Pedlow, S. E., & Herman-Giddens, M. E. (2001). Earlier onset of puberty in girls: Relation to increased body mass index and race. *Pediatrics, 108*, 347–353.

Karmi, N. (2012, Jan. 20). Iran shuts down shops selling Barbie dolls, news agency says. *USA Today.* Retrieved from http://www.usatoday.com/money/world/story/2012-01-20/iran-barbie-shops/526985901

Karney, B. R., Beckett, M. K., Collins, R. L., & Shaw, R. (2007). *Adolescent romantic relationships as precursors of health adult marriages: A review of theory, research, and programs.* Santa Monica, CA: RAND Corporation.

Keller, S. N., & Brown, J. D. (2002). Media interventions to promote responsible sexual behavior. *The Journal of Sex Research, 39*(1), 67–72.

Kelly, A. E., & Rodriguez, R. R. (2006). Publicly committing oneself to an identity. *Basic and Applied Social Psychology, 28*, 185–191.

Kim, J. L., Collins, R. L., Kanouse, D. E., Elliott, M. N., Berry, S. H., Hunter, S. B., … & Kunkel, D. (2006). Sexual readiness, household policies, and other predictors of adolescents' exposure to sexual content in mainstream entertainment television. *Media Psychology, 8*, 449–471.

Kim, J. L., & Ward, M. (2004). Pleasure reading: Associations between young women's sexual attitudes and their reading of contemporary women's magazines. *Psychology of Women Quarterly, 28*, 48–58.

Kunkel, D., Farrar, K. M., Eyal, K., Biely, E., Donnerstein, E., & Rideout, V. (2007). Sexual socialization messages on entertainment television: Comparing content trends 1997–2002. *Media Psychology, 9*, 595–622.

Lafraniere, S., Wines, M., & Wong, E. (2011, Oct. 26). China reins in entertainment and blogging. *New York Times.* Retrieved from http://www.nytimes.com/2011/10/27/world/asia/china-imposes-new-limits-on-entertainment-and-bloggers.html?_r=1

Lenhart, A. (2009). *Teens and sexting.* Pew Research Center's Internet & American Life Project. Retrieved from http://www.pewinternet.org/Reports/2009/Teens-and-Sexting.aspx

Lo, V., Wei, R., & Wu, H. (2010). Internet pornography and teen sexual attitudes and behavior. *China Media Research, 6*(3), 66–75.

Marcia, J. E. (1980). Identity in adolescence. In J. Adelson (Ed.), *Handbook of adolescent psychology* (pp. 159–187). New York, NY: Wiley & Sons.

Martin, J. A., Hamilton, B. E., Sutton, P. D., Ventura, S. J., Matthews, T. J., Kirmeyer, S., & Osterman, M. J. K. (2010a). Births: Final data for 2007. *National Vital Statistics Reports,*

58(24). National Center for Health Statistics. Retrieved from http://www.cdc.gov/nchs/data/nvsr/nvsr58/nvsr58_24.pdf

Martin, J. A., Hamilton, B. E., Sutton, P. D., Ventura, S. J., Matthews, T. J., & Osterman, M. J. K. (2010b). Births: Final data for 2008. *National Vital Statistics Reports, 59*(1). National Center for Health Statistics. Retrieved from http://www.cdc.gov/nchs/data/nvsr/nvsr59/nvsr59_01.pdf

Milbrath, C., Ohlson, B., & Eyre, S. L. (2009). Analyzing cultural models in adolescent accounts of romantic relationships. *Journal of Research on Adolescence, 19*(2), 313–351.

Monroe, S. M., Rhode, P., Seeley, J. R., & Lewinsohn, P. M. (1999). Life events and depression in adolescence: Relationship loss as a prospective risk factor for first onset of major depressive disorder. *Journal of Abnormal Psychology, 108*, 606–614.

Montgomery, M. J., & Sorell, G. T. (1998). Love and dating experience in early and middle adolescence: Grade and gender comparisons. *Journal of Adolescence, 21*, 677–689.

Moreno, M. A., Brockman, L., & Christakis, D. A. (2009). "Oops, I did it again:" A content analysis of adolescents' sexual references on Myspace. *Journal of Adolescent Health, 44*(2), S22–S23.

Moyer-Gusé, E., Chung, A., & Jain, P. (2011). Identification with characters and discussion of taboo topics after exposure to an entertainment narrative about sexual health. *Journal of Communication, 61*, 387–406.

Moyer-Gusé, E., & Nabi, R. L. (2011). Comparing the effects of entertainment and education television programming on risky sexual behavior. *Health Communication, 26*, 416–426.

Munshi, S. (2001). *Images of the "modern woman" in Asia: Global media, local meanings*. Richmond, Surrey, UK: Curzon.

Murnen, S. K., & Stockton, M. (1997). Gender and self-reported sexual arousal in response to sexual stimuli: A meta-analytic review. *Sex Roles, 37*, 135–153.

Nabi, R. L., & Clark, S. (2008). Exploring the limits of social cognitive theory: Why negatively reinforced behaviors on TV may be modeled anyway. *Journal of Communication, 58*, 407–427.

Neemann, J., Hubbard, J., & Masten, A. S. (1995). The changing importance of romantic relationship involvement to competence from late childhood to late adolescence. *Development and Psychopathology, 7*, 727–750.

Nielsen. (2009). *How teens use media: A Nielsen report on the myths and realities of teen media trends*. Chicago, IL: The Nielsen Company.

Noar, S. M., Pierce, L. B., & Black, H. G. (2010). Can computer-mediated interventions change theoretical mediators of safer sex? A meta-analysis. *Human Communication Research, 36*, 261–297.

Noll, J. G., Shenk, C. E., Barnes, J. E., & Putnam, F. W. (2009). Childhood abuse, avatar choices, and other risk factors associated with Internet-initiated victimization of adolescent girls. *Pediatrics, 123*, 1078–1083.

O'Hara, R. E., Gibbons, F. X., Gerrard, M., Li, Z., & Sargent, J. D. (2012). Greater exposure to sexual content in popular movies predicts earlier sexual debut and increased sexual risk taking. *Psychological Science, 23*, 984–993.

Pardun, C. J., L'Engle, K. L., & Brown, J. D. (2005). Linking exposure to outcomes: Early adolescents' consumption of sexual content in six media. *Mass Communication & Society, 8*(2), 75–91.

Parker, A., & Fischhoff, B. (2005). Decision-making competence: External validity through an individual-differences approach. *Journal of Behavioral Decision Making, 18*, 1–27.

Peter, J., & Valkenburg, P. M. (2008). Adolescents' exposure to sexually explicit Internet material, sexual uncertainty, and attitudes toward uncommitted sexual exploration: Is there a link? *Communication Research, 35*, 579–601.

Peter, J., & Valkenburg, P. M. (2010). Processes underlying the effects of adolescents' use of sexually explicit internet material: The role of perceived realism. *Communication Research, 37*, 375–399.

Pinkleton, B. E., Austin, E. W., Cohen, M., Chen, Y.-C., & Fitzgerald, E. (2008). Effects of a peer-led literacy curriculum on adolescents' knowledge and attitudes toward sexual behavior and media portrayals of sex. *Health Communication, 23*, 462–472.

Quinn, N., & Holland, D. (1987). Culture and cognition. In D. Holland & N. Quinn (Eds.), *Cultural models in language and thought* (pp. 3–40). Cambridge, UK: Cambridge University Press.

Regmi, P. R., van Teijlingen, E. R., Simkhada, P., & Acharya, D. R. (2011). Dating and sex among emerging adults in Nepal. *Journal of Adolescent Research, 26,* 675–700.

Reyna, V. F., & Farley, F. (2006). Risk and rationality in adolescent decision making: Implications for theory, practice, and public policy. *Psychological Science in the Public Interest, 7*(1), 1–44.

Rice, E., Rhoades, H., Winetrobe, H., Sanchez, M., Montoya, J., Plant, A., & Kordic, T. (2012). Sexually explicit cell phone messaging associated with sexual risk among adolescents. *Pediatrics, 130,* 667–673.

Rideout, V. J., Foehr, U. G., & Roberts, D. F. (2010). Generation M2: Media in the lives of 8- to 18-year-olds. Retrieved from http://www.kff.org/entmedia/upload/8010.pdf

Rohn, U. (2010). *Cultural barriers to the success of foreign media content: Western media in China, India and Japan.* New York, NY: Peter Lang.

Roskos-Ewoldsen, D. R., Roskos-Ewoldsen, B., & Carpentier, F. R. D. (2002). Media priming: A synthesis. In J. Bryant & D. Zillmann (Eds.), *Media effects: Advances in theory and research* (2nd ed.) (pp. 97–120). Mahwah, NJ: Lawrence Erlbaum Associates.

Segrin, C., & Nabi, R. L. (2002). Does television viewing cultivate unrealistic expectations about marriage? *Journal of Communication, 52*(2), 247–263.

Shafer, A. S., Bobkowski, P. S., & Brown, J. D. (2013). Sexual media practice: How adolescents select, engage with, and are affected by sexual media. In K. E. Dill (Ed.), *Oxford handbook of media psychology* (pp. 223–251). New York, NY: Oxford University Press.

Sharpe, T. H. (2003). Adolescent sexuality. *The Family Journal: Counseling and Therapy for Couples and Families, 11*(2), 210–215.

Silva, W. I. D., Karunathilake, K., & Perera, R. (2009). Patterns of sexual vulnerability among adolescents and youths in Sri Lanka. *Asian Population Studies, 5*(1), 41–59.

Silverberg, S. B., & Steinberg, L. (1987). Adolescent autonomy, parent-adolescent conflict, and parental well-being. *Journal of Youth and Adolescence, 16*(3), 293–312.

Simon, W., & Gagnon, J. H. (1987). The scripting approach. In J. Geer & W. O'Donoghue (Eds.), *Theories of human sexuality* (pp. 363–383), New York, NY: Plenum.

Singhal, A., & Rogers, E. M. (2001). The entertainment-education strategy in communication campaigns. In R. E. Rice & C. Atkins (Eds.), *Public communication campaigns* (3rd ed.) (pp. 343–356). Thousand Oaks, CA: Sage Publications.

Snell, W. E., Jr. (2001). Measuring multiple aspects of the sexual self concept: The Multidimensional Sexual Self-concept Questionnaire. In W. E. Snell, Jr. (Ed.), *New directions in the psychology of human sexuality: Research and theory.* Cape Girardeau, MO: Snell Publications. Retrieved from http://cstl-cla.semo.edu/snell/books/sexuality/sexuality.htm

Snell, W. E., Jr., Fisher T. D., & Schuh, T. (1992). Reliability and validity of the sexuality scale: A measure of sexual-esteem, sexual-depression, and sexual-preoccupation. *Journal of Sex Research, 29,* 261–273.

Steele, J. R. (1999). Teenage sexuality and media practice: Factoring in the influences of family, friends, and school. *The Journal of Sex Research, 36,* 331–341.

Steinberg, L. (2008). A social neuroscience perspective on adolescent risk-taking. *Developmental Review, 28,* 78–106.

Strasburger, V. C., & Wilson, B. J. (2002). *Children, adolescents & the media.* Beverly Hills, CA: Sage Publications.

Strasburger, V. C., Wilson, B. J., & Jordan, A. B. (2009). *Children, adolescents, and the media* (2nd ed.). Thousand Oaks, CA: Sage Publications.

Straubhaar, J. D. (2007). *World television: From global to local.* Los Angeles, CA: Sage Publications.

Turner, J. S. (2011). Sex and the spectacle of music videos: An examination of the portrayal of race and sexuality in music videos. *Sex Roles, 64,* 173–191.

Uddin, J., & Choudhury, A. M. (2008). Reproductive health awareness among adolescent girls in rural Bangladesh. *Asian-Pacific Journal of Public Health, 20*(2), 117–128.

Valkenburg, P. M., & Peter, J. (2011). Online communication among adolescents: An integrated model of its attraction, opportunities, and risks. *Journal of Adolescent Health, 48*, 121–127.

Wallis, C. (2011). Performing gender: A content analysis of gender display in music videos. *Sex Roles, 64*, 160–172.

Ward, L. M. (2003). Understanding the role of entertainment media in the sexual socialization of American youth: A review of empirical research. *Developmental Review, 23*, 347–388.

Ward, L. M., Hansbrough, E., & Walker, E. (2005). Contributions of music video exposure to black adolescents' gender and sexual schemas. *Journal of Adolescent Research, 20*, 143–166.

Ward, L. M., & Friedman, K. (2006). Using TV as a guide: Associations between television viewing and adolescents' sexual attitudes and behavior. *Journal of Research on Adolescence, 16*, 133–156.

Ward, L. M., & Rivadeneyra, R. (1999). Contributions of entertainment television to adolescents' sexual attitudes and expectations: The role of viewing amount versus viewer involvement. *Journal of Sex Research, 36*, 237–249.

World Health Organization. (2012). *Adolescent health and development.* Retrieved from http://www.searo.who.int/en/Section13/Section1245_4980.htm

Wright, P. (2011). Mass media effects on youth sexual behavior: Assessing the claim for causality. In C. T. Salmon (Ed.), *Communication Yearbook* (pp. 343–386). New York, NY: Routledge Press.

Wright, P. J., & Randall, A. K. (2012). Internet pornography exposure and risky sexual behavior among adult males in the United States. *Computers in Human Behavior, 28*, 1410–1416.

Ybarra, M. L., & Mitchell, K. J. (2005). Exposure to Internet pornography among children and adolescents: A national survey. *CyberPsychology & Behavior, 8*, 473–486.

Ybarra, M. L., Mitchell, K. J., Hamburger, M., Diener-West, M., & Leaf, P. J. (2010). X-rated material and perpetration of sexually aggressive behavior among children and adolescents: Is there a link? *Aggressive Behavior, 37*(1), 1–18.

Ybarra, M. L., Mitchell, K. J., & Korchmaros, J. D. (2011). National trends in exposure to and experiences of violence on the Internet among children. *Pediatrics, 128*(6), e1376–e1386.

Zimmerman, R. S., Palmgreen, P. M., Noar, S. M., Lustria, M. A., Hung-Yi, H., & Horosewski, M. (2007). Effects of a televised two-city safer sex mass media campaign targeting high-sensation-seeking and impulsive-decision-making young adults. *Health Education & Behavior, 34*, 810–826.

Zurbriggen, E. L., & Morgan, E. M. (2006). Who wants to marry a millionaire? Reality dating television programs, attitudes toward sex, and sexual behaviors. *Sex Roles, 54*(12), 1–17.

CHAPTER 7

The Positive and Negative Effects of Video Game Play

Sara Prot, Craig A. Anderson, Douglas A. Gentile,
Stephanie C. Brown, and Edward L. Swing

Introduction

Video games have become an incredibly popular and pervasive form of entertainment. Video game use has increased steadily over time (Rideout, Foehr, & Roberts, 2010) and today 9 out of 10 American children and teens play video games (Gentile, 2009; Gentile & Walsh, 2002). On average, youth play video games for two hours a day (Rideout, Foehr, & Roberts, 2010). However, a significant percentage of males report playing four hours a day or more (e.g., Bailey, West, & Anderson, 2010). This fact that such a large number of children and adolescents frequently play video games makes understanding video game effects on players an important research goal.

The rising popularity of video games has brought about an explosion of research on video game effects (Barlett, Anderson, & Swing, 2009). The increasingly large research literature on this topic consistently shows that video game effects are not trivial; significant effects of video game play are found in short-term and long-term contexts, and across a wide range of domains (e.g., Anderson, Gentile, & Dill, 2012). Some of these effects have been extensively researched and are well established, such as the effects of violent video games on aggression (e.g., Anderson & Dill, 2000). However, recent research has revealed a number other positive and negative consequences of video game play, such as beneficial effects of prosocial games on helping (Greitemeyer & Osswald, 2010), positive effects of action games on visual-spatial skills (Green & Bavelier, 2007), harmful effects of fast-paced games on cognitive control (Bailey, West and Anderson, 2010), and the phenomenon of video game addiction (Gentile et al., 2011).

This chapter provides an overview of current research findings in the area of video game effects. First, two theoretical perspectives are described that can be used to understand the mechanisms through which video games affect players. Next, research findings are reviewed concerning a wide range of positive and negative video game effects. Finally, several conclusions are drawn and key unanswered questions are identified that need to be addressed in future research.

Theoretical Frameworks

Several theoretical frameworks have provided useful insights for understanding positive and negative video game effects. Two different approaches are described in this section: (1) the general aggression model and the general learning model and (2) the five dimensions of video game effects perspective.

The general aggression model (GAM; e.g., Anderson & Bushman, 2002; Anderson & Carnagey, 2004; Anderson & Huesmann, 2003; Barlett & Anderson, 2013; DeWall, Anderson, & Bushman, 2011) has guided a large amount of research in the media violence domain, including research on violent video game effects (e.g., Anderson & Dill, 2000; Möller & Krahe, 2009). The GAM integrates key ideas from a number of more specific models of aggression (e.g., Bandura, 1973, 1983; Berkowitz, 1984; Huesmann, 1986, 1998) and provides a holistic framework for understanding how social, personological, and biological factors interact to bring about aggressive behavior. GAM can be used to understand both short-term effects of media violence on aggression in the immediate situation and long-term processes that aid the development of an aggressive personality. An overview of both the long-term and short-term processes in GAM is shown in Figure 7.1. According to GAM, media violence can increase the likelihood of aggression in the short term through its influence on a person's present internal state, which includes affective, cognitive, and arousal states. For example, playing a violent video game can prime aggressive thoughts, increase hostile affect, and create physiological arousal. In turn, internal state variables affect appraisal and decision making processes. Decision making can result either in impulsive or in thoughtful action, which can be aggressive or nonaggressive. For example, if provoked immediately after playing a violent game, the likelihood of choosing an aggressive response is increased due to heightened arousal and primed aggressive thoughts and feelings. Factors that increase the accessibility of aggressive thoughts or feelings tend to increase the likelihood of aggressive behavior emerging from the decision process. Once a behavioral response has been chosen, this feeds back into the situation and can influence later thoughts, feelings, and actions. Over time, the outcomes of each encounter can exert an influence on one's personality (e.g., strengthening habitual patterns of responding), creating

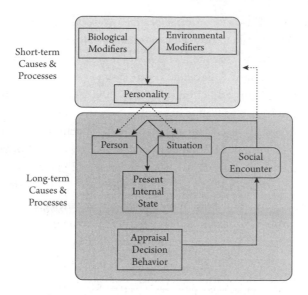

Figure 7.1 The General Aggression Model: Overall View. Source: Anderson & Carnagey (2004).

a feedback loop. Through this cycle, repeated long-term exposure to media violence leads to the development and rehearsal of aggressive knowledge structures, causing harmful consequences such as more positive attitudes toward violence, greater expectations of aggression by others, hostile attribution bias, and desensitization to violence (Carnagey & Anderson, 2003).

The general learning model (GLM; Buckley & Anderson, 2006; Gentile et al., 2009; Gentile, Groves, & Gentile, 2014; Maier & Gentile, 2012; Swing & Anderson, 2008) incorporates multiple domain-specific learning theories into one larger meta-theory. The GLM describes how multiple learning mechanisms (e.g., habituation, classical conditioning, observational learning, etc.) can work both serially and in parallel to produce learning outcomes from any experience (Gentile, Groves, & Gentile, 2014). In the long term, the GLM describes how beliefs, attitudes, and affective traits (such as trait empathy and trait hostility) can be changed and developed as a result of learning experiences. The developmental and learning processes posited by GLM can be applied not only to aggression, but to any kind of social behavior. For example, much of the empirical support for GLM comes from the literature on media effects on prosocial behavior and helping (e.g., Bushman & Anderson, 2009; Gentile et al., 2009; Greitemeyer, 2009; Greitemeyer & Osswald, 2009, 2010).

The five dimensions of video game effects approach (Gentile, 2011; Gentile & Stone, 2005; Khoo & Gentile, 2007; Stone & Gentile, 2008) posits that video games can affect players on at least five different dimensions—amount of play, content, context, structure, and mechanics. Each dimension can produce specific types of effects. The amount of play can produce effects regardless of game content by displacing time players spend in other activities. The amount of game play has been associated with lower academic performance (Chan & Rabinowitz, 2006; Sharif & Sargent, 2006), risk of childhood obesity (Berkey et al., 2000), and gaming addiction (Gentile, 2009; Gentile et al., 2011). Game content has been shown to lead to content-specific learning. Educational games have been successfully used to teach a number of school subjects (Corbett, Koedinger, & Hadley, 2001). Violent video games have been shown to increase aggression (Anderson et al., 2010), whereas prosocial video games have been shown to increase empathy and helping (Greitemeyer & Osswald, 2010). The context of video game play may moderate effects of other game characteristics on specific outcomes. For example, it is possible that playing a game with friends may change the way video game content affects players (Anderson, Gentile, & Dill, 2012). The way a video game is structured and displayed on a screen may significantly affect visuospatial processing. For example, a number of studies have demonstrated that playing fast-paced video games may have positive effects on a number of visual and spatial skills, such as faster visual reaction times, and improved target localization and mental rotation (Achtman, Green, & Bavelier, 2008; Green & Bavelier, 2003, 2007). Finally, game mechanics can lead to improvements in specific motor skills. For example, video game play experience has been shown to predict surgical skill among laparoscopic surgeons (Rosser et al., 2007). Exercise games have been successfully used in physical therapy (Betker et al., 2006; Deutsch et al., 2008). Because research on video game effects has often been contentious, this approach is useful for helping to explain why different studies appear to find different types of effects. Many findings that initially appear contradictory are often focused on different levels of analysis, and are in fact complementary when examined through this dimensional approach.

VIOLENT VIDEO GAME EFFECTS

Much of the research done on video game effects has focused on the effects of violent video games on aggression. Findings from experimental studies, correlational studies, longitudinal studies, as well as a number of meta-analyses confirm that violent video game play can increase aggressive cognitions, affect, and behavior both in immediate and long-term contexts (e.g., Anderson & Dill, 2000; Anderson, Gentile, & Buckley, 2007; Anderson et al., 2010). More recent research has also shown that violent video game play leads to desensitization to violence (Bartholow, Bushman, & Sestir, 2005), diminished empathy, and a lower likelihood of prosocial behavior (Bushman & Anderson, 2009).

Experimental studies have been used to demonstrate causal relationships between violent video game play and aggression in the short-term. Laboratory experiments have shown that even a brief episode of violent video game play leads to more aggressive thoughts (e.g., Anderson & Dill, 2000), hostile affect (e.g., Carnagey & Anderson, 2005) and an increased likelihood of aggressive behavior (e.g., Konijn, Bijvank and Bushman, 2007). Correlational studies make it possible to examine associations between violent video game exposure and real-world aggression. Findings from correlational studies show that violent video game effects found in the laboratory generalize to real-life situations. For example, greater amounts of violent video game play in real life are significantly associated with more positive attitudes toward violence (e.g., Funk et al., 2004), higher trait hostility (e.g., Anderson, Gentile, & Buckley, 2007), and an increased likelihood of involvement in physical fights (e.g., Gentile, Lynch, Linder, & Walsh, 2004). Longitudinal studies can be used to determine long-term relations between violent video game play and aggression. For example, one study tracked a sample of adolescents over a period of two years and showed violent video game play to be a significant predictor of later violence and delinquency, even after controlling for relevant covariates (Hopf, Huber, & Weib, 2008).

Each research design contributes to the study of video game effects on aggression and strong causal conclusions depend on consistent results across all types of designs (Abelson, 1995; Swing & Anderson, 2010). Different types of research designs make different methodological assumptions, so when a result is repeatedly shown using different designs, we can be confident that it is not just a byproduct of methodological flaws. Testing a hypothesis using different methodologies and in different contexts allows researchers to triangulate, with the hope of identifying a true causal factor (Anderson, 1989). Scientific confidence can be increased by aggregating results from different studies using meta-analytic techniques.

The most comprehensive meta-analysis of violent video game effects on aggression and related variables to date was conducted by Anderson and colleagues (2010). This meta-analytic review included 136 research papers with 381 effect size estimates involving more than 130,000 participants. The sample consisted of both published and unpublished studies and included studies from both Eastern and Western cultures. Main findings from this meta-analysis based on the subsample of studies that met all the best practices criteria (the "best raw" sample in Anderson et al., 2010) are shown in Figure 7.2. Playing violent video games was shown to increase the likelihood of physically aggressive behavior, aggressive thinking, aggressive affect, and physiological arousal. Violent video game exposure was also shown result in desensitization/low empathy and a decreased likelihood of prosocial behavior. Significant effects of violent video games on all six outcomes were found both for men and for women and for samples from both Eastern and Western cultures. Importantly, the pattern of results for different outcomes was consistent across all three types of research designs (experimental, cross-sectional, and longitudinal).

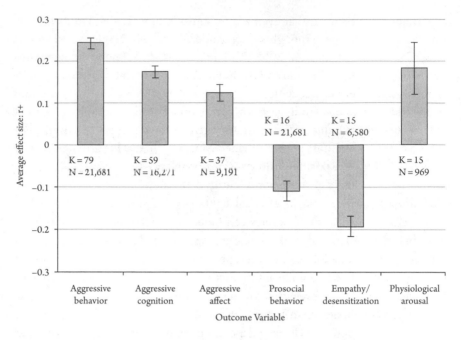

Figure 7.2 Effects of Violent Video Games on Aggressive Behavior, Aggressive Cognition, Aggressive Affect, Physiological Arousal, Empathy/Desensitization, and Prosocial Behavior. Notes: Results from the "best raw" sample (Anderson et al., 2010). K = number of effects; N = total sample size. Vertical capped bars are the upper and lower 95% confidence intervals.

These findings represent strong evidence that exposure to violent video games is a causal risk factor for increased aggressive behavior, aggressive cognition, and aggressive affect, and for decreased empathy and prosocial behavior. Are the effect sizes large enough to be considered important? Because aggression is influenced by a large number of risk factors, no single factor can explain more than a small fraction of variability in aggression (Anderson & Huesmann, 2003). However, when effects accumulate across time and when a large proportion of the population is exposed to a risk factor, even small effects can have large practical consequences (Abelson, 1985). In fact, the obtained effect size of violent video games on aggression (longitudinal effect after controlling for sex and earlier levels of aggression, r+ = .152) is in the same range as the effects of substance use, abusive parents, and poverty on aggression (U.S. Department of Health and Human Services, 2001).

In our view, findings from the extensive meta-analysis by Anderson and colleagues (2010) provide conclusive proof that violent video game play has both short-term and long-term influences on aggression and related variables. However, the topic of media violence effects on aggression is still under debate both by popular culture scholars (Jenkins, 2006) and researchers in the field of psychology (e.g., Ferguson & Kilburn, 2010). Several smaller meta-analytic reviews of the effects of violent video games on aggression (e.g., Ferguson, 2007a, 2007b) seem to show nonsignificant findings contradictory to those of Anderson et al. (2010). However, a careful examination of findings from these meta-analyses reveals that the data tend to agree for both proponents and critics of video game research, but they interpret the results differently (see Table 7.1). A recent study found that traditional approaches to analysis may actually underestimate the size of the effect of violent media (Gentile & Bushman, 2012). This same study, however, also demonstrated that media violence deserves neither special concern nor special denial as a risk factor for aggression—it acts similarly to other known risk factors, and by itself is not sufficient to cause serious aggressive acts.

CRITICS AND PROPONENTS OF VIOLENT VIDEO GAME RESEARCH: POINTS OF AGREEMENT

Seven meta-analyses of violent video games have been published (Anderson, 2004; Anderson & Bushman, 2001; Anderson et al., 2004; Anderson et al., 2010; Ferguson, 2007a, 2007b; Sherry, 2001). There are two fascinating aspects of these meta-analyses. First, although they vary greatly in terms of how many studies they include, they find almost identical effect sizes for violent video games on aggressive thoughts, feelings, and behaviors (Table 7.1). The empirically defined effect sizes are in the small to moderate range. Second, although they find almost identical effect sizes, Sherry and Ferguson interpret the effect as unimportant, whereas Anderson and colleagues interpret it as highly important. It is certainly normal for scientists to differ in their interpretations of empirical data, and that has definitely been the case with the data with regard to violent video games. Nonetheless, the numbers are empirically derived, and all of these meta-analyses seem to agree with each other.

It is also interesting that although these authors appear to disagree with regard to how to interpret the link between violent game exposure and aggressive behavior, they do not disagree about the other effects. That is, although Ferguson (2007a, p. 479) feels that the evidence on violent games and aggressive behaviors is not compelling, he believes that the effects on aggressive thoughts, prosocial behaviors, and physiological arousal "appear to be more sound."

Note that well-tested psychological theories agree that media can influence our thoughts and feelings, and thoughts and feelings are related to behaviors. Our summary at this point, then, is that much of the disagreement about the effects of violent video games is more apparent than real. Meta-analyses agree that there is a nonzero relation between violent gaming and aggressive thoughts,

Table 7.1 **Effect Size Findings from Seven Meta-Analytic Reviews of Violent Video Game Effects on Aggression and Related Variables**

	Anderson & Bushman (2001)	Sherry (2001)	Anderson (2004)	Anderson et al. (2004)	Ferguson (2007a)	Ferguson (2007b)	Anderson et al. (2010)
Number of independent estimates	54	25	86	55	25	21	381
Number of participants	4,262	1,716	11,014	15,491	4,205	3,602	130,295
Aggressive thoughts	.27	–	.24	.31/.24*	.25	–	.16
Physiological arousal	.22	–	.16	.22	.27	–	.18
Aggressive feelings	.18	–	.16	.29/.16*	–	–	.14
Aggressive behaviors	.19	.16	.20	.23/.28*	.29/.15+	.14	.19
Prosocial behaviors	–.16	–	–.21	–.25/–.30*	–.30	–	–.10

*Studies split into experimental and correlational studies, and no overall estimate was given; The first number shown in each cell (e.g. +.29) is the empirically derived estimate, whereas the second number (e.g. .15) is the theoretically derived estimate revised to account for potential publication bias.

feelings, arousal, and behaviors. It is also clear that the effect is not overwhelming—these are generally small to moderate effect sizes. This also fits well with existing theory and data about aggression—aggression is multicausal, and therefore no single environmental factor should overwhelm all others (including genetic, personality, and situational factors).

ATTENTION PROBLEMS AND EXECUTIVE FUNCTIONS

Recent research has linked video game playing with greater attention problems[1] and several conceptually related abilities (i.e., impulsiveness, self-control, executive functioning, and cognitive control). This body of research remains considerably smaller than research on other negative outcomes, such as aggression, and the strength of evidence for a causal effect is more limited. Nonetheless, the evidence to date is consistent with negative effects of video game exposure on attention problems and other related variables.

Several cross-sectional studies have found that children and adolescents who play more video games also tend to have more attention problems (e.g., Chan & Rabinowitz, 2006). Furthermore, longitudinal studies have found that video game exposure is related to greater subsequent attention problems, even when earlier attention problems are statistically controlled for (Gentile, Swing, Lim, & Khoo, 2012; Swing, Gentile, Anderson, & Walsh, 2010). This suggests that the link between video game playing and attention problems is not simply the result of those with attention problems being more attracted to video games.[2] These studies have also ruled out a number of alternative variables, such as sex, age, race, and socioeconomic status. We are not aware of any experimental studies to date testing the effect of repeated video game exposure on attention problems. Thus, though most of the evidence so far is consistent with a causal effect of video games on attention problems, it remains possible that some alternative variable not yet tested accounts for this association.

The extent to which specific video game dimensions matter beyond the overall amount of video game exposure is less clear. Violent video game playing is related to greater attention problems (Hastings et al., 2009). This violent content link seems to explain some unique variance beyond the overall hours of video game playing (Gentile et al., 2012). However, when initial attention problems are also controlled for, only overall time spent playing video games remains a uniquely significant predictor of attention problems. Future research may clarify these mixed findings regarding violent content. Additionally, the possibility that other video game dimensions (e.g., fast pacing) are specifically linked to attention problems needs to be investigated.

Several studies have also found certain executive functions to be impaired by video game playing (e.g., Kirsh, Olczak, & Mounts, 2005; Mathews et al., 2005). Participants experimentally assigned to play a violent video game performed worse on an emotional Stroop task compared to those assigned to play a nonviolent video game (Kirsh et al., 2005). Specifically, those who played a violent video game were less able to ignore the meaning of emotion-related words in a color-naming Stroop task. Another study found that proactive cognitive control, a type of executive function involving the maintenance of information in working memory, is lower in habitual violent video game players compared with nonviolent video game players (Bailey, West, & Anderson, 2010).

THEORETICAL EXPLANATIONS

How these apparent video game effects on attention problems and related outcomes are explained depends to some extent on whether certain video game dimensions, such as violent content or fast pacing, are thought to underlie the effects. To the extent that the number of hours spent playing video games best predicts attention problems, this would support the displacement hypothesis (i.e., that this effect results from the displacement of time away from tasks that contribute to the development of sustained attention and impulse control; Gentile et al., 2012). American children and adolescents (ages 8–18) spend approximately 7.5 hours per day with various forms of electronic media, which makes a considerable amount of displacement of other activities plausible (Rideout, Foehr, & Roberts, 2010). To the extent that video games and other forms of electronic media do not lead to the development of impulse control and sustained attention, their use may cut into time that otherwise would have been spent on activities that would have improved these abilities.

Alternatively, if violent content, fast pacing, or other video game dimensions play a particularly important role in the negative effects of video games on attention problems, this would support the excitement hypothesis (Gentile et al., 2012). That is, video games that are exciting and contain a number of cues that naturally attract attention (e.g., violence, rapid movement, flashing lights) might lead a person to be less able to focus in contexts that lack these features. For example, school classrooms and work environments typically require individuals to direct their attention in a purposeful way without much guidance from external stimuli. Those who have spent a great deal of time playing action-packed video games may be more reliant on external cues and less able to direct their attention based on goals or expectations, leading to greater distraction or decreased persistence.

SCHOOL PERFORMANCE

A number of studies have documented a significant negative association between the amount of time spent with screen-based media (television, movies, and video games) and school performance (e.g., Anderson & Dill, 2000; Chan & Rabinowitz, 2006; Cordes & Miller, 2000; Gentile, 2009; Sharif & Sargent, 2006). For example, a recent survey done on a large, nationally representative sample of American children and adolescents found that nearly half (47%) of heavy media users get poor grades, compared to 23% of light media users (Rideout, Foehr, & Roberts, 2010). A longitudinal study of elementary school children showed that total screen time significantly predicts poorer grades later in the school year, even while controlling for other relevant covariates (Anderson Gentile, & Buckley, 2007).

Why is media use associated with poorer grades? The displacement hypothesis posits that electronic media can negatively influence school performance by displacing time that would have been spent in other educational activities (such as reading and homework; Gentile et al., 2004). There has been some empirical support for this hypothesis. For example, adolescent video gamers have been found to spend 30% less time reading and 34% less time doing homework than nongamers (Cummings & Vandewater, 2007). However, it is also possible that children who have trouble at school choose to spend more time playing video games in order to experience feelings of mastery or that attention problems cause both preference for video games and poorer school performance (Gentile, 2009). More research is needed in this area to explore other mechanisms that might also contribute to the link between media use and school performance.

VIDEO GAME ADDICTION

There are now scores of studies looking at what is being called pathological gaming or video game "addiction." Many researchers define pathological use of video games in the same way as pathological gambling, focusing on damage to family, social, school, occupational, and psychological functioning (Sim, Gentile, Bricolo, Serpelloni, & Gulamoydeen, 2012). Like gambling, playing video games starts as a form of entertainment. It becomes pathological for some people when video games start producing negative life consequences (Sim et al., 2012).Currently, video game addiction is not classified as a formal disorder in the Diagnostic and Statistic Manual of Mental Disorders (DSM). The category of "internet use gaming disorder" has been in the appendix of the new DSM-V with the goal of encouraging further research in this area (American Psychiatric Association, 2013).

Overall, studies examining pathological video gaming show good reliability and validity (Gentile, Coyne, & Bricolo, 2013). Regarding the prevalence, one national study conducted in the United States with a sample of 1,100 youth found that 8.5% of youth gamers could be classified as pathological (Gentile, 2009). Similar percentages are found in several other countries, including 8.7% in Singapore (Choo et al., 2010), 10.3% (Peng & Li, 2009) and 10.8% (Lam, Peng, Mai, & Jing, 2009) in China, 8.0% in Australia (Porter, Starcevic, Berle, & Fenech, 2010), 11.9% in Germany (Grüsser, Thalemann, & Griffiths, 2007), and 7.5% in Taiwan (Ko, Yen, Yen, Lin, & Yang, 2007). These studies have not used a common methodology or definition, however, so each estimate of prevalence should be considered to be preliminary (although it is interesting that the percentages are so similar, given the vast differences in methods and populations).

Pathological gamers show patterns of comorbidity similar to those found in other addictions. Researchers have measured other clinical disorders and have found that pathological technology users often show comorbidity with psychiatric disorders (e.g., Shapira, Goldsmith, Keck, Khosla, & McElroy, 2000). Shapira and colleagues (2003) summarized those studies and noted that the most typical comorbid or primary disorders were mood disorders, substance use disorders, anxiety disorders, impulse control disorders, and personality disorders. Other studies have found that pathological use is also comorbid with ADHD and anxiety/depression (e.g., Gentile, 2009; Gentile et al., 2011). Most of the studies that have looked at potential outcomes of pathological use have found significant problems, such as poorer school performance, insomnia, suicidal thoughts, financial problems, and more relationship problems (Gentile Coyne, & Bricolo, 2013).

A question that is just beginning to be answered is whether pathological gaming is a problem in its own right, or whether it is simply symptomatic of other problems (such as depression). Longitudinal studies are needed to answer this question. To date, only one longitudinal study of pathological gaming has been published (although there has been one on pathological internet use; Lam & Peng, 2010). In it, 3,034 Singaporean children and adolescents were followed across two years, testing whether variables such as depression and poor school performance are predictors of or are predicted by pathological video gaming (Gentile et al., 2011). Because of the large sample size, the researchers were able to classify gamers into four types: those who never were pathological gamers across the two years, those who became pathological gamers, those who were pathological gamers at the start but stopped being pathological, and those who were and stayed pathological gamers. Somewhat surprisingly, depression became worse if youth became pathological gamers. Furthermore, anxiety, social phobia, and school performance also became worse after becoming a pathological gamer. Additionally, if children stopped being pathological gamers, their depression, anxiety, social phobia, and school performance all improved. This pattern suggests that these are likely to be outcomes of pathological technology use rather than predictors of it. At a minimum, it suggests that these conditions are truly comorbid, such that they can influence each other. The fact that depression, anxiety and social phobia worsened after becoming a pathological gamer supports the idea that pathological gaming is a distinct mental health disorder rather than being just a symptom of other conditions. On the other hand, it is likely that such mental health issues have reciprocal relationships and share common risk factors.

At the time of this writing, the early research on pathological gaming appears to suggest that it is highly similar to other addictions in its pattern of comorbidity and outcomes. Additional research is clearly needed to determine its etiology, risk factors, and course, as well as the best approaches for treatment.

Positive Video Game Effects

VISUAL-SPATIAL SKILLS

Playing video games has been associated with performance superiority and improvement on many visual and spatial tasks. Specific visual-spatial skills and tasks that incorporate those skills can be improved through games that require the player to practice extracting spatial information from the screen. Positive effects of video game play on visual-spatial skills have been found both in correlational studies (e.g., Green & Bavelier, 2003) and experimental studies (e.g., Okagaki & Frensch, 1994). Gamers have been found to outperform nongamers on a number of visual and spatial tasks, demonstrating faster visual reaction times and improved target localization and mental rotation (Green & Bavelier, 2003; Achtman, Green, & Bavelier, 2008; Green & Bavelier, 2007). Experimental studies have shown that only 10 hours of video game play can improve spatial attention and mental rotation (Feng, Spence, & Pratt, 2007; Green & Bavelier, 2003). It should be noted that most studies that have found video game effects on visual-spatial skills have used fast-paced video games, which are typically violent. This serves as a reminder that video games do not conform to a good-bad dichotomy—they engender many effects that can be both positive and negative.

NONVIOLENT VIDEO GAME EFFECTS

Prosocial Video Games

Prosocial video games are centered on helping other game characters, distinct from hero-centered violent video games in which the player's character kills (or helps another character kill) enemies. In the laboratory, prosocial video game play has been shown to reduce aggressive thoughts, feelings, and behavior while increasing prosocial thoughts, empathy, and helping behavior (Narvaez, Mattan, MacMichael, & Squillace, 2008; Sestir & Bartholow, 2010; Anderson et al. 2012). Several studies have reported long-term effects of prosocial video game play, finding increases in cooperation, sharing, empathy, and helping behavior in adolescents (Gentile, 2009) and increases in prosocial behavior among children (Sestir & Bartholow, 2010). Playing prosocial games not only increases prosocial behavior but also decreases aggression. Research by Greitemeyer and Osswald (2009) found that even a brief prosocial gaming experience leads to a decrease in the hostile expectation bias (a tendency to perceive other people's provocative actions as hostile instead of accidental) and in the accessibility of antisocial thoughts.

Educational Video Games

Educational video games have been found to be effective teaching aids in a wide range of domains. Video games reinforce the student's behavior often, are engaging enough for the student to play the games on multiple occasions, provide clear objectives, and require active involvement (Gentile and Gentile, 2008). Educational video games have been successfully used to teach students a number of school subjects, such as mathematics, reading, and biology (Murphy, Penuel, Means, Korbak, & Whaley, 2001; Corbett, Koedinger, & Hadley, 2001). Employers have also recognized the power of the video games to teach and have incorporated games to teach employees needed job skills. For example, Volvo has used an online game to train car salesmen (Entertainment Software Association, 2011b).

Educational video games can also be used to explain health conditions and encourage healthier lifestyles. A number of studies have shown video games to be effective teaching tools for helping youth understand health conditions such as cancer and diabetes (Brown et al., 1997; Kato, Cole, Bradlyn, & Pollock, 2008; Lieberman, 2001). These games can also bring about behavioral change. For example, after six months of playing a video game on diabetes self-management, diabetic youth decreased their number of visits to the emergency room as compared to those in the control condition (Lieberman, 2001).

Exergames

Exergames can be classified as interactive video games that require some type of exercise to play. These games can take the form of traditional exercise, such as yoga or boxing, or can incorporate movement through more creative means, such as dodging a ball or jumping over an obstacle. Exergame research has focused on three areas: energy expenditure, activity time, and activity preference. The excitement provided by exergames contributes to all three areas, enabling players to get into the game and expend more energy, to play the game longer and with more frequency over time, and to prefer exergames over traditional exercise (Biddiss & Irwin, 2010; Graf, Pratt, Hester, & Short, 2009; Mellecker & McManus, 2008). Klein and Simmers (2009) found that even those with a low motivation to exercise were still willing to engage in an exergame. In a period in which American children spend more than six hours a day watching television and playing video games (Rideout, Foehr, & Roberts, 2010), it's no wonder that the preference for exergames in children has caused enthusiasm in parents and pediatricians alike. These video games do more than contribute to physical fitness; they contribute to psychological health as well. In a study conducted by Rosenberg et al. (2010), senior citizens living in a community had an increased quality of life and exhibited improvement in subsyndromal depression after only three months of playing Wii sports.

Conclusions and Unanswered Questions

Video games are at the center of a public debate concerning what is beneficial or harmful to children and adolescents. Views expressed in this debate have often been extreme, either idealizing or vilifying video games. Critics of video games, such as now-disbarred attorney Jack Thompson, have called video games "murder simulators" and pointed to violent video games as clear causes of school shootings (e.g., Cavalli, 2008). On the other hand, the Entertainment Software Association recognizes only positive outcomes of video game play (such as positive influences of video games on perceptual skills) and discounts the existence of any harmful effects (e.g., Entertainment Software Association, 2011a). The critics and the proponents tend to ignore research evidence supporting the views of the opposing camp and label video games as clearly "good" or "bad."

In contrast, the research findings reviewed in this chapter lead to the conclusion that video game effects are complex and are better understood in terms of multiple dimensions than a good or bad dichotomy. Significant effects of video game play have been demonstrated in a wide range of domains. Some of these effects are desired by parents, such as the effect of prosocial video games on empathy and helping (Greitemeyer & Osswald, 2010). Other video game effects are worrisome to parents, such as the effects of violent video games on aggression (e.g., Anderson & Dill, 2000), although it should be noted that this is a desired effect by the armed services who train soldiers with violent video games. Even a single game can have multiple effects on a person, some of which are harmful and some of which are beneficial (e.g., a violent game which improves visuospatial functioning, but which also increases the risk of physical aggression).

The rapid growth in research on video game effects has helped greatly improve our understanding of how video games influence players. Effects of violent video games on aggression and related variables have received an especially large amount of attention and are now fairly well understood (Anderson et al., 2010). Other areas of research are newer and still contain a number of unanswered questions that need to be addressed. More research is needed to increase our understanding of how prosocial video games exert their effects on empathy and helping, to explore video game effects on attention and cognitive control, and to increase our knowledge of symptoms and consequences of gaming addiction. Given the large proportion of children and adolescents who play video games, increasing our understanding of both positive and negative video game effects is a relevant research topic that has important implications for public policy debates, for theory development, and for planning potential intervention strategies designed to increase positive effects and reduce negative effects of playing video games.

Notes

1. The term *attention problems* refers to problems associated with attention disorders, such as attention-deficit/hyperactivity disorder. These problems are generally assessed as a continuous variable, rather than a diagnostic category. Attention problems should not

be confused with "visual attention." Attention problems include difficulty in sustained effortful processing and impulse control, whereas visual attention refers to fast and accurate extraction or processing of information from the visual field.

2. However, video game playing increasing attention problems and attention problems increasing video game playing are not mutually exclusive possibilities. Indeed, Gentile et al. (2012) found evidence for bidirectional causality between these variables.

References

Abelson, R. P. (1985). A variance explanation paradox: When a little is a lot. *Psychological Bulletin*, 97, 129–133.

Abelson, R. P. (1995). *Statistics as principled argument*. Hillsdale, NJ: Lawrence Erlbaum Associates.

Achtman, R. L., Green, C. S., & Bavelier, D. (2008). Video games as a tool to train visual skills. *Restorative Neurology and Neuroscience*, 26, 435–446.

American Psychiatric Association. (2013). *Diagnostic and statistical manual of mental disorders (5th ed.)*. Arlington, VA: American Psychiatric Publishing.

Anderson, C. A. (1989). Temperature and aggression: Ubiquitous effects of heat on occurrence of human violence. *Psychological Bulletin*, 106, 74–96.

Anderson, C. A. (2004). An update on the effects of playing violent video games. *Journal of Adolescence*, 27, 113–122.

Anderson, C. A., & Bushman, B. J. (2001). Effects of violent video games on aggressive behavior, aggressive cognition, aggressive affect, physiological arousal, and prosocial behavior: A meta-analytic review of the scientific literature. *Psychological Science*, 12, 353–359.

Anderson, C. A., & Bushman, B. J. (2002). Human aggression. *Annual Review of Psychology*, 53, 27–51.

Anderson, C. A., & Carnagey, N. L. (2004). Violent evil and the general aggression model. In A. Miller (Ed.), *The social psychology of good and evil* (pp. 168–192). New York, NY: Guilford Publications.

Anderson, C. A., Carnagey, N. L., Flanagan, M., Benjamin, A. J. J., Eubanks, J., & Valentine, J. C. (2004). Violent video games: Specific effects of violent content on aggressive thoughts and behavior. *Advances in Experimental Social Psychology*, 36, 199–249.

Anderson, C. A., & Dill, K. E. (2000). Video games and aggressive thoughts, feelings, and behavior in the laboratory and in life. *Journal of Personality and Social Psychology*, 78, 772–790.

Anderson, C. A., Gentile, D. A., & Buckley, K. E. (2007). *Violent video game effects on children and adolescents: Theory, research, and public policy*. New York, NY: Oxford University Press.

Anderson, C. A., Gentile, D. A., & Dill, K. E. (2012). Prosocial, antisocial, and other effects of recreational video games. In D. G. Singer & J. L. Singer (Eds.), *Handbook of children and the media* (2nd ed.) (pp. 249–272). Thousand Oaks, CA: Sage.

Anderson, C. A., & Huesmann, L. R. (2003). Human aggression: A social-cognitive view. In M. A. Hogg & J. Cooper (Eds.), *Handbook of social psychology* (pp. 296–323). London, UK: Sage Publications.

Anderson, C. A., Shibuya, A., Ihori, N., Swing, E. L., Bushman, B. J., Sakamoto, A., ... & Saleem, M. (2010). Violent video game effects on aggression, empathy, and prosocial behavior in Eastern and Western countries. *Psychological Bulletin*, 136, 151–173.

Bandura, A. (1973). *Aggression: A social learning analysis*. Englewood Cliffs, NJ: Prentice-Hall.

Bandura, A. (1983). Psychological mechanisms of aggression. In R. G. Geen & E. Donnerstein (Eds.), *Aggression: Theoretical and empirical reviews* (pp. 1–40). New York, NY: Academic Press.

Bailey, K., West, R., & Anderson, C. A. (2010). A negative association between video game experience and proactive cognitive control. *Psychophysiology*, 47, 34–42.

Barlett, C. P., & Anderson, C. A. (2013). Examining media effects: The general aggression and general learning models. Chapter in E. Scharrer (Ed.), *Media effects/media psychology*. Boston, MA: Wiley-Blackwell.

Barlett, C. P., Anderson, C. A., & Swing, E. L. (2009). Video game effects—confirmed, suspected, and speculative: A review of the evidence. *Simulation & Gaming, 40,* 377–403.

Bartholow, B. D., Bushman, B. J., & Sestir, M. A. (2005). Chronic violent video game exposure and desensitization to violence: Behavioral and event-related brain potential data. *Journal of Experimental Social Psychology, 42,* 283–290.

Berkey, C. S., Rockett, H. R. H., Field, A. E., Gillman, M. W., Frazier, A. L., Camargo, C. A., & Colditz, G. A. (2000). Activity, dietary intake, and weight changes in a longitudinal study of preadolescent and adolescent boys and girls. *Pediatrics, 105,* e56.

Berkowitz, L. (1984). Some effects of thoughts on anti- and prosocial influences of media events: A cognitive-neoassociation analysis. *Psychological Bulletin, 95,* 410–427.

Betker, A. L., Szturm, T., Moussavi, Z. K., & Nett, C. (2006). Video game–based exercises for balance rehabilitation: A single-subject design. *Archives of Physical Medication and Rehabilitation, 87,* 1141–1149.

Biddiss, E., & Irwin, J. (2010). Active video games to promote physical activity in children and youth. *Archives of Pediatrics and Adolescent Medicine, 164,* 664–672.

Brown, S. J., Lieberman, D. A., Gemeny, B. A., Fan, Y. C., Wilson, D. M., & Pasta, D. J. (1997). Educational video game for juvenile diabetes: Results of a controlled trial. *Medical Informatics, 22*(1), 77–89.

Buckley, K. E., & Anderson, C. A. (2006). A theoretical model of the effects and consequences of playing video games. In P. Vorderer & J. Bryant (Eds.), *Playing video games—motives, responses, and consequences* (pp. 363–378). Mahwah, NJ: Lawrence Erlbaum Associates.

Bushman, B. J., & Anderson, C. A. (2009). Comfortably numb: Desensitizing effects of violent media on helping others. *Psychological Science, 20,* 273–277.

Carnagey, N. L. & Anderson, C. A. (2003). Theory in the study of media violence: The general aggression model. In D. Gentile (Ed.) *Media violence and children* (pp. 87–106), Westport, CT: Praeger.

Carnagey, N. L., & Anderson, C.A. (2005). The effects of reward and punishment in violent video games on aggressive affect, cognition, and behavior. *Psychological Science, 16,* 882–889.

Cavalli, E. (2008). Jack Thompson reaches out to Take-Two exec's mother. *Wired.* Retrieved from http://www.wired.com/gamelife/2008/04/jack-thompson-p/

Chan, P. A., & Rabinowitz, T. (2006). A cross-sectional analysis of video games and attention deficit hyperactivity disorder symptoms in adolescents. *Annals of General Psychiatry, 5*(16). doi:10.1186/1744-859X-5-16

Choo, H., Gentile, D. A., Sim, T., Li, D., Khoo, A., & Liau, A. K. (2010). Pathological video-gaming among Singaporean youth. *Annals of the Academy of Medicine Singapore, 39,* 822–829.

Corbett, A. T., Koedinger, K. R., & Hadley, W. (2001). Cognitive tutors: From the research classroom to all classrooms. In P. S. Goodman (Ed.), *Technology enhanced learning* (pp. 235–263). Mahwah, NJ: Lawrence Erlbaum.

Cordes, C., & Miller, E. (2000). *Fool's gold: A critical look at computers in childhood.* College Park, MD: Alliance for Childhood.

Cummings, H. M. M., & Vandewater, E. A. P. (2007). Relation of adolescent video game play to time spent in other activities. *Archives of Pediatric and Adolescent Medicine, 161,* 684–689.

Deutsch, J. E., Borbely, M., Filler, J., Huhn, K., & Guarrera-Bowlby, P. (2008). Use of a low-cost, commercially available gaming console (Wii) for rehabilitation of an adolescent with cerebral palsy. *Physical Therapy, 88,* 1196–1207.

DeWall, C. N., Anderson, C. A., & Bushman, B. J. (2011). The general aggression model: Theoretical extensions to violence. *Psychology of Violence, 1,* 245–258.

Entertainment Software Association (2011a). 2011 essential facts about the computer and video game industry. Retrieved from http://www.theesa.com/facts/pdfs/ESA_EF_2011.pdf

Entertainment Software Association (2011b). Games: Improving education. Retrieved from http://www.theesa.com/games-improving-what-matters/ESA_FS_Education_2011.pdf

Feng, J., Spence, I., & Pratt, J. (2007). Playing an action video game reduces gender differences in spatial cognition. *Psychological Science, 18,* 850–855.

Ferguson, C. J. (2007a). Evidence for publication bias in video game violence effects literature: A meta-analytic review. *Aggression and Violent Behavior, 12,* 470–482.

Ferguson, C. J. (2007b). The good, the bad and the ugly: A meta-analytic review of positive and
negative effects of violent video games. *Psychiatric Quarterly, 78,* 309–316.

Ferguson, C. J., & Kilburn, J. (2010). Much ado about nothing: The misestimation and over-
interpretation of violent video game effects in Eastern and Western nations: Comment on
Anderson et al. (2010). *Psychological Bulletin, 136,* 174–178.

Funk, J. B., Baldacci, H. B., Pasold, T., & Baumgardner, J. (2004). Violence exposure in real-life,
video games, television, movies, and the internet: is there desensitization?. *Journal of
Adolescence, 27*(1), 23–39.

Gentile, D. A. (2009). Pathological video game use among youth 8 to 18: A national study.
Psychological Science, 20, 594–602.

Gentile, D. A. (2011). The multiple dimensions of video game effects. *Child Development
Perspectives, 5,* 75–81.

Gentile, D. A., & Bushman, B. J. (2012). Reassessing media violence effects using a risk and resi-
lence approach to understanding aggression. *Psychology of Popular Media Culture 1,* 138–151.

Gentile, D. A., Anderson, C. A., Yukawa, N., Saleem, M., Lim, K. M., Shibuya, A., . . ., Sakamoto, A.
(2009). The effects of prosocial video games on prosocial behaviors: International evidence
from correlational, longitudinal, and experimental studies. *Personality and Social Psychology
Bulletin, 35,* 752–763.

Gentile, D. A., Choo, H., Liau, A. K., Sim, T., Li, D., Fung, D., & Khoo, A. (2011). Pathological
video game use among youths: A two-year longitudinal study. *Pediatrics, 127,* e319–e329.

Gentile, D. A., Coyne, S. M., & Bricolo, F. (2013). Pathological technology addictions: What is
scientifically known and what remains to be learned. In K. E. Dill (Ed.), *Oxford Handbook of
Media Psychology.* New York, NY: Oxford University Press.

Gentile, D. A., & Gentile, J. R. (2008). Video games as exemplary teachers: A conceptual analysis.
Journal of Youth and Adolescence, 37, 127–141.

Gentile, D. A., Groves, C., & Gentile, J. R. (2014). The general learning model: Unveiling the
learning potential from video games. In F. C. Blumberg (Ed.) *Learning by playing: Video
Gaming in Education* (pp. 121–142). New York: Oxford University Press.

Gentile, D. A., Lynch, P. J., Linder, J. R., & Walsh, D. A. (2004). The effects of violent video game
habits on adolescent aggressive attitudes and behaviors. *Journal of Adolescence, 27,* 5–22.

Gentile, D. A., & Stone, W. (2005). Violent video game effects on children and adolescents: A review of the literature. *Minerva Pediatrica, 57,* 337–358.

Gentile, D. A., Swing, E. L., Lim, C. G., & Khoo, A. (2012) Video game playing, attention problems, and impulsiveness: Evidence of bidirectional causality. *Psychology of Popular Media
Culture, 1*(1), 62–70.

Gentile, D. A., & Walsh, D. A. (2002). A normative study of family media habits. *Journal of Applied
Developmental Psychology, 23,* 157–178.

Graf, D. L., Pratt, L. V., Hester, C. N., & Short, K. R. (2009). Playing active video games increases
energy expenditure in children. *Pediatrics, 124,* 534–540.

Green, C. S., & Bavelier, D. (2003). Action video game modifies visual selective attention. *Nature,
423,* 534–537.

Green, C. S., & Bavelier, D. (2007). Action video game experience alters the spatial resolution of
attention. *Psychological Science, 18*(1), 88–94.

Greitemeyer, T. (2009). Effects of songs with prosocial lyrics on prosocial thoughts, affect, and
behavior. *Journal of Experimental Social Psychology, 45,* 186–190.

Greitemeyer, T., & Osswald, S. (2009). Prosocial video games reduce aggressive cognitions.
Journal of Experimental Social Psychology, 45, 896–900.

Greitemeyer, T., & Osswald, S. (2010). Effects of prosocial video games on prosocial behavior.
Journal of Personality and Social Psychology, 98, 211–221.

Grüsser, S. M., Thalemann, R., & Griffiths, M. D. (2007). Excessive computer game playing: Evidence for addiction and aggression? *CyberPsychology & Behavior, 10,* 290–292.

Hastings, E. C., Karas, T. L., Winsler, A., Way, E., Madigan, A., & Tyler, S. (2009). Young children's video/computer game use: Relations with school performance and behavior. *Issues in Mental Health Nursing, 30,* 638–649.

Hopf, W. H., Huber, G. L., & Weib, R. H. (2008). Media violence and youth violence: A 2 year longitudinal study. *Journal of Media Psychology: Theories, Methods and Applications, 20,* 79–96.

Huesmann, L. R. (1986). Psychological processes promoting the relation between exposure to media violence and aggressive behavior by the viewer. *Journal of Social Issues, 42,* 125–139.

Huesmann, L. R. (1998). The role of social information processing and cognitive schema in the acquisition and maintenance of habitual aggressive behavior. In R. Geen & E. Donnerstein (Eds.) *Human aggression: Theories, research, and implications for policy* (pp. 73–109). New York, NY: Academic Press.

Jenkins, H. (2006). The war between effects and meaning: Rethinking the video game violence debate. In D. Buckingham & R. Willett (Eds.), *Digital generations: Children, young people, and new media* (pp. 19–31). Mahwah, NJ: Erlbaum.

Kato, P. M., Cole, S. W., Bradlyn, A. S., & Pollock, B. H. (2008). A video game improves behavioral outcomes in adolescents and young adults with cancer: A randomized trial. *Pediatrics, 122,* 305–317.

Khoo, A., & Gentile, D. A. (2007). Problem-based learning in the world of games. In O. S. Tan and D. Hung (Eds.), *Problem-based learning and e-learning breakthroughs* (pp. 97–129). Singapore: Thomson Publishing.

Kirsh, S. J., Olczak, P. V., & Mounts, J. R. (2005). Violent video games induce affect processing bias. *Media Psychology, 7,* 239–250.

Klein, M. J., & Simmers, C. S. (2009). Exergaming: Virtual inspiration, real perspiration. *Young Consumers, 10,* 35–45.

Ko, C. H., Yen, J. Y., Yen, C. F., Lin, H. C., & Yang, M. J. (2007). Factors predictive for incidence and remission of internet addiction in young adolescents: A prospective study. *Cyberpsychology & Behavior, 10,* 545–551.

Konijn, E. A., Bijvank, N. M., & Bushman, B. J. (2007). I wish I were a warrior: The role of wishful identification in effects of violent video games on aggression in adolescent boys. *Developmental Psychology, 43,* 1038–1044.

Lam, L.T., Peng, Z., Mai, J., & Jing, J. (2009). The association between internet addiction and self-injurious behaviour among adolescents. *Injury Prevention, 15,* 403–408.

Maier, J. A. & Gentile, D. A. (2012).Learning Aggression through the Media: Comparing psychological and communication Approaches. In L.J. Shrum (Ed.)*The Psychology of Entertainment Media: Blurring the Lines Between Entertainment and Persuasion* (2nd Edition, pp.267–299). New York: Taylor & Francis

Möller, I., & Krahé, B. (2009). Exposure to violent video games and aggression in German adolescents. *Aggressive Behavior, 35,* 75–89.

Lam, L. T., & Peng, Z. W. (2010). Effect of pathological use of the internet on adolescent mental health: A prospective study. *Archives of Pediatrics & Adolescent Medicine, 164,* 901–906. doi:10.1001/archpediatrics.2010.159

Lieberman, D. A. (2001). Management of chronic pediatric diseases with interactive health games: Theory and research findings. *Journal of Ambulatory Care Management, 24*(1), 26–38.

Mathews, V. P., Kronenberger, W. G., Wang, Y., Lurito, J. T., Lowe, M. J., & Dunn, D. W. (2005). Media violence exposure and frontal lobe activation measured by functional magnetic resonance imaging in aggressive and nonaggressive adolescents. *Journal of Computer Assisted Tomography, 29,* 287–292.

Mellecker, R. R., & McManus, A. M. (2008). Energy expenditure and cardiovascular responses to seated and active gaming in children. *Archives of Pediatrics and Adolescent Medicine, 162,* 886–891.

Murphy, R., Penuel, W., Means, B., Korbak, C., & Whaley, A. (2001). *E-desk: A review of recent evidence on the effectiveness of discrete educational software.* Menlo Park, CA: SRI International.

Narvaez, D., Mattan, B., MacMichael, C., & Squillace, M. (2008). Kill bandits, collect gold or save the dying: The effects of playing a prosocial video game. *Media Psychology Review, 1*(1).

Okagaki, L., & Frensch, P. A. (1994). Effects of interactive entertainment technologies on development. *Journal of Applied Developmental Psychology, 15*, 33–58.

Peng, L. H., & Li, X. (2009). A survey of Chinese college students addicted to video games. *China Education Innovation Herald, 28*, 111–112.

Porter, G., Starcevic, V., Berle, D., & Fenech, P. (2010). Recognizing problem video game use. *Australian and New Zealand Journal of Psychiatry, 44*, 120–128.

Rideout, V. J., Foehr, U. G., & Roberts, D. F. (2010). Generation M2: Media in the lives of 8- to 18-year olds. Retrieved from http://www.kff.org/entmedia/entmedia012010nr.cfm

Rosenberg, D., Depp, C. A., Vahia, I. V., Reichstadt, J., Palmer, B. W., Kerr, J., Norman, G., & Jeste, D. V. (2010). Exergames for subsyndromal depression in older adults: A pilot study of a novel intervention. *American Journal of Geriatric Psychiatry, 18*, 221–226.

Rosser, J. C., Lynch, P. J., Cuddigy, L., Gentile, D. A., Klonsky, J., & Merrell, R. (2007). The impact of video games on training surgeons in the 21st century. *Archives of Surgery, 142*, 181–186.

Sestir, M. A., & Bartholow, B. D. (2010). Violent and nonviolent video games produce opposing effects on aggressive and prosocial outcomes. *Journal of Experimental Social Psychology, 46*, 934–942.

Shapira, N. A., Goldsmith, T. D., Keck, P., Khosla, U., & McElroy, S. (2000). Psychiatric features of individuals with problematic internet use. *Journal of Affective Disorders, 57*, 267–272.

Shapira, N. A., Lessig, M. C., Goldsmith, T. D., Szabo, S. T., Lazoritz, M., Gold, M. S., & Stein, D.J., (2003). Problematic internet use: proposed classification and diagnostic criteria. *Depression and Anxiety, 17*, 207–216.

Sharif, I., & Sargent, J. D. (2006). Association between television, movie, and video game exposure and school performance. *Pediatrics, 118*, e1061–e1070.

Sherry, J. L. (2001). The effects of violent video games on aggression. *Human Communication Research, 27*, 409–431.

Sim, T., Gentile, D. A., Bricolo, F., Serpelloni, G., & Gulamoydeen, F. (2012). A conceptual review of research on the pathological use of computers, video games, and the internet. *International Journal of Mental Health and Addiction*. DOI 10.1007/s11469-011-9369-7

Stone, W., & Gentile, D. A. (2008, August). The five dimensions of video game effects. Paper presented at the annual convention of the American Psychological Association, Boston, MA.

Swing, E. L., & Anderson, C. A. (2008). How and what do video games teach? In T. Willoughby & E. Wood (Eds.) *Children's learning in a digital world* (pp. 64–84). Oxford, UK: Blackwell.

Swing, E. L., & Anderson, C. A. (2010). Media violence and the development of aggressive behavior. In M. DeLisi & K. M. Beaver (Eds.) *Criminological theory: A life-course approach.* (pp. 87–108). Sudbury, MA: Jones and Bartlett.

Swing, E. L., Gentile, D. A., Anderson, C. A., & Walsh, D. A. (2010). Television and video game exposure and the development of attention problems. *Pediatrics, 126*, 214–221.

U.S. Department of Health and Human Services (2001). *Youth violence: A report of the Surgeon General.* Retrieved from http://www.surgeongeneral.gov/library/youthviolence/chapter4/sec3.html

CHAPTER 8

Risk and Harm on the Internet

▪

Sonia Livingstone

The Internet in Children's Everyday Lives

The speed with which children and families are gaining access to new media technologies today has not been experienced before in the history of technological innovation. Not only are people in many parts of the world acquiring, learning to use, and finding a purpose for the Internet in their daily lives, but it seems that everyday practices of communication, education, entertainment, commerce, and participation are being rewritten through the use of online digital technologies, especially mobile and social media. Moreover, children and young people have tended to lead in this effort to get online, resulting in claims that these "digital natives" (Helsper & Eynon, 2010) are gaining skills and opportunities little understood by those traditionally tasked with supporting them and keeping them safe. Often having to play catch-up with both innovative youth and the continually changing technology, diverse stakeholders—governments, schools, industry, child welfare groups, and civil society—seek to maximize online opportunities while minimizing the risk of harm associated with Internet use. All this poses some fascinating challenges for families, for the wider society—and for research. How do children gain access to and experience new media, especially the Internet, in their home, school, and community? Does the reconfiguring of identity, knowledge, social relations, and intimacy afford children more risks than opportunities? What are the priorities and the dilemmas for governments, for educators, for industry, and even for individuals? In this chapter, I reflect on the emerging patterns of findings from research, focusing the thorny and often misunderstood question of the relation between risk and harm.

A starting point is the hotly contested agenda of questions debated in the public domain, strongly focused on values and social change. This agenda tends to articulate a technologically determinist perspective in which new technological developments are framed as a potentially transformative influence entering into an otherwise stable social reality. Sometimes this is optimistic—suggesting that Internet access at school can motivate children to learn, that civic websites will reinvigorate apathetic youth, or that the World Wide Web enhances children's knowledge in ways that libraries never managed to do. However, although techno-optimism is strong, in relation to children it is the anxieties, even moral panics, that dominate the agenda—just as they always have in the history of new media. Public pronouncements in the media, government, and everyday discourse are supremely technologically determinist in their vision of the Internet as a corrupter of innocence, disrupting traditional authority relations between adults and children. Hence the media headlines convey worry that the Internet is now raising our children, that social networking sites have undermined children's sense of privacy, that mobile media bring pedophiles into the child's bedroom, and so on. The result is that many parents are anxious about their children's online activities, and schools have often banned the use of social or mobile media on the premises, thereby directly undermining society's hopes for e-learning and new forms of engagement. Such anxieties in turn fuel calls to governments to regulate the internet industry, although until just a decade ago, the Internet was commonly likened to a virtual Wild West, a realm separate from the online world in both its content (being full of pornography and pedophiles) and its processes and structures (being both technically very complex and seemingly able to elude the grasp of national jurisdictions).

But in thinking about what's new, three critiques of such technologically determinist perspectives are important. First, technologies such as the Internet are far from pure bundles of hardware and wires—rather, they are socio-technical systems that have been designed, planned, regulated, and implemented in particular cultural-economic contexts, and these help shape what we think "the Internet" is (Selwyn, 2012). Second, when we talk of the dangers of "the Internet," we are often not referring to the technology itself but rather how people use it—people design and spread viruses, or post pornography on websites, or seek to groom children. Third, as is implied in both these critiques, gaining mass access to the Internet is not the only recent change in an otherwise stable reality, for accompanying every stage in the Internet's diffusion are the social processes of innovation, design, marketing, distribution, regulation, adoption, and appropriation. And it may be any or all of these processes, not just the technology, that really explains why e-learning has taken off but e-participation is struggling, or why online pornography is now commonplace but online grooming remains rare. Interestingly, while many of the social actors shaping the power and potential of the Internet are influential organizations in their own right—governments, major corporations, systems of health care or education or city planning—ordinary householders also have a role to play. And recognizing the role of children and parents in shaping what the Internet is and could be is part and parcel of the same research project that aims to map the opportunities and risks it affords. Indeed, these different roles are complementary in complex but fascinating ways: for example, the more that parents oversee children's Internet safety, the less need for government top-down regulation; the more creatively children find online workarounds, the more canny must designers be in managing the online experience.

However, this is not to say that the Internet, as socially shaped and used in our lives, is neutral or even irrelevant in explaining the conditions of contemporary childhood. To grasp its role, the concept of affordances is helpful—this alerts us not to the intrinsic features of an object but to the meaningfulness of certain features as we particularly perceive them: unlike a glass of water, a hot cup of tea is thirst-quenching for me but not for my cat; a French film affords pleasure to me but not to my monoglot daughter; and a social networking site affords a chance for intimacy to my daughter but a chance for abuse to a pedophile. In short, to understand any object, especially complex communication technologies, we must seek to understand the specific interaction between the character of the technology and that of the user. It is the dynamic of technology-in-use that matters. Furthermore, such use is not to be understood in terms of the individual; it is fundamentally social. My daughter does not social-network alone. A film is not made in French if no one speaks the language. The affordances of the technology are locked in mutual determination with the wider circuit of culture—encompassing production, distribution, and consumption. And here questions of culture, economy, and inequality enter. My daughter social-networks in a world with many actual friends, vast numbers of potential friends, and a few pedophiles. Unless they are native speakers, people generally need access to education in order to learn French.

To be sure, as danah boyd (2008) and others have persuasively argued, the Internet's affordances matter in modern societies—adapting boyd's list, we can point to the importance of *persistence* (content is recorded, always visible, difficult to erase), *scalability* (simple interactions can be rapidly made available to vast audiences), *asynchronicity* (enabling interaction management), *replicability* (permitting seamless editing and manipulation of content), *searchability* (both extending and permitting specialization within networks of information and relationships), *audience uncertainty* (regarding who is listening and who is speaking), and *collapsed contexts* (absence of conventional boundaries for social situations, a key consequence being blurring of the public and private domains) (Livingstone, 2013a). All this, research is now revealing, is sustaining a highly immersive networked culture of expressivity, sociality, and competing information sources, with many implications for ways in which children live their lives. But to understand the array of online opportunities and risks afforded to children or, more important, the actual benefits and harms that they experience, we must inquire into the social shaping and social consequences of Internet use-in-context (Bakardjieva, 2005; Lievrouw & Livingstone, 2006). That requires multidimensional research—preferably multidisciplinary, multimethod research. Any answers will be provisional, and any normative recommendations will be context-dependent. After all, it is one thing to ask whether children are adversely affected by exposure to online pornography or bullying; it is more complex to ask whether the fact that such exposure occurs via the Internet really makes a difference, recognizing that pornography and bullying have always existed, inserting themselves into children's lives in different ways depending on the cultural and media environment of the times. Research is making some headway in relation to these questions (for recent reviews, see Gasser, Maclay, & Palfrey, 2010; Hasebrink, Livingstone, Haddon, & Ólafsson, 2009; Palfrey, boyd, & Sacco, 2008; OECD, 2011), but there is much more to do.

Online Risks: From Fears to Findings

Reliable data on the incidence of online risk encountered by children are surprisingly hard to find—and, as the EU Kids Online network discovered when designing a survey to answer this basic question, it is also hard to produce. The Safer Internet Program of the European Commission had funded our network of some 100 multidisciplinary researchers in 25 countries to ask children about online risk in the most conscientious way we could. After much consultation with child welfare and survey design experts, we determined on interviewing children where they would be most relaxed—at home, but with as much privacy from both parents and the interviewer as could be managed. Questions were presented either on a page that the child could put in a self-sealed envelope or on a computer screen turned to the child; interviewers were on hand to explain anything tricky to understand, and they also did their best to encourage parents to leave the room. A number of ethical issues inevitably arose, since researchers should not introduce new ideas to the child (for instance, asking about pornography when a child hadn't heard of this before), and nor should they promise unconditional confidentiality, lest they learn that a child was in danger and be unable to intervene. Given these and related issues, the network decided to interview 9- to 16-year-olds (on the assumption that younger children would require a different approach) about a range of risks (phrased in ordinary, descriptive language) that they may have experienced in the recent past (without directly asking about the present).

In both its breadth and depth, as well as in the fact that it addressed detailed searching questions of Internet use directly to 9- to 16-year-old children, this survey provides a unique and unprecedented insight into the nature of children's online experience. In terms of theory, we trace the path of children's online experiences from Internet use (amount, devices, location) through online activities (opportunities, skills, risky practices) to the risks encountered online and then the outcomes experienced (whether harmful or not, how children cope). Crucially, we recognize that because not all children encounter risk and not all risks result in harm, research must identify the protective factors (e.g., coping) that reduce the likelihood of harm and the risk factors that increase it. Last, in order to inform evidence-based policy, the study has—from inception to interpretation of findings—been conducted in dialogue with policymakers (Livingstone, 2013b). To start, however, we had to define *risk* and, also surprisingly, this was not obvious. The media headlines scream about pornography and pedophiles. But evidence of cyberbullying also is rising. And some qualitative research suggested new or neglected risks—visiting suicide sites, for example. One of our earliest and most effective contributions, therefore, which was widely taken up by policymakers, was to classify risk in a manner that gave clarity and order to the otherwise inchoate set of fears that shifted every time the media discovered a new and tragic case (see Table 8.1). It was particularly important to us as child-centered researchers to complicate the roles that children themselves could play in relation to risk—not simply as victims but, in various ways, as receivers, participants and actors, sometimes as both perpetrator and victim, and often as something more ambiguous—especially in the days of Web 2.0 and user-generated content. Challenging the simple vision of the innocent child is important: children are often reluctant to seek help for anything that worries them online precisely because their own participation will thereby be revealed, and then they fear punishment for tarnishing their "innocent" image.

The purpose of the survey, then, was to put some numbers to the cells. We didn't ask about all the risks in the survey, but for those we did ask about, the incidence reported by 9- to 16-year-olds (note that we asked only the 11- to 16-year-olds about racism, "sexting," harmful user-generated content, and data misuse) were lower than many had feared. Based on incidence, policymakers should focus less on bullying than on sexting, and not only on pornographic content but also on other potentially harmful user-generated content—pro-anorexia sites, for instance. In what follows, limitations of space permit only a short summary of key findings. These present the findings across all 25 European countries; interestingly, although the incidence of risk varies (Livingstone, Haddon, Görzig, & Ólafsson, 2011), the factors that differentiate among children, and the patterning of variables that predict who encounters more or less risk, proved to be strikingly similar across countries (Livingstone, Haddon, & Görzig, 2012).

Table 8.1 **Risks Relating to Children's Internet Use (Exemplars Only)**

	Content Receiving mass-produced content	*Contact Participating in (adult-initiated) online activity*	*Conduct Perpetrator or victim in peer-to-peer exchange*
Aggressive	Violent / gory content	Harassment, stalking	Bullying, hostile peer activity
Sexual	Pornographic content	"Grooming," sexual abuse or exploitation	Sexual harassment, "sexting"
Values	Racist / hateful content	Ideological persuasion	Potentially harmful user-generated content
Commercial	Embedded marketing	Personal data misuse	Gambling, copyright infringement

Sexual Content

Society has long worried about children's exposure to sexual content of one kind or another, and research in recent years has begun to examine exposure online as a particular focus (Lenhart, 2009; Peter & Valkenburg, 2009; Wolak, Mitchell, & Finkelhor, 2007). Key findings from the EU Kids Online survey are shown in Box 8.1.

What are the policy implications of these findings? Although public concern over online sexual content is justified, the extent of children's exposure should not be exaggerated, nor should it be assumed that all children are upset or harmed by such exposure—the present findings do not support some of the moral panics surrounding this issue. Although the Internet makes sexual content more readily available to all, with many children reporting exposure via accidental pop-ups, the regulation of more established media (television, video, magazines, etc.) remains important. Private access also matters—children who go online via their own laptop, mobile phone or, especially, a handheld device are more likely to have seen sexual images or received sexual messages. Similarly, those who go online in their bedroom, at a friend's house, or "out and about" are more likely to see sexual content online. The advice from the early days of the Internet, namely that parents should put the computer in a public room, should be revised now that many children have personal and mobile devices, and thus new safety tools and guidance are needed. Perhaps most important, the high public concern over teenage boys' supposedly deliberate exposure to sexual content tends to eclipse attention to other problems. These include the distress that inadvertent exposure to pornography and violent content may cause girls (and some boys), younger children, and those facing psychological difficulties in their lives (Livingstone, Kirwil, Ponte, & Staksrud, in press).

Box 8.1 **Children's Exposure to Sexual Content Online and Offline**

- Children encounter pornography online and offline: 14% of 9- to 16-year-olds have seen sexual images online, and 4% (that is, about 25% of those who had seen an image) were upset by this. However, 23% of 9- to 16-year-olds have seen sexual images whether online or elsewhere: for example, 12% have seen them on television or on videos or DVDs, and 7% have seen them in magazines or books.

- A minority of online content is sexually explicit—among 11- to 16-year-olds, 11% have seen nudity, 8% have seen someone having sex, 8% of seen genitals, and 2% have seen violent sex. Also, 2% have been asked to talk about sexual acts with someone online, and 2% have been asked for an image of their genitals.

- Sexual content is not just found on websites but is now circulated among peers: 15% of 11- to 16-year-olds have received sexual messages, and 4% (about 25% of those who had received a message) said they had been upset by this. Also, 3% say they have sent sexual messages to someone.

- Age and gender make a difference: older more than younger children report exposure to sexual content, and more boys than girls have seen sexual images; a third of teenage boys say they have seen these, with a quarter of teenage boys having seen them online. Vulnerability also matters—those who report more psychological difficulties are also more likely to have seen sexual images or received sexual messages online, and they are more often upset by the experience.

- Risks migrate: those who have encountered a range of risks offline are more likely to encounter sexual content online. However, risk and harm are not the same: older children and boys encounter more sexual content, but younger children and girls are more upset when they encounter this. Also, children who score highly on "sensation seeking" encounter more content and yet are less upset about it—possibly the very act of seeking and finding new content builds resilience for some.

- Parents are insufficiently aware of their children's exposure to sexual content: among children who have seen sexual images online, 40% of their parents are unaware of this. Among the groups more upset by what they see, that is, among girls and younger children, half of their parents are unaware that they have had such an experience. Relatedly, among children who have received sexual messages, 52% of their parents are unaware of this, and again this is more common among parents of girls and younger children.

Online Bullying

Building on growing concerns about cyberbullying, and bearing in mind debates over definitions (and problems of translation, since the term *bully* does not exist in many languages), the EU Kids Online survey asked children whether they had been treated, or had treated other people, in a hurtful or nasty way on the Internet, whether as a single, repeated, or persistent occurrence (see also Patchin & Hinduja, 2012; Smith, Mahdavi, & Carvalho, 2008; Vandebosch & Cleemput, 2009). Key findings are summarized in Box 8.2.

Notably, although relatively few children report being bullied, this is the risk that upsets them most, more than sexual images, sexual messages, or meeting online contacts offline. Hence the policy implications are pressing. In countries where there is more bullying, there tends to be more bullying online. This suggests that as Internet use increases, so will bullying online. Thus antibullying initiatives should accompany efforts to promote Internet use. Online and offline bullying should be seen as connected, part of a vicious cycle in which perpetrators reach their victims through diverse means and victims find it hard to escape. Yet, those who bully may also be vulnerable, and they are often victims themselves, so sensitive treatment is required. Although children have a range of coping responses, this risk does upset them, and more support is needed—fewer than half tell a parent or other adult, and fewer than half know how to block the person or delete their messages, so further awareness-raising is vital.

Meeting New Contacts Online

Communicating, making new friends, developing intimacy—all this is fraught with difficulties and embarrassment for young people. The Internet, it seems, offers a space for privacy, control over communication, and experimentation. It also lets children easily get to know many new people, whether like themselves or quite different. Traditionally, in face-to-face encounters, it has been clear who children are in touch with because (1) children can see who they are talking to; (2) parents can oversee who the child is talking to; and (3) the child's own identity is not in doubt. But on the Internet, none of this can be assumed: online, famously, no one knows whether you are a dog—or a child; nor is it clear whether you are talking to a child or an adult, or an adult pretending to be a child. No longer can parents oversee their children's friends— they are no longer present in the house or on the street, only on the computer, often inaccessible even to curious or concerned parents. Unsurprisingly, then, nowhere has the public anxiety been greater than over the tension between "meeting strangers" (as many adults see it) and "making new friends"

Box 8.2 **Children's Exposure to Bullying Online and Offline**

- Among 9- to 16-year-old Internet users, 6% report having been bullied online and 3% confess to having bullied others. Far more have been bullied offline, however, with 19% saying they have been bullied at all—and 12% saying they have bullied someone else. In some countries, bullying is much more common than in others.

- Offline and online bullying are closely related. About half (56%) of online bullies said they had also bullied people face-to-face, and about half (55%) of online victims said they have also been bullied face-to-face. So it is not the case that bullying takes place either online or offline, but rather that bullying migrates from one domain to the other, making it hard for the victim to escape.

- Bullying and being bullied tend to go together. Among those who do not bully others, being bullied is relatively rare: 8% of children experienced offline bullying only and 4% experienced online bullying. But, among those who have bullied others offline, nearly half have also been bullied offline (and fewer online). On the other hand, among those who have bullied others online, nearly half have been bullied online (and fewer offline).

- Which children bully or are bullied? Children who bully and who are bullied online report rather more psychological difficulties than children with no experience of bullying online. Also, those who bully tend to be higher in sensation seeking, while those who are bullied are more often ostracized by their peers.

- As for the question of harm, the 6% of children who have been bullied online divide fairly evenly into those who were very upset (31%), fairly upset (24%), a bit upset (30%) and, the smallest category, not at all upset (15%). Girls experience feeling more upset than boys (37% vs. 23% "very upset").

- Children have some resources at their disposal to cope with being bullied online: about one-third (36%) try to fix the problem, most tell someone (77%, usually a friend but often a parent), and nearly half (46%) block the person sending the hurtful messages.

(as children may see it). Meeting strangers is a risk. Making new friends is an opportunity. Distinguishing between the two may depend on the child and the circumstances. Avoiding the emotionally charged terms *stranger* and *friend*, we asked children in the survey about the people they are in touch with online and whether they also know them offline (see Box 8.3).

Box 8.3 **Children's Exposure to New Contacts Online and Offline**

- Among European 11- to 16-year-olds, 87% say that online they are in touch with people they first met face-to-face; 39% are in touch with people they met on the Internet who are friends or family of people they know; and 25% are in touch with people they met online who have no connection with their existing social circle.
- Among 9- to 16-year-olds, 30% have had contact online with someone they haven't met face-to-face, but only 9% have gone to an offline meeting with such a person.
- Among those children who have met online contacts offline, half have met one or two people in the past year, and half have met more. Also, 57% met a friend of a friend (someone in their social circle), while 48% met someone unconnected with their life before meeting them online.
- Among those children who did meet an online contact offline, 61% of their parents were not aware of this, rising to 68% among the younger children. Parents were least aware of such meetings in Ireland, the UK, Cyprus, and Portugal.
- Several factors predict who makes contacts online: being higher in self-efficacy or sensation seeking; engaging in risky online and offline activities; and having parents who place fewer restrictions on the child's Internet use. Interestingly, those who go to meet new contacts offline show a similar pattern, except they are also more likely to have psychological difficulties, so children's vulnerability is part of what makes some go to face-to-face meetings with "new friends."
- Among those children who went to offline meetings with contacts made online, 11% (i.e., 1% of all children surveyed) were bothered or upset by what happened—the vast majority, then, were not upset by such meetings. For ethical reasons, the survey didn't ask much about what happened, though we know that two-thirds of those upset met someone about their own age; a fifth said something hurtful was said and a few said something sexual happened. The findings also showed that those who were upset were more likely to be younger, lower in self-efficacy and higher in psychological difficulties—in short, they tended to be the more vulnerable children.

Meeting new people online is now commonplace for young people, and only in a small minority of cases is there cause for serious concern. From the perspective of policymakers, it is therefore important to distinguish the common occurrence of making new online contacts from the less common occurrence of actually going to meet them. It is equally important to recognize that for the most part, meeting online contacts is harmless, probably even fun. But for a minority of children, meeting online contacts is harmful, and these children tend already to be the more vulnerable. Because their parents are often unaware of what has happened, awareness-raising efforts should be increased so that parents of younger or otherwise more vulnerable children recognize the risk, without undermining the chance for most children to have fun making new friends.

Newer Risks

Public anxiety often focuses on pornography, sexting, bullying, and meeting strangers, especially for young children. But there are other risks that worry children, including many teenagers, as illustrated in Box 8.4.

Survey findings showed in particular that negative user-generated content is becoming common: 12% of 11- to 16-year-olds have seen hate sites in the past year; 10% have seen pro-anorexic sites, and among 14- to 16-year-old girls, the rate rises to about one in five; 7% have seen self-harm sites; 5% have seen drug

---

Box 8.4 **What Upsets Children on the Internet (Examples)**

- "When somebody says that he/she is going to commit suicide" (boy, 15, Germany)
- "Girlfriends, who I thought were my friends, have been awful. They took my identity to have my boyfriend" (girl, 15, France)
- "Bloodthirsty websites that show how someone is beating himself bloody or how someone is scratching himself" (girl, 15, Austria)
- "Showing sexual practices, offering drugs and weapons, religious groups" (boy, 15, Czech Republic)
- "When human beings are killed; when human beings are hurt while other people are watching" (girl, 10, Germany)
- "Torturing ourselves, attempts at suicide, using drugs" (boy, 15, Hungary)
- "Pictures of naked people and of people who want to lose weight very quickly" (girl, 10, Portugal)
- "Somebody that would 'crack' my password, I mean to access my account, to impersonate me and to make people in my contact list believe that I'm lying to them etc." (girl, 12, Romania)
- "The influence of bad websites such as things like diet to lose weight so you could be known as the pretty one. Like vomiting things" (girl, 15, Ireland)

sites; and 5% have seen suicide sites. In all, one in five 11–16 year olds have seen one or more of these kinds of sites. It is, therefore, vital to listen to children to learn what new risks they are experiencing. Addressing risks associated with peer-to-peer conduct (user-generated content and personal data misuse) poses a critical challenge to policymakers. While younger children have fewer resources to cope with online risk, the evidence shows that they are also more willing to turn to parents for help; meanwhile, teenagers face particular risks that worry them and that they may struggle with alone, so they need particular coping strategies and support.

What's the Harm?

Risk, as framed by the mass media, seems inherently a "bad thing" (Mascheroni, Ponte, Garmendia, Garitaonandia, & Murru, 2010). But risk, as defined by risk theorists, refers to the likelihood of harm, and this likelihood may be very low (Klinke, Dreyer, Renn, Stirling, & Van Zwanenberg, 2006). In short, policymakers need to know the likelihood of harm, which is rarely 100%; they also need to know the magnitude or severity of the potential harm, for this is rarely devastating, although it can be. In the EU Kids Online survey, four in ten children said they had encountered one or more of the risks we asked about, but only one in eight said they were bothered or upset by something online. Admittedly, with children it is hard to measure actual harm, especially in a survey. But if we do not try, we may reinforce the misinterpretation of risk as harm—i.e., that the mere exposure to pornography or to bullying messages, or the mere fact of meeting an online contact offline, becomes in itself a measure of harm. Here the popular analogy of comparing safety on the Internet to safety on the roads (Criddle, 2006) goes awry, because sad to say, we know not only how many kids have road accidents each year—in the UK, it's about 40,000—but we also know how many are killed (about 300) (Madge & Barker, 2007). But online, we tend to report the figures for "accidents," as it were, without knowing whether and when kids pick themselves up and turn out to be just fine—or not. So on the Internet, we tend to confuse the higher numbers who are exposed to the risk (which we can measure) with the presumably-lower numbers who actually experience harm (which we have not measured well so far). Hence the public anxiety. Assessing whether a child is damaged in the long term by exposure to pornography or bullying is a hard challenge for future research.

In our survey, given our child-centered approach, we took just one small step in this direction by asking the kids for their perspective. We found that for the main risks we asked about, as noted above, among those who had encountered the risk, the incidence of some degree of upset—arguably, of harm—was relatively low. Most children claimed to be fine with seeing pornography or meeting so-called strangers—who usually turned out to be another child in their community. Bullying, however, was generally not fine. Moreover, the patterns among children are interesting. Generalizing across risks, we have found that children who are older, who are higher in self-efficacy and sensation seeking, who do more online activities, and who report more psychological problems encounter more risks of all kinds online. By contrast, children who are younger, who are lower in self-efficacy and sensation seeking, who do fewer online activities, have fewer digital skills, or who have more psychological problems are more likely to be upset by the risks that they encounter. In other words, kids who are vulnerable to harm may or may not be those especially likely to encounter risks online. Indeed, our analysis of protective and vulnerability factors strongly suggests that kids who are vulnerable offline are more likely to be vulnerable online—if they encounter the risks in the first place, that is. It is hard to communicate to policymakers, however, that the conditions that increase risk differ from those that increase harm.

To be sure, this is just a beginning, for in trying to understand harm (and, then, vulnerability), we are limited to what children tell us at the time—though this has its own value—as illustrated by the quotations in Box 8.4. But the risk theorists would require us next to measure the magnitude as well as the likelihood of harm—here the story of meeting online contacts offline might tell a different and a more worrying story for the small minority who report being upset (Finkelhor, 2008), not to mention the long-term consequences of serious or repeated exposure to risk. So that's a priority for future research, if it can be done. The point is this: to report that 14% of European kids have seen sexual images online is an important part of the picture (after all, it isn't the 100% so often feared), but even this figure does not report the risk of harm itself; rather, it reports the "risk of the risk," where the harm itself remains elusive (and in need of further research).

But there is scope for further complication. On the roads—and elsewhere in their lives, it seems—children live in an increasingly risk-averse culture (Gill, 2007). Adults today, it seems, carry with them a picture in their minds of the freedoms they enjoyed in their locality that today's children are denied. Indeed, a focus on risk seems to ignore the benefits of Internet use, and living in a risk-averse culture (with phones and Facebook often banned in school and with parents anxiously watching over the child's shoulder at home) means that the Internet is a pretty restricted place for many children. Since in reality only a small minority of children upload as well as download, create as well as receive, or explore freely beyond Google, Facebook, and YouTube (Livingstone & Helsper, 2007), society still faces the significant task of maximizing the opportunities of the Internet for children as well as in minimizing its risks (or, better, in minimizing harm).

Moreover, many activities fall into a gray area between risks and opportunities—the Internet affords, indeed, risky opportunities. In our survey, half of 11- to 16-year-olds say, "I find it easier to be myself on the Internet than when I am with people face-to-face," and this may help explain why, further:

- 40% of 9- to 16-year-olds have "looked for new friends on the Internet";
- 34% have "added people to my friends list or address book that I have never met face-to-face";
- 16% have "pretended to be a different kind of person on the Internet from what I really am";
- 15% have "sent personal information to someone that I have never met face-to-face"; and
- 14% have "sent a photo or video of myself to someone that I have never met face-to-face."

This is partly a matter of Internet design—to post content online, you must provide personal details; to make new friends you must contact "strangers"; to explore widely may expose you to inappropriate content; to seek guidance on your diet may lead to healthy or pro-anorexic advice. Navigating all this is a challenge for adults as well as children—and this doesn't simply reflect our lack of digital literacy, or theirs, but also the fact that most of the Internet is designed for commercial purposes—it is far from a trustworthy, accountable, and enabling sphere designed for the public good. But it is also the case that these kinds of ambiguous "risky opportunities" allow children to experiment online with relationships, intimacy, and identity. This is vital for growing up if children are to learn to cope with the adult world. But risky opportunities are linked to vulnerability as well as resilience. In pursuing why some children undertake these risky online activities, analysis revealed that several influential factors – as predicted by a range of hypotheses (Livingstone, Haddon, & Görzig, 2012). Specifically, the following groups of children were more likely to engage in risky online activities:

- Children who were older, male, or higher in self-efficacy (Schwarzer & Jerusalem, 1995) and sensation seeking (Stephenson, Hoyle, Palmgreen, & Slater, 2003).
- Children who used the Internet in more places, for longer, and for more activities, as predicted by the hypothesis that more use makes for more opportunities but also more risks (Livingstone & Helsper, 2010).
- Children who encountered more offline risks (e.g., say "yes" to "Had so much alcohol that I got really drunk," "Missed school lessons without my parents knowing," "Had sexual intercourse," "Been in trouble with my teachers for bad behavior," "Been in trouble with the police"), as predicted by the hypothesis that offline risks migrate online (Livingstone, Haddon, & Görzig, 2012).

- Children with more psychological difficulties, as predicted by the hypothesis that those vulnerable offline will also be vulnerable online (Livingstone, Haddon, & Görzig, 2012).
- Children who said it is "very true" that "I find it easier to be myself on the Internet," as predicted by the hypothesis that people seek online to compensate for the social problems they suffer offline (Valkenburg & Peter, 2009).
- Children with more digital literacy and safety skills, suggesting that online experimentation can enhance skills, though greater skill is also linked to more (not fewer) online risky activities.

Unsurprisingly, then, our research shows that risks and opportunities tend to go hand in hand—more risk is associated with more opportunity, and vice versa (Livingstone & Helsper, 2010), which poses a challenge for policymakers seeking to change the balance between the two. Yet it is unsurprising when we think of, say, teaching children to cycle on the roads: there, too, more skill leads to more opportunities but also more risk. Challengingly, though, this means that initiatives to improve digital skills appear to increase not only the opportunities but also the risks (although perhaps not the harm). Last, a world without risk is undesirable. Children must learn to face the unexpected, to take calculated risks and, within reason, to cope when things go wrong. Developmental psychologists are clear—without facing some degree of adversity, children do not become resilient (Schoon, 2006) and, although safety remains important, it is as important, or even more important, to empower children to become confident and resilient in exploring their world and seeking out its benefits.

Conclusion

In this chapter, I have presented the main findings and policy recommendations that emerge from the EU Kids Online project, focusing on the relation between opportunities, risk, and harm. Although both research and policy have tended to treat these as separable parts of children's experience, the two are inextricably intertwined. The evidence shows that as use of the Internet increases—at the level of individuals and countries—so too does risk. However, fewer children report being harmed by online risks. Being bullied online is the risk that upsets children the most, even though it is among the least common. Meeting new people offline—the risk that the public worries about the most—very rarely upsets children, although when it does upset them the consequences can be very serious. While society may judge, on moral grounds, that children should not be exposed to sexual content, children are only upset by such exposure in a few circumstances, while in others such exposure may be pleasurable. Moreover, as discussed above, research has made some progress in identifying the factors that help explain which children are likely to encounter online risk and for which children this may be experienced as harmful.

In short, I have argued that it is unrealistic to consider how children can learn from the Internet or participate online without also considering the risks that such activities may bring with them, often inadvertently. Similarly, it is inappropriate to seek strategies for reducing the risks that the Internet poses to children without recognizing that some strategies may—often also inadvertently—result in curtailing children's online freedoms. It is vital, therefore, that children's Internet use is understood in the round, neglecting neither the risks nor the opportunities nor, indeed, the practicalities of internet use in everyday contexts.

Certainly it is too simple to call for restrictions on children's use of the Internet. But ways must be found to manage risk without unduly restricting opportunities. As with riding a bike or crossing the road, everyday activities online carry a risk of harm, but this harm is far from inevitable—indeed, it is fairly rare. The EU Kids Online survey provides clear empirical support for policy efforts both to manage children's encounters online so as to reduce harm (though not necessarily to reduce risk). This should be achieved both by designing the online environment to build in safety considerations and to increase children's digital skills, coping, and resilience. In some countries, the need for such efforts is already pressing. In others, it may be anticipated that as use rises, so too will the need for greater policy efforts regarding children's safety, empowerment, and well-being.

Acknowledgments

This chapter draws on findings reported in Livingstone, S., Haddon, L., Görzig, A., & Ólafsson, K. (2011). *EU Kids Online II: Final Report*. London, UK: EU Kids Online. http://eprints.lse.ac.uk/39351/

The EU Kids Online network is funded by the EC (DG Information Society) Safer Internet plus Programme (project code SIP-KEP-321803); see www.eukidsonline.net. Thanks to all network members for their many and thoughtful contributions to EU Kids Online. For full details of the research methodology employed to produce findings summarized in this chapter, please see the 2010 technical report and user guide available at http://eprints.lse.ac.uk/45271/.

References

Bakardjieva, M. (2005). *Internet society: The Internet in everyday life*. London, UK: Sage.
boyd, D. (2008). Why youth ♥ social network sites: The role of networked publics in teenage social life. In D. Buckingham (Ed.), *Youth, identity, and digital media*, Vol. 6, (pp. 119–142). Cambridge, MA: MIT Press.

Criddle, L. (2006). *Look both ways: Help protect your family on the Internet.* Redmond, WA Microsoft Press.

Finkelhor, D. (2008). *Childhood victimization: Violence, crime, and abuse in the lives of young people.* New York, NY: Oxford University Press.

Gasser, U., Maclay, C., & Palfrey, J. (2010). *Working towards a deeper understanding of digital safety for children and young people in developing nations.* Cambridge, MA: Berkman Center for Internet & Society.

Gill, T. (2007). *No fear: Growing up in a risk averse society.* London, UK: Calouste Gulbenkian Foundation.

Hasebrink, U., Livingstone, S., Haddon, L., & Ólafsson, K (2009). *Comparing children's online opportunities and risks across Europe: Cross-national comparisons for EU Kids Online* (2nd ed.). London, UK: EU Kids Online.

Helsper, E., & Eynon, R. (2010). Digital natives: where is the evidence? *British Educational Research Journal, 36,* 502–520.

Palfrey, J., boyd, d., & Sacco, D. (2008). Enhancing child safety and online technologies: Final report of the ISTTF to the multi-State working group on social networking of state attorney generals of the United States. Cambridge, MA: Berkman Center for Internet and Society at Harvard University.

Klinke, A., Dreyer, M., Renn, O., Stirling, A., & Van Zwanenberg, P. (2006). Precautionary risk regulation in European governance. *Journal of Risk Research, 9,* 373–392.

Lenhart, A. (2009). *Teens and sexting: How and why minor teens are sending sexually suggestive nude or nearly nude images via text messaging.* Washington, DC: Pew Internet & American Life Project.

Lievrouw, L., & Livingstone, S. (2006). Introduction to the updated student edition. In L. Lievrouw & S. Livingstone (Eds.), *Handbook of new media: Social shaping and social consequences* (pp. 1–14).

Livingstone, S. (2013a). Children's Internet culture: Power, change and vulnerability in twenty-first century childhood. In D. Lemish (Ed.), *Routledge handbook on children, adolescents and media* (pp. 111–119). London, UK: Routledge.

Livingstone, S. (2013b). "Knowledge enhancement": On the risks and opportunities of generating evidence-based policy. In B. O'Neill, E. Staksrud, and S. McLaughlin (Eds.), *Children and Internet safety in Europe: Policy debates and challenges* (pp. 91–107). Goteborg, Sweden: Nordicom.

Livingstone, S., Haddon, L., & Görzig, A. (Eds.) (2012). *Children, risk, and safety online: Research and policy challenges in comparative perspective.* Bristol, UK: The Policy Press.

Livingstone, S., Haddon, L., Görzig, A., & Ólafsson, K. (2011). *Risks and safety on the Internet: The perspective of European children. Full findings.* London, UK: EU Kids Online.

Livingstone, S., & Helsper, E. J. (2007). Gradations in digital inclusion: Children, young people and the digital divide. *New Media & Society, 9,* 671–696.

Livingstone, S., & Helsper, E. J. (2010). Balancing opportunities and risks in teenagers' use of the Internet: The role of online skills and Internet self-efficacy. *New Media & Society, 12,* 309–329.

Livingstone, S., Kirwil, L., Ponte, C., & Staksrud, E. (in press). In their own words: what bothers children online? *European Journal of Communication.*

Madge, N., & Barker, J. (2007). *Risk & childhood.* London, UK: The Royal Society for the Encouragement of Arts, Manufactures & Commerce.

Mascheroni, G., Ponte, C., Garmendia, M., Garitaonandia, C., & Murru, M. F. (2010). Comparing media coverage of online risks for children in southern European countries: Italy, Portugal and Spain. *International Journal of Media and Cultural Politics, 6,* 25–44.

OECD. (2011). The protection of children online: Risks faced by children online and policies to protect them. Retrieved from http://www.oecd-ilibrary.org/docserver/download/5kgcjf71pl28.pdf?expires=1384404156&id=id&accname=guest&checksum=2093F58CEB4ED35318EFAE7356AE9DE3

Patchin, J. W., & Hinduja, S. (2012). *Cyberbullying prevention and response: Expert perspectives.* New York, NY: Routledge.

Peter, J., & Valkenburg, P. M. (2009). Adolescents' exposure to sexually explicit Internet material and sexual satisfaction: a longitudinal study. *Human Communication Research, 35,* 171–194.

Schoon, I. (2006). *Risk and resilience: Adaptations in changing times.* New York, NY: Cambridge University Press.

Schwarzer, R., & Jerusalem, M. (1995). Generalized self-efficacy scale. In J. Weinman, S. Wright, & M. Johnston (Eds.), *Measures in health psychology: A user's portfolio* (pp. 35–37). Windsor, UK: NFER-Nelson.

Selwyn, N. (2012). Making sense of young people, education, and digital technology: the role of sociological theory. *Oxford Review of Education, 38,* 81–96.

Smith, P. K., Mahdavi, J., & Carvalho, M. (2008). Cyberbullying: its nature and impact in secondary school pupils. *Journal of Child Psychology and Psychiatry, 49,* 376–385.

Stephenson, M. T., Hoyle, R. H., Palmgreen, P., & Slater, M. D. (2003). Brief measures of sensation seeking for screening and large-scale surveys. *Drug and Alcohol Dependence, 72,* 279–286.

Valkenburg, P. M., & Peter, J. (2009). Social consequences of the Internet for adolescents: a decade of research. *Current Directions in Psychological Science, 18*(1), 1–5.

Vandebosch, H., & Cleemput, K. V. (2009). Cyberbullying among youngsters: Profiles of bullies and victims. *New Media & Society, 11,* 1349–1371.

Wolak, J., Mitchell, K., & Finkelhor, D. (2007). Unwanted and wanted exposure to online pornography in a national sample of youth Internet users. *Pediatrics, 119,* 247–257.

CHAPTER 9

Technology and Public Health Interventions

■

Michele Ybarra

Importance of the Area

The influence that technology has in our lives today cannot be overstated. According to recent data, 82% of adults (Pew Internet & American Life Project, 2012b) and 95% of adolescents (Pew Internet & American Life Project, 2012c) use the internet. Cell phone ownership is close behind, with 88% of adults (Pew Internet & American Life Project, 2012a) and 77% of adolescents reporting ownership (Pew Internet & American Life Project, 2012d). As technology becomes ever more ubiquitous, so too does its convergence; the lines between "online" and "offline" are blurred to the point where this distinction is less and less clear. Questions such as "How many hours a day are you online?" befuddle young people, who invariably respond, "All of the time." For those who have smartphones, internet access is continuous. As technology becomes the place where people "are," interest in how it can be harnessed to impact the public's health has increased.

Public health aims to positively affect healthy development at the population level. There will always be a need for individualized care. The aim of public health is not to replace individual health care providers but rather to reduce the number of people who need direct intervention, thereby reducing the burden on the health care system so that scarce resources can be better allocated. Technology has transformed public health efforts (Howitt et al., 2012): health behavior change programs can be made accessible to anyone who has internet access; electronic medical records can increase the accuracy and completeness of patient data, while also making information accessible across health care settings; diagnoses can be made thousands of miles away from the patient through video and, more recently, picture text messaging, just to name a few examples. Technology-based interventions, those that use the internet, cell phone text messaging, or both, combine the wide reach of mass media campaigns with the individual, tailored approach of clinical interventions. But this promise is not without pitfalls.

In this chapter, we discuss the benefits and drawbacks of technology in public health and examine instructive examples of how technology can be used to affect the public's health to illuminate opportunities for future programming.

Benefits and Drawbacks of Technology in Public Health

Technology-based interventions offer several potential advantages over traditional interventions (Howitt et al., 2012; Muñoz, 2012; Ybarra & Eaton, 2005). More and more, technology is able to reach people where they "are," in a time and space that is comfortable and convenient for them. As such, technology-based interventions lack many of the access issues of traditional interventions, including competition for time among other activities. People who live in areas without nearby in-person public health programming (e.g., smoking cessation programs, weight loss programs) are able to easily access programs on the internet or via cell phone. And, interventions targeting sensitive topics such as sex or violence can be accessed privately and anonymously through technology. Technology-based interventions are scalable and cost effective because there are fewer personnel and infrastructure costs (Ybarra & Eaton, 2005). Furthermore, technology allows the tailoring of the program to the individual's motivations for behavior change (e.g., health), demographic characteristics (e.g., biological sex), and stage of behavior change (e.g., planning, relapse) (Strecher, 1999; Strecher et al., 1994; Strecher et al., 2005), while also maintaining fidelity. In-person interventions can be similarly tailored, but also can suffer from variability of implementation across facilitators.

Compared to the internet, text messaging–based programs may be superior in some cases, because of their always-on nature (Cole-Lewis & Kershaw, 2010; Déglise, Suggs, & Odermatt, 2012; Wei, Hollin, & Kachnowski, 2011). Intervention messages are never far from the person's reach. Moreover, messages are received automatically instead of requiring the participant to go to a computer and log on to a specific website, as with internet-based interventions. This proactive method (i.e., a message is scheduled and initiated by the service) rather than a reactive method (i.e., the participant contacts the service to receive the message) may be more effective in promoting behavior change (Sherman et al., 2008). In our work, we found that text messaging was an effective way to engage adolescents and young adults in data collection efforts (see below in

Recent Successes of Technology in Public Health). Perhaps compared to the internet, text messaging allows people to engage with content at a time—and in an amount of time—that feels manageable, whereas other modes may be perceived as more intensive and therefore more burdensome.

Certainly, the benefits of technology need to be tempered by the potential drawbacks. For traditional prevention and intervention programs, the costs are on the back end via implementation and dissemination (e.g., through facilitator training). In contrast, the costs for technology-based programs are on the front end in development. Once the program is developed, it is relatively inexpensive to roll out and test. Most research grant programs are structured so that feasibility first needs to be demonstrated before a larger amount of money is awarded. This structure works well for traditional programs, but is counter to the cost trajectory of technology-based interventions, because the (expensive) software needs to be developed before feasibility can be tested. Even bare-bones beta versions of a technology-based program can be costly to develop.

Another challenge lies in distinguishing between fads and transcendent technological advances. On the one hand, we need to anticipate trends and develop programs ahead of the curve so that they are ready and waiting when usage has increased; on the other hand, we want to avoid costly development and testing of what ultimately becomes last year's "Big Thing." Many changes in technology, however, are related to the applications themselves and not the underlying modes. For example, Facebook is essentially an application that marries popular modes: instant messaging, blogging, emailing, and so on. While Facebook, like MySpace before it, may eventually lose appeal among certain groups of people, the communication modes it supports are unlikely to fade away. As another example, applications (i.e., "apps") are becoming less common in favor of mobile-accessible websites because apps are operating system-specific; one has to be developed for the iPhone, another for the Android, and so on. Mobile-accessible websites can be designed to behave like an app (e.g., by having an icon downloaded to the phone) but can run on all phones equivalently. Public health efforts that are based on these transcendent communications (e.g., instant messaging, text messaging) are likely to be relevant beyond evolutionary changes in the technology or platform.

The use of technology also raises important ethical issues. As we know from the too-frequent instances of companys' servers being hacked, internet security is fallible. We researchers do the best we can to protect the data, and we hope that people will be less interested in our patient data than credit card data; but the data may be vulnerable. Another ethical issue involves the identification and referral of people in crisis. When someone presents in person or over the telephone, their distress and need for follow-up care can be more easily identified and addressed quickly, whereas online someone may express their need for intervention at a website that may not be monitored. There are ways to program triggers so that someone who would like immediate follow-up can push a crisis button on the intervention website, or text a specific code in a text messaging intervention. Thus, with careful consideration, a crisis protocol can be put into place to keep youth safe even in these environments where we cannot actually touch, see, or even hear them. Another ethical issue involves the unintentional disclosure of data. This is especially of concern with applications that may store text messages or other data on patients' phones. This can be mitigated by encouraging patients to password-protect their phones. We must also be conscious of the type of messages we are sending to patients in the same ways we are when we leave messages on a patient's home telephone answering machine. The issues of personal privacy are similar to those that arose with previous technologies. The protocols need to be translated, however, to ensure privacy is maintained in these new environments that present different access points (e.g., cell phones). What it means to obtain as researchers and provide as participants informed consent about the collection of personal data via technology is another key ethical issue. While participants may indicate that they understand the potential risk of having certain types of messages on their phone, or agree to have GPS tracking data communicated from their phone to the research team, they may not appreciate the full extent of what they are agreeing to until, for example, they are presented with their GPS data or experience consequences.

Unlike structured settings that have a captive audience, such as schools, users of technology-based interventions need to be self-motivated to engage with the program over and over. Creators of technology-based programs therefore need to be clear about why their target population will be interested enough in the intended health behavior change to engage with the content of their own volition. For example, although public health professionals are concerned about reducing HIV rates, people who do not feel at risk for contracting HIV are unlikely to self-engage in a multilesson online program. This is probably why retention rates of online programs are low (Brouwer et al., 2011). It is promising that text messaging–based intervention research is reporting higher retention rates than previous online research (Cole-Lewis & Kershaw, 2010; Déglise et al., 2012).

Finally, we need to resist the temptation to use technology for all populations in every case. Technology-based interventions are not for everyone. Indeed, it is unlikely that a "single bullet" or unique intervention can be developed that will address everyone's needs and interests. Interventionists need to be clear about their population, and also what the population's motivation and ability to access the program via technology would be. For example, if parents are uninterested in attending an after-school meeting, it seems unlikely that their interest would inherently increase simply because the information is now online, unless their objections focused on issues related to scheduling and convenience. We also need to remember that technology is simply the communication mode through which we deliver our intervention content; it is not the intervention itself. Just as with traditional programming, what we say and how we say it is still the foundation of behavior change.

Recent Successes of Technology in Public Health

There are several useful reviews of how technology has been used to affect youth behavior change, including in the fields of smoking cessation (Rodgers et al., 2005; Whittaker et al., 2009) and HIV prevention (Chiasson et al., 2006; Ybarra & Bull, 2007). Here, two technology-based projects are discussed in depth to help the reader think through some of the issues of using technology in public health interventions.

CYBERSENGA

CyberSenga is an internet-based HIV prevention program that was developed and tested among adolescent high school students in Mbarara, Uganda. Mbarara municipality, with a population of 69,000 (based on the 2002 census), is the sixth largest urban center in Uganda (Uganda Bureau of Statistics, 2005). The greater Mbarara district is second in population only to the Kampala district, yet it falls in the bottom half of districts in terms of population density. Mbarara municipality is perhaps best described as an urban center serving mainly a rural population.

The *Senga* is the name given to the paternal aunt who traditionally advised girls as they came of age on issues related to running a household, including sexuality and sexual health. Although the *senga* is less common in today's Uganda society, it still has strong cultural resonance. The CyberSenga program was desgined around a virtual *senga* (and a *kojja*, the male equivalent, for boys), who embodied a trustworthy role model who imparted sexual health program content.

CyberSenga content was motivated by the Information-Motivation-Behavior model of HIV preventive behavior (Bryan, Fisher, & Benziger, 2000; Fisher, Fisher, Bryan, & Misovich, 2002; Fisher, Fisher, Williams, & Malloy, 1994; Kalichman et al., 2006; Linn et al., 2001). Extensive formative research informed the development of the intervention. Steps included: focus groups with adolescents and adolescent health professionals, a technology assessment of adolescent computer and internet skills, and two field tests to test out the logistics of the protocol as well as understand how young people would interact with the intervention (Bull, Nabembezi, Birungi, Kiwanuka, & Ybarra, 2010; Mitchell,

Bull, Kiwanuka, & Ybarra, 2011; Ybarra, Biringi, Prescott, & Bull, 2012; Ybarra, Kiwanuka, Emenyonu, & Bangsberg, 2006; Ybarra, Korchmaros, Kiwanuka, Bangsberg, & Bull, 2012). Six 1-hour modules were created: (1) HIV prevention information (e.g., what HIV is and how it is prevented); (2) problem solving and communication skills (e.g., steps to solving a problem; strategies for communicating your solution to others assertively); (3) norms for sexual behavior (e.g., reasons why adolescents choose to be abstinent or to have sex); (4) condom skills (e.g., demonstration of correct condom use; testimonials from people like the users who used condoms); (5) healthy relationships (e.g., the components of healthy relationships; identifying coercive gifts); and (6) a review. The full program can be found at www.cybersenga.com.

Once the intervention website was finalized, the program's impact on HIV preventive behavior was measured in a randomized controlled trial with 366 adolescents (Ybarra et al., 2013; Ybarra, Bull, Prescott, & Birungi, 2013; Ybarra, Korchmaros, Prescott, & Birungi, under review). Youth were randomly assigned to either the intervention group or a treatment-as-usual control group. Those randomized to the intervention group completed one module a week online over a five-week period. The sixth module was delivered as a 'booster' to half of the intervention, about 3 months after they completed the previous five modules (Ybarra et al., 2013; Ybarra et al., under review).

We created a "mobile cyber café" in a designated room at each of the schools because two of our partner schools did not have internet or computer access at school. Netbooks were connected to the internet through a router that was powered by a car battery given that consistent electricity in the schools could not be assumed. Research assistants actively sought out participants to come to the mobile café and complete their session. They also provided technological assistance and answered questions about the program or the survey when they arose.

Both program completion rates and follow-up rates were extremely high and are much higher than other HIV-related online interventions: More than 90% of intervention participants completed all five modules (Ybarra, Bull, Prescott, & Birungi, 2013), and over 90% of participants provided 3-month and 6-month follow-up data. The high response rates may be because the intervention was delivered online but had a human component in the form of the research assistants (Brouwer et al., 2011). It may also be because the internet is relatively unique and therefore intriguing to youth in Uganda. Part of the interest in the program was being able to access to accurate and detailed information about sex and HIV; but another part was in being able to use the internet—even if use was restricted solely to the intervention content. Another reason may be because the population was motivated: about one in three youth reported knowing someone who had died of AIDS and about two in five had been tested for HIV themselves.

The sense of personal risk for contracting HIV is simply higher in Uganda than it is, for example, in the United States.

This project was initially funded in 2007 by the National Institutes of Health. Since that time, access to cell phones and text messaging in Uganda (and other developing countries) has skyrocketed, while internet access has increased but not at the same rate (Central Intelligence Agency, 2013). We wondered if perhaps text messaging would have been a better delivery mode—until we learned that it was against the rules in many of our partner schools for students to have a cell phone while at school. Given that boarding school is a common student experience, this is not an inconsequential limitation. Had we developed a text messaging–based program without understanding the specific needs and in this case, restrictions, of our population, we would have missed reaching the youth entirely. At the same time, it is not yet clear how long it will take for the internet to reach a penetration rate such that youth in schools will have regular access. It may be that more traditional delivery modes, such as in-person programming, are better suited to this environment. The problem is resources. Muyinda and colleagues (2003) developed a community-based *senga* program. Well-respected women in the community were trained to be "community *sengas*" and were assigned a group of adolescent women with whom to intervene on topics related to sexual health. The program demonstrated positive results but has not been sustained or further disseminated because of lack of funding. Internet-based programs remain promising, because they do not require additional funding for dissemination. Recent improvements in internet delivery have reduced the cost of internet connections; hopefully, access will accordingly increase.

The example of the CyberSenga program highlights the importance of understanding the target population and the cultural differences that may enhance (or in other examples, decrease) the likelihood of program dissemination. Again, the search for a "single bullet" is a false one: it is unlikely and unrealistic to expect one specific mode of delivery to be sufficient. In the case of HIV prevention, where public health efforts need to be extensive, it is appropriate to expect and therefore develop a wide range of programs that are accessible across multiple modes so that accurate and behavior-changing information is available whenever and however that particular person is looking for it. Thus, the question is not necessarily whether the website is a better delivery mechanism than text messaging or in-person contact, but rather whether there are people who may look for HIV prevention information online, and if so, what we need to do to ensure that it is easily accessible.

STOP MY SMOKING (SMS)

Stop My Smoking is a six-week text messaging–based smoking cessation program for adolescents and young adults. It was initially developed for adult smokers in

Ankara, Turkey (Ybarra et al., 2011; Ybarra, Bağcı Bosi, Korchmaros, & Emri, 2012; Ybarra, Holtrop, Bağcı Bosi, & Emri, 2012; Ybarra, Holtrop, Bağcı Bosi, Bilir, Korchmaros, & Emri, 2013) and went through extensive formative development, including focus groups and field testing, to tailor the content to 18- to 25-year-old smokers in the United States (Ybarra, Prescott, & Holtrop, in press). Research suggests that quitting is a process that is marked by different stages (Strecher, 1999; Strecher et al., 1994; Strecher et al., 2005). First, people need to prepare to quit, by understanding when and why they smoke and identifying ways to address potential challenges when quitting. It also is critical to identify a quit day, the day on which the smoker commits to quitting. When the quit day arrives, it is critical to ensure that the smoker is ready and has the resources available to make it smoke-free for the entire day. The first week after the quit day is key—if the person can make it without smoking this first week, the chances of long-term success are greatly improved. After the first week when physical withdrawal is complete, it is important for the now-former smoker to focus on relapse prevention and maintaining a smoke-free lifestyle by focusing on behavioral changes. The text messaging program content mirrored these stages in the quitting process. Smokers received two weeks of pre-quit messages aimed at encouraging them to clarify reasons for quitting and to understand their smoking patterns and tempting situations/triggers/urges. Early quit messages, the week following the quit day, talked about common difficulties and discomforts associated with quitting and emphasized the use of coping strategies. Late quit messages helped participants think about different situations in which they were triggered to smoke—and to recognize that these situations were likely different than they were when the person was smoking. The content provided actionable information about how to deal with issues that arise as a nonsmoker (e.g., stress, moods). Based on telephone quit line research that suggests most smoking relapse occurs within the first week (Zhu et al., 1996), smokers were contacted at 2 days post-quit and again at 7 days post-quit. At each point, if participants reported smoking, they were pathed to content that focused on helping them get back on track and to recommit to quitting. If participants were smoking at *both* 2 and 7 days post-quit, they were pathed to an encouragement arm that focused on norms for quitting and suggested that the participant try quitting at later time when he or she was more prepared. Based on a similar smoking intervention developed in New Zealand (Rodgers et al., 2005), we also included a "text buddy": pairs of smokers in the program were sequentially assigned to one another, so that they could text one another for support anonymously through the program. A "text crave" feature, which provided immediate, on-demand messages aimed at distracting the participant from a craving was additionally provided. Crave messages were sent to participants after they texted one of two key words, *crave* or *smoke*, to the program.

The SMS program was tested among 164 adolescent and young adult smokers 18–25 years old across the United States. One hundred and one youth were randomly assigned to the smoking cessation program and 63 to a control group that received the same number of text messages but with content focused on improving one's sleep and fitness (Ybarra, Holtrop, Prescott, Rahbar, & Strong, 2013). The program is unique because few smoking cessation programs exist for adolescents and young adults. The randomized controlled trial design is unique because programs that do exist have almost exclusively been tested in college and university settings (Murphy-Hoefer et al., 2005). We recruited young people online, most frequently using Craigslist to reach out to smokers. The use of technology allowed us to reach a diverse sample of young people both in and out of tertiary school settings, from across the United States, representing a variety of income levels and metropolitan settings.

Retention rates were high: over 85% of participants responded at 4 weeks post-quit and 80% responded at 12 weeks post-quit (Ybarra, Holtrop, et al., 2013). These rates likely reflect the relative ease of responding to surveys via text messaging and online. In further support of this hypothesis, three different follow-up strategies were tested in our 12-week follow-up effort: Group 1 was given follow-up as usual (i.e., an initial email invitation to complete the online survey, along with a link and text message alerting them to check their email; reminder telephone calls, texts, and emails to nonresponders). Group 2 was given follow-up as usual with an additional incentive of $10 offered to nonresponders 1 week after the initial survey invitation if they completed the survey within 24 hours. Group 3 was invited to complete a brief text message survey for $10, with the option to also complete the online survey to receive the same incentive as the other groups receive (Ybarra, Holtrop, Prescott, & Strong, under review). The sample was divided into thirds, and participants were assigned to one of the three follow-up methodologies sequentially (i.e., the first third of the sample who moved into the 12-week follow-up was assigned to Group 1). Seventy-four percent of participants in Group 1, 78% of participants in Group 2, and 89% of participants in Group 3 provided follow-up data at 12 weeks post-quit ($p = 0.12$). Of the 12 participants who completed the brief text message survey in Group 3, 10 (83%) also completed the online survey after completing the brief text version. This mini-experiment suggests that text messaging surveys may result in higher response rates than online surveys, but also that text messaging may be a good gateway to improved response rates for longer online surveys.

Like the CyberSenga example, the Stop My Smoking example demonstrates the ability of technology to deliver public health messaging to engage people and affect behavior change. This example also highlights the impact that burdensome data collection can have on response rates and provides clues about how we might use text messaging and other technologies that are in the hands of adolescents as a way to increase their engagement in this process.

Unanswered Questions

As technology continues to evolve, challenges as well as opportunities will continue to present themselves. For example, one of initial lures of technology was that it could stand alone. researchers could create it, consumers would come, and we wouldn't have to expend any additional money on upkeep or personnel. The reality is a bit more complex. We are finding that even if we build it, people won't necessarily come. While not unique to technology-based interventions, this truth disabused us of the idea that technology was a magical panacea saving us from the headaches of first convincing people of the need for behavior change, and then keeping them engaged long enough to get the dosage necessary to effect behavior change. Perhaps, as we move forward into the next wave of technology-based interventions, standalone programming will transition toward models that use technology, especially perhaps using websites as a gateway to more traditional services. Or, we may start using technology to enhance in-person clinical experiences and patient-provider relationships: consumers talk to their provider about losing weight, and then are signed up for a 4-week text messaging or online program to help them reach their goal, for example.

Sustainability is another unanswered question. While the costs to deliver a standalone website once it is developed are relatively small (essentially, the cost of the server and the fee for the URL), there are potentially high costs in paying a programmer to keep the code compatible with never-ending software upgrades. For example, the CyberSenga program stopped functioning properly only six months after the close of the trial because of an upgrade to the flash program on which the back end was built. Text messaging programs additionally require ongoing financial support to send the text messages. This challenge will be compounded for programs that integrate technology and humans, such as live chat on crisis websites (e.g., the National Suicide Prevention Line). Whether and how public health campaigns can secure this funding—even if it is less expensive than personnel costs—remains to be seen.

Talk of technology must necessarily include a discussion of the digital divide, both within and across countries (Cole-Lewis & Kershaw, 2010; Howitt et al., 2012). In the United States, the gap in internet access across groups of different races and incomes seems to be closing—and this is largely due to internet-accessible mobile phones that minority and low-income youth are using to access the internet (Lenhart, Ling, Campbell, & Purcell, 2010). Certainly, access to technology differs between developed and developing countries

(World Economic Forum, 2012). Interestingly, the trends are different for SMS and internet: because it required less infrastructure, SMS technology was more popular in developing countries than in the United States for many years. Internet access has lagged behind in developing countries, however. Concerns about the potential ethical and health implications introduced by this digital divide seem to be based on the assumption that technology-based public health efforts are de facto superior to more traditional efforts, such that those who do not have access to them are always at a disadvantage. Perhaps instead of considering how emerging public health efforts may marginalize certain populations, the discussion could center more on how technology can and cannot be used to invigorate the health of marginalized populations. Certainly, the answer to this question will continue to evolve along with technology.

Conclusion

As access to and use of newer technologies have increased, so too has the recognition that these tools can potentially be used as effective public health intervention delivery mechanisms, both because this is more and more where adolescents "are," but also because of other strengths that technology may have over more traditional communication modes. At the same time, technology is not a panacea and should not be seen as the go-to answer for all adolescent prevention and intervention efforts. Understanding when, why, and how to use technology is integral for today's public health professionals.

Acknowledgments

The SMS USA smoking cessation project was supported by Award Number R21CA135669 from the National Cancer Institute at the National Institutes of Health. It was implemented in collaboration with Dr. Jodi Holtrop at Michigan State University, Dr. Hossein Rahbar at the University of Texas Health Science Center at Houston, and consultants, Drs. Amanda Graham and David Strong.

The CyberSenga project was supported by Award Number R01MH080662 from the National Institute of Mental Health. It was developed in collaboration with Drs. Sheana Bull at the University of Colorado at Denver, David Bangsberg at Harvard University, and Julius Kiwanuka at the Mbarara University of Science and Technology.

In both cases, content herein is solely the responsibility of the author and does not necessarily represent the official views of the National Institutes of Health.

References

Brouwer, W., Kroeze, W., Crutzen, R., de Nooijer, J., de Vries, K. N., Brug, J., & Oenema, A. (2011). Which intervention characteristics are related to more exposure to internet-delivered healthy lifestyle promotion interventions? A systematic review. *Journal of Medical Internet Research, 13*, e2. doi:10.2196/jmir.1639

Bryan, A. D., Fisher, J. D., & Benziger, T. J. (2000). HIV prevention information, motivation, behavioral skills and behaviour among truck drivers in Chennai, India. *AIDS, 14*, 756–758. doi:10.1097/00002030-200004140-00021

Bull, S., Nabembezi, D., Birungi, R., Kiwanuka, J., & Ybarra, M. L. (2010). Cyber-Senga: Ugandan youth preferences for content in an internet-delivered comprehensive sexuality education programme. *East African Journal of Public Health, 7*, 58–63.

Central Intelligence Agency. (2013). The world factbook: Uganda. Retrieved from https://www.cia.gov/library/publications/the-world-factbook/geos/ug.html

Chiasson, M. A., Parsons, J. T., Tesoriero, J. M., Carballo-Dieguez, A., Hirshfield, S., & Remien, R. H. (2006). HIV behavioral research online. *Joural of Urban Health, 83*, 73–85. doi:10.1007/s11524-005-9008-3

Cole-Lewis, H., & Kershaw, T. (2010). Text messaging as a tool for behavior change in disease prevention and management. *Epidemiologic Reviews, 32*, 56–69. doi:10.1093/epirev/mxq004

Déglise, C., Suggs, L. S., & Odermatt, P. (2012). Short message service (SMS) applications for disease prevention in developing countries. *Journal of Medical Internet Research, 14*, e3. doi:10.2196/jmir.1823

Fisher, J. D., Fisher, W. A., Bryan, A. D., & Misovich, S. J. (2002). Information-motivation-behavioral skills model-based HIV risk behavior change intervention for inner-city high school youth. *Health Psychology, 21*, 177–186. doi:10.1037/0278-6133.21.2.177

Fisher, J. D., Fisher, W. A., Williams, S. S., & Malloy, T. E. (1994). Empirical tests of an information-motivation-behavioral skills model of AIDS-preventive behavior with gay men and heterosexual university students. *Health Psychology, 13*, 238–250.

Howitt, P., Darzi, A., Yang, G.-Z., Ashrafian, H., Atun, R., Barlow, J., ... & Wilson, E. (2012). Technologies for global health. *Lancet, 380*, 507–535. doi:10.1016/S0140-6736(12)61127-1

Kalichman, S. C., Simbayi, L. C., Cain, D., Jooste, S., Skinner, D., & Cherry, C. (2006). Generalizing a model of health behaviour change and AIDS stigma for use with sexually transmitted infection clinic patients in Cape Town, South Africa. *AIDS Care, 18*, 178–182. doi:10.1080/09540120500456292

Lenhart, A., Ling, R., Campbell, S., & Purcell, K. (2010). Teens and mobile phones. Washington, DC: Pew Internet & American Life Project. Retrieved from http://www.pewinternet.org/Reports/2010/Teens-and-Mobile-Phones.aspx

Linn, J. G., Garnelo, L., Husaini, B. A., Brown, C., Benzaken, A. S., & Stringfield, Y. N. (2001). HIV prevention for indigenous people of the Amazon basin. *Cellular and Molecular Biology (Noisy-le-grand), 47*, 1009–1015.

Mitchell, K. J., Bull, S., Kiwanuka, J., & Ybarra, M. L. (2011). Cell phone usage among adolescents in Uganda: Acceptability for relaying health information. *Health Education Research, 26*, 770–781. doi:10.1093/her/cyr022

Muñoz, R. (2012). Using evidence-based Internet interventions to reduce health disparities worldwide. *Journal of Medical Internet Research, 12*, e60. doi:10.2196/jmir.1463

Murphy-Hoefer, R., Griffith, R., Pederson, L. L., Crossett, L., Iyer, S. R., & Hiller, M. D. (2005). A review of interventions to reduce tobacco use in colleges and universities. *American Journal of Preventive Medicine, 28*, 188–200. doi:10.1016/j.amepre.2004.10.015

Muyinda, H., Nakuya, J., Pool, R., & Whitworth, J. (2003). Harnessing the senga institution of adolescent sex education for the control of HIV and STDs in rural Uganda. *AIDS Care, 15*, 159–167. doi:10.1080/0954012031000105414

Pew Internet & American Life Project. (2012a). Adult gadget ownership over time (2006-2012). Retrieved from http://pewinternet.org/Static-Pages/Trend-Data-%28Adults%29/Device-Ownership.aspx

Pew Internet & American Life Project. (2012b). Demographics of Internet users. Retrieved from http://pewinternet.org/Static-Pages/Trend-Data-%28Adults%29/Whos-Online.aspx

Pew Internet & American Life Project. (2012c). Demographics of teen Internet users. Retrieved from http://pewinternet.org/Static-Pages/Trend-Data-%28Teens%29/Whos-Online.aspx

Pew Internet & American Life Project. (2012d). Teen gadget ownership. Retrieved from http://www.pewinternet.org/Static-Pages/Trend-Data-(Teens)/Teen-Gadget-Ownership.aspx

Rodgers, A., Corbett, T., Bramley, D., Riddell, T., Wills, M., Lin, R. B., & Jones, M. (2005). Do u smoke after txt? Results of a randomised trial of smoking cessation using mobile phone text messaging. *Tobacco Control, 14*, 255–261. doi:10.1136/tc.2005.011577

Sherman, S. E., Takahaski, N., Kalra, P., Gifford, E., Finney, J. W., Canfield, J., ... & Kuschner, W. (2008). Care coordination to increase referrals to smoking cessation telephone counseling: a demonstration project. *American Journal of Managed Care, 14*, 141–148.

Strecher, V. J. (1999). Computer-tailored smoking cessation materials: A review and discussion. *Patient Education and Counseling, 36*, 107–117. doi:10.1016/S0738-3991(98)00128-1

Strecher, V. J., Kreuter, M., Den Boer, D. J., Kobrin, S., Hospers, H. J., & Skinner, C. S. (1994). The effects of computer-tailored smoking cessation messages in family practice settings. *Journal of Family Practice, 39*, 262–270.

Strecher, V. J., Marcus, A., Bishop, K., Fleisher, L., Stengle, W., Levison, A., ... & Nowak, M. (2005). A randomized controlled trial of multiple tailored messages for smoking cessation among callers to the cancer information services. *Journal of Health Communication, 10*, 105–118. doi:10.1080/10810730500263810

Uganda Bureau of Statistics. (2005). 2005 statistical abstract. Kampala, Uganda: Uganda Bureau of Statistics.

Wei, J., Hollin, I., & Kachnowski, S. (2011). A review of the use of mobile phone text messaging in clinical and healthy behaviour interventions. *Journal of Telemedicine and Telecare, 17*(1), 41–48. doi:10.1258/jtt.2010.100322

Whittaker, R., Borland, R., Bullen, C., Lin, R. B., McRobbie, H., & Rodgers, A. (2009). Mobile phone–based interventions for smoking cessation. *Cochrane Database of Systematic Reviews*, CD006611. doi:10.1002/14651858.CD006611.pub2

World Economic Forum (2012). The global information technology report 2012. Living in a hyperconnected world. Retrieved from http://reports.weforum.org/global-information-technology-2012/, accessed 01/11/13

Ybarra, M. L., Bağcı Bosi, A. T., Bilir, N., Holtrop, J. S., Korchmaros, J., & Emri, A. K. S. (2011). Interest in technology-based and traditional smoking cessation programs among adult smokers in Ankara, Turkey. *Tobacco Induced Diseases, 9*, 10. doi:10.1186/1617-9625-9-10

Ybarra, M., Bağcı Bosi, A. T., Korchmaros, J., & Emri, S. (2012). A text messaging-based smoking cessation program for adult smokers: randomized controlled trial. *Journal of Medical Internet Research, 14*, e172. doi: 10.2196/jmir.2231

Ybarra, M. L., Biringi, R., Prescott, T., & Bull, S. S. (2012). Usability and navigability of an HIV/AIDS Internet intervention for adolescents in a resource limited setting. *Computer Informatics in Nursing, 30*, 587–595. doi:10.1097/NXN.0b013e318266cb0e

Ybarra, M. L., & Bull, S. (2007). Current trends in Internet- and cell phone–based HIV prevention and intervention programs. *Current HIV/AIDS Reports, 4*, 201–207. doi:10.1007/s11904-007-0029-2

Ybarra, M. L., Bull, S. S., Prescott, T. L., & Birungi, R. (2013). Acceptability and feasibility of CyberSenga: an Internet-based HIV-prevention program for adolescents in Mbarara, Uganda. *AIDS Care*. Advance online publication. doi: 10.1080/09540121.2013.841837

Ybarra, M. L., & Eaton, W. W. (2005). Internet-based mental health interventions. *Mental Health Services Research, 7*, 75–87. doi:10.1007/s11020-005-3779-8

Ybarra, M. L., Holtrop, J. S., Bağcı Bosi, A. T., Bilir, N., Korchmaros, J. D., & Emri, A. K. S. (2013). Feasibility and acceptability of a text messaging based smoking cessation program in Ankara Turkey. *Journal of Health Communication, 18*, 960–973. doi: 10.1080/10810730.2012.75739

Ybarra, M. L., Holtrop, J. S., Bağcı Bosi, T., & Emri, S. (2012). Design considerations in developing a text messaging program aimed at smoking cessation. *Journal of Medical Internet Research, 14*, e103. doi:10.2196/jmir.2061

Ybarra, M. L., Holtrop, J. S., Prescott, T. L., Rahbar, M. H., & Strong, D. (2013). Pilot RCT results of Stop My Smoking USA: a text messaging-based smoking cessation program for young adults. *Nicotine & Tobacco Research, 15*, 1388–1399. doi: 10.1093/ntr/nts339

Ybarra, M. L., Holtrop, J. S., Prescott, T. L., & Strong, D. (under review). Feasibility and acceptability of SMS USA, a text messaging-based smoking cessation program for young adults.

Ybarra, M. L., Kiwanuka, J., Emenyonu, N., & Bangsberg, D. R. (2006). Internet use among Ugandan adolescents: Implications for HIV intervention. *Public Library of Science: Medicine, 3*, e433. doi:10.1371/journal.pmed.0030433

Ybarra, M. L., Korchmaros, J., Kiwanuka, J., Bangsberg, D., & Bull, S. (2012). Examining the applicability of the IMB model in predicting condom use among sexually active secondary school students in Mbarara, Uganda. *AIDS and Behavior, 17*, 1116–1128. doi: 10.1007/s10461-012-0137-x

Ybarra, M. L., Korchmaros, J. D., Prescott, T. L., & Birungi, R. (under review). Examining the influence of CyberSenga, an internet-based HIV and healthy sexuality program in Mbarara, Uganda, on HIV-related information, motivation, and behavioral skills. *Health Psychology.*

Ybarra, M. L., Prescott, T. L., & Holtrop, J. S. (in press). Steps in tailoring a text messaging–based smoking cessation program for young adults. *Journal of Health Communication.*

Zhu, S. H., Strecher, V. J., Balabanis, M., Rosbrook, B., Sadler, G., & Pierce, J. P. (1996). Telephone counseling for smoking cessation: effects of single-session and multiple-session interventions. *Journal of Consulting and Clinical Psychology, 64*, 202–211. doi:10.1037/0022-006X.64.1.202

CHAPTER 10

Using Media to Aid Children in War, Crisis, and Vulnerable Circumstances[1]

Dafna Lemish

The idea that media can aid children during a war, crisis, and other vulnerable circumstances is often met with quite cynical reactions. How could a television program, a book, or even a sophisticated website help children who lost their homes in an earthquake in Haiti or a tsunami or nuclear disaster in Japan? How could media help an orphan in Zimbabwe who lost his parents to AIDS, a girl sold to the sex industry in Thailand, a homeless boy living with gangs in the streets of Rio de Janeiro; or a child caught in a street shooting by rebels while fleeing from a bombarded home in Syria? Obviously, I will not suggest here that media will or can restore peace, put food on the table, or bring dead loved ones back to life. However, many initiatives around the world advocate and demonstrate that, when used appropriately, media can bring comfort and hope, teach skills for competent response to an emergency, promote resilience, and even contribute to the improvement of the lives of children and their families. Thus, the purpose of this chapter is to document some of these initiatives and to discuss the extant, albeit scarce, formative and/or evaluative research available from these media endeavors. In addition, I will share my own input into these efforts, and finally sketch the future work that still needs to be advanced in this area.

Existing Research to Date

Extant research focuses on three interrelated domains: the roles that producers of children's media see for themselves in harnessing the media to aid children in war, crisis, and vulnerable circumstances; the study of interventions on behalf of children in this domain; and the space provided to children to voice their own opinions, needs, and anxieties over their life circumstances. Below, I review these three themes (for an elaborated review, see Lemish & Götz, 2014).

STUDIES OF PRODUCERS' VIEWS AND STRATEGIES

Studies of producers of media for children offer insights into their decision making processes, policies, and views of their role in keeping an appropriate balance between, on the one hand, the need to inform children about the harsh realities of war, conflict, natural disasters, and other crisis circumstances and, on the other hand, the need to do so in an age-appropriate way that promotes children's healthy development and well-being. In interviews conducted with 135 producers of quality television for children from 65 countries around the world (Lemish, 2010), I collected dozens of examples of programs that addressed crises and conflicts (e.g., HIV/AIDS and rape prevention animations in South Africa; fiction narratives exposing the negative implications of domestic violence in Latin American machismo culture; or efforts to confront the tradition of girl-brides in the Middle East and to advocate for girls' rights for education).

Several studies, in particular, examined producers' views and strategies in relationship to the onset of the war in Iraq in 2003. In her survey of 31 broadcasters from 23 countries, Strohmaier (2007) examined the ways they perceived their responsibilities and roles during the war in Iraq and the practices they adopted in trying to help children around the world. She found that despite their good intentions, most of the broadcasters surveyed did not have formal plans or strategies regarding the portrayal of the war, but rather they seemed to strategize based on their intuitions and assumptions about their child-audience's needs and desires. Nikken and Walma van der Molen (2007) examined various consolation strategies used by Dutch and German news producers during the first week of the war in their attempts to help children cope with the fear evoked by the news coverage, including their careful selection of news topics, their limiting the presentation of distressing photos, their use of animations, their consoling comments, and the like. My own study (Lemish, 2007) of three children's television channels in Israel in the weeks of uncertainty before the outbreak of the war in Iraq uncovered some of the dilemmas that producers of children's media faced when confronted with an existential threat.

Finding the appropriate balance between maintaining a broadcast routine with which children are familiar and comfortable and that gives them a sense of security and stability, while at the same time addressing the harsh realities of a war period, seemed to present the greatest challenge to all broadcasters. They considered children's unique needs during a time of crisis: their need to stay safe and busy at home, to have outlets for tension relief, and to be informed; all tasks, they noted, that media can help facilitate. However, although clearly the need to keep children busy, relaxed, and informed seemed to be acknowledged by all, finding the delicate balance between these special efforts and the regular broadcasting schedule remained a major issue in helping children cope with the prewar tension building up in their society.

Applying conflict resolution constructs in order to analyze programs produced for children in several deeply conflicted regions in the world (including former Yugoslavian countries, Israel-Palestine, Colombia, and the Philippines) provides another means by which to infer producers' use of media for children living in deeply conflicted societies (P. Lemish, 2007). For example, Lemish and Scholote (2009) examined a selection of quality television programs focusing on conflict, which had been submitted in the last decade as entries to the *Prix Jeunesse International Festival,* and found that producers employed a rich and diverse approach to the presentation of conflicts and their resolution to assist children in understanding the political as well as social conflicts taking place in their own and other societies. More specifically, an analysis of initiatives for the use of media to advance conflict transformation in Northern Ireland suggests that a rich corpus may be available to help young people, their families, and educators understand a range of issues involved in the transition from violent confrontation to democratic, nonviolent management of conflicts and crises in social life (Lemish, 2008).

STUDIES OF THE EFFECTIVENESS OF INTERVENTIONS

What is missing, however, is systematic research that examines the effectiveness of documented as well as advocated interventions in achieving their goals. Such a research project has the potential, as well, to provide professionals involved in producing these programs with valuable feedback on the benefits and accomplishments of their creative efforts. Insights into such potential can be found in the following review of research conducted that has examined the effectiveness of a limited number of interventions.

Sesame Workshop has been the leading force, to date, in efforts to systematically explore ways to use media in early childhood to better the lives of young children in areas of conflict and vulnerable circumstances, as well as in studying the effectiveness of several of these efforts. For example, evaluation studies of the co-production *RechovSumsum / Shaar'aSimsim* aimed at reconciliation efforts between Israeli and Palestinian preschoolers (Brenick, Lee-Kim, Killen, Fox, Raviv & Leavitt, 2007; Warshel, 2007) suggested that such interventions are powerful in that they can challenge negative stereotypes by exposing children to peaceful, normalized relationships between groups constantly portrayed on television news as violent enemies. Such alternative representations offer children momentary relief from reality and a vision of an alternative future. Similarly, in

Bangladesh, the assessment of the co-production, *Sisimpur*, found that family members thought that the program had positive influences on children who viewed the series, as well as on adult caregivers, with regard to literacy, acquisition of social-cultural knowledge, and promoting diversity and girls' education (Jain & Kibria, 2009; Lee, 2007). *Sesame Street Panwapa Project* was found to be effective in promoting global citizenship and helping young children living in a conflict-ridden world understand and appreciate the world's diversity (Cole & Lee, 2009). *Sesame Tree,* a more recent initiative in Northern Ireland, designed to contribute to the reconciliation between the Catholic and Protestant communities, is currently under investigation (Cochrane, 2010). *Sesame Street* co-productions also inspired the series *Nashe Maalo* ("Our Neighborhood") in Macedonia, following the war in the former Yugoslavia. The program was designed to promote multicultural understanding and respect among ethnic Albanian, Macedonian, Roma, and Turkish children. A study that examined the effectiveness of the series documented that regular viewing was associated with both familiarity and knowledge acquisition about the various minority groups, more positive attitudes toward them, as well as expression of willingness to invite home children from groups other than one's own (Shochat, 2003).

Several media-related conflict resolution and peace-building initiatives for children took place in Northern Ireland through the years of the Troubles, including *Off the Walls,* a series of programs for use in schools and youth clubs, and the *Respecting Difference* series for preschoolers, both of which were designed to promote mutual respect and tolerance among Northern Ireland children (Lemish, 2008). One initiative in Ireland received particular research attention. A series of brief animated episodes aimed at preschoolers, named *Media Initiatives for Children,* was designed to promote acceptance and appreciation of differences among people in order to promote greater understanding and less strife among children in conflicted societies. These short spots, similar to public service announcements, were broadcast regularly on television in both Northern Ireland and the Republic of Ireland between 2003 and 2009 and were also integrated within the preschool curriculum. Several studies of the impact of this project found that viewing the series within an integrated preschool curriculum contributed to positive changes in recognizing differences and exclusion, and that children exposed to this intervention were more willing to play with all children, compared with those who were not part of the project (Connolly, 2009; Connolly, Fitzpatrick, Gallagher, & Harris, 2006).

Thus, the accumulated literature suggests that age-appropriate, well-designed, and well-executed educational media interventions for young children and caregivers can have the intended effects on cognitive, social, and emotional development. Such projects do seem to enable children to change the framing through which a contested issue is being viewed and to think about it from different perspectives (Prasad, 2009; Singhal, Cody, Rogers, & Sabido, 2004). Discussion of these interventions included the need to apply a non-Western perspective to such interventions around the world in order to enhance their social relevancy and effectiveness (Dutta, 2006).

However, evaluating the effectiveness of such interventions is a complicated endeavor, as it depends to a large degree on the project's goals, the target age group, and the definitions of short- and long-term effectiveness. It requires funding and a base of skills and technology, often scarce in low-resource societies. Nevertheless, those interventional experimentations privileged to be evaluated demonstrate the positive potential that media can have for children in crisis and vulnerable situations.

PROVIDING CHILDREN WITH OPPORTUNITIES FOR EXPRESSION AND INVOLVEMENT

Finally, media can aid children by giving voice to their opinions, emotions, and experiences during a crisis. Unfortunately, most of the evidence in this line of research comes from privileged countries were children have access to a rich media environment and develop the literacy skills necessary to master new technologies. For example, researchers in Germany and the Netherlands (Nikken & Götz, 2007) and the United Kingdom (Carter, 2007; Carter, Messenger Davies, Allan, Mendes, Milani, & Wass, 2009) examined children's reactions to news coverage of wars and conflict, among others, through their postings on the web and creating their own news programs. Such outlets allowed children to express their thoughts, feelings, and opinions, and desire to be informed. They also provided children an opportunity to be involved in contemporary social and political debates. Such opportunities serve to contribute to children's well-being by empowering them to become active participants rather than passive victims.

Studies of youth-made media from around the world (e.g., Fisherkeller, 2011) suggest that many such efforts are directed toward creating "participatory culture" and redressing social inequalities; providing support and opportunities for social change; and bettering the lives of disadvantaged children and youth. Stuart and Mitchell (2013) adopt the concept of "youth as knowledge producers" in order "to refer to the ways in which young people can serve both as resources to each other and play a key role as protagonists in the production of knowledge about their everyday lives" (p. 360). They report on several projects in South Africa that allow children to share their experiences through digital storytelling and photovoicing regarding HIV/AIDS transmission and sexual relationships in a society devastated by the epidemic. In another example from Stuart and Mitchell (2013), children in Nepal used participatory video to express their experiences with the effects of climate change and the resulting floods, droughts, and landslides on their access to water and the resulting effects on their physical and emotional well-being. These productions also served to benefit children directly in the material world, as they informed decision makers and these insights were used to formulate policy-oriented actions (e.g., including categories related to safety and security in the area of water, sanitation, and child protections policy).

These few case studies serve to illustrate some of the initiatives that attempt to realize the communication rights of children, as delineated in the United Nations Convention on the Rights of the Child (United Nations, 1989), including the right to be heard and to be taken seriously; to free speech and to information; to maintain privacy; to develop cultural identity; and to be proud of one's heritage and beliefs. Yet these rights are rarely realized: whether girls and boys live in deprived, resource-poor societies or in overwhelmingly commercialized, profit-driven ones, few children's voices are heard in the media or taken seriously. This is even more infrequent for children under the age of 8 and those from minority and marginalized groups (United Nations, 1989). Even in cases when young children appear to be provided space to offer their "voice," the voice heard often reflects the perspective of the dominating class of adults. There are just too few possibilities for them to express their needs and opinions, which, in and of itself, can help children cope with hardships.

A UNICEF Global Resource Package

The United Nations International Children's Emergency Fund (UNICEF) headquarters and country offices often take the lead in developing creative media materials in low-resource countries. For example, gender equality was promoted in the *Meena* series in South Asia and the *Sarah* series in Africa. Both series feature a girl protagonist as a role model who deals with issues of gender equity specific to those parts of the world (e.g., the right for education; prevention of early marriage). UNICEF supported local adaptations of *Sesame Street* in countries such as Mexico, Kosovo, and South Africa. It also contributed to the development of culturally specific programs, such as the animated preschool series *The Magic Journey* in Kyrgyzstan (Komerecki, 2010). UNICEF-sponsored media products have been developed, as well, for both children and caregivers in Lesotho, the Maldives, Myanmar, the Pacific Islands, Tanzania, Turkmenistan, and Vietnam, among others. The focus of these interventions was mostly on supporting the psychosocial needs of vulnerable children, such as orphans, children with disabilities or HIV/AIDS, and children struggling with the impact of an emergency, such as a tsunami.

In an attempt to map and pull together exemplary work done in many countries around the world, UNICEF sponsored the development of a resource package, entitled "Communicating with Children: Principles and Practices to Nurture, Inspire, Excite, Educate and Heal" (Kolucki & Lemish, 2011). This resource package also offers principles and related guidelines to educators, media producers, caregivers, and others on how to communicate with children in ways that are age-appropriate, child-friendly, holistic, positive, culturally sensitive, and inclusive. It is designed to provide users of the package with the tools to use communication to help build children's (and their caretakers') self-esteem, confidence, and resilience, and to aid in healing the wounds of injustice, prejudice, and poverty inflicted on children. It embarks on this journey with the hope of nurturing the belief that communication is one of the most empowering ways to improve the lives of children and their families, particularly those most vulnerable, marginalized, and disadvantaged (pp. vii–viii).

This collaboration between my colleague Barbara Kolucki[2] (a practitioner with more than 25 years of experience in more than 20 countries in the developing world in building local media and staff capacity) and myself (as a scholar with expertise in the field of media and children) involved reviewing hundreds of media texts from around the world and resulted in the following conceptual framework of principles and guidelines. These principles and guidelines serve as a checklist for producing children's media and for evaluating existing materials. The principles are illustrated by positive examples from a range of countries and a variety of media forms and genres, and address the needs of different age groups (detailed discussion and all the resources is available at http://www.unicef.org/cwc):

- Principle 1, "Communication for children should be age-appropriate and child-friendly," is supported by guidelines to
  - use child-appropriate language, characters, stories, music; and humor;
  - encourage and model positive interaction and critical thinking; and
  - use special effects judiciously and wisely.
- Principle 2, "Communication for children should address the child holistically," is supported by guidelines to
  - use an integrated rather than a single-issue approach to communication;
  - offer positive models for adults in their relationships with children as full human beings in their own right; and
  - create "safe havens."

(continued)

- Principle 3, "Communication for children should be positive and strengths-based," is supported by guidelines to
  - build self-confidence as well as competence;
  - use positive modeling;
  - include children as active citizens learning about and modeling social justice; and
  - do no harm.
- Principle 4, "Communication for children should address the needs of all, including those who are most disadvantaged," is supported by guidelines to
  - reflect the dignity of each and every child and adult;
  - be inclusive and celebrate and value all types of diversity;
  - ensure communication is free of stereotypes; and
  - reflect and nurture the positive aspects of local cultures and traditions.

Dozens of examples are provided to illustrate the principles and guidelines in an integrative manner, as they apply to the three different age groups. For example, the issue of water is dealt with in many ways. The book *Thar Thar Takes a Bath* is designed to teach parents to help a toddler who survived the tsunami in Myanmar overcome fear of water as s/he agrees to take a bath. A poster entitled *"Let's Wash Hands"* targets young schoolchildren in Indonesia and aims to teach them the basic hygienic behavior of hand washing; it also incorporates counting of fingers and singing a song via a strong girl role model. *Be Prepared*, a book from Myanmar for the entire family, teaches how to divide responsibilities in preparation for survival given the prospect of a future flood that might destroy their homes. *Remembering Mommy* is a book for young children developed in South Africa to help AIDS orphans deal with their grief; the book models sharing memories and maintaining routines while handling their experience of death. This book also serves as a local model to introduce sensitive topics such as illness, death, trauma, emergency, and other difficult circumstances in ways that acknowledge the pain; the book also provides comfort and support for other caring adults, and helps children build resilience and restore a sense of hope for a better future. *"See Something Say Something"* (United Kingdom), a series of short films about bullying, demonstrates interactions between the bully, the bullied, and the witness to bullying as a part of an antibullying campaign. An animation spot in Moldova, *No More Playing with Chickens*, presents the story of a girl whose grandfather explains to her why she cannot play with chickens anymore during the avian influenza epidemic. In Iraq, an animated television spot, *Landmine Injury Reduction Education,* tells the story of two boys playing with a kite, and it models appropriate behavior when discovering a landmine in their field.

Bringing together scholarship with experience in the field in communication for development enabled us to recommend working strategies for putting the guidelines into practice that have been shown to be effective in field work (Lemish & Kolucki, 2013). These include, first and foremost, as a necessary condition, collaboration among all stakeholders and partners (e.g., government agencies, parents, teachers, and creative media experts) in the creation of innovative media when all partners are guided by a holistic understanding of the developmental needs of children. We recommended that a top priority for creative efforts should be given to the "critical needs of young children and their caregivers living in especially difficult circumstances such as HIV/AIDS, emergencies, child protection, gender inequality, or other child rights issues" (Lemish & Kolucki, 2013, p. 336). We also emphasized that media interventions "should complement and support the nurturing, responsive care provided to young children by parenting caregivers as well as care by front-line workers and the broader community. Communication can mobilize these workers and the community, building skills and instilling in them a sense of confidence in their ability to support the development of young children in all circumstances" (p. 336).

What's Next?

While this rich resource package from UNICEF pulls together decades of academic and practical experience globally, formative and evaluative research that can assist us on very many levels is sorely missing at this time. In relation to the UNICEF project, for example, we need to evaluate the merit of each individual communication intervention recommended in our package (posters, oral stories, books, animation spots, television programs, radio broadcasts, puppet shows, web links, etc.). We reviewed a wealth of materials from which we have gleaned but a few of the positive examples in order to illustrate the principles and guidelines, while representing a wide range of countries, media, and experiences. In doing so, we had to build on anecdotal data from use of these productions in the field. This was necessary because we did not have systematic research at our disposal to support our grounded, hands-on knowledge and/or our own evaluation of their quality. This gap in the research can be attributed to many causes, including a lack of resources and skilled researchers in these nations; a lack of interest and support for research in these areas of the world; and the historic dominance of research on the negative impact of media on children's lives.

In addition, since the resource package was just launched by UNICEF in fall 2011, we have yet to follow the entire project with systematic evaluative research. Such a project would seek to answer many questions: How helpful is such a resource for various stakeholders who work with children in crisis situations worldwide? What can caregivers, policymakers, educators, development agents, media professionals, and other invested people take from this resource that will help them promote the empowerment of children and families? How do they employ these principles if given opportunities to do so? Such an evaluation endeavor would require a host of longitudinal, multimethod, and multicultural research projects that also seek to account for indirect policy interventions and changes.

As processes of technological and cultural globalization intensify, children's access to various media will become more prevalent, even in the low-resource parts of the world. Several pilot projects have already introduced children living in remote areas to media technologies on an experimental basis, including solar-powered radios, computers, the internet, and mobile phones (e.g., Bachan & Raftree, 2011; Education Development Center, 2009). These innovations have been used in diverse places, such as Rwanda and Afghanistan, and in diverse emergencies, such as earthquakes and hurricanes. Yet, issues of unequal access and inappropriate use of media continue to challenge us to consider certain questions: How can we reach children (and their caregivers) and enrich their lives by using media wisely and responsibly for their well-being and healthy development? How can we use different means of communication to make a difference, most specifically to vulnerable and disadvantaged children, in ways that build resilience, help them to survive and thrive, and set them off on a trajectory toward a better life? The work to answer these questions has only begun.

Notes

1. This chapter is based on previous work, including Kolucki & Lemish, 2011; Lemish & Götz, 2007; Lemish & Götz, 2014; and Lemish & Kolucki, 2013.
2. I am indebted to my colleague Barbara Kolucki and to the Communication for Development Unit of UNICEF for allowing me to share our joint project and to build on their invaluable expertise and insights.

References

Bachan, K., & Raftree, L. (2011). Integrating information and communication technologies into communication for development strategies to support and empower marginalized adolescent girls. Paper presented at the XIIth UN Round Table on Communication for Development, New Delhi, India.

Brenick, A., Lee-Kim, J., Killen, M., Fox, N. Raviv, A., & Leavitt, L. (2007). In D. Lemish & M. Götz (Eds.) *Children and media in times of war and conflict* (pp. 287–308). Cresskill, NJ: Hampton Press.

Carter, C. (2007). Talking about my generation: A critical examination of children's BBC *Newsround* web site discussions about war, conflict, and terrorism. In D. Lemish & M. Götz (Eds.) *Children and media in times of war and conflict* (pp. 121–142). Cresskill, NJ: Hampton Press.

Carter, C., Messenger Davies, M., Allan, S., Mendes, K., Milani, R., & Wass, L. (2009). What do children want from the BBC? Children's content and participatory environments in the age of citizen media. Retrieved from http://www.bbc.co.uk/blogs/knowledgeexchange/cardif-ftwo.pdf

Cochrane, A. (2010). "It shows you how stupid your own side is"—children, media and sectarian division: Studies with primary and preschool children in the UK and Ireland. Paper presented at the conference Growing Up in Divided Societies, Queen's University, Belfast, Ireland.

Cole, C., & Lee, J. (2009). Creating global citizens: The Panwapa Project. *Communication Research Trends, 28*(3), 25–30.

Connolly, P. (2009). Developing programmes to promote ethnic diversity in early childhood: Lessons from Northern Ireland. Working Paper No. 52. The Hague, The Netherlands: Bernard van Leer Foundation.

Connolly, P., Fitzpatrick, S., Gallagher, T., & Harris, P. (2006). Addressing diversity and inclusion in the early years in conflict-affected societies: A case study of the Media Initiative for Children—Northern Ireland. *International Journal of Early Years Education, 14*(3), 263–278.

Dutta, M. J. (2006). Theoretical approaches to entertainment education campaigns: A subaltern critique, *Health Communication, 20*(3), 221–231.

Education Development Center, Inc. (2009). Radio instruction to strengthen education (RISE) in Zanzibar. Retrieved from http://archive.idd.edc.org/resources/print/radioinstruction-zanzibar.pdf

Fisherkeller, J. (Ed.) (2011). *International perspectives on youth media: Cultures of production and education*. New York, NY: Peter Lang.

Jain, S., & Kibria, N. (2009). *Sisimpur, Sesame Street* in Bangladesh: Exploring the challenges in early childhood development. *Journal of Children and Media, 3*(1), 95–100.

Kolucki, B., & Lemish, D. (2011). Communicating with children: Principles and practices that nurture, inspire, excite, educate and heal. Retrieved from http://www.unicef.org/cwc/files/CwC_Web(2).pdf

Komerecki, M. (2010). Documenting capacity development: "Keremet Koch/The Magic Journey." A case study of UNICEF's approach and practice. UNICEF Division of Policy and Practice Working Paper series (draft).

Lee, J. H. (2007). The educational and cultural impact of *Sisimpur*. *TelevIZIon, 20E*, 51–53.

Lemish, D. (2007). Israeli children's TV going to war with Iraq. In D. Lemish & M. Götz (Eds.) *Children and media in times of war and conflict* (pp. 201–214). Cresskill, NJ: Hampton Press.

Lemish, D. (2010). *Screening gender on children's television: The views of producers around the world*. New York, NY: Routledge.

Lemish, D., & Götz, M. (Eds.) (2007). *Children and media in times of war and conflict*. Cresskill, NJ: Hampton Press.

Lemish, D., & Götz, M. (2014). Conflict, media and child well-being. In A. Ben-Arieh, F. Casas, I. Førnes, & J. E. Korbin (Eds.), *Handbook of child well-being: Theories, methods and policies in global perspective* (Volume 4, pp. 2013–2029). Dordrecht, Germany: Springer.

Lemish, D., & Kolucki, B. (2014). Media and early childhood development. In P. L. Britto, P. L. Engle, & C. M. Super (Eds.), *Handbook of early childhood development research and its impact on global policy* (pp. 329–347). New York, NY: Oxford University Press.

Lemish, P. (2007). Developing children's understanding of conflict resolution through quality television. In D. Lemish & M. Götz (Eds.), *Children and media in times of war and conflict* (pp. 215–236). Cresskill, NJ: Hampton Press.

Lemish, P. (2008). Peacebuilding contributions of Northern Ireland producers of children and youth-oriented media. *Journal of Children and Media, 2*(3), 282–299.

Lemish, P., & Scholote, E. (2009). Media portrayals of youth involvement in social change: The roles of agency, praxis, and conflict resolution processes in TV programs. In T. Tufte & F. Enghel (Eds.), *Youth engaging with the world—media, communication, and social change* (pp. 193–215). Göteburg, Sweden: NORDICOM.

Nikken, P., & Götz, M. (2007). Children's writings on the internet about the war in Iraq: A comparison of Dutch and German submissions to guestbooks on children's TV news programs. In D. Lemish & M. Götz (Eds.), *Children and media in times of war and conflict* (pp. 99–119). Cresskill, NJ: Hampton Press.

Nikken, P., & Walma van der Molen, J. H. (2007). "Operation Iraqi freedom" in the children's news: A comparison of consolation strategies used by Dutch and German news producers. In D. Lemish & M. Götz (Eds.), *Children and media in times of war and conflict* (pp. 177–200). Cresskill, NJ: Hampton Press.

Prasad, K. (2009). Communication for development: Reinventing theory and action. New Delhi, India: B.R. World of Books.

Shochat, L. (2003). Our neighborhood: Using entertaining children's television to promote interethnic understanding in Macedonia. *Conflict Resolution Quarterly, 21*(1), 79–93.

Singhal, A., Cody, M., Rogers, E., & Sabido, M. (Eds.) (2004). *Entertainment-education and social change: History, research, and practice.* Mahwah, NJ: Lawrence Erlbaum.

Strohmaier, P. (2007). How TV producers dealt with the war in Iraq in their children's programs. In D. Lemish & M. Götz (Eds.), *Children and media in times of war and conflict* (pp. 143–162). Cresskill, NJ: Hampton Press.

Stuart, J., & Mitchell, C. (2013). Media, participation and social change: Working within a "youth as knowledge producers" framework. In D. Lemish, D. (Ed.), *The Routledge international handbook of children, adolescents and media* (pp. 359–365). New York, NY: Routledge.

United Nations. (1989). Text of the UN Convention on the Rights of the Child. Retrieved from http://www.un.org/documents/ga/res/44/a44r025.htm

Warshel, Y. (2007). "As though there is peace": Opinions of Jewish-Isaeli children about watching *Rechov Sumsum/Shara'a Simsim* amidst armed political conflict. In D. Lemish & M. Götz (Eds.), *Children and media in times of war and conflict* (pp. 309–332). Cresskill, NJ: Hampton Press.

CHAPTER 11

Early Learning, Academic Achievement, and Children's Digital Media Use

Ellen Wartella and Alexis R. Lauricella

Early Learning and Academic Achievement

In 1966, *Sesame Street* founders Joan Ganz Cooney and Lloyd Morrisett asked, "Can television be used to teach young children?" (Sesame Workshop, n.d.). More than 45 years later, we have sufficient evidence that preschool children can learn from quality educational television programming (e.g., Anderson, Huston, Schmitt, Linebarger, & Wright, 2001; Friedrich & Stein, 1973, Wright et al., 2001), but today we are left with many unanswered questions about children's early learning and academic achievement in relation to newer digital media use.

Since the late 1960s when *Sesame Street* and *Mister Rogers' Neighborhood* first aired, many subsequent children's educational television shows have been developed. As a result of these initial educational preschool programs, there is considerable literature on the impact of curriculum-based educational programming on preschool viewers. Decades of research have demonstrated that for preschool-age children, quality educational television can have a positive effect on academic achievement both during the preschool years and beyond (Anderson et al. 2001; Penuel et al., 2012, Wright et al., 2001). However, today, television programs and DVDs are created specifically for very young children (e.g., Baby Einstein), children from birth to age 8 are engaging with media on a range of screen platforms beyond traditional television (Common Sense Media, 2011), and interactive media have been recommended as tools that can be used for education in early childhood programs (National Association for the Education of Young Children and the Fred Rogers Center for Early Learning and Children's Media, 2012). As times and technology have changed, it is important to adapt the original question that sparked the creation of *Sesame Street* to "How can *digital media* best be used to teach young children?"

Importance of the Area

ACCESS AND USE

Today, young children are spending vast amounts of time with media starting at very young ages (Common Sense Media, 2011). The most recent national survey of young children's media use found evidence of young children using a variety of media products starting as young as 6 months of age (Common Sense Media, 2011). This report found that, while TV still dominates children's media use (1 hour and 44 minutes per day), time spent with new media devices is increasing. Access to mobile devices ranges depending on the study and the source. Common Sense Media (2011) reports that more than half (52%) of children have access to newer mobile devices (smartphones, video iPods, iPads or other tablet devices) whereas PlayScience (2011) reports that almost 80% of children between the ages of 2 and 5 and 73% of children between the ages of 6 and 9 have access to a smartphone. Children's access to iPod Touch also increases as children get older, with only 35% of 2- to 5-year-olds having access, compared to 49% of 6- to 9-year-olds (PlayScience, 2011). Newer mobile technology is increasing in access and use by young children, but computers remain a popular and frequently used media device at home. Computers, which most parents (69%) believe help rather than hurt learning (Rideout & Hamel, 2006), are still used frequently among 4- to 8-year-old children (Common Sense Media, 2011).

Technology use is not only occurring in the home; schools are also increasing their use of technology in their classrooms. Recently, schools have increased their access to and use of digital technologies, especially computers with internet, in classrooms (National Education Association, 2008). Specifically, in 1998 the Federal Communications Commission started the E-rate program, subsidizing internet access for public schools serving lower-income students (Federal Communications Commission, 1997). With increased access, more teachers are able to incorporate technology into their classrooms and curriculum. A report by Grunwald Associates (2009) found that K–12 teachers are using digital media often and pre-K teachers (33%) use media in their classrooms with preschool-aged children. Even more recent findings suggest that while home access to newer mobile technologies is increasing rapidly (Common Sense Media, 2013), new technology access remains low for early childhood programs (Wartella, Blackwell, Lauricella, & Robb, 2013). More specifically, research indicates that family child care providers are more likely to have and use TV-based (TV, DVD, VRC) and digital technologies (computers, internet, electronic toys) with young children than teachers in center-based programs (Wartella, Schomburg, Lauricella, Robb, & Flynn, 2010). Recently, the National Association for the Education of Young Children and the Fred Rogers Center for Early Learning and Children's Media (2012) released a joint position statement that encouraged child care professionals to include digital technology as educational tools in their classrooms, suggesting that technology and media can enhance experiences when integrated into the environment, curriculum, and routines of early childhood programs. The decrease in cost of digital technologies together with an endorsement for proper use and increased teacher interest in technology is likely to continue to increase the use of digital technologies for learning outside of the home.

CONTENT AND LEARNING

Not surprisingly, coinciding with the increase in use of media both at home and in school, the range of content available for children from birth to age 8 is vast and growing. Through the Ready to Learn initiative on PBS, as well as the advent of such cable channels devoted to young children as Sprout, Nick Jr., Disney, and Baby First TV, there were more than 50 preschool television shows for child viewers as of 2008 (Hayes, 2008). While for most of the last 45 years television sets provided the major source of educational screen media content, that has changed in the past decade. Now children can access old and newer television content online via YouTube, Netflix, and other online video sites on demand. Moreover, newer digital content is being developed for mobile devices such as smartphones and tablet devices, which seem to be especially successful at capturing the interest of very young learners. Beyond child interest, parents feel that they need media to help them with their children's education (Rideout & Hamel, 2006), and parents frequently report purchasing apps for younger children that focus on literacy or reading, art and creativity, or social-emotional skills (PlayScience, 2011). These beliefs that out-of-school educational media are important to prepare their young children for school success have helped to fuel the explosion of these educational products. Research, however, on these newer devices and on attempts to educate children beyond the core math and literacy concepts has been slow to develop. The combination of increased digital technology use at home and at school, the recent surge in types of digital media products for young children, and the wide array of child-directed content is resulting in new questions about the potential of these digital media and their impact on academic achievement overall.

Major Research Findings

The vast majority of research on early learning and academic achievement from media is based on preschoolers' learning from television content. Two major research studies examined the impact of educational television programs, specifically *Sesame Street*, on current learning and academic achievement (Anderson et al., 2001) and the long-term impact of viewing *Sesame Street* on high school grades and achievement (Huston, Anderson, Wright, Linebarger, & Schmitt, 2001). Educational television programs created with specific academic focuses like literacy or science have also demonstrated success as educational learning tools for kindergarteners and young elementary school–aged children (Penuel et al., 2009; Penuel et al., 2012) in the classroom environment.

HOME MEDIA USE

Decades of research with preschool-aged children have demonstrated that watching educational media at home is positively associated with preschoolers' development of literacy, mathematics and science skills, and prosocial behavior (Comstock & Scharrer, 2007; Fisch, 2004; Friedrich & Stein, 1973; Anderson et al., 2000). Empirical evidence indicates that preschoolers actively watch television (Anderson & Lorch, 1983) and that television viewing in the preschool years can be positively associated with academic and cognitive outcomes. Studies conducted immediately after *Sesame Street* began airing found that preschool-aged children who watched the most *Sesame Street*, learned the most (Ball & Bogatz, 1970). For example, children who viewed more *Sesame Street* performed better on tasks assessing their knowledge of the alphabet, numbers, and shapes, all concepts that had been presented in *Sesame Street* episodes. Similarly, *Reading Rainbow* and *Sesame Street* viewers have better literacy and numeracy skills than their nonviewing peers (Zill, Davies, & Daly, 1994). Research on *Blue's Clues*, a preschool show created to teach problem solving skills, demonstrated that viewing can have positive effects on cognitive development, including performance on pattern perception, creative thinking, and general problem solving tasks (Anderson et al., 2000).

Importantly, the positive effects associated with viewing educational preschool television seem to be even more powerful for at-risk children. The initial studies of *Sesame Street* found that, compared to their advantaged peers, disadvantaged children improved more on academic measures from pretest to posttest after watching *Sesame Street*.(Ball & Bogatz, 1970). More recently, viewing episodes of *Between the Lions*, a preschool educational television program dedicated to improving literacy skills, demonstrated improvements in multiple literacy skills for young children (Linebarger, Kosanic, Greenwood, & Doku,

2004). More specifically, children who were moderately at risk demonstrated gains across all areas of emergent literacy that were featured in the *Between the Lions* episodes.

Not only can viewing educational preschool television programming have a positive impact on current academic skills, but children who viewed educational programs as preschoolers also showed educational benefits some years later. Wright and colleagues (2001) found that children from lower income families who watched *Sesame Street* at ages 2 or 3 had better vocabulary and math skills when they were 5 years old, compared to children who didn't watch *Sesame Street*. Further, high school students who had frequently watched educational television programs, particularly *Sesame Street*, as preschoolers had better grades in their high school years (Anderson et al., 2001; Huston et al., 2001). The authors use the early learning model to explain these findings (Huston et al., 2001), suggesting that early viewing of these educational programs as preschoolers teaches children basic skills that are foundational for future cumulative learning that occurs in their formal education experiences. Therefore, children who watched *Sesame Street* as preschoolers may be entering school more ready to learn than children who did not watch. The authors also acknowledge that other important variables may influence performance including parent involvement and the ways in which watching *Sesame Street* may be related to children's motivation and interest to learn.

Parents and teachers have generally viewed computers more positively than other forms of media, such as TV, in terms of educational potential, largely because they feel that computers are something their children will have to learn to use as working adults (Rideout & Hamel, 2006). Research largely supports that interactive media, primarily computers, can have positive effects on learning (Jackson et al., 2006). Studies of preschoolers' learning from computers found positive effects in multiple domains, including social and emotional development, language and literacy skills, and cognition and general knowledge (see review by Children Now, 2007). As with television programs, the content is essential. Computers are most effective when preschoolers use age-appropriate software. Conversely, Haugland (1992) demonstrated when content is not developmentally appropriate for the audience; creativity can be diminished with use.

CLASSROOMS

For preschoolers, viewing educational television programs as part of a curriculum within a school or center-based program has been associated with increased academic achievement, especially for low-income or at-risk children. Classrooms that participated in a *Between the Lions* intervention in which episodes of the program were shown in the classroom, and where the curriculum was developed around key concepts, improved performance on reading tasks (Linebarger, 2009). Literacy intervention programs that used three different preschool educational television programs (*Super WHY!*, *Sesame Street*, and *Between the Lions*) with low-income preschoolers found these media supplements had positive effects on children's basic literacy skills, including letter recognition and letter sounds (Peneuel et al., 2009; Penuel et al., 2012). Beyond literacy, interventions using *Sid the Science Kid* and *Peep and the Big Wide World*, both science television programs created for preschoolers, in combination with hands-on activities resulted in increased science-related talk at home for low-income preschoolers (Penuel et al., 2010).

Use of computers in preschooler's classrooms has demonstrated positive effects on traditional learning skills and those related to social and emotional development (see ChildrenNow, 2007, for review). A few studies have demonstrated that computer use in the classroom can have positive effects on communication with the teacher (Van Scoter, Ellis, & Railsback, 2001) and other children (Clements, 1994, Haugland & Wright, 1997). Other studies have demonstrated that providing access to computers with reading and math software can positively influence reading readiness skills for kindergarteners (Hess & McGarvey, 1987). In contrast, simply providing access to technology does not automatically result in benefits (Jordan, 2005). Research suggests that many teachers are using technologies to prepare to teach and to communicate but rarely are students in the classroom using the technology (Russell, Bebell, O'Dwyer, & O'Connor, 2003).

EARLY LEARNING FROM MEDIA AND THE VIDEO DEFICIT

Unlike the decades of research available on preschool media use, the focus on infant and toddler media use is relatively new. For the past decade, since the creation of the Baby Einstein series of products in the late 1990s, researchers have begun to explore whether infants and toddlers could learn from media, specifically television and DVDs, in the same way that preschoolers do. To date, there remains scholarly disagreement and many unanswered questions about whether media can be used to enhance early learning and academic achievement for infants and toddlers.

Initial research of infant and toddler media found that infants and toddlers learn better from a real-world adult than they do from a video presentation, thus leading Anderson and Pempek (2005) to coin the term *video deficit*. Evidence in support of this hypothesis has been demonstrated in a range of imitation studies (Barr & Wyss, 2008; Barr & Hayne, 1999; Hayne, Herbert, & Simcock, 2003; Strouse & Troseth, 2008) and object-search task studies (Schmitt & Anderson,

2002; Deocampo & Hudson, 2005; Schmidt, Crawley-Davis, & Anderson, 2007; Troseth & DeLoache, 1998; Troseth, 2003) with infants and toddlers between 12 months and 3 years old. Also, infants and toddlers learn language skills better from a live experience than from a video or televised presentation (Kuhl, Tsao, & Liu, 2003; Naigles & Kako, 1993; Richert, Robb, Fender, & Wartella, 2010). Together there is considerable support for the video deficit effect for infants and toddlers.

However, there is also evidence that under certain circumstances the video deficit effect can be ameliorated and that learning from video can occur. First, repetition of the video presentation increases learning with 12- and 18-month-old infants (Barr, Muentener, Garcia, Fujimoto, & Chavez, 2007). Additionally, with object-search tasks, young children who are given training or opportunities to engage with the television screen acting as a provider of information are better able to use a video presentation as information to successfully find a hidden toy (Nielsen, Simcock, & Jenkins, 2008; Troseth, 2003; Troseth, Saylor, & Archer, 2006). Furthermore, aspects of commercially made videos have also been tested to evaluate learning. Infants can learn a cognitively meaningful seriation task (ordering objects according to size) better from a video presentation when the character on the screen is familiar compared to when the character is unfamiliar (Lauricella, Gola, & Calvert, 2011). Also, toddlers successfully imitated the behaviors demonstrated on video when the video contained a voice-over that provided labels during the demonstration (Barr & Wyss, 2008). These research studies provide some specific examples of opportunities in which young children did learn from media.

However, whether infants and toddlers can learn language from videos is still unclear An experimentally controlled study demonstrated that infants who were exposed to Baby Einstein around age 1 showed greater learning of specific words from the DVD compared to children in the control group who did not view the video (Vandewater, 2011). In contrast, other studies examining infants' language learning from commercially created infant-directed videos have failed to find learning gains (DeLoache et al., 2010; Kuhl et al., 2003; Richert et al., 2010). Overall, the research exploring early learning from media is influenced largely by the context, content, and media platform that the child is engaging with, leaving researchers and parents with more questions about how to use these products with very young children.

New Research and Unanswered Questions

Today young children are growing up in a world surrounded by digital media devices and interactive screens. Young children are using these devices at early ages and their use and access appears to be increasing quickly (Common Sense Media, 2011). Given the vast array of digital media with content created specifically for young children, there are many questions about whether learning can occur from these devices and optimism that these devices can be used to enhance academic achievement. However, to date we have more questions than empirical research to provide answers.

TECHNOLOGY IN THE CLASSROOM

Does technology in the classroom enhance early learning and academic achievement? Many elementary schools in the US have begun to introduce iPads to kindergarten classrooms (Toboni, 2011) but not all schools are collecting data, and it is too early for any longitudinal data to be available. One initial finding from a kindergarten iPad initiative has demonstrated increases in literacy test scores (Roscorla, 2012). Research with older children is beginning to demonstrate the effective use of computers and interactive digital technologies in the classroom and for informal learning (e.g., Kafai & Giang, 2008) but less research has been conducted with younger children in the United States. In Chile, more than 1,200 first- and second-grade students from economically disadvantaged schools participated in an in-school study to determine the effects of video games on learning, motivation, and classroom dynamics (Rosas et al., 2003). Evidence from this study demonstrates that the use of educational video games in the classroom can have positive effects on certain academic skills, including reading comprehension, spelling, and math skills. Also, use of these video games in classrooms results in increased motivation to learn and a positive impact on classroom dynamics (Rosas et al., 2003).

APPS

Do apps on mobile multitouch technologies such as smartphones and tablets enhance learning and academic achievement? The Apple AppStore has an education category for apps and nearly 80% of the top-selling apps in the education category target children (Shuler, 2012). The "general early learning" category is the most popular subject within the AppStore (Shuler, 2012). Not only are there apps created for and targeted to young children, but almost 80% of 2- to 5-year-old children have access to a smartphone, and parents tend to choose apps for their younger children that focus on literacy or math, art and creativity, social-emotional skills, and healthy habits (PlayScience, 2011). While these apps are reported as educational on the AppStore where they are purchased, there has been no published research to date that has evaluated whether children do learn from these app game experiences.

E-BOOKS AND INTERACTIVE BOOKS

Do e-books or computer-based interactive books enhance early learning and academic achievement? There are still many questions about the use of e-books for learning and literacy. Research with traditional books has demonstrated the important role that parent-child interaction has on expressive language (e.g., Whitehurst et al., 1988) and the effect of parent-child reading on emergent literacy and reading achievement (see Bus, van Ijzendoorn, & Pelligrini, 1995, for review). Further, when parents read with young children and ask questions about the story, provide labels explaining aspects of the book, or make requests that the child relate the story content to their own life, children often have higher vocabulary acquisition (Zevenbergen & Whitehurst, 2003). Early studies on electronic books found that parents do engage in some of the same reading styles as they do with traditional books (Fisch, Shylman, Akerman, & Levin, 2002). Research on "talking books," computer-based books that the child can click on to have the character read the words, demonstrates that these types of digital books can improve children's phonological skills (Chera & Wood, 2003). However, other studies of interactive books in which the online book has interactive features that the child can touch, thereby interacting with the actual story, have indicated that the interactive features of the books can influence the books' effectiveness, both positively and negatively (Labbo & Kuhn, 2000). A recent small-scale study by the Joan Ganz Cooney Center found that the enhanced e-book prompted more non-content-related interactions with parents, compared with either the traditional book or the basic e-book (Chiong, Ree, Takeuchi, & Erickson, 2012).

EXECUTIVE FUNCTION AND FUTURE LEARNING

Most of the focus on newer technologies has been on exploring concrete academic-focused learning from digital media. Another question is whether experiences using these devices can have any effect on the development of more global skills that may positively influence learning. Over the last decade, there has been a considerable focus on executive functioning skills and the role that they play on future learning (e.g., Blair & Razza, 2007). Research should examine how interactive technologies like apps that require children to tax and practice their executive functioning abilities (e.g., keeping information in mind, inhibition, planning, and attention) can affect executive function development or general learning skills.

Our Thoughts and Summary

During the television era, *Sesame Street* demonstrated that educational TV could teach children useful content and prepare them for schooling. *Sesame Street's* success was largely a result of an impressive production model, which has continued to be used for the past four decades and which many other successful educational television programs have adapted and used (Cole, Richman, & Brown, 2001). The *Sesame Street* model is to define the educational aim of the program; enlist creative writers and performers to create an engaging show; use formative research to shape and inform the program; and study the effects of the program on child audiences through evaluation research. Today, creators should follow the same model for new digital media: educational aims are crucial and these aims should be appropriate given the unique affordances of new technology. The use of both formative and evaluation research to test and assess the learning objects of digital media products should become routine. Through such research we can develop an understanding of the effectiveness of the special characteristics and affordances for learning from these newer digital technologies.

We are hopeful that we will begin to answer the many questions that arise around new digital technologies, but in order to do so, research needs to be conducted, evaluated, and implemented by those who are creating the new media. In 1996, Joan Ganz Cooney wasn't sure whether television could teach young children, but through research we now know that when television producers create high quality, age-appropriate, educational content, children can learn. More research is needed to fully understand whether and how young children can use new digital media to enhance leaning and academic achievement, but through research we can begin to understand the unique characteristics of digital media that should and can be exploited to make optimal learning materials for young children.

References

Anderson, D. A., Bryant, J., Wilder, W., Santomero, A., Williams, M., & Crawley, A. M. (2000). Researching *Blue's Clues*: Viewing behavior and impact. *Media Psychology, 2,* 179–194.

Anderson, D. A., & Lorch, E. P. (1983). Looking at television: Action or reaction? In Bryant, J. & Anderson, D. (Eds.), *Children's understanding of television*. New York, NY: Academic Press.

Anderson, D. R., Huston, A. C., Schmitt, K. L., Linebarger, D. L., & Wright, J. C. (2001). Early childhood television viewing and adolescent behavior: The recontact study. *Monographs of the Society for Research in Child Development, 66,* 1–147.

Anderson, D. R., & Pempek, T. (2005). TV and very young children, *The American Behavioral Scientist, 48,* 505–522.

Ball, S., & Bogatz, G. A. (1970). First year of *Sesame Street:* An evaluation; a report to the Children's Television Workshop. Princeton, NJ: Educational Testing Service.

Barr, R., & Hayne, H. (1999). Developmental changes in imitation from television during infancy. *Child Development, 70,* 1067–1081.

Barr, R., Muentener, P., Garcia, A., Fujimoto, M., & Chavez, V. (2007). The effect of repetition on imitation from television during infancy. *Developmental Psychobiology, 49,* 196–207.

Barr, R., & Wyss, N. (2008). Reenactment of televised content by 2-year-olds: Toddlers use language learned from television to solve a difficult imitation problem. *Infant Behavior and Development, 31,* 696–703.

Blair, C., & Razz, R. P. (2007). Relating effortful control, executive function, and false belief understanding to emerging math and literacy ability in kindergarten. *Child Development, 78,* 647–663.

Bus, A. G., van Ijzendoorn, M. H., & Pellegrini, A. D. (1995). Joint book reading makes for success in learning to read: A meta-analysis on intergenerational transmission literacy. *Review of Educational Research, 65,* 1–21. doi:10.3102/00346543065001001

Chera, P., & Wood, C. (2003). Animated multimedia "talking books" can promote phonological awareness in children beginning to read. *Learning and Instruction, 13,* 33–52.

Children Now. (2007). The effects of interactive media on preschoolers' learning: A review of the research and recommendations for the future. Retrieved from http://www.childrennow. org/uploads/documents/prek_interactive_learning_2007.pdf

Chiong, C., Ree, J., Takeuchi, L., & Erickson, I. (2012). Print books vs. e-books: Comparing parent-child co-reading on print, basic, and enhanced e-book platforms. Retrieved from http://www.joanganzcooneycenter.org/wp-content/uploads/2012/07/jgcc_ebooks_ quickreport.pdf

Clements, D. H. (1994). The uniqueness of the computer as a learning tool: Insights from research and practice. In J. L. Wright & D. D. Shade (Eds.), *Young children: Active learners in a technological Age* (pp. 31–49). Washington, DC: National Association for the Education of Young Children.

Cole, C. F., Richman, B. A., & Brown, S. A. M. (2001). The world of *Sesame Street* research. In S. M. Fisch & R. T. Truglio (Eds.), *"G" is for growing: Thirty years of research on children and Sesame Street* (pp. 147–180). Mahwah, NJ: Lawrence Erlbaum Associates.

Common Sense Media (2011). Zero to eight: Children's media use in America. Retrieved from http://www.commonsensemedia.org/sites/default/files/research/zerotoeightfinal2011.pdf

Comstock, G., & Scharrer, E. (2007). *Media and the American child.* Burlington, MA: Academic Press.

DeLoache, J. S., Chiong, C., Sherman, K., Islam, N., Vanderborght, M., Troseth, G. L.,...& O'Doherty, K. (2010). Do babies learn from baby media? *Psychological Science, 21,* 1570–1574. doi:10.1177/0956797610384145

Deocampo, J. A., & Hudson, J. A. (2005). Two-year-olds use of video representations to find a hidden toy. *Journal of Cognition and Development, 6,* 229–258.

Federal Communications Commission. (1997). "Commission Implements Telecom Act's Universal Service Provisions," Report No. CC 97–24, CC Docket No. 96–45. Retrieved from http://transition.fcc.gov/Bureaus/Common_Carrier/News_Releases/1997/nrcc7032. html

Fisch, S. M. (2004). *Children's learning from educational television: Sesame Street and beyond.* Mahwah, NJ: Lawrence Erlbaum Associates.

Fisch, S. M., Shulman, J. S., Akerman, A., & Levin, G. A. (2002). Reading Between The Pixels: Parent-Child Interaction While Reading Online Storybooks. *Early Education & Development, 13*(4), 435–451. doi:10.1207/s15566935eed1304_7

Friedrich, L. K., & Stein, A. H. (1973). Aggressive and prosocial television programs and the natural behavior of preschool children. *Monographs of the Society for Research in Child Development, 38,* 1–64.

Grunwald Associates. (2009). Digitally inclined. Annual survey of educators' use of media and technology. Arlington, VA: Public Broadcasting Services.

Haugland, S. W. (1992). The effect of computer software on preschool children's developmental gains. *Journal of Computing in Childhood Education, 3*(1), 15–30.

Haugland, S. W., & Wright, J. L. (1997). *Young children and technology: A world of discovery.* Boston, MA: Allyn and Bacon.

Hayes, D. (2008). *Anytime playdate: Inside the preschool entertainment boom or how television became my baby's best friend.* New York, NY: Free Press.

Hayne, H., Herbert, J., & Simcock, G. (2003). Imitation from television by 24- and 30-months-olds. *Developmental Science, 6,* 254–261.

Hess, R.D., & McGarvey, L. J. (1987). School-relevant effects of educational use of microcomputers in kindergarten classrooms and homes. *Journal of Educational Computing Research, 3,* 269–287.

Huston, A. C., Anderson, D. A., Wright, J. C., Linebarger, D. L, & Schmitt, K. L. (2001). Sesame Street viewers as adolescents: The recontact study. In S. M. Fisch & R. T. Truglio (Eds.), *"G" is for growing: Thirty years of research on children and Sesame Street* (pp. 131–145). Mahwah, NJ: Lawrence Erlbaum Associates.

Jackson, L. A., von Eye, A., Biocca, R. A., Barbatsis, G., Zhao, Y., & Fitzgerald, H. E. (2006). Does home Internet use influence the academic performance of low-income children? *Developmental Psychology, 42,* 429–435. doi:10.1037/0012-1649.42.3.429

Jordan, A. B. (2005). Learning to use books and television: An exploratory study in the ecological perspective. *American Behavioral Scientist, 48,* 523–538. doi:10.1177/0002764204271513

Kafai, Y. B., & Giang, M. T. (2008). Virtual playgrounds: Children's multi-user virtual environments for playing and learning with science, in T. Willoughby and E. Wood, Eds., *Children's learning in a digital world* (pp.). Oxford, UK: Blackwell Publishing Ltd. doi:10.1002/9780470696682.ch8

Kuhl, P. K., Tsao, F-M., & Liu, H.-M. (2003). Foreign-language experience in infancy: Effects of short-term exposure and social interaction on phonetic learning. *Proceedings of the National Academy of Science, 100,* 9096–9101.

Labbo, L. D., & Kuhn, M. R. (2000). Weaving chains of affect and cognition: A young child's understanding of CD-ROM talking books. *Journal of Literacy Research, 32,* 187–210.

Lauricella, A. R., Gola, A. H., & Calvert, S. L. (2011). Toddlers' learning from socially meaningful video characters. *Media Psychology, 14,* 216–232.

Linebarger, D. L (2009). Evaluation of the *Between the Lions* Mississippi literacy initiative: 2007–2008. Retrieved from http://pbskids.org/lions/parentsteachers/pdf/Linebarger_2009.pdf

Linebarger, D. L., Kosanic, A. Z., Greenwood, C. R., & Doku, N. S. (2004). Effects of viewing the television program *Between the Lions* on the emergent literacy skills of young children. *Journal of Educational Psychology, 96,* 297–308. doi:10.1037/0022-0663.96.2.297

Naigles, L. R., & Kako, E. T. (1993). First contact in verb acquisition: Defining a role for syntax. *Child Development, 64,* 1665–1687.

National Education Association (2008). Access, adequacy and equity in education technology: Results of a survey of America's teachers and support professionals on technology in public schools and classrooms. Retrieved from http://www.edutopia.org/pdfs/NEA-Access,Adequacy,andEquityinEdTech.pdf

National Association for the Education of Young Children and the Fred Rogers Center for Early Learning and Children's Media. (2012). Technology and interactive media as tools in early childhood programs serving children from birth through age 8. Joint position statement. Retrieved from http://www.naeyc.org/files/naeyc/file/positions/PS_technology_WEB2.pdf

Nielsen, M., Simcock, G., & Jenkins, L. (2008). The effect of social engagement on 24-month-olds' imitation from live and televised models. *Developmental Science, 11,* 722–731.

Penuel, W. R., Bates, L., Gallagher, L. P., Pasnik, S., Llorente, C., Townsend, E., ... & Vanderborght, M. (2012). Supplementing literacy instruction with media-rich intervention: Results of a randomized controlled trial. *Early Childhood Research Quarterly, 27,* 115–127.

Penuel, W. R., Bates, L., Pasnik, S., Townsend, E., Gallagher, L. P., Llorente, C., & Hupert, N. (2010). The inmpact of a media-rich science curriculum on low-income preschoolers' science talk. In *Proceedings of the 9th International Conference of the Learning Sciences, 1,* 238–245. ICLS'10. Chicago, Illinois: International Society of the Learning Sciences, 2010. http://dl.acm.org/citation.cfm?id=1854360.1854391.

Penuel, W. R., Pasnik, S., Bates, L., Townsend, E., Gallagher, L. P., Llorente, C., & Hupert, N. (2009). Preschool teachers can use a media-rich curriculum to prepare low-income children for school success: Results of a randomized controlled trial. New York, NY, and Menlo Park, CA: Education Development Center, Inc. and SRI International.

PlayScience. (2011). Mobile playgrounds: Kids, families, and mobile play. *PlayScience LabReport, 2,* 1–4. Retrieved from http://playsciencelab.com/LabReport/MobilePlaygrounds_LabReport. pdf

Richert, R. A., Robb, M. B., Fender, J. G., & Wartella, E. (2010). Word learning from baby videos. *Archives of Pediatrics & Adolescent Medicine, 164,* 432–437.

Rideout, V., & Hamel, R. (2006). The media family: Electronic media in the lives of infants, toddlers, preschoolers, and their parents. Menlo Park, CA: Kaiser Family Foundation.

Rosas, R., Nussbaum, M., Cumsille, P., Marianov, V., Correa, M., Flores, P., ... & Salina, M. (2003). Beyond Nintendo: Design and assessment of educational video games for first and second grade students. *Computers & Education, 40,* 71–94.

Roscorla, T. (2012, February 16). iPad kindergarten research starts turning up results. *Converge.* Retrieved from http://www.convergemag.com/classtech/iPad-Kindergarten-Research.html

Russell, M., Bebell, D., O'Dwyer, L., & O'Connor, K. (2003). Examining Teacher Technology Use Implications for Preservice and Inservice Teacher Preparation. *Journal of Teacher Education, 54*(4), 297–310. doi:10.1177/0022487103255985

Schmidt, M. E., Crawley-Davis, A. M., & Anderson, D. R. (2007): Two-year-olds' object retrieval based on television: Testing a perceptual account, *Media Psychology, 9,* 389–409.

Schmitt, K. L., & Anderson, D. R. (2002). Television and reality: Toddlers' use of visual information from video to guide behavior. *Media Psychology, 4,* 51–76.

Sesame Workshop (n.d.). 40 years and counting. Retrieved from http://www.sesameworkshop. org/our impact/40-years.html

Shuler, C. (2012). iLearnII: An analysis of the education category of the iTune AppStore. New York, NY: The Joan Ganz Cooney Center at Sesame Workshop

Strouse, G. A., & Troseth, G. L. (2008). "Don't try this at home": Toddlers' imitation of new skills from people on video. *Journal of Experimental Child Psychology, 101,* 262–280.

Toboni, G. (2011, September 14). Apple iPad for kindergarten students? Schools try them. *ABC Good Morning America.* Retrieved from http://abcnews.go.com/Technology/apple-ipad-learning-tool-kindergarten-maine-tennessee-south/story?id=14509290#.UAmlsDFWqxo

Troseth, G. L. (2003). Getting a clear picture: young children's understanding of a televised image. *Developmental Science, 6,* 247–253.

Troseth, G. L., & DeLoache, J. S. (1998). The medium can obscure the message: Young children's understanding of video. *Child Development, 69,* 950–965.

Troseth, G. L., Saylor, M. M., & Archer, A. H. (2006). Young children's use of video as a source of socially relevant information. *Child Development, 77,* 786–799.

Vandewater, E. A. (2011). Infant word learning from commercially available video in the US. *Journal of Children and Media, 5,* 248–266. doi: 10.1080/17482798.2011.584375

Van Scoter, J., Ellis, D., & Railsback, J. (2001). Technology in early childhood education: finding the balance. Portland, OR: Northwest Regional Educational Laboratory. Retrieved from http://www.netc.org/earlyconnections/byrequest.pdf

Wartella, E., Schomburg, R. L., Lauricella, A. R., Robb, M., & Flynn, R. (2010). Technology in the lives of teachers and classrooms: Survey of classroom teachers and family child care providers. Report for the Fred Rogers Center. Latrobe, PA.

Wartella, E., Blackwell, C. K., Lauricella, A. R., & Robb, M. (2013). Technology in the lives of educators and early childhood programs. Report for the Fred Rogers Center, Latrobe, PA and the Center on Media and Human Development, Evanston, IL.

Whitehurst, G. J., Falco, F. L., Lonigan, C. J., Fischel, J. E., DeBaryshe, B. D., Valdez-Menchaca, M. C., & Caulfield, M. (1988). Accelerating language development through picture book reading. *Developmental Psychology, 24*(4), 552–559. doi:10.1037/0012-1649. 24.4.552

Wright, J. C., Huston, A. C., Murphy, K. C., St Peters, M., Pinon, M., Scantlin, R., & Kotler, J. (2001). The relations of early television viewing to school readiness and vocabulary of children from low-income families: The early window project. *Child Development, 72,* 1347–1366. doi: 10.1111/1467-8624.t01-1-00352

Zevenbergen, A. A., & Whitehurst, G. J. (2003). Dialogic reading: A shared picture book reading intervention for preschoolers. In A.Van Kleeck, S. A. Stahl, & E. B. Bauer (Eds.), *On reading books to children: Parents and teachers* (pp. 170–194). Mahwah, NJ: Lawrence Erlbaum.

Zill, N., Davies, E., & Daly, M. (1994). Viewing of Sesame Street by preschool children in the United States and its relation to school readiness. Rockville, MD: Westat, Inc.

CHAPTER 12

Children's Parasocial Relationships

Sandra L. Calvert and Melissa N. Richards

Children's Parasocial Relationships

Children's media have historically been rooted in characters—from the early days of Captain Kangaroo and Howdy Doody to the contemporary era of Dora the Explorer and Elmo. Unlike any previous technological age, however, characters now travel across media platforms such as television, computers, and mobile technologies through programs, advertisements, games, and mobile apps. This transmedia experience is enhanced by a transenvironment experience that brings onscreen characters into homes through this multitude of screen media and branded toys, foods, and clothes. More than any other generation, our children live in a world that is populated with influential media characters from the earliest days of their lives.

Little is known, however, about the underlying reasons for why or how characters influence children's learning or interests. We argue here that parasocial relationships—one-sided, emotionally tinged friendships that develop between an audience member and a media character (Horton & Wohl, 1956)—are a key underlying reason for media characters' influence on children's developmental outcomes. More specifically, we propose that children perceive their favorite media characters as persons who become trusted friends, a perception that then influences the credibility that they give to the character's messages about a range of topics, including prosocial behaviors, STEM (i.e., Science, Technology, Engineering, and Mathematics) and language learning, and food consumption. In this chapter, we examine what parasocial relationships are, how they influence children's learning and behavior, how they develop, and how to measure them.

Similarities between Children's Relationships with People and Media Characters

Children's worlds are densely populated with media characters from very early ages. Media characters are invited into children's homes through television and video programs, movies, online interactive programs at websites, video game play, and apps played on mobile media, such as tablets (e.g., iPads) and mobile phones (Common Sense Media, 2013). Children play with toys that are replicas of their favorite characters and wear clothing depicting their favorite characters (Rideout & Hamel, 2006). Children also see these characters when they leave their homes, e.g., at a grocery store or fast food restaurant on food and beverage packaging. Through these transenvironment experiences that bridge the symbolic and actual worlds of children, media characters are accessible virtually everywhere children are.

Although media characters saturate children's transmedia environments, 0- to 8-year-old children's primary exposure to media characters is through screen media, in which they invest an average of 1 hour and 55 minutes per day (Common Sense Media, 2013). Learning from screens, however, can be considerably challenging for very young children. Research demonstrates that prior to age 3, very young children learn from live presentations better than from video ones, a phenomenon known as the video deficit (Anderson & Pempek, 2005; see also chapter 11).

Arguments have also been advanced that children's learning is superior from live rather than animated media characters, and that this pattern continues throughout the preschool years (Richert, Robb, & Smith, 2011). One reason that young children's learning from video is presumably better from live characters is due to the reality versus fantasy status of actual people versus animated characters (Richert et al., 2011). However, parents report that their preschool-aged children think that their *favorite* onscreen characters are *real*, can see and hear what they are saying, and experience life beyond the screen, even when that character is animated (Bond & Calvert, in press; Dorr, 1986). Similarly, Hawkins and Pingree (1981) found that young children believed that television characters lived in the television set and that these characters heard the child viewers talking to them.

Why do some young children think and act like their favorite media characters are real? Consider the qualities of face-to-face interpersonal relationships and those of parasocial relationships. Both social and parasocial companions have names, an important indicator of *personhood* (Calvert, 2002). Media characters are embodied; they have human-like features such as eyes, ears, a nose, and a mouth, just like people do. Characters have a gender and often an ethnic background, both of which are important determinants of friendship patterns with actual children (Graham & Cohen, 1997), and of character preferences (Calvert, Strong, Jacobs, & Conger, 2007). When depicted in programs, media characters, like real people, have friends, and some have families or pets (e.g., Emily's big, red animated dog named Clifford). Often characters have life stories that include experiences that are familiar to children, such as when the Taiwanese character DoDo jumps in puddles after it rains or invites his friends to his birthday party (Calvert, 2012). Media characters also experience the negotiations that are needed to find cooperative solutions with other media friends during the inevitable conflict situations that occur in close relationships.

Media characters play with each other onscreen as children play with one another, and they are also readily accessible to children as toys in their homes, making them potential playmates. Early childhood is a time in development characterized by imaginative activities and beliefs in imaginary friends and in mythological cultural icons, such as Santa Claus and the Easter Bunny (Calvert, 1999; Singer & Singer, 2005; Valkenburg & Calvert, 2012). Many parents encourage their children to believe that these beings, as well as certain media characters, are real. During play sessions, for instance, parents foster children's beliefs that these characters are "persons" by asking their child to show affection toward the character (e.g., by hugging or kissing them), and by encouraging their child to nurture the character by pretending to feed them and put them to sleep (Calvert, Richards, & Kent, 2013; Gola, Richards, Lauricella, & Calvert, 2013). These behaviors are consistent with young children's characteristic style of animistic thinking in which children give human attributes to inanimate objects, such as bestowing life, consciousness, and will upon them (Piaget, Tomilson, & Tomilson, 2007).

Repeated exposure to a media character has been correlated with perceptions of realism. For instance, 5- and 7-year-old children who watched more educational children's programs or cartoons were more likely to perceive the characters in those programs as real (Wright, Huston, Reitz, & Piemyat, 1994). Now the main characters in children's programs often speak directly to children and simulate contingency by having a character ask questions and then pause for the child to respond, a practice that facilitates interaction with the onscreen character that is also similar to how children interact with their friends (Anderson, et al., 2000; Calvert, 2006; Calvert et al., 2007; Giles, 2002). Finally, just as in real friendships, children "break up" with media characters as their parasocial relationships wane over time. Children may outgrow the character, find a new character that is more appealing, or get bored with the character, much as they do with their off-screen friends (Bond & Calvert, 2013). Not surprisingly, the older children are, the more likely they are to have broken up with a favorite media character: only 0.1% of children under the age of 2, 37% of 2- to 5-year-old children, and 75% of 5- to 8-year-old children had broken up with a favorite media character, as reported by their parents (Bond & Calvert, 2013).

Characters also break up with child audiences. For instance, the live character Steve from the children's program *Blue's Clues* left the program to be replaced by the live character Joe. The way that children feel when they break up with a media character may depend largely on the strength of the relationship that they have with that character. For instance, research on parasocial breakups in young adults suggests that stronger parasocial relationships were positively associated with more distressed feelings when their favorite character's television show went off the air (Eyal & Cohen, 2006).

The relationships that children develop with media characters, then, bear considerable similarity to children's off-screen social relationships (Giles, 2002). Rather than wonder why many young children think that their favorite characters are real, a better question may be to ask why young children would *not* think these characters are real and potentially worthy of their trust.

Influences of Parasocial Relationships with Media Characters

Given the parallels between the way that children bond in their interpersonal relationships with face-to-face others and with media characters, emerging questions to ask include how important these relationships are to children and whether they influence children's learning and behavior. Relationships with media characters certainly influence adults. Early research suggested that adult audiences bestowed considerable trust on newscasters that the audience selectively viewed (Rubin, Perse, & Powell, 1985). The term *parasocial interaction* was used to describe these relationships, as newscasters looked directly into the camera lens while speaking to the audience. The adult literature is now drawing a distinction between parasocial interactions, which can occur at one point in time, and a parasocial relationship, which involves cross-situational exposures to a character in which a deeper, ongoing relationship develops (Schramm & Hartmann, 2008).

In the children's literature, Krcmar (2010) drew a similar distinction between social meaningfulness and social contingency. When comparing toddlers' imitation of their onscreen mother (i.e., a socially meaningful other) to their imitation of an onscreen stranger (i.e., a socially irrelevant other), Krcmar (2010) found that toddlers imitated their mother more often than the stranger, thereby supporting the importance of social meaningfulness in early learning from screens. Consistent with these arguments, we found that viewing a video demonstration by a meaningful media character increased toddlers' seriation of objects (a STEM task), but observing an unknown media character did not (Lauricella, Gola, & Calvert, 2011).

In a follow-up study, we were able to build a meaningful, parasocial relationship between toddlers and the unknown character through exposure to videos and to parent-child toy play with a puppet of the character. The familiarized character group subsequently performed better on a seriation task that was demonstrated by that character when compared to a no-exposure control group. By contrast, an unfamiliar character group who viewed the seriation demonstration did not perform any better than the no-exposure control group. Within the familiarized character condition, engaging in prosocial nurturant behaviors directed at a puppet version of the character during prior play sessions predicted toddlers' subsequent seriation scores. These emotionally tinged nurturing behaviors, such as putting the character down for a nap, demonstrated the early formation of children's parasocial relationships with a media character (Gola et al., 2013).

Interactive media also provide opportunities to create a parasocial relationship as a character responds contingently to what children do, as well as to who they are. When compared to a control group who did not receive an interactive toy, for example, toddlers learned a subsequent seriation task from a video presentation better when the toddlers had previously played over time with an interactive character who had been personalized to them (e.g., the character called the child by his or her name, was the same gender as the child, had the same favorite food); by contrast, toddlers did not learn better than the control group when they had played over time with an interactive character who was dissimilar to them (e.g., the character called the child a generic name, was not the same gender as the child, had a different favorite food from the child; Calvert, Richards, & Kent, 2013). Similarly, contingent replies by meaningful characters can increase children's language skills. In particular, 3- to 7-year-old children who played a *Martha Speaks: Dog Party* app demonstrated vocabulary gains for targeted words, and literacy gains also emerged for children who played a *SuperWhy!* app (Chiong & Shuler, 2010). Interactivity may assist learning, in part, because the characters respond contingently to children and/or because children become very engaged with the characters and the content (Calvert, Strong, & Gallagher, 2005).

An additional function that media characters serve is to represent and to sell specific brands of foods, most of which have been documented to be low in nutrients and high in calories (Institute of Medicine, 2006). Consequently, the role that these characters play in the worldwide pediatric obesity crisis has been under considerable scrutiny (Institute of Medicine, 2006, 2012). Branded characters like McDonald's Ronald McDonald and General Mills's Trix Rabbit appear in numerous settings where children come into contact with them, such as television commercials, online marketing, grocery stores, and quick serve restaurants (Calvert, 2008). An evidentiary review of the extant literature on marketing and obesity led Institute of Medicine committees in 2006 and 2012 to recommend changes in marketing practices directed at children. In particular, the IOM committees suggested that marketers use the power of media characters to "sell" healthy rather than unhealthy products to children because of children's unique relationships with these characters, such as placing their trust in them.

By 2 to 6 years of age, children already recognize branded characters and associate them with products (Lapierre, Vaala, & Linebarger, 2011). These positive feelings about characters—which represent a dimension of a parasocial relationship—also influence children's food preferences. For example, children who saw popular media characters on a cereal box liked the taste of the breakfast cereal more than children who saw a nearly identical cereal box without those media characters, an outcome which was attributed to classical conditioning (Lapierre et al., 2011; Roberto, Baik, Harris, & Brownell, 2010). Similarly, Kotler, Schiffman, and Hanson (2012) found that young children were more likely to select foods paired with a picture of familiar *Sesame Street* characters than to select foods with unfamiliar generic characters when the two foods were similar (e.g., two vegetables). However, the characters were not as influential if the food paired with the popular character did not taste as good (e.g., a vegetable versus a salty or sugary snack). Nor were Dutch children who saw the popular U.S. characters of Dora the Explorer or SpongeBob SquarePants on their food packages more likely to select that food for a snack than foods that had a picture of an unfamiliar animated character on them (DeDroog, Valkenburg, & Buijzen, 2011).

A limitation of the existing research is that these studies use familiarity and overall audience popularity as a way to index the power of the character to influence children's preferences, rather than measuring the children's parasocial relationship with specific characters. Indeed, the underlying reason that these characters may lead to positive feelings about brands, and hence be effective in influencing children's perceptions of taste, may be because children develop a personal relationship with specific media characters; that is, the strength of a parasocial relationship with a meaningful character may influence the character's relative persuasiveness, as was the case in children's learning of seriation tasks (Calvert et al., 2013; Gola et al., 2013).

Measuring Children's Parasocial Relationships with Media Characters

Even though meaningful onscreen characters and people are influencing children's early learning, we have few measures for assessing the strength of parasocial relationships (Hoffner, 2008). What exactly is a parasocial relationship in childhood? At what point is the indicator of a parasocial relationship more than mere familiarity with the character? Nurturing the character is a behavioral approach for operationalizing an emotionally tinged, parasocial relationship with a media character (Calvert et al., 2013; Gola et al., 2013). Another approach is to investigate children's favorite characters, an approach that has been used to tap into the construct of parasocial relationships among grade school children (Hoffner, 1996) and, we believe, would likely be an appropriate method with even younger children.

Using a parent survey consisting of Likert scale items to describe their 6-month to 8-year-old children's parasocial relationships with characters (which were called "favorite characters" in the survey), Bond and Calvert (in press) found that parents (n = 146) reported three major components of children's parasocial relationships. These are *character personification* (e.g., the child trusts the character, treats the character as a friend, thinks the character has thoughts and emotions); *attachment* (e.g., the character makes the child feel safe; the character's voice soothes the child); and *social realism* (e.g., the child thinks the character is real). These three factors accounted for 58.89% of the variance in parents' descriptions of their children's parasocial relationships with favorite media characters (see Figure 12.1).

Many parents encourage their children to treat characters as if they have thoughts and intentions (i.e., that the characters have minds), which is an essential part of *character personification* (Bond & Calvert, in press). As friends and playmates, characters also offer children opportunities to practice social skills that are part of the vertical relationships (parent-to-child or teacher-to-child) in which initial social skills are acquired, as well as horizontal relationships (peer-to-peer) in which children refine those social skills by practicing them with their friends (Hartup, 1989). For instance, children can engage in vertical prosocial caretaking behaviors with toy versions of characters (e.g., feeding them), practicing the same kinds of actions that their parents do with them (Calvert et al., 2013; Gola et al., 2013). Children can also play with toy versions of a character on an equal basis as a friend in a horizontal relationship (e.g., pretend play).

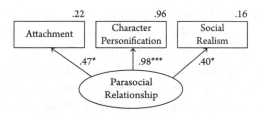

Figure 12.1 Components of Children's Parasocial Relationships with Favorite Media Characters.

As children come to think of characters as *persons*, they may also begin to trust them as friends. When Corriveau and Harris (2009) exposed 3- to 5-year-old children to a video featuring a familiar or unfamiliar teacher who was accurate or inaccurate in labeling words that the children knew, the teacher's accuracy made little difference for 3-year-olds who continued to trust her when she labeled objects that were unfamiliar to them. The 5-year-olds showed even stronger preferences for the familiar teacher if she had been accurate in labeling familiar objects. The authors argued that children's trust in the familiar over the unfamiliar teacher, particularly at the youngest ages, is based on their prior positive emotional feelings experienced during repeated interactions with their teachers. We argue that very young children may come to trust familiar media characters more so than unfamiliar characters because of their extensive, personal experience with them.

Attachment, a motivational-behavioral control system that is preferentially responsive to a small number of caregivers (Bowlby, 1969), may be a key component of parasocial relationships, because the warmth and predictability of characters may result in the child feeling secure (Bond & Calvert, in press). Media characters are highly predictable over time because they are scripted (Calvert, 2012). Television and computer programs (and now apps) are experienced repeatedly, allowing children to predict what will come next, and children may develop emotional relationships with some of these characters. Because characters are readily available across multiple platforms, children can seek out security in these characters in a variety of settings. For example, a child who identifies Dora from the animated television program *Dora the Explorer* as her favorite character may see Dora on television at home, interact with her on a mobile device while waiting in line with parents at the grocery store, or play with her as a plush toy at the doctor's office. Characters in the form of plush toys can provide contact comfort for young children, just as teddy bears have traditionally been used in Western cultures: children may cuddle up and sleep with them each night or hold on to them as they wait at the doctor's office.

Finally, *social realism*—that the child thought the character was real—emerged as a component of parasocial relationships (Bond & Calvert, in press). This finding puts us at odds with those who argue that preschool-aged children know that media characters are imaginary, and hence, that these characters should have less influence than real people (Richert et al., 2011). Rather, our findings are consistent with those indicating that 5- and 7-year-old children believe that their favorite characters are real (Wright et al., 1994): parents in our study of 6-month to 8-year-old children reported no age differences in the belief that the characters were real (Bond & Calvert, in press). In fact, preoperational thought continues until age 7 on average

(Piaget et al., 2007), so children may still believe that their favorite characters are real as they spend considerable time viewing and interacting with these preferred "persons."

The Development of Children's Parasocial Relationships

At what point in development do parasocial relationships emerge? What role do environmental factors play in this development? To answer these questions, Bond and Calvert (in press) also asked parents Likert-type questions to test a model of early parasocial relationship development between their children and their favorite media characters. This model is depicted in Figure 12.2.

Our model suggests an integral role for parents in the development of their children's parasocial relationships. Specifically, parents who encourage their children to treat a media character "as if" that character is a friend who has thoughts, emotions, feelings, needs, and wants are most likely to have children who develop a parasocial relationship with that character. Another significant effect is found for children's play with a toy media character and the development of a parasocial relationship with that character. That is, children who play with toy versions of their favorite media character are more likely to develop a parasocial relationship with that media character. Repeated exposure to a media character across platforms was mediated by parasocial interaction, that is, the frequency with which the child tried to interact with onscreen characters while using media devices. Parasocial interaction then directly predicted parasocial relationship development. Toy play and parental mediation can also go through parasocial interaction en route to influencing the development of a parasocial relationship, though they can also take a direct route, bypassing the

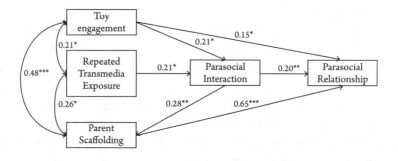

Figure 12.2 The Development of Children's Parasocial Relationships with Favorite Media Characters.

parasocial interaction. Put another way, a direct route means that engagement with a toy media character per se can lead to the development of a parasocial relationship with that character. Overall, then, we found that environmental influences outside of media screens play an extremely important role in the development of parasocial relationships with characters who have their origins onscreen.

Future Research Directions

The emerging literature on children's parasocial relationships with media characters provides a glimpse of the promise that they hold for children's developmental outcomes. A key future research direction involves the development of more accurate, concise, and valid measures of parasocial relationships that young children, rather than their parents, can complete. Measures need to move away from current practices of overall audience trends to more specific examinations of favorite characters as well as behavioral measures, such as personalization scores during play with toy representations of media characters. This type of delineation would add to our understanding of how specific characters influence children's learning in everyday settings where they choose exposure, rather than as a captive audience in experimental media studies.

Another goal is to separate and then link parasocial relationships (which involve the deep-rooted meaningfulness of a child for a character) from parasocial interactions (circumstances in which characters talk to and interact with children and children reply to them). Are children, for instance, more likely to form parasocial relationships with characters who talk to them versus those who do not? If one looks at practices of young children's television programs, it appears that this belief is the popular consensus of broadcasters, because many characters in young children's programming now pause and interact with the audience (Calvert, 2006).

Additionally, an examination of the links among parasocial relationships and role models is needed. In vertical relationships, friends sometimes serve as models that can guide another's behaviors through a desire or wish to be like them. Friendships can also be horizontal relationships, where the two individuals typically have equal power. The link between the kinds of processes that occur in children's vertical and horizontal relationships with media characters should be studied to uncover the important implications for how and how well media characters can serve as children's early teachers.

Research is needed about how characters and parental scaffolding of parasocial relationships seamlessly unify children's multiplatform digital world. More investigation is needed to elucidate how children easily switch platforms and environments with the help of media characters. In addition, understanding the role that parents play in their child's formation of parasocial relationships with these media characters will likely enhance our understanding of the foundations and widespread nature of parasocial relationships.

Finally, not all parasocial relationships may lead to desirable outcomes. For instance, relationships with media characters that market unhealthy foods may be a driving force of the obesity crisis (Institute of Medicine, 2006, 2012), or even of antisocial behavior if children choose a villain as a favorite character. Research is needed to determine which children are most likely to form parasocial relationships with characters that may have adverse effects on their development, and how those relationships can be terminated in favor of healthier ones.

Conclusion

Parasocial relationships have enormous potential to influence children's developmental outcomes, including prosocial behaviors, STEM learning, language acquisition, and consumption of specific foods. A challenge for this line of research involves measurement: an actual parasocial relationship with a media character needs to be separated from proxies like familiarity and the overall audience popularity of a media character. Adults and children alike know many people quite well who they do not like or trust, and the same can be said for their feelings about media characters. Behavioral measures, such as those that tap into the personal relationships that children form with media characters, are one such option.

What can be said with certainty is that media characters permeate the worlds of children, and that children's relationships with characters are often treated just as their relationships with real children. As scholars and educators, we should seize this moment and optimize the opportunities that children's parasocial relationships with media characters afford for early constructive social, cognitive, and physical developmental outcomes.

Acknowledgments

This chapter was supported by grants from the National Science Foundation (NSF#0126014; NSF#1252113; NSF#1251745). We gratefully acknowledge their support of this research.

References

Anderson, D. A., & Pempek, T. A. (2005). Television and very young children. *American Behavioral Scientist, 48*, 505–522.

Anderson, D. R., Bryant, J., Wilder, A., Santomero, A., Williams, M., & Crawley, A. M. (2000). Researching *Blue's Clues*: Viewing behavior and impact. *Media Psychology, 2*, 179–194. doi:10.1207/S1532785XMEP0202_4

Bond, B. J., & Calvert, S. L. (in press). A model and measure of U.S. parents' perceptions of young children's parasocial relationships. *Journal of Children and Media.*

Bond, B. J. & Calvert, S.L. (2013b). Parasocial breakup with media characters during early childhood. Paper presented at the National Communication Association, Washington, DC.

Bowlby, J. (1969). *Attachment and loss.* New York, NY: Basic Books.

Calvert, S. L. (1999). *Children's journeys through the information age.* Boston, MA: McGraw Hill.

Calvert, S. L. (2002). Identity on the internet. In S. L. Calvert, A. B. Jordan, & R. R. Cocking (Eds.), *Children in the digital age: Influences of electronic media on development* (pp. 57–70). Westport, CT: Praeger.

Calvert, S. L. (2006). Media and early development. In K. McCartney & D. A. Phillips (Eds.) *Blackwell Handbook of Early Childhood Development* (pp. 843–879). Boston, MA: Blackwell.

Calvert, S. L. (2008). Children as consumers: Advertising and marketing. *The Future of Children, 18*, 205–225.

Calvert, S. L. (2012). Educational media. Invited presentation given at the U.S. State Department, Skyope, Macedonia.

Calvert, S. L., Richards, M. N., & Kent, C. (2013). Interactive media characters for toddlers' early STEM learning. Paper presented at the Society for Research in Child Development, Seattle, WA.

Calvert, S. L., Strong, B., & Gallagher, L. (2005). Control as an engagement feature for young children's attention to, and learning of, computer content. *American Behavioral Scientist, 48*, 578–589. doi:10.1177/0002764204271507

Calvert, S. L., Strong, B. L., Jacobs, E. L., & Conger, E. E. (2007). Interaction and participation for young Hispanic and Caucasian children's learning of media content. *Media Psychology, 9*(2), 431–445. doi:10.1080/15213260701291379

Chiong, C., & Shuler, C. (2010). Learning: Is there an app for that? New York, NY: The Joan Ganz Cooney Center at Sesame Workshop.

Common Sense Media (2013). *Zero to eight: Children's media use in America.* San Francisco, CA: Common Sense Media. Retrieved from http://www.commonsensemedia.org/research/zero-to-eight-childrens-media-use-in-america-2013

Corriveau, K., and Harris, P. L. (2009), Choosing your informant: weighing familiarity and recent accuracy. *Developmental Science, 12*, 426–437. doi:10.1111/j.1467-7687.2008.00792.x

DeDroog, S. M., Valkenburg, P. M., & Buijzen, M. (2011).Using brand characters to promote young children's liking of and purchase requests for fruit. *Journal of Health Communication, 16*, 79–89. doi:10.1080/10810730.2010.529487

Dorr, A. (1986). *Television and children: A special medium for a special audience.* Beverly Hills, CA: Sage Publications.

Eyal, K., & Cohen, J. (2006). When good friends say goodbye: A parasocial breakup study. *Journal of Broadcasting and Electronic Media, 50*, 502–523. doi:10.1207/s15506878jobem5003_9

Giles, D. C. (2002). Parasocial interaction: A review of the literature and a model for future research. *Media Psychology, 4*, 279–305. doi:10.1207/S1532785XMEP0403_04

Gola, A. A. H., Richards, M. N., Lauricella, A. R., & Calvert, S. L. (2013). Building meaningful parasocial relationships between toddlers and media characters to promote early mathematical skills. *Media Psychology, 16,* 390–411. doi:10.1080/15213269.2013.783774

Graham, J. A., & Cohen, R. (1997). Race and sex as factors in children's sociometric ratings and friendship choices. *Social Development, 6,* 355–372. doi:10.1111/j.1467–9507.1997. tb00111.x

Hartup, W. (1989). Social relationships and their developmental significance. *American Psychologist, 44,* 120–126. doi:10.1037/0003–066X.44.2.120

Hawkins, R. P., & Pingree S. (1981). Using television to construct social reality. *Journal of Broadcasting, 25,* 347–364. doi:10.1080/08838158109386459

Hoffner, C. (1996). Children's wishful identification and parasocial interaction with favorite television characters. *Journal of Broadcasting & Electronic Media, 40,* 389–402. doi:10.1080/08838159609364360

Hoffner, C. (2008). Parasocial and online social relationships. In S. L. Calvert & B. J. Wilson (Eds.), *The handbook of children, media, and development* (pp. 309–333). Malden, MA: Wiley-Blackwell.

Horton, D., & Wohl, R. R. (1956). Mass communication and para-social interaction: Observations on intimacy at a distance. *Psychiatry, 19,* 215–229.

Institute of Medicine. (2006). *Food marketing to children and youth: Threat or opportunity?* Washington, DC: The National Academies Press.

Institute of Medicine. (2012). *Accelerating progress in obesity prevention: Solving the weight of the nation.* Washington, DC: The National Academies Press.

Kotler, J. A., Schiffman, J. M., & Hanson, K. G. (2012). The influence of media characters on children's food choices. *Journal of Health Communication, 17,* 886–898. doi:10.1080/1081 0730.2011.650822

Krcmar, M. (2010). Can social meaningfulness and repeat exposure help infants and toddlers overcome the video deficit? *Media Psychology, 13,* 31–53. doi:10.1080/15213260903562917

Lapierre, M. A., Vaala, S. E., & Linebarger, D. L. (2011). Influence of licensed spokescharacters and health cues on children's ratings of cereal taste. *Archives of Pediatric & Adolescent Medicine, 165,* 229–234. doi:10.1001/archpediatrics.2010.300

Lauricella, A. R., Gola, A. A. H., & Calvert, S. L. (2011). Toddlers' learning from socially meaningful video characters. *Media Psychology, 14,* 216–232. doi:10.1080/15213269.2011.573465

Piaget, J., Tomilson, J., & Tomilson, A. (2007). *The child's conception of the world: A 20th century classic of child psychology.* Lanham, MD: Rowman & Littlefield.

Richert, R. A., Robb, M. B., & Smith, E. I. (2011). Media as social partners: The social nature of young children's learning from screen media. *Child Development, 82,* 82–95. doi:10.1111/j.1467-8624.2010.01542.x

Rideout, V., & Hamel, E. (2006). *The media family: Electronic media in the lives of infants, toddlers, and preschoolers.* Menlo Park, CA: Kaiser Family Foundation.

Roberto, C. A., Baik, J., Harris, J. J., & Brownell, K. D. (2010). The influence of licensed characters on children's taste and snack preferences. *Pediatrics, 126,* 88–93. doi:10.1542/peds.2009-3433

Rubin, A. M., Perse, E. M., & Powell, R. A. (1985). Loneliness, parasocial interaction, and local television news viewing. *Human Communication Research, 12,* 155–180. doi:10.1111/j.1468-2958.1985.tb00071.x

Schramm, H., & Hartmann, T. (2008). The PSI-process scales. A new measure to assess the intensity and breadth of parasocial processes. *Communications: The European Journal of Communication Research, 33,* 385–401. doi:10.1515/COMM.2008.025

Singer, D. G., & Singer, J. L. (2005). *Imagination and play in the electronic age.* Boston, MA: Harvard University Press.

Valkenburg, P. M., & Calvert, S. L. (2012). Television and the child's developing imagination. In D. Singer & J. Singer (Eds.), *Handbook of children and the media* (2nd ed.) (pp. 121–134). Thousand Oaks, CA: Sage.

Wright, J. C., Huston, A. C., Reitz, A. L., & Piemyat, S. (1994). Young children's perceptions of television reality: Determinants and developmental differences. *Developmental Psychology, 30*(2), 229–239. doi:10.1037/0012-1649.30.2.229

CHAPTER 13

Behind the Scenes

WORKING WITH HOLLYWOOD TO MAKE POSITIVE
SOCIAL CHANGE

Marisa Nightingale

Introduction

There is ample research to demonstrate that media influence teens in a variety
of ways, ranging from attitudes to intent to action. According to Brown (2003),

> The notion that popular media can be used to positively educate audi-
> ences in regards to health issues is becoming more widely accepted as
> a growing body of evidence suggests that attitudes and behaviors can
> be positively affected by the mass media. The entertainment-education
> strategy (E-E) relies on embedding educational messages in popular
> entertainment content in hopes of increasing knowledge, raising aware-
> ness, affecting attitudes in a positive way, and encouraging audiences to
> make responsible health decisions in their own lives. Television is par-
> ticularly effective in its ability to educate audiences because it can include
> characters audiences relate to as they struggle with similar real-life issues.
> Research suggests that audiences are less likely to be skeptical of health
> messages or resist them when they are skillfully embedded in their favor-
> ite TV shows and experienced by characters the audience identifies with.

What follows is an exploration of what happens when social science research
findings are applied in Hollywood—in real time, and in an industry that changes
rapidly. Can Hollywood be a force for good in efforts to prevent teen pregnancy?
What kinds of obstacles do we run into as we try to integrate prevention messages into popular entertainment media that young people and their parents

consume? Is there any evidence of success? Can teen pregnancy prevention media strategies be applied to other social issues? In this chapter, I try to answer these questions and highlight some important lessons learned over 17 years of work to get popular media to help prevent teen pregnancy. I will focus primarily on work with TV shows, since that is still one of the biggest and most influential elements of teens' media diet.

Entertainment media have tremendous reach and credibility with young people and their parents—our primary target audiences. The National Campaign to Prevent Teen and Unplanned Pregnancy, a nonpartisan, nonprofit organization whose goal is to improve the well-being of children and families by reducing teen and unplanned pregnancy, engages a variety of sectors—including entertainment media—to make prevention a priority. However, the National Campaign could never print enough brochures to reach the more than 3 million viewers who eagerly tuned in to *Secret Life of the American Teenager* (whose mid-season premiere was ABC Family's most watched telecast of all time with 12- to 34-year-old viewers) or the more than 13 million who watch ABC's *Modern Family* each week. And, even if we could, brochures would not be nearly as entertaining or compelling as these shows. So, finding ways to be part of these and other shows' relationships with viewers gives us a much better chance to reach our audiences where they are, and where they want to be. This approach is efficient and effective: it fosters conversation between peers and parents about their own views and values.

Why is message integration particularly valuable to efforts to reduce teen and unplanned pregnancy? When it comes to subjects like relationships, dating, sex, pregnancy and contraception, the message is nuanced. Unlike messages related to violence, tobacco, or drug abuse, for which the message to teens is, at the core, "Don't do this—it's harmful and can hurt or kill you," sex and pregnancy are an important part of life and can be meaningful and wonderful, when the timing and situation are right. So the message is more complex: rather than "never," the message is "not yet." Prevention, we've been told by teens, is what you do when you never want something—like a disease. Pregnancy is something most people want, someday—so we increasingly focus on messages about *delaying* pregnancy when communicating with teens.

Integrating messages into entertainment content in order to help prevent teen pregnancy relies on the power of narrative to engage and motivate teens and their parents. An engaged audience is primed (1) to learn new information; (2) to truly feel that teen pregnancy could happen to them or their children; (3) to discuss what they see on TV and relate it to their own views and values; and (4) to feel motivated to do whatever it may take to prevent teen pregnancy. According to polling, 76% of U.S. teens say that what they see in the media about sex, love, and relationships can be a good way to start conversations about these topics (The National Campaign to Prevent Teen and Unplanned Pregnancy, 2012).

Identifying with characters in favorite TV shows can help this engagement last beyond any single episode, and helps viewers personalize what they're seeing in ways that other, more general media campaigns cannot. In fact, 3 out of 4 teens agree with this statement: "When a TV show or character I like deals with teen pregnancy, it makes me think more about my own risk (of becoming pregnant/causing a pregnancy) and how to avoid it" (The National Campaign to Prevent Teen and Unplanned Pregnancy, 2012). Research has long shown that this kind of active participation can move individuals along the continuum from awareness of an issue toward behavior change. The real magic—and learning—happens when entertainment and education coexist and complement each other.

Teen Pregnancy and Teen Media

Over the past two decades, much has changed in teenage pregnancy and in teen media. Between 1990 and 2009, teen pregnancy has declined 51%, among non-Hispanic whites and non-Hispanic black teens, and has declined 40% among Hispanic teens (Martin et al., 2012). Rates have declined across all racial and ethnic groups, (National Center for Health Statistics, 2013) even though teen pregnancy was once thought to be inevitable and intractable. Still, nearly 3 in 10 girls in the U.S. get pregnant as teens, and one in six will be a teen mother (National Center for Health Statistics, 2013). Despite historic declines, the U.S. still has the highest teen pregnancy rate of any comparable Western nation (Hamilton, Martin, & Ventura, 2012). We care about reducing teen and unplanned pregnancy because it is one of the most effective ways to reduce child poverty (Committee on Ways and Means Democrats, 2004). The consequences for babies born to teens are numerous and lasting: children of teen mothers are more likely to be born prematurely and low birth-weight (Martin et al., 2009); they are more likely to fail in school (Hoffman, 2006); to suffer abuse and neglect (Martin et al., 2009); to grow up in poverty (US Census Bureau, 2011); and to become teen parents themselves (Perper, Peterson, & Manlove, 2010). Babies born from unplanned pregnancies to single young adults don't fare much differently. What inspires us and our media partners is that teen pregnancy is 100% preventable—and it is a sure-fire way to improve the lives of this generation and the next. Reasons for the sharp decline in teen pregnancy over the past two decades are as complex as are the reasons that teens get pregnant in the first place, and no single factor can be pointed at as the solution.

Over this same period, as teen pregnancy has declined, sexual content in media has increased—as have prevention messages, according to the Kaiser Family Foundation (2005)—just not at the same rate (Kunkel, Eyal, Finnerty,

Biely, & Donnerstein, 2005). Teens are now accustomed to sexual content in their media, and polls from the National Campaign to Prevent Teen and Unplanned Pregnancy show that teens don't want less sex in their media, but 3 out of 4 teens say they do want to see more of the consequences of sex—including teen pregnancy—in the media they consume (The National Campaign, 2012).

A study by Rebecca Collins and colleagues (2004) found that teens who watched the largest amount of sexual content on TV were twice as likely as those who watched the smallest amount "to initiate sexual intercourse during the following year or to progress to more-advanced levels of other sexual activity" (RAND Health, 2004. See Collins, et al., 2004, p. 2). While it may be the case that sexual content in media is encouraging teens to experiment with sex, it may also be the case that teens who are curious about sex and feel ready to have sex are also seeking out media with more sexual content. Regardless, Collins and colleagues note that "entertainment shows that include portrayals of sexual risks and consequences can potentially have two beneficial effects on teen sexual awareness: they can teach accurate messages about sexual risks, and they can stimulate a conversation with adults that can reinforce those messages" (RAND Health, p. 3, 2004). So, what role do the media ultimately play in teens' attitudes toward and decisions about sex? Hollywood did not cause the teen pregnancy problem in America, but many people believe that it has been a key part of the decline. In fact, nearly 6 in 10 adults in the United States agree that the decline in teen pregnancy is due in part to increased media attention to the issue (The National Campaign to Prevent Teen and Unplanned Pregnancy, 2012). Two specific shows—MTV's *16 and Pregnant* and *Teen Mom*—have been credited specifically with a reduction in teen births among viewers (Kearney & Levine, 2014).

Young people want information and discussions about sex from their favorite media. Adolescents report intentionally seeking information about sex from television, magazines and the Internet. In a national sample of high school students, more than half said they had learned about birth control, contraception, or preventing pregnancy from magazines and/or television (Brown, 2003). When young people grow accustomed to media portrayals of sex without protection or consequences, and when these portrayals are not balanced out elsewhere with examples of what prevention looks like, the concern is that young people will believe that such risk-taking is "expected and appropriate and will apply those norms in their sexual lives" (Brown, 2003).

While media are blamed for a wide range of social ills, I would posit that this is due to an overblown and unrealistic sense of what entertainment media can—and can't do—when it comes to teen sex and pregnancy. Here's what entertainment media such as TV shows, magazine articles, blogs, and other web content *can* do.

SET THE SOCIAL SCRIPT

As noted above, when teens see teen characters in their favorite TV shows deal-ing with a sexual situation, they may not copy exactly what they see, but they may perceive what they see as "normal." So, if teens' favorite shows depict sexual situ-ations with few serious consequences or rare mentions of contraception, they may begin to assume that sex doesn't actually have real consequences or that contraception is not a "normal" part of sex. One teen told me that in the shows she watches, teens tend to have sex first, then get to know each other. Though that's not what she observed among her classmates, it did make her wonder whether or not that was the way things were "supposed to be." Teens also love to discuss their favorite shows with their friends, and teen marketing experts note that as teens try on different images and identities, and bond with other teens, they use their favorite TV shows as a way to and seek out like-minded peers.

MAKE A VAGUE, GENERAL TOPIC PERSONALLY RELEVANT

Campaign polling shows that 50% of teens have never thought about how a preg-nancy would affect their lives. If they've never thought about it before, why should they think about it now, and why should they be motivated to prevent it? If teens have a relationship with a beloved character in a TV show (what Brown, 2003, refers to as a "super-peer"), this character's experiences can seem like they're hap-pening to an actual friend—which can help break through teens' wall of denial and get them to start thinking that sexually risky situations might actually happen to them. Such personalization of risk is an important step toward prevention.

SHOW CONSEQUENCES

Characters on TV—whether fictional or part of a reality show—can show audi-ences the real consequences of their actions, both in the short term and over the long term. In scripted series, I often advise writers that it may be even more help-ful to show consequences over time, if the TV show allows, rather than to show risk, consequences, and resolution all tied up in a bow in a single episode. One of the best things about working with scripted series is that the consequences of something that happens in the beginning of a season can show up many episodes later, and viewers who are attached to that character and show will remember what happened long after that particular storyline has concluded. We learned this firsthand in our work with the WB show *Dawson's Creek*. In response to an audience survey to assess the effect of prevention messages on the attitudes of the show's most avid viewers, many respondents discussed a pregnancy scare – never mentioned in the survey questionnaire— that had happened in a previous season. They remembered this story line and cited it in their survey responses as the reason that a particular character chose not to have sex with a new partner in the show's subsequent season (National Campaign, 2003).

DRAW ATTENTION, GENERATE INTEREST, AND SPARK REACTIONS

Entertainment media are particularly well-suited to go beyond raising awareness (which public service announcements are also very well-equipped to do) and can help motivate action and point viewers toward helpful resources. The Kaiser Family Foundation has not only worked to integrate messages about sexual health into entertainment content and provided a robust array of resources through ItsYourSexLife.com; the foundation has also conducted extensive research on the ways that entertainment programming has informed viewers about emergency contraception and HIV transmission, with viewers learning new information and reporting that they were motivated to ask their doctors about it. According to a 1997 Kaiser Family Foundation study of an episode of *ER* that included information about emergency contraception shortly after it became available: "The number of *ER* viewers who knew that a woman has options for preventing pregnancy even after unprotected sex increased by 17 percentage points (from 50% to 67%) in the week after the April 10th episode, which included a brief mention of the topic." We know from experience at the National Campaign that web traffic spikes on our teen site when a show includes both in-show messaging about teen pregnancy and then runs a PSA immediately following the show, referring viewers to our site (www.StayTeen. org) as a place for teens to go to get more information. The storylines make viewers aware and pique their interest; and a PSA after a relevant episode can send them—at the moment when they are most interested—to a helpful resource that will offer much more information than any entertainment program would or could.

PROVIDE A PLACE TO REACT

Every TV show aimed at teens now has a robust life in social and digital media, to extend its relationship with viewers beyond individual episodes of shows and to keep this relationship fresh and evolving between episodes. Through character blogs, web extras, Facebook posts, tweets (in character and from the actors or producers), audiences interact with their favorite TV shows, give their opinions about what they're watching, and are frequently given the opportunity to answer questions from the show or its creators. This opportunity to respond to what they're seeing has become a seamless and expected part of the TV viewing experience that did not exist 15 years ago. When teens weigh in with their own opinions about how a character may have handled a risky sexual situation, they are by definition exploring their own views on the subject—and thereby personalizing the issue.

MAKE A CONNECTION WITH THE AUDIENCE

One of the most important and valuable things popular media can do is to forge a strong connection with the audience. This is equally important to anyone who is trying to work with the media to create social change: if there is no connection with the audience, no learning can take place. However, the power of popular media in forging and sustaining these strong connections between the fictional (or sometimes real) world they portray and the viewer's personal attachment to that world lies at the heart of what it possibly the best that entertainment media can do to help solve social problems: forge a relationship with teens that compels them to come back week after week, tuning in, paying attention, and talking about it afterward.

ALLOW VIEWERS TO IDENTIFY WITH THEIR FAVORITE CHARACTERS

Many teens are drawn to their favorite shows because they see themselves in one of the characters. How such characters handle risky sexual situations can create a safe, positive place for viewers to "try on" what they're seeing before they are in that situation themselves. We know that one of the most powerful things a parent can do to help their teens avoid pregnancy is to help them come up with a plan for what they'll do in the heat of a sexual situation before they're actually in it. Popular TV shows often show outsize personalities that teens love to follow because they are outrageous—but many teens also follow a TV "pseudo-peer" whose actions can be instructive in that teen's own life, whether this beloved character makes mistakes and suffers consequences, or makes a more prudent decision after careful thought and consideration.

Just as there are important things that entertainment media can do, there are also important things that such media cannot do—nor should they be expected to.

BE A SUBSTITUTE FOR CARING ADULTS

No matter how pervasive various media are in a young person's life, teens have told us year after year, for a decade and a half, that parents are the top influence on their decisions about sex (The National Campaign, 2012). Unfortunately, parents consistently say that they think peers and media are more influential. Media are indeed a powerful force in teens' lives, and if parents abdicate their influential role, other forces will step in. Still, teens want and need to hear from their parents more than anyone else about sex, love, and how to tell the difference.

REPLACE THE INTENSE INTERVENTION OF A PREVENTION PROGRAM OR CURRICULUM

There is no way that a TV show or magazine—no matter how compelling—could do the job of an effective teen pregnancy prevention program. Many such interventions have shown success in delaying sex and reducing teen pregnancy among specific populations and after rigorous scientific evaluation. Media cannot fill the same role. Media are pervasive, but their primary purpose is to entertain, whereas prevention programs are carefully designed specifically to reduce teen pregnancy. These two approaches can complement each other well but are not interchangeable.

BE SEEN AS A SOLO SOLUTION

When popular media include helpful prevention messages, real progress can be made when teens are also surrounded by helpful prevention messages at home, in school, and beyond. Media messages alone are not likely to change behavior. When they exist as part of a more integrated whole, they can be a powerful force in grabbing teens' attention, helping them think about their own risk, giving them specific ideas about why and how to find out more information, and motivating them to talk about what they are seeing with peers, partners, and parents. These are all important steps on the path towards behavior change. Some promising new research is starting to demonstrate more direct links between media messages and specific behavioral outcomes—an exciting new development in this field (Kearney and Levine, 2014).

Youth Media Environment

Over the past two decades, almost everything about the teen media landscape has changed. It has changed so much, in fact, that the media environment in which teens are growing up today bears little or no resemblance to that of the mid-1990s. On average, 8- to 18-year-olds spend 7 ½ hours per day consuming media—mostly watching TV—which adds up to more time spent with media than in school over the course of a year. In addition, 75% of 12- to 17-year-olds own cell phones, and 8- to 18-year-olds send an average of 3000 text messages per month; fully 40% of teens multitask when using electronic devices. Their average Facebook visits last 20.5 minutes (Rideout, Foehr, & Roberts, 2010).

While teens have always been avid media consumers, they are multitasking more than ever, increasing the total time spent with media. According to the Kaiser Family Foundation, teens are not abandoning TV for digital media but rather using multiple media simultaneously: watching TV while surfing the web, listening to music, and updating their Facebook statuses. According to the Kaiser Family Foundation (2010), "High levels of media multitasking also contribute to the large amount of media young people consume each day. About 4 in 10 7th-12th graders say they use another medium 'most' of the time they're listening to music (43%), using a computer (40%), or watching TV (39%)" (Rideout et al., 2010). These profound changes have opened some exciting new avenues of opportunity for social change, and have fundamentally altered the way teens view themselves in relation to their favorite media. While teens have always been heavy media consumers, they are no longer passive users.

Teens are media content creators and active participants who expect to have a conversation with their favorite shows. Teens create their own videos, websites, Tumblrs, and social media personae—and have never lived any other way. They expect to weigh in on TV shows' Facebook pages, lobby networks to save their shows from cancellation, comment on blogs written by their favorite characters, and get special previews and exclusive content online, having a relationship with their favorite TV shows well beyond whichever screen (TV, computer, or mobile device) they use to watch them. Their conversations with favorite characters and shows, which happen with or without issue experts' participation, provide researchers and advocates with exciting new opportunities to participate in conversations and, if done carefully, inform viewers in a way that works seamlessly in the media environment they already inhabit. Teens watch what they want to watch on their schedules—not when the TV networks say they should watch. They can skip ads that don't interest them. They are in charge of what, when, and how they watch.

The past two decades have also seen the advent of unscripted "reality" television. Ever since the debut of MTV's *The Real World* in 1992, unscripted series have become a staple of broadcast and cable television and have created a spinoff universe in the tabloids in which ordinary people become celebrities just by opening their lives up to a camera crew. Teen viewers have grown just as attached to these "characters" as they have to fictional ones (and many would argue that a heavy dose of fiction is inherent in "reality" television). This form of television is cheaper to produce than scripted series are, and can withstand writers' strikes and other forces in the "real world" of the media business. Working in partnership with these shows is still possible, but it requires a keen understanding of how these shows are produced and where the opportunities lie.

Despite these seismic changes in the way entertainment media are created and consumed, one critical element has stayed the same: a good story is still king. Viewers will always relish—and always have—good storytelling and compelling characters. This connection to characters, especially when it evolves and deepens over time, is where the magic happens, both for the those who create these stories and for the causes that want to be part of this strong bond between media and audience.

There are many examples—particularly in developing countries—of "education-entertainment" campaigns that show real results in disease prevention and health promotion. A number of soap operas and radio programs in the developing world integrate health messages into media content with enormous, measurable success. However, in many cases, those efforts exist in countries in which the government controls media content, or the audience can be reached at a saturation level by a handful of media outlets. Because the United States has free and independent media, this means that, by definition, those who develop media content are harder to influence and are in many cases reluctant to be given ideas or information by any outside group, whether it's the government or a nonprofit.

Public Service Announcements (PSAs) can be very valuable, but PSAs are proving to be an increasingly difficult way to reach and connect with audiences in a reliable way. Reaching an audience effectively through advertising is a challenge both nonprofits and corporations are facing: audiences can skip ads whenever they want to; PSAs that rely on donated "remnant" space deliver uncertain and unpredictable reach; PSAs compete against ads with much larger production and placement budgets; and, most important, teens in particular can see "good for you" messages coming from a mile away. PSAs are good ways to grab attention, to reinforce messages, to point audiences toward resources, and in particular, to reach an audience that cannot be reached through content (e.g., the National Campaign's efforts to reach teen boys through their favorite shows have included PSA placements that air during *The Simpsons*, the Teen Choice Awards, and other shows that are popular with our target but that simply don't lend themselves to content integration).

With PSAs, makers have total control over content and almost zero control over where even the most spectacular, well-produced PSAs will be placed. With message integration into content, one has basically no control over the final script, but the best possible placement: the message is woven into content that your target audience is actually seeking out. Message integration can give audiences nuance and complexity not possible in a short PSA, and stories can unfold over a long period of time, which gives content creators an opportunity to explore many facets of the teen pregnancy issue, and not just as a one-off. In essence, PSAs can be effective if you have a *captive* audience; message integration happens as part of a conversation with a *captivated* audience.

Research in Action: Getting Prevention Messages in Media Content

Social science research tells us that it's not enough for someone in your target audience to hear a message; they need to engage with it. Message integration often delivers high audience engagement. When it comes to teens and sex, media researchers recommend more messages about prevention; more portrayals of condom negotiation between partners and more characters choosing to delay sex; more examples of parents having helpful conversations with teens; and more demonstrations of the consequences of sex—emotional and physical. Can we actually make these recommendations come to life? Yes. But this "yes" comes with many caveats, some hard-won knowledge, and an understanding that the price of admission into Hollywood includes getting comfortable giving up full control over your message.

Over the past decade and a half, my colleagues and I have worked closely with television executives, writers, producers, show-runners, magazine editors, online content producers—an array of people who create the media content that young people and their parents consume. We have honed our approach over the years and are committed to remaining flexible in order to sustain long-term relationships in the media industry, which is in a constant state of evolution and innovation, both creatively and from a business perspective.

What follow are some real-life lessons about what it takes to do this kind of work, what you must give up, what can be gained, and how research principles about the impact of media on youth can be put to work in the "real world," or, at least, Hollywood. The National Campaign is by no means the only organization with robust partnerships in entertainment media—in fact, the Kaiser Family Foundation, the Robert Wood Johnson Foundation, The Norman Lear Center/CDC's Hollywood, Health and Society, and others have been doing excellent work in partnership with Hollywood on a range of social issues for decades. I am writing about my own experiences and those of my colleagues, but commend these efforts and know that those of us who do this work have learned a lot from one another and support each other's work.

WHAT'S IN IT FOR HOLLYWOOD?

In thinking about placing your messages in entertainment media, you first need to consider, "What's in it for Hollywood?" —and the answer is, "That depends." These are not people who get up every day to prevent teen pregnancy. That's our job. Their job is to get up every day and deliver entertaining content to their viewers. Our other job is to help them see that we can both meet our goals through their work. For the most part, my colleagues and

I do not generally bring funds to these content partnerships (though we have experimented with some sponsored content on a small scale). What we do bring is an issue that is important to their audience, and the heft and credibility of an organization that is science-based, nonpartisan, nongovernmental, and that works on other fronts beyond media (e.g., policy, research, community action, and national partnerships). This matters a lot to media partners. Our chief goal when cultivating new media partnerships is to show media executives—clearly and in their terms—what they will get out of working with the National Campaign to Prevent Teen and Unplanned Pregnancy. We never promise more viewers; but what we can promise—and then deliver—is good, solid research and messages about what science says can prevent teen and unplanned pregnancy; and we support them when they do tell these stories, whether it's to praise their efforts in the press or offer more information to viewers once a story is on the air.

DON'T ASSUME THEY CARE: MAKE THEM CARE

We know why teen pregnancy is such an important problem—and how directly connected it is to reducing child poverty and improving children's health and well-being. But any interaction with a media partner has to begin with the assumption that they may not know anything, let alone care about our issue. We have developed a variety of videos and other material—all grounded in solid research—to put real human faces on the numbers, to tell a story that moves those who are professional storytellers. We have to remember that they have many other issue groups who also want their time and attention. Therefore, just as we are enlisting their help in making teen pregnancy relevant to their viewers, it is our job first to make teen pregnancy relevant to them.

NO PREACHING, NO ENTITLEMENT

I would not welcome people coming into my office and telling me that I owed it to them to help them do their job. So I would never do that to one of my media partners. If we can't show potential media partners why collaborating would benefit them, it means we have no business knocking on their door. Yet.

KNOW YOUR AUDIENCE(S)

Our target audiences are teens, young adults, and their parents. We make a serious effort to find out what they think about teen and unplanned pregnancy and how to prevent it. What do they think about sex, love, and values?

What do they want more of or less of from their peers? Their parents? Their media? What motivates them? What stops them from using contraception? Is it embarrassing to admit to being a virgin? We often conduct joint original surveys with our magazine partners—such as *Seventeen* (which reaches 2 million teenage girls each month) and *ESSENCE* (which reaches more than 3 million African American women each month). These surveys not only strengthen our relationships with these outlets and their audiences; they also provide our entire array of media partners and community groups with keen insight into our shared audiences. In a survey conducted by McKinsey & Co., one of the nation's leading management consulting firms and experts on impact evaluation, 94% of entertainment media executives who have worked with the National Campaign say our work together has helped them present teen pregnancy prevention in interesting and appropriate ways to their audiences (McKinsey & Company, 2003).

SEX IS SEXY

At some point, almost all media (whether scripted or unscripted, print or broadcast) tell stories about sex, relationships, dating—it always has been and always will be the stuff of dramas and comedies in real life, in fiction, and in all areas in between. Sex, pregnancy, relationships, love—our issue is an inherently complex, dramatic, and funny one. It benefits our prevention effort that we are not asking media executives to take on an entirely new subject; rather, we are trying to enhance and add dimensions to a subject that is already of great interest to them and to their audiences. Rather than positioning preventing teen and unplanned pregnancy as a public health issue, we position it as a topic with many facets that is relevant to all kinds of characters and situations—whether it's a dramatic pregnancy scare scenario, a heartfelt conversation between a parent and teen, a love story, or a funny sex-fail moment.

KNOW YOUR SHOWS

We need our media partners in order to do our jobs; they don't need us to do theirs. We are aware that we are piggybacking on the carefully crafted, extremely valuable relationship they've built with their audiences. Therefore, we are committed to watching their shows. We find out: What kind of tone does the show take with its viewers? Why do fans watch it? How have they addressed our issues in the past? We get to know the characters, the voice of the show in social media. It's insulting to Hollywood executives to go to them and have no idea about the world they have so meticulously created and in which they spend every waking moment. We need to be part of the universe they've brought to life, not drag them into ours.

EDUCATION HAS TO ENHANCE—NOT CANCEL OUT—ENTERTAINMENT

It is critical that media partners feel that advocates and issue groups are on their side, rather than working against them when it comes to making entertainment. One example of an entertainment program that was deeply educational and extremely entertaining from the outset is the 2010 Lifetime original movie, *The Pregnancy Pact*. The executive producer worked in close partnership with the Campaign throughout the script's development, including many Campaign messages and wanting very much to get the facts straight, but not at the expense of good storytelling. *The Pregnancy Pact* was a ratings success story: it was the number-one original movie on ad-supported cable among 18- to 34-year-old women in more than a decade, with more than 23 million viewers watching the movie's first four airings. The National Campaign wrote online discussion guides and information for parents and teens; scripted a PSA that Lifetime produced and aired at the end of the movie; collaborated on press materials; provided information to the cast; and more. Lifetime distributed more than 400 free DVDs with our discussion guides to educators and youth programs nationwide, and the movie continues to air on the Lifetime Movie Network.

THERE ARE MANY DECISION-MAKERS ON EACH SCRIPT

We may propose to a writer that he or she consider incorporating a scene in which partners negotiate condom use, and that writer may love the idea. However, the script still has to go through extensive rewrites, has to meet the approval of network executives, and has to fit into strict time parameters. That and countless other behind-the-scenes negotiations that we are not privy to are a big part of the process that any script goes through from story idea to production. Things change. And change back again. So, while we know from research that giving viewers models for how to talk about contraception is what teens, researchers, and advocates want to see more of on television, getting that to happen is not a linear process. When it does happen, we applaud it, promote it, and find creative ways for advocates to use the show in educational settings. But when it doesn't happen, we are aware that many competing forces are at play and the omission is not a reflection of any resistance to our goals. This is why it is critical to offer content creators multiple messages—it gives them more opportunities to weave issues into storylines and allows them to include the topic in various ways throughout the life of the show.

IT'S THEIR CONTENT, NOT OURS

We serve as a resource, a sounding board, and a source of information and material; we are not script writers or producers. If a TV show wants to publicize its involvement with the Campaign, we do so happily, but always at their request. Such media partners as Lifetime Television, *ESSENCE, Seventeen,* and MTV have always been eager to publicize our collaboration; others prefer to keep things behind the scenes. We follow their lead and never take credit for their work.

STAY INFORMED ABOUT THE MEDIA BUSINESS

Changes in the media industry can affect the way content integration efforts take shape. It is critical that we follow our partners and their companies in the industry trades, such as *Variety, The Hollywood Reporter,* and *Advertising Age.* We need to know what kinds of challenges they're facing (mergers? writers' strike? ad revenue down?) and incorporate that into our planning when we think about whom to target and when. Advertisers are increasingly developing multidimensional partnerships with TV shows, going well beyond product placement in shows into brand integration in social media and online. Many corporate brands now sponsor original content with media partners and co-produce original webisodes and other new material. Nonprofits are experimenting with sponsored content as well and are starting to learn more about its effectiveness. When the National campaign asks writers to include our messages in their storylines, we must be mindful that they are getting similar requests not only from other causes, but also from paying advertisers. They have to balance these requests with their creative story ideas, and must deliver entertaining programming to audiences that doesn't feel like a mash-up of ads and PSAs, served up in the guise of a TV show.

CARROTS, NOT STICKS

Our campaign's approach to our media partners has always been to applaud them and shine a spotlight on them when they get it right, not to scold them if they get it wrong. After all, it's their content, not ours. We have worked hard to build trust with our media partners, and over time, this trust leads to closer collaboration and a wider variety of opportunities to do creative work together.

TAKE THE LONG VIEW

Integrating messages about teen and unplanned pregnancy into entertainment media content is not something that can be done on a short timeline. This work is most effective when the right people are in the right decision-making roles at media companies that reach our audiences. It takes years to cultivate these relationships, and even when all other elements are lined up just right (e.g., an executive wants to work with us; a show has just the right story opportunities and audience), we still may not succeed in getting a storyline to deal with our issue. We assure our media partners that we are in this for the long haul, and that we'd rather wait for all the necessary conditions to align perfectly than to try to force something that doesn't really work for them. Social change happens over long spans of time, and for a complex variety of reasons. Messages integrated into media take time to play out and resonate with audiences. For example, TeenNick's hit show *Degrassi* has included Campaign messages in every single teen pregnancy–related storyline the show has aired since 1997. This was the result of an ongoing, ever-evolving relationship and trust between the network and the National Campaign over many years. As a result of this growing partnership, TeenNick often features blog posts with relevant episodes and has aired the National Campaign's StayTeen PSAs an average of 30 times per month for free from 2007 to 2012, giving viewers exposure to our messages multiple times and in a variety of ways on the network.

STRATEGY AND OPPORTUNITY

Our campaign's media team approaches this work with a carefully honed strategy, but also a willingness and readiness to take advantage of new and unexpected opportunities whenever they arise. We target specific outlets and work with our media partners to forge relationships in just the right places; but we have also benefited enormously from those occasions when media partners approach us and enlist our help with a show we may not have thought to target. If a media executive or creator wants to work with us, we are committed to providing help with as much enthusiasm and rigor as we do with those partners we have been cultivating for years.

Examples of In-Depth, Effective Media Partnerships

Here are three examples of true "360-degree" Campaign media partnerships over the past decade. Each case is one that includes message integration as well as collaboration online, in social media and beyond. Since TV shows are always on the verge of obsolescence, I have chosen examples that I think will have lasting implications, long after these specific shows are off the air:

DAWSON'S CREEK

We had the pleasure and privilege of working closely with the hit teen series *Dawson's Creek* on the WB Network, from its pilot episode in 1998 to its series finale in 2003. Our relationship began when the president of entertainment at the WB (now a National Campaign board member), introduced us to the show's creator, gave her blessing to the show to work with us, and encouraged us to maintain a close relationship with the show. It was critical to our success to have such support from the right person at the right time. Thanks to her leadership, enthusiasm, and commitment to handling our topic in an accurate and helpful way, we were given a warm welcome by the show's executive producer, writers, online content producers, and network marketing executives and deepened these relationships over time. The show's executive producer was very committed to getting things "right" and welcomed our participation, knowing that his show would be able to explore sexual topics in a responsible way while remaining addictively entertaining to its teen audience. The show and the network agreed to collaborate with the National Campaign on an audience evaluation in the show's final season, a challenging research effort that required them to give us access to scripts before shows aired, as well as access to the show's most committed viewers online.

Dawson's Creek tackled sex and relationships in nearly every episode (and was considered quite racy at the time), and treated teen characters as smart, savvy, and worldly people whose often clueless parents made more mistakes in relationships than their kids did, who tried to be good parents but often fumbled, or who were too wrapped up in their own relationship dramas to be of any help to their kids. In the universe of *Dawson's Creek*, teens got their wisdom from their peers. The show boasted high ratings (averaging 7 million 13- to 24-year-old viewers each week) and very high audience engagement, and a desire among viewers to have ongoing conversations with these characters even when the show was on summer hiatus.

We discussed with the writers the fact that while only about half of high school–aged teens were sexually active, most teens way overestimated the number of their peers who were having sex, and that 2 out of 3 teens who had had sex said they wished they'd waited longer. We told them that boys rarely get the message that it's okay to delay sex—and that it's okay to say no to sex, even if they'd said yes before. In the show's second season, Pacey—a sexually active teen boy—decides that he is not ready to have sex with his new girlfriend, Andie (a virgin), even though she wants to. He decides that it's such a big deal that they should wait. While the writers and producers gather information from a wide variety of sources, they found a way to bring to life the idea of a sexually active teen boy taking sex seriously and deciding to turn it down for emotional reasons. They chose the angle that suited their show and characters, and they helped get an important message across to viewers as part of a key storyline.

In 2003, in collaboration with the WB and the market research team at General Mills, we did an "attitude tracker" evaluation of 3,700 committed

Dawson's Creek viewers, ages 13–21, surveying them over a period of six weeks, immediately after they watched new episodes of the show. We wanted to find out whether they were aware of—and how they responded to—teen pregnancy prevention messages that had been present throughout the show's lifespan. Efforts to embed public health messages and information into entertainment content "are more successful if the messages are simple, presented by characters and on shows that young people like, and are frequent and sustained over time" (Brown, 2003). *Dawson's Creek* was an early example for others in Hollywood that education can accompany—and even enhance entertainment. Key findings from our evaluation include the following:

- *Dawson's Creek* producers/writers incorporated campaign messages into programming, though the messages were often indirect or part of subplots. Viewers confirmed that they were aware of various campaign messages in storylines.
- Of the 13- to 17-year-old viewers surveyed, 68% said that *Dawson's Creek* made them more aware of the risks and consequences of sex.
- Of the 13- to 21-year-old viewers surveyed, 49% said that watching *Dawson's Creek* helped them decide to be more cautious about sex.
- Whether characters do the "right" or the "wrong" thing, the storylines seem to lead teen viewers to examine their own attitudes and beliefs.
- Nearly half of teens (49%) said the show taught them a positive message about teen relationships.
- Of all teens surveyed, 68% said that they talked to their friends about the themes in *Dawson's Creek* episodes.
- Nearly one out of five viewers talked to parents about show themes. Those who did found the episodes helped initiate conversations about sex and relationships, which teens often find hard to do with parents.
- Open-ended responses from teens in the survey illustrate the way they identified with characters in the show and thought about their own views and values:

> "I am glad they didn't throw Joey and Charlie together and have them sleep together. They can have an intimate relationship without sex."
> "The episode was good and…a guy that carries condoms if he's your boyfriend is not always pressuring you to have sex because sex in my opinion is not a planned act but a spontaneous one and being prepared is smart."
> "The show…helped me see that I didn't need to be having sex with my boyfriend to keep him with me. I only wished I waited longer before I did and I wish I had seen these episodes before I had sex."

"Watching these shows I learned from quotes that Joey uses, and I use them in my life…"

"I loved this episode I watch it with my mom all the time and we talk about the show. There is definitely more sex in this season's DC but I think the way you go about it is really good."

PARENTHOOD

Parents are a critical audience for our teen pregnancy prevention efforts, so the campaign's media team pursues partnerships with media that parents of teens consume with as much energy and focus as we do with teen and young adult outlets. NBC's *Parenthood* is an hour-long drama about the lives of adult siblings and their parents, children, friends, and relationships. It has consistent critical acclaim and a devoted fan base. Its audience is highly engaged with the show, and every episode features some facet of parent-teen relationships. The parent characters on the show are smart, devoted, realistic, and flawed—as are their teenage children. The family relationships are not idealized, but their devotion to one another is at the core of the series. The show averages about 5 million viewers each week and is most popular among 18- to 49-year-olds.

Our campaign has had the privilege of providing information for storylines, online content, and the show's social media since its first season. In the show's 2011–2012 season, as part of an ongoing storyline about a sexually active teenage girl (Haddie) dating an older guy (Alex), one episode culminates in her telling her parents (Adam and Christina) that she is sexually active—after having denied it repeatedly. Her parents' reactions are imperfect, relatable, and deeply moving. After the episode in which Christina talks to her daughter about sex and its emotional as well as physical consequences, the National Campaign worked with NBC.com on slideshows with tips for parents to help them talk with their teens about sex; a guest blog post, and other links and resources. We also collaborated with the show's social media producers, who posted a question on the show's Facebook page, asking its nearly 500,000 Facebook fans what they thought of the way Adam and Christina handled the sex talk with their daughter. Overnight, viewers posted nearly 1,200 responses, describing their own family conversations about sex and demonstrating high viewer engagement. Many parents watched the show with their teens, and saw themselves in the story and characters:

"Wow—my teenage girls had their mouths open WIDE during this episode—they were appalled! THEY told me she was so inappropriate to have sex in the first place. But I have to say—I'd do the same as Christina (but way more info on birth control) because I want my kids to know that whatever they do, they can always talk to me."

"I think they hit the nail on the head in showing the difficulties in handling a sensitive situation like that. Parents do not always share the same views and do not have ALL the answers. Staying involved and "showing up" is the key. I love this show! "Having been in a very similar situation with my 17-year-old son last month, I think the depiction was so realistic it hurt. I've begun to wonder if there are secret cameras in our house that they are taking material from...."

MTV'S 16 AND PREGNANT AND TEEN MOM

It is almost impossible to capture here the depth and the breadth of the impact that 16 and Pregnant and its spin-off, Teen Mom, (which includes Teen Mom 2 Teen Mom 3) have had on the National Campaign's media work and on the teen pregnancy issue overall. Exciting research by a team of economists asserts that these shows led to a 5.7 percent reduction in teen births – or about one-third of the decline in teen births in the 18 months following the preiere of 16 and Pregnant in June 2009 (Kearney & Levine, 2013). The teen birth rate declined steadily between 1991 and 2012, and researchers say that MTV's shows helped accelerate the decline during the period they studied (Kearney & Levine, 2013). To determine how these shows influenced teens' thinking and behavior, the researchers analyzed Nielsen ratings data, metrics from Google searches and Twitter chatter, and teen birth rates using Vital Statistics Natality microdata. They conclude that 16 and Pregnant, Teen Mom and Teen Mom 2 not only influenced viewers' thinking about contraception, the shows "led teens to noticeably reduce the rate at which they give birth" (Kearney & Levine, 2013). This research model is tremendously useful for other efforts to understand the effect of media on teen behavior.

16 and Pregnant and the series of Teen Mom seasons follow the lives of real teenage mothers, their partners, and their parents—many of whom are beloved by fans and feel like real friends to many viewers. These shows have not only demonstrated that media can be linked to positive behavior change among teens, they have also changed the national conversation about teen pregnancy and parenthood. Many argue that tabloid coverage of these teen mothers has turned them into celebrities and glamorized teen pregnancy, sending the wrong message to teens (though often those who make this claim have never watched the show) (Kearney & Levine, 2014). In fact, campaign polling found that 77% of American teens say MTV's 16 and Pregnant and Teen Mom help teens better understand the challenges of pregnancy and parenting (The National Campaign, 2012).

The concept for the show was MTV's, but they welcomed the National Campaign as a full partner from the beginning. We have provided information, expertise, and support behind the scenes to the producers, the network, the publicists, the online content creators, and more. National Campaign staff produces discussion guides for *16 and Pregnant* and blog posts for *Teen Mom*, and works hand-in-hand at all levels of the network to provide information and alert them to breaking news; Campaign staff also frequently speaks to journalists about the impact of these shows. Given our close relationship, many have mistakenly referred to the shows as the National Campaign's—in fact, our ability to speak about the shows' positive impact is more credible because these shows are created by MTV, not by us.

Unlike scripted series, the storylines in unscripted series have to follow the real conversations and actions of the people whose lives they are chronicling. The opportunity for an organization like the National Campaign to offer information and support on storylines must, by definition, take a different form. Unscripted shows have to go where the "characters" take them. MTV has been a true leader in its effort to give the National Campaign access to these shows' producers, allowing us to talk with them about our issue and equip them with information and questions to keep in mind when they are out in the field, following these young women around and then deciding what footage to include in the final product.

The producers and MTV network executives have made sure that *16 and Pregnant* and *Teen Mom* include frequent, detailed discussions about of contraception—weaving a prevention theme into shows that are primarily about chronicling the lives of teen parents. MTV.com provides information and resources online, through www.ItsYourSexLife.com (a partnership with the Kaiser Family Foundation), as well as through blog posts, social media, online videos, and more. These series have been tremendous ratings successes for the network and have kept a national spotlight on teen pregnancy and parenthood in a way that is unprecedented and unparalleled. The notion that there would be two hit shows on the air—on MTV no less—that are solely focused on teen pregnancy and parenthood would have been unthinkable 17 years ago, when our campaign was getting started. When the opportunity arose to work in partnership with these shows, our campaign jumped at the chance and we have had the privilege of deepening and extending this partnership with each passing year. In the spring of 2012, *16 and Pregnant* ranked number one among all cable shows in its timeslot, and the show had tremendously high engagement among viewers:

- *16 and Pregnant* was streamed more than 38 million times online through 2012.
- There are nearly 60 million unique visitors to MTV.com each month for its combined web sites.
- *Teen Mom* has more than 8 million Facebook fans.

- On average, more than 90,000 people comment on the *Teen Mom* Facebook fan page the same day an episode airs.

These comments from fans on the *16 and Pregnant* Facebook page illustrate strong viewer reaction and personalization:

> "I don't want it to end…this show gave me the courage to go to college and start trying to move on…being a single mom isn't the best thing in the world but I know one day my child will look back and learn how to make better decisions."
>
> "Why do some people think this show 'promotes' teen pregnancy? Unless you're lucky enough to have parents like Farrah, Maci, and Chelsea, that foot the bill for everything, it's a rough road. It cuts off your social life, your future, your relationships. It's hard, it's time consuming, expensive, it's life-changing and this show represents just that. If anything, it's a good wake up call to young girls."

MTV has made several seasons of *16 and Pregnant* available to the National Campaign to distribute on DVD with comprehensive discussion guides (created by the National Campaign and approved by MTV).Thousands of educators and parents are using these DVDs and discussion guides to extend the conversation in classrooms. In 2013, the Campaign sponsored *16 and Pregnant: Where Are They Now*, a series of webisodes that caught up with some of the young moms from the show and discussed contraception in detail. Regardless of how long these shows last on-air, the National Campaign and its community partners will be able to draw on them for educational purposes for years to come.

In 2010, the Campaign conducted an evaluation to assess the impact of MTV's *16 and Pregnant* on teen viewers' attitudes about teen pregnancy. In partnership with the Boys & Girls Clubs of America, a total of 162 10- to 19-year-olds completed both the pre- and post-test. Some were assigned to a treatment group (which included watching episodes of the show and participating in a guided discussion afterwards); those in the control group did not watch the episodes or participate in a discussion, but did complete the same pre- and post-tests. Some key findings include these:

- *16 and Pregnant* got teens talking and thinking about teen pregnancy. The majority of teens who watched and discussed the show in a group also later talked to a friend about the show, and 40% talked to a parent afterward; about one-third spoke to a sibling or a girlfriend or boyfriend.
- The teens in this study enjoyed watching and discussing the *16 and Pregnant* episodes and thought that the show was realistic. Neither the boys nor girls

who watched the episodes wanted to imitate the teens in the episodes they watched. In fact, nearly all teens (93%) who watched the show agreed (53% strongly agreed) with the statement, "I learned that teen parenthood is harder than I imagined from these episodes."

Conclusion

Ultimately, message integration is not an end in itself; rather it is a conversation-starter, giving young people and their families an appealing way to have conversations that are essential but often difficult to begin. Whether these conversations happen in social media or are guided by discussion materials in classrooms or living rooms, entertainment media provide an excellent entry point to open the lines of communication about one's own views, values, and plans for prevention. There are numerous examples of the positive role Hollywood plays in reducing teen and unplanned pregnancy, and I believe these examples can inspire other collaborative and creative media partnerships.

There are some research challenges for the next generation of media researchers to consider, as we look ahead to a media environment that will be increasingly mobile and interactive:

- How do we know whether integrated messages are reaching the target in an effective way?
- How do we understand the effects of message integration over a number of episodes or seasons?
- How do we measure the specific impact of an organization's involvement in a show when the media industry itself is struggling to measure the impact of its interactions with viewers?
- How do we know whether our audience thinks or acts differently because of messages that have been incorporated into their media content, especially when it is hard to have a true "control group"?

Despite the challenges, there are some promising new approaches to using social media activity, viewer numbers, and other data to demonstrate the impact of media messages on specific behavioral outcomes (Kearny & Levine, 2013).

Social and digital media provide advocates and researchers with a tremendous opportunity to learn and to take action. One such opportunity for researchers would be to mine conversations already happening in social media for evidence of engagement and for clues to the impact that integrated messages may be having. Advocates can build on and inform these conversations—highlighting portrayals they do like and correcting myths and misperceptions they don't like. Armed with creative new approaches, scholars and advocates have never had such broad and abundant opportunities to forge partnerships with popular media and to join and shape the rich discussions that young people are having with their media and with each other.

References

Albert, B. (2012). *With one voice 2012: America's adults and teens sound off about teen pregnancy.* Washington, D.C.: The National Campaign to Prevent Teen and Unplanned Pregnancy. Retrieved from http://www.thenationalcampaign.org/resources/pdf/pubs/WOV_2012.pdf

Brown, J. (2003). Introduction to Assessing the Impact of Teen Pregnancy Prevention Messages in *Dawson's Creek*: A Survey of Dedicated Viewers (unpublished paper). The National Campaign to Prevent Teen and Unplanned Pregnancy, Washington, DC.

Collins, R. L., Elliott, M. N., Berry, S. H., Kanouse, D. E., Kunkel, D., Hunter, S. B., & Miu, A. (2004). Watching sex on television predicts adolescent initiation of sexual behavior. *Pediatrics, 114*(e280). doi: 10.1542/peds.2003-1065-L

Committee on Ways and Means Democrats. (2004). *Steep Decline in Teen Birth Rate Significantly Responsible for reducing Child Poverty and Single-Parent Families.* (Committee Issue Brief, April 23, 2004). Washington, DC: Author.

Curtin, S. C., Abma, J. C., Ventura, S. J, & Henshaw, S. K. (2013). Pregnancy Rates for U.S. women continue to drop. *NCHS data brief, 136.* Hyattsville, MD: National Center for Health Statistics. Retrieved from http://www.cdc.gov/nchs/data/databriefs/db136.pdf

Hamilton, B. E., Martin, J. A., & Ventura, S. J. (2013). Births: Preliminary data for 2012. *National vital statistics reports, 62*(3). Hyattsville, MD: National Center for Health Statistics. Retrieved from http://www.cdc.gov/nchs/data/nvsr/nvsr62/nvsr62_03.pdf

Hamilton, B. E., & Ventura, S. J. (2012). Birth rates for U.S. teenagers reach historic lows for all age and ethnic groups. *NCHS data brief, 89.* Hyattsville, MD: National Center for Health Statistics. Retrieved from http://www.cdc.gov/nchs/data/databriefs/db89.pdf

Hoffman, S. D. (2006). *By the numbers: The public costs of adolescent childbearing.* Washington, DC: The National Campaign to Prevent Teen Pregnancy.

Kearney, M. S., & Levine, P. B. (2014). Media influences on social outcomes: The impact of MTV's "16 and Pregnant" on teen childbearing. *NBER working paper, 19795.* Cambridge, MA: The National Bureau of Economic Research. Retrieved from http://www.nber.org/papers/w19795.pdf?new_window=1

Kunkel, D., Eyal, K., Finnerty, K., Biely, E., & Donnerstein, E. (2005). *Sex on TV 4.* Menlo Park, CA: The Henry J. Kaiser Family Foundation. Retrieved from http://kaiserfamilyfoundation.files.wordpress.com/2013/01/sex-on-tv-4-full-report.pdf

Martin, J. A., Hamilton, B. E., Sutton, P. D., Ventura, S. J., Menacker, F., Kirmeyer, S. & Matthews, T. J. (2009). Births: Final data for 2006. *National vital statistics reports, 5* (7).

Martin, J. A., Hamilton, B. E., Ventura, S.J., Osterman, M.J.K., Wilson, E.C., & Mathews, T.J. (2012). Births: Final data for 2010. *National vital statistics reports, 61*(1). Retrieved from http://www.cdc.gov/nchs/data/nvsr/nvsr61/nvsr61_01.pdf

McKinsey & Company. (2003). The National Campaign to Prevent Teen Pregnancy: A study of its impact on five key customer groups. Unpublished report.

The National Campaign to Prevent Teen and Unplanned Pregnancy. (2012). Early Childhood Longitudinal Study (ECLS-B), 9 month collection using the Data Analysis System (DAS) [Data file]. Unpublished raw data.

Perper, K., Peterson, K., & Manlove, J. (2010). Diploma attainment among teen mothers. *Child trends fact sheet.* Washington, DC: Child Trends. Retrieved from http://childtrends.org/wp-content/uploads/2010/01/child_trends-2010_01_22_FS_diplomaattainment.pdf

RAND Health. (2004). Does watching sex on television influence teens' sexual activity?. *Research Highlights*. Santa Monica, CA: Author. Retrieved from http://www.rand.org/content/dam/rand/pubs/research_briefs/2005/RB9068.pdf

Rideout, V. J., Foehr, U. G., & Roberts, D.F. (2010). *Generation M2: Media in the lives of 8- to 18-year-olds*.Menlo Park, CA: Henry J. Kaiser Family Foundation. Retrieved from http://kaiserfamilyfoundation.files.wordpress.com/2013/04/8010.pdf

U.S. Census Bureau. (2011). Table C8: poverty status, food stamp receipt, and public assistance for children under 18 years by selected characteristics: 2010. *America's Families and Living Arrangements: 2010*. Retrieved from http://www.census.gov/population/www/socdemo/hh-fam/cps2010.html

CHAPTER 14

Sesame Workshop's *Talk, Listen, Connect*

A MULTIPLE MEDIA RESOURCE TO BENEFIT MILITARY
FAMILIES WITH YOUNG CHILDREN

David Cohen, Jeanette Betancourt, and Jennifer Kotler

Introduction

The number of young children in military families and the types of challenges they face as a result of the global War on Terrorism are significant. There are more than 700,000 children under 6 years old in military families (Secretary of Defense, 2010). Multiple deployments, frequent moves, and having a parent injured or die are realities for many of these children, and these events can be a source of psychological stress. Thus, children in military families experience high rates of trauma, as well as mental health and related problems (Huebner & Mancini 2005; Orthner and Rose, 2005). Despite research showing that programs and resources to support families can mitigate military children's negative experiences (Behnke, MacDermid, Anderson, & Weiss, 2010; Beardsley et al., 2011), few age-appropriate resources exist that specifically target younger children and their families.

To respond to the need of military families with young children, Sesame Workshop launched *Talk, Listen, Connect* (*TLC*), a four-part multiple-media initiative. The bilingual (English/Spanish) project includes a variety of materials—video, print, online, and digital resources, as well as a live USO show and nationally broadcast television specials—and addresses a range of issues central to the military family's experience: deployments and homecomings; changes, such as a parent returning injured; and grief following the death of a parent. A separate set of materials was devoted specifically to each of these issues. In addition, four separate evaluations were conducted on each set of materials, namely deployment, homecoming, changes, and grief.

This chapter provides an overview of the *Talk, Listen, Connect* initiative and of the findings from evaluations of the impact that this media-based initiative has had on military families with young children. The chapter also describes how *TLC* resources were developed to successfully address the critical needs of military families with young children experiencing deployments, or children with a parent who dies or returns injured; it also describes recommendations for best practices for providing assistance via media that may benefit military children and their families. It concludes with a discussion of how lessons learned from this initiative might improve the ways in which we deal with children's social and emotional needs through age-appropriate media content.

Background

Despite the large number of military families with young children and the challenges they face, the general public has been largely unaware of these families and their experiences. Sesame Workshop was drawn into the lives of these families after a series of news articles that focused on the plight of military families whose homes were being foreclosed while one of the parents was deployed (Haddock, 2003; Henriques, 2005). Inquiries by Sesame Workshop into the experiences of these families indicated what was already apparent to the military community: there are large numbers of military families with preschool children, and these families experience unique challenges. Further, few materials were designed specifically to meet the needs of these families and their young children. Recognizing its unique expertise in creating media content that addresses this age group's socioemotional and cognitive needs, Sesame Workshop decided to investigate how it might devote the power of its creative and educational resources toward producing materials for military families with young children.

Helping through Media

The idea that media can have a positive impact on the emotional well-being of children in vulnerable circumstances is often met with skepticism. Indeed, the popular press and some research suggest media might have quite the opposite effect on children's social and mental health (Villani, 2001; Singer et al., 1999; Schooler, Ward, Merriwether, & Caruthers, 2004). However, media produced in a way that carefully caters its content to the needs of its audience and their particular circumstances can result in positive outcomes (Austin & Husted, 1998; Bond, 2011; Snyder, 2007; Connolly, Fitzpatrick, Gallagher, &

Harris, 2006; see also Chapter 10, this volume). Sesame Workshop has a history of demonstrating its effectiveness through the media it has produced for young children and families living in challenging situations. In areas of conflict, such as Northern Ireland, Kosovo, Israel, and the Palestinian territories, Sesame Workshop has created media that help children, both socially and emotionally. Children who viewed Sesame Workshop's television shows produced in these areas showed greater gains in prosocial reasoning, or taking another's perspective (MediaKidz, 2012), cooperation, sharing, helping (Sesame Workshop, 2011), and/or mutual respect and understanding (Cole & Lee, in press).

How It's Done: The Workshop Model

To produce effective media for children, Sesame Workshop employs its "model," which enables three key players in the development of the material—producers, educators, and researchers—to coordinate their distinct areas of expertise (see Figure 14.1). Producers are responsible for the creative aspects of the material, educators develop and set the curricular goals, and researchers serve as the voice of the target audience to provide information on the materials' effectiveness (Cole, Richman, & McCann Brown, 2001).

The process of production for the *TLC* initiative closely resembles that used by Sesame Workshop's international projects (Cole, Labin,& Galarza, 2008; see Figure 14.2), in which initial phases involve a series of seminars led by experts familiar with the target population to determine the extent of need, identify the intended audience, and develop curriculum goals. These seminars are attended by producers, researchers, and educators so that ideas can be aired, goals can be clarified, and all those responsible for the project's success can share a common vision. The outcome of these seminars is a document that includes the main

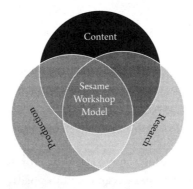

Figure 14.1 The Workshop Model.

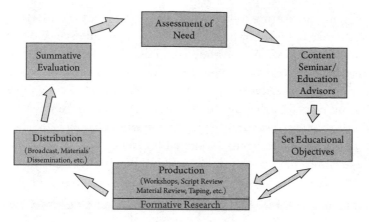

Figure 14.2 Cycle of Content in the Workshop Model.

curriculum goals of the project and describes how these goals can be addressed via media; this serves as a guide for creating content.

As content is created, formative research is conducted to inform on the production of materials. Draft materials are presented to the target audience to gauge comprehension, utility, and appeal. Reactions to materials are shared with producers and educators working on the project, and materials are revised accordingly. This iterative process is repeated with subsequent drafts of materials, as time and necessity permit, to help ensure the final product meets the needs of the target audience. After materials are produced and distributed, a summative evaluation may be conducted to determine the impact of the media project on its intended audience (Cole et al., 2001).

Talk, Listen, Connect: The Model at Work

Planning and executing a media initiative to help young children in military families cope was a challenging task. However, it was made manageable through the experience gained and through the methods developed by Sesame Workshop, described earlier. Each phase of the project followed the process developed around the Sesame Workshop model, and will be summarized in the sections that follow. Describing how *TLC* was developed may help others interested in producing media that aims to improve children's emotional well-being.

The Beginning: Advisory Seminar

To launch *TLC*, Sesame Workshop convened a meeting in 2005 with a group of advisors, including leading experts in child development, mental health, and programs supporting military families. The aim of the meeting was to outline the needs of military families with young children and determine whether and how Sesame Workshop could develop a set of media resources to assist military families with young children with the transitions and challenges they face. The advisory meeting clarified the experiences of military families and helped further define their needs. One clear message, for example, was that "when a parent is deployed, the whole family is deployed," and therefore any resources being developed for military families should target the whole family, not just the child. In addition, advisors explained that aiding parents and caregivers in helping their young children cope could also positively affect the parents' own ability to cope. Thus, materials aimed at helping young children could also be meaningful to the adults who care for them (Sesame Workshop, 2005).

Because of the stigma associated with seeking mental health–related assistance among military families (Hoge et al., 2004; Milliken, Auchterlonie, & Hoge, 2007), the advisors noted that *Sesame Street*, with characters who are appealing and familiar to both parents and their children, not imposing or threatening, might be an ideal vehicle to deliver important information to families with young children. Further, it was decided that the materials should aim to teach and encourage caregivers about ways to attend to their young children and provide strategies on how to talk with the children about the stresses and challenges they face. Thus, the *TLC* curriculum focused on:

- modeling age-appropriate conversations between preschoolers and adults using the *Sesame Street* characters;
- modeling age-appropriate strategies and activities to help cope with the stress of military life, specifically deployments, relocations, homecomings, death, and injury;
- teaching adult caregivers the importance of communication and strategies to promote communication with young children about the experiences they are going through;
- promoting the notion that enabling adult caregivers to help their children learn to cope will help the caregivers and the entire family cope as well; and
- using *Sesame Street*'s nonthreatening, and even inviting content, to avoid the stigma, common in the military community, of asking for assistance.

The materials would aim to reach as wide an audience as possible within the military community, with resources available in English and Spanish.

Figure 14.3 The *Talk, Listen, Connect*
Website.

Figure 14.4 *Talk, Listen Connect.*

Talk, Listen Connect: The Multiple Media Kits

Table 14.1 provides a brief description of the goals of each set of *Talk, Listen, Connect* materials. These bilingual (English/Spanish) multimedia outreach kits included DVDs for children and adults starring the Muppets from *Sesame Street*, as well as live-action footage of military families coping with the various phases of deployment and grief. Print materials for children, facilitators, parents, and other adult caregivers were also part of the kits, and included a storybook, parent guide, and posters. All of the materials are also available online at http://www sesamestreet.org/parents/topicsandactivities/toolkits/TLC.

The first set of resources, *Talk, Listen, Connect* (*TLC I*) was produced in 2006. Subsequent materials (*TLC II—Homecomings* and *TLC II—Changes*) were created to respond to the increased need of military families for resources regarding multiple deployments and parents returning with visible and/or "invisible" injuries (e.g., traumatic brain injuries, post-traumatic stress) (Clark et al., 2007). A final set of materials, *Talk, Listen, Connect: When Families Grieve*, was produced for those families who experienced the death of a parent (*TLC III—Grief*).

As with the broader initiative, advisory meetings were held to ascertain the main goals for each project, and formative research was conducted with the target audience

Table 14.1 **Brief Descriptions of the *Talk, Listen, Connect* resources**

Title	Sesame Street DVD Story*	Goals
Talk, Listen, Connect (2006)	Elmo learns to adjust after he discovers his father has to go away for an extended period of time.	• Help military families with young children between the ages of two and five build a sense of stability and resiliency during times of separation by offering age appropriate strategies for coping when a parent is deployed.
Talk, Listen, Connect—Homecomings (2008)	The DVD stories recounts age-appropriate situations regarding multiple deployment with the familiar *Sesame Street* characters, and with live action films of real military families.	• Assist parents with ways to help their children cope with multiple deployments by offering age-appropriate strategies for coping when a parent returns home, and must deploy again.
Talk, Listen, Connect—Changes (2008)	With the help of her Sesame Street friends and family, Rosita learns how to cope after her father is injured.	• Assist parents with ways to help young children gain an age-appropriate understanding of a parent's injury by including them and the entire family in the rehabilitation process. • Reassure children that they are loved and secure and that together with their families, they can learn new ways of supporting one another, and have hope for the future.
*Talk, Listen, Connect—When Families Grieve*** (2010)	Features a *Sesame Street* Muppets story about, and documentary footage of, families who have experienced the death of a parent due to a variety of situations including illness, suicide, accidents, and other sudden or natural causes	• Enable caregivers to help their children cope with the anxiety and confusion their children may experience following the death of a parent. • Provide families with age-appropriate tools to support and comfort children, including ways to talk about death with a young child. • Reassure children that they are loved and safe and that families can learn ways of supporting one another and move forward.

* Included in each of the DVDs is live-action footage of military families (and nonmilitary families) modeling appropriate coping and communication behaviors regarding the particular challenges addressed in each initiative. All sets of the *TLC* materials included video, print, and online materials for children and their adult caregivers.

**Two versions of *When Families Grieve* were produced, one for military and one for nonmilitary families.

to ensure the content was useful, relevant, and comprehensible. Finally, an evaluation was conducted to gauge the impact of the media resources on the target population.

However, even before these resources were fully developed, Sesame Workshop conducted formative research to inform on the production of the materials and ensure their relevance and utility for the intended audience.

Formative and Summative Research

The formative research for *TLC* involved presenting rough drafts of the video, online, and print materials to parents and caregivers of young children in military families. Based on responses to the drafts of the materials, the content and/or its presentation were revised to make certain the final product met the needs of military families with young children. This formative research included groups of parents or other primary caregivers, who were mostly female partners of deployed military service members. All five branches of the military were represented in the groups (Army, Marines, Navy, Air Force, and Coast Guard), as well as groups representing both the Reserve component (National Guard and Reserves) and active duty. In addition, because the materials are fully bilingual (English/Spanish), groups were conducted with both Spanish-speaking and English-speaking caregivers.

The reactions to these early drafts of the materials were positive and enthusiastic. To a great extent these reactions appeared to be driven by the fact that currently available information is both scarce and scattered, and what is available is antiquated. The participants described having to spend inordinate amounts of time searching for materials in an attempt to deal with the myriad of situations, issues, and challenges that arise for a military family with young children. Participants also pointed to the appeal and trust both they and their children felt for *Sesame Street* and its characters (Sesame Workshop, 2007).

However, the participants clearly felt important aspects of their experiences needed to be included or highlighted further. For example, participants noted that the *TLC I* materials should further reinforce the notion that "when a service member is deployed, the whole family is deployed." They felt that materials should therefore focus not only on helping children cope, but on how parents can also better cope by helping their children. Participants also stated that they did not experience deployment as a distinctly three-step process (predeployment, deployment, and homecoming), but more as one long continuous period fraught with a series of preparations and adjustments that typically extend past the time the family is reunited (Sesame Workshop, 2005).

Formative research conducted around *TLC II—Changes* and *TLC II—Homecomings* made it apparent that separate booklets and DVDs were necessary to address each of the topics of multiple deployment and injury. While many of the participants who reviewed drafts of the multiple deployment materials were

Figure 14.5 Talk, Listen, Connect:
Deployment, Changes, & Homecoming.

interested in exploring the *TLC II— Changes* content, they also wanted to have some control over how that content would be viewed by their young children. Participants in the *TLC II* formative research also suggested more appropriate phrases to use when discussing topics around injury with young children, for example that the injured parents be described as having had an "incident" not an "accident"; that children be told that "the injury occurred on their job," and that parents didn't "lose" a limb, but rather they "gave" one. Also, participants suggested that Elmo's house in the video portion of the materials should not appear too neat and organized, as this is not a realistic portrayal of a typical military household with children going through difficult circumstances (Sesame Workshop, 2007).

Formative research provided particularly valuable information that helped the development of the *TLC III—Grief* initiative. Participants described a number of challenges that families with young children need assistance with when a parent dies, such as how to

- explain death in concrete terms so that a child understands that it is permanent, and answer those questions that will likely arise (e.g., "Why did he/she die?" "Will he/she be coming back?" "Where is he/she now?");
- deal with the changes in family routine and structure that lie ahead, such as the surviving parent returning to work, moving, new responsibilities and routines, and so on;
- address the dual loss that military families experience, specifically the loss of a parent in the military coupled with the loss of the family's military home/ identity; and
- address differences in the way military families and families in the general public experience the initial period following the death of a parent.

Among those in the general public interviewed, most described the time between learning of the death and planning the funeral as quick, confusing

talk,
listen,
connect

When Families Grieve™

THIS KIT INCLUDES:
A Sesame Street DVD
A Guide for Parents and Caregivers
A Children's Story

Figure 14.6 Talk, Listen, Connect: When Families Grieve.

and overwhelming. By contrast, military families appear to have a support system in place to help guide them through these difficult moments and the questions and issues that immediately arise upon learning of the death of a loved one. As one provider serving military families explained, "In 24 hours most families have already gone through this process" (Sesame Workshop, 2010).

The producers at Sesame Workshop took the results of the formative research into consideration, and incorporated them into the final versions of the materials. The positive findings of the evaluations of these materials, described in Figure 14.3 below, along with their high appeal and use, may be due in part to these revisions.

Discussion

The results of the above evaluations clearly show that the *Talk, Listen, Connect* materials were appealing and well used, and indicate willingness among caregivers to share the materials with their young child despite the sensitive themes addressed. There is also evidence that the materials promoted positive change in caregivers' behavior and attitudes around helping their child cope with deployments, injury, and the death of a parent. While these evaluations did not include direct observations of parents or children, these results are hopeful and point to the potential for media to make a positive difference for military families experiencing traumatic or disruptive events.

Lessons for All Media Addressing the Emotional Needs of Children and their Caregivers

The elements that contributed to the success of *TLC* as an initiative for military families may be applied to the production of media for all children and families

Table 14.2 **Impact of Talk, Listen, Connect**

Title	Design	Sample	Findings
Talk, Listen, Connect	Pre-/post-	The sample of 367 participants represented a mix of military branches: active duty, guard, and reserve.	After using the materials, respondents • reported they were better able to handle future deployments; • reported they were more comfortable helping their preschooler cope with deployment; and • reported declines in weekly frequency of experiencing low interest and involvement in life and in feelings of depression or hopelessness (Russell Research, 2006).
Talk, Listen, Connect— Homecomings	Quasi-experimental*	The sample included a total of 232 participants representing a mix of military branches (active duty, guard, and reserve) who cared for children 2 to 5 years old. Most were mothers/spouses of military members.	Caregivers who received the TLC II—Homecomings kit were significantly more likely than v in the comparison group to report that • the kit changed the way they helped their child cope with deployment; and • they were more comfortable helping their child cope after using the kit than those in comparison group (Military Family Research Institute, 2009).
Talk, Listen, Connect— Changes	Quasi-experimental*	The sample of 153 caregivers included mostly mothers of children 2 to 8 years old who had a spouse injured while in the military.	Caregivers who received the TLC II—Changes kit were significantly more likely than those in the comparison group to report that • they had greater ease in dealing with their child's negative emotions, responding to their child's requests for help; • they had increased feelings of parenting support; • they had fewer feelings of being alone and felt more socially engaged;

(continued)

Table 14.2 Continued

Title	Design	Sample	Findings
			• they identified that their home environment was significantly less chaotic and their children less inhibited after using the kit; and • their children screamed or yelled significantly less and got into significantly fewer peer conflicts (Military Families Research Institute, 2009).
*Talk, Listen, Connect— When Families Grieve***	Quasi-experimental**	A total of 93 caregivers participated, and included mostly women. The majority of the deceased were fathers of children in the study. The majority of children in the baseline and post-exposure groups were between the ages of 2 and 8 years, with girls and boys equally represented. Because materials were aimed at nonmilitary and military families, both types of families were included in this evaluation.	Compared to the comparison group, participants who used the *TLC III* kit materials were • significantly more likely to report that the materials had a positive impact on their child's coping with grief; and • significantly more likely to report that the materials had a positive impact on their own coping with grief (Uniformed Services University of the Health Sciences, 2011).

*Participants were randomly assigned to a test group, which received the *Talk, Listen, Connect* materials to use for four weeks, or to a control group. The control group received a different *Sesame Street* outreach kit called *Healthy Habits for Life*, which promoted nutrition and physical activity, to use for the four weeks. The *Healthy Habits for Life* kit included components similar to those found in the *Homecomings and Changes* kit (a DVD, print materials for parents and children) but focused on nutrition.

**Participants were randomly assigned to a test group, which received the *Talk, Listen, Connect* materials to use for four weeks, or to a control group. The control group received a different *Sesame Street* outreach kit called *Let's Get Ready: Planning Together for Emergencies*, about emergency preparedness, to use for the four weeks. The *Let's Get Ready* kit included components similar to those found in the grief kit (a DVD, print materials for parents and children) but focused on emergency preparedness.

Figure 14.7 Engaging Audiences.

facing difficult circumstances. The lessons learned from producing *TLC* will shed light on how to develop media that can benefit the well-being of not only children in military families, but all children.

ENGAGE AUDIENCES

For any type of intervention, all participants must be engaged in the materials being developed and find the materials relevant to their needs. Past research has suggested that successful interventions for military families have both the support and commitment from the military community they are intended to serve, both at the administrative level, and at the level of the local installations and outlying communities where participating families live. In military communities this can be somewhat more complex, as each installation and branch may have significant differences both culturally and on a community level (Beardslee et al., 2011).

A similar strategy was used in the development of the Baby Elmo parenting program, designed for incarcerated teen fathers. The program intentionally engaged the staff of the prisons and jails where the project was being implemented, which not only helped encourage the adoption of the program in the different sites where it was implemented, but encouraged the staff to complement the program with their own ideas (e.g., graduation ceremonies for those completing the program) and to feel an investment in the success of the project (Brito et al., 2012). The importance of engaging the target audience is also emphasized with regard to media campaigns around nutrition. For example, Snyder (2007) states that engaging members of the target population and community organizations in campaign design and implementation—through community boards, hiring staff from the target population to be involved in campaign design, and conducting formative research with the target population— helps nutrition campaigns succeed.

USE FAMILIAR CHARACTERS

The familiarity and appeal of *Sesame Street* and its characters across a wide audience was a distinct advantage for the *Talk, Listen, Connect* initiative. No matter the geographic location or military branch, parents likely felt comfortable with the initiative and were likely to commit their time and effort to using its resources, because these were trusted characters. Indeed, the *Sesame Street* characters and brand were mentioned often in participants' reasons for finding the materials appealing and deciding to use them appeal and use of the materials. As studies on successful health-related media campaigns have found, to increase messages' acceptance, campaigns must select credible spokespeople and organizations that balance trustworthiness and expertise (McGuire, 1989; Kotler, Roberto, & Lee, 2002). For the families who received the *TLC* materials, *Sesame Street* seems to fall squarely into those categories. Moreover, the familiarity and appeal of *Sesame Street* and its characters may also explain the positive impact the materials had on families. Current research suggests that children learn better from television characters they know and like than from unknown characters (Lauricella, Gola, & Calvert, 2011). It may be that the positive impact of *TLC* that parents reported for their children may be due in part to the prior relationship the children had with the *Sesame Street* characters.

Figure 14.8 Use of Familiar Characters.

BE AWARE OF POTENTIAL BARRIERS AND HOW
TARGETING THE CHILD MAY HELP

Initiatives that deal with emotional well-being may also have to address the stigma that is sometimes associated with seeking assistance. An initiative may have the best intentions and resources, but without an audience it cannot succeed. *Talk, Listen, Connect,* by using familiar and child-friendly content, is able to subtly promote positive mental health messages in a way that is neither didactic nor judgmental. Because the information is conveyed through the eyes of a child (via a *Sesame Street* character), children and their parents are introduced to behaviors and ideas they might not otherwise be receptive to. Interestingly, other mental health–related campaigns have used this family-based strategy to overcome the stigma adults might believe is associated with seeking help, by providing services directed at the child. For example, Rishel (2012) notes that in regard to programs designed to assist depressed mothers, who are often reluctant to accept services for themselves, the focus may need to be initially on their children. Rishel explains that mothers overcome many barriers to seek services for their children, and therefore may be more willing to accept intervention approaches if providers focus these approaches on how they will benefit their children.

INVOLVE PARENTS AND OTHER CAREGIVERS

At the same time, adult caregivers should also be a focus of any media initiative designed to promote the emotional well-being of children. The *TLC* initiative was aimed at trying to support military children in the face of potentially difficult challenges imposed by the demands of their parent's military service, and while research has shown that several factors contribute to children's successfully facing these challenges, the strongest and most consistent is the behavior of parents (MacDermid et al., 2008). Similarly, the Baby Elmo project developed by Barr (2011) for incarcerated teen fathers focuses on the parent as well as the child because, as Barr explains, children show lower levels of aggressive behavior and better regulation of emotion when their biological fathers remain in contact with them (Barr et al., 2011).

LEVERAGE THE ACCESSIBILITY AND PRIVACY OF MEDIA

Media resources have "the advantage of being able to be accessed, in the privacy of the home" by groups who "may otherwise be difficult to reach" (Sander, Montgomery, & Brechman-Toussaint, 2000). *Talk, Listen, Connect,* as a set of media-based materials that can be used in the privacy of one's home, might be attractive to parents who might otherwise feel stigmatized for seeking assistance

Figure 14.9 Involving Parents and Caregivers.

Figure 14.10 Accessibility and Privacy of Media at Home.

for the family's emotional health. Moreover, the materials are portable and can be used wherever a military family's home might be, as long as they have internet access and/or a DVD player. This is particularly useful for military families, who relocate significantly more frequently than other families. Public health campaigns have also seen the value of media in reaching individuals in need who might not be ready pursue mental health assistance. Initiatives like the National Institute of Mental Health's "Real Men Real Depression," for example, use videos and the internet to raise awareness about depression, and researchers suggest that these media-based programs are valuable because they are able to reach individuals experiencing mental health issues who might not otherwise recognize their symptoms or seek treatment (Hammer & Vogel, 2010; Rochlen & Hoyer, 2005).

CONSIDER CULTURE

One must always work to make sure that media materials are sensitive to the distinct needs and norms of the culture they aim to serve. In the *TLC* initiative, we recognized the importance of being familiar with the workings of each branch of the military when producing materials. Depending on its focus, an initiative may require different versions of resources specific for each branch. Or an initiative might seek to create a single resource that would be relevant to the entire military community and provide resources that focus on goals that are general enough to be applicable to all branches. *Talk, Listen, Connect* attempted the latter strategy. The choice is often dictated by the intended audience, as well as available funding and time. This was the case when Sesame Workshop embarked on a rural literacy project. There was broad support within the targeted communities, but specific differences emerged. For example, libraries, which were a suggested resource for families with limited resources, were not a realistic option for some families. Materials therefore had to be adapted to accommodate different communities' needs (Sesame Workshop, 2005).

On another level, Sesame Workshop's international co-productions seek to create media relevant to the countries where they are being produced, because that will be most effective in reaching the children in those countries. Whether

Figure 14.11 Considering the Norms and Needs of Culture.

in Egypt, China, Russia, or Kuwait, each co-production must consider the culture of the country in which it is produced. While some curricular goals, such as health or numeracy, may not be unique to each country's co-production, the ways they are presented are culturally specific and unique (e.g., in the choices of accompanying music/songs, settings, clothing). As Cole and colleagues (2001) note, children learn best from the cultural context in which they live, and therefore a successful co-production must create media that are culturally relevant.

Conclusions

There are few resources for military families that target both parents and the young children in their care; even fewer of these resources have been evaluated

Figure 14.12 The TLC Project—Considering the Emotional Well-Being of Children.

in any way. Sesame Workshop's *Talk, List, Connect* project provides an example of how a media-based initiative functioned and performed with military families. The media component was a distinct advantage for this initiative in addressing the needs of a military family audience. While it may be that part of what accounted for the high appeal and use of the materials was the familiarity and popularity of *Sesame Street* and its characters, the formats of the materials—the DVD, print and online materials—and their packaging into a convenient kit—were probably an added feature that contributed to the use and impact of the materials. It is unclear whether an intervention that required families to attend workshops or clinical evaluations would be as popular, particularly with a population that might be reluctant to seek mental health assistance. The portability and easy access of a media-based resource can therefore also be seen as a positive aspect of the initiative for families and should not be underestimated.

There are limitations to the evaluations described above, including self-report and the absence of direct observations of children and parents, as well as the absence of a comparison group in the initial *TLC I* evaluation. It would also be useful to examine whether and how the combination of the all *TLC* media resources—DVDs, online materials, live shows, television specials, and print resources—may affect military families' well-being. Nevertheless, the findings point to the positive impact a media-based intervention might have on military families with young children. Moreover, the characteristics of the *TLC* project that contributed to its success, namely that it is deemed relevant by the target audience, produced from a trusted source, and appeals to children as well as their caregivers, can be applied to all types of media-based initiatives designed to promote the emotional well-being of vulnerable children and families.

References

Austin, L. S., & Husted, K. (1998). Cost-effectiveness of television, radio, and print media programs for public mental health education. *Psychiatric Services, 49*(6), 808–811.

Barr, R., Brito, N., Zocca, J., Reina, S., Rodriguez, J., & Shauffer, C. (2011). The Baby Elmo program: Improving teen father–child interactions within juvenile justice facilities. *Children and Youth Services Review, 33*(9), 1555–1562.

Brito, N., Barr, R., Rodriguez, J., & Shauffer, C. (May, 2012). Developing an effective intervention for incarcerated teen fathers. *Zero to Three, 32*(5), 26–32.

Beardslee, W., Lester, P., Klosinski, L., Saltzman, W., Woodward, K., Nash, W.,...& Leskin, G. (2011). Family-centered preventive intervention for military families: Implications for implementation science. *Prevention Science, 12*(4), 339–348.

Behnke, A. O., MacDermid, S. M., Anderson, J. C., Weiss, & Howard M. (2010). Ethnic variations in the connection between work-induced family separation and turnover intent. *Journal of Family Issues, 31*(5), 626–655.

Bond, B. J. (2011). Sexuality in the media and emotional well-being among lesbian, gay, & bisexual adolescents. (Unpublished doctoral dissertation). University of Illinois, Urbana-Champaign.

Clark, M., Bair, M., Buckenmaier, C., Gironda, R., & Walker, R. (2007). Pain and combat injuries in soldiers returning from Operations Enduring Freedom and Iraqi Freedom: Implications for research and practice. *Journal of Rehabilitation Research and Development*, 44(2), 179–194.

Cole, C. F., Labin, D., & Galarza, M. (2008). Begin with the children: What research on Sesame Street's international coproductions reveals about using media to promote a new more peaceful world. *International Journal of Behavioral Development*, 32(4), 359–365.

Cole, C. F., & Lee, J. H. (In press). Using media to foster mutual respect and understanding among children in a post-conflict region: The Rruga Sesam/Ulica Sezam project in Kosovo. In C. Ramirez-Barat (Ed.), *Transitional justice, culture, and society*. New York, NY: International Center for Transitional Justice.

Cole, C. F., Richman, B. A., & McCann Brown, S. A. (2001). The world of *Sesame Street* research. In S. Fisch & R. Truglio (Eds.), *"G" is for Growing*. Mahwah, NJ: Erlbaum.

Haddock, S. (2003, December 5) Soldier's family facing eviction. *Deseret Morning News*. Retrieved from http://www.deseretnews.com/article/565036557/Soldiers-family-facing-eviction.html?pg=all

Hammer, J. H., & Vogel, D. L. (2010). Men's help seeking for depression: The efficacy of a male-sensitive brochure about counseling. *The Counseling Psychologist*, 38, 296–313.

Henriques, D. B. (2005, March 28). Some creditors make illegal demands on active duty soldiers. *The New York Times*. Retrieved from http://www.nytimes.com/2005/03/28/national/28military.html?_r=0

Hoge, C. W., Castro, C. A., Messer, S. C., McGurk, D., Cotting, D. I., & Koffman, R. L. (2004). Combat duty in Iraq and Afghanistan, mental health problems, and barriers to care. *The New England Journal of Medicine*, 351(1), 13–22.

Huebner, A. J., & Mancini, J. A. (2005, June). Adjustments among adolescents in military families when a parent is deployed. *Final report to the Military Family Research Institute and Department of Defense Quality of Life Office*. Retrieved from http://www.cfs.purdue.edu/mfri/pages/research/Adjustments_in_adolescents.pdf

Lauricella, A. R., Gola, A. A. H., & Calvert, S. L. (2011). Toddlers' learning from socially meaningful video characters. *Media Psychology*, 14(2), 216–232.

MacDermid, S. M., Samper, R, Schwarz, R, Nishida, J., & Nyaronga, D. (2008). Understanding and promoting resilience in military families. West Lafayette, IN: Military Family Research Institute at Purdue University.

McGuire, William J. (1989). Theoretical foundations of campaigns. In R. E. Rice and C.A. Atkin (Eds.), *Public communication campaigns* (2nd ed.) (pp. 43–65). Newbury Park, CA: Sage.

MediaKidz Research & Consulting. (2012). Rechov Sumsum experimental study: Learning among Jewish preschoolers in Israel. Unpublished manuscript.

Milliken, C. S., Auchterlonie, J. L., & Hoge, C. W. (2007). Longitudinal assessment of mental health problems among active and reserve component soldiers returning from the Iraq war. *The Journal of the American Medical Association*, 298(18), 2141–2148.

Orthner, D. K., & Rose, R. (2005). *SAF V survey report:Adjustment of army children to deployment separations*. Chapel Hill, NC: The University of North Carolina at Chapel Hill.

Rishel, C. W. (2012). Pathways to prevention for children of depressed mothers: A review of the literature and recommendations for practice. *Depression Research and Treatment*. Retrieved from http://www.hindawi.com/journals/drt/2012/313689/

Rochlen, A. B., & Hoyer, W. D. (2005). Marketing mental health to men. *Journal of Clinical Psychology*, 61, 675–684.

Sanders, M. R., Montgomery, D. T., & Brechman-Toussaint, M. L. (2000). The mass media and the prevention of child behavior problems: The evaluation of a television series to promote positive outcomes for parents and their children. *Journal of Child Psychology and Psychiatry*, 41(7), 939–948.

Schooler, D. L., Ward, M., Merriwether, A., & Caruthers, A. (2004). Who's that girl: Television's role in the body image development of young white and black women. *Psychology of Women Quarterly, 28*, 38–47.

Secretary of Defense. (2010). *2010 Demographics profile of the military community.* Retrieved from http://www.militaryonesource.mil/12038/MOS/Reports/2010_Demographics_Report.pdf

Sesame Workshop. (2005). Rural literacy: Findings of focus groups to inform on the production of literacy materials for rural children and their caregivers in Mississippi. Unpublished manuscript.

Sesame Workshop. (2007). Formative Research on Phase II of Sesame Workshop's Military Families Outreach Initiative. Unpublished manuscript.

Sesame Workshop. (2010). Talk, Listen, Connect III: Families Coping with Death: a Project for Military and Civilian Families with Young Children. Focus Group Research. Unpublished manuscript.

Sesame Workshop. (2011). The educational impact of *Shara'a Simsim* on children in the West Bank. Unpublished manuscript.

Singer, M. I., Miller, D. B., Guo, S., Flannery, D. J., Frierson, T., & Slovak, K. (1999). Contributors to violent behavior among elementary and middle school children. *Pediatrics, 104*(4), 878–884.

Snyder, L. B. (2007). Health communication campaigns and their impact on behavior. *Journal of Nutrition Education and Behavior, 39*(2), 32–40.

Villani, S. (2001). Impact of media on children and adolescents: a 10-year review of the research. *Journal of the American Academy of Child and Adolescent Psychiatry, 40*(4), 392–401.

CHAPTER 15

Perspectives on Parenting in a Digital Age

■

Anne Collier

"We're growing a bunch of people who see what they do as social and collaborative and as parts of joining online communities," said Arizona State University professor James Paul Gee in an interview for PBS's *Frontline* (2009). He talked about how naturally our kids work and play in what the business world calls "cross-functional teams," where everybody on the team is an absolute expert in something, but they know how to integrate their expertise with everybody else's. They know how to understand the other person's expertise so they can pull off an action together in a complicated world...a very important way of being in the world in the 21st century....And kids are ready for this world" (Frontline, 2009).

Parents don't get that message about the digital age a lot. Instead, for the past decade and a half, the messages they've been hearing much more often—in the news media, from their children's schools, from policymakers and even children's advocates—are that this new media environment we're all experiencing is quite likely harmful to children. For example, these are titles of breakout sessions at a national law enforcement conference in 2009: "Facebook, the Sex Offenders' Catalog," "MySpace. The predator's new playground," and "How the Media Is Killing Our Children" (http://www.nasro.org).

While largely well-intentioned, probably, the messaging about digital media's risks to children's well-being—predators, cyberbullying, multitasking, video game violence, sexting, and so on—replaces curiosity, communication, and collaboration with fear of and disrespect for something that is engaging our children in many ways. "What we decide to pay attention to determines what we see," is how Cathy Davidson, a professor of ____English at Duke University, explained "attention blindness" in an interview about her latest book, *Now You See It*, for the MacArthur Foundation's Spotlight on Digital Media (Ray, 2011). Davidson was talking about education; I apply this argument also to the way we view and approach our children's experiences with technology—and our parenting. If we focus on the risks, victimization and fear that dominate the news coverage and political messaging about youth and technology, we're missing valuable information about our children's use of new media, including the kind that comes with calm conversations with our kids themselves.

"Parents receive so little advice about how to confront the real challenges of navigating the digital environment which is unfamiliar to them and often to their children," wrote Henry Jenkins, professor of communication at the University of Southern California introducing a talk he gave to parents of his students (Jenkins, 2010). "Most often, [parents] are told, 'just say no.' The more you restrict media use, the better parent you are. And for God's sake, keep the computer out of the kid's bedroom. But none of that feels adequate for a world where there is real learning taking place online, where learning to navigate the new media environment is going to be key for your offspring's future success." John Seely Brown, scientist and visiting scholar at USC, punctuated that point about 18 months later in a keynote speech at the Digital Media & Learning conference in March 2012, saying that "the most unsafe thing you could do is not let your kids start to understand how to interact with the world" (http://dml2012.dmlhub.net).

The Problem of "Juvenoia"

So why does society seem so inclined to believe the opposite—that new media are harmful to children? I think one answer is too little "signal" from research, cutting through all the "noise" from the technopanic—shorthand for the moral panic the developed world has experienced over the media shift—or an unwillingness to trust the research (Marwick, 2008). That, blended with the usual parental fears about influences over our children which we can't control and the usual human fear of that which we don't understand, make for what seems to be an unusually and actually inappropriately acute case of "juvenoia" for this generation of parents. I'll get to the inappropriate part in a minute, but first: juvenoia.

The term was coined by David Finkelhor, director of the Crimes Against Children Research Center at the University of New Hampshire, for "the exaggerated fear of the influence of social change on youth." It's not new, he says. It seems to afflict every generation as it forgets its own growing-up years. In a talk he gave in late 2010, the professor pointed out an observation attributed to Aristophanes around 400 B.C.: "The children now love luxury, they have bad manners, contempt for authority...and love chatter in place of exercise" (Aristophanes foretold Facebook chat!)—and a similar one by medieval monk Peter the Hermit saying, somewhere around the 12th or 13th century, that "the young people of today think of nothing but themselves [reminding me of current claims of a narcissism epidemic].... They are impatient of all restraint." Fast-forward a handful of centuries, and you have the U.S. comic-book panic of the '50s, complete with congressional hearings on comic books' impact on America's youth, and a number of other modern-day examples Finkelhor cited (http://vimeo.com/16900027).

So if adults have always had this anxiety around the necessarily self-focused, identity-exploring ways of adolescents as they get ready to leave and find new caves, continents, or careers, why is the internet seen as a threat that—in today's parental minds—may equal or exceed the draft, rock 'n' roll, the antiwar movement, and the sexual revolution? "Exposure" is the short answer. And not exposure to technology, but the exposure that the internet and digital media afford.

24/7 Exposure to Somebody Else's Values?

Finkelhor, who is a parent too and jokingly paused before taking questions to "monitor my son's Facebook profile," has talked about "the biosocial parental investment in offspring" and what we see as threats to our offspring. What the internet affords is the newest seeming threat to that investment: a combination of maximum diversity and 24/7 exposure to a diversity of values.

This goes deeper than technophobia and describes what's unique about today's media sea change. But first let's look back to what it contrasts with. Consider what ancient tribal society was like for parents, and compare it to today. As Finkelhor has suggested, back then the whole tribe shared the same values, so the inputs all around a child supported his or her parents' inputs. Now, in today's user-driven media environment, children are constantly exposed to a vast array of values from all directions: not just from regulated, professionally produced media, but from potentially everybody, because anybody—including our children's peers—can be a media producer now. So to an unprecedented degree, "Virtually every parent from every station in life," Finkelhor said, "sees him or herself as raising children in *opposition* to the common culture [which includes the internet and which certainly doesn't have much commonality]. Parents feel undermined by it—pitted, depending on their point of view, against consumerism, secularism, sexual licentiousness, government regulation, violence, junk food, public schools, religious and racial bigotry.... Of course the internet is one of the institutions that increased the diversity of that exposure, and this leads to a constant anxiety about [children's exposure to] external threats" to "our family's values" (http://vimeo.com/16900027).

A Parental Siege Mentality

As I listened to Finkelhor's talk, the phrase "siege mentality" came to mind. It seems to be based on a feeling that this generation of young people is somehow increasingly—and unprecedentedly—different from the older generation because of our children's comparative comfort with a new media environment we so often hear is threatening to them, and thus to our ability to raise them properly. Finkelhor sums it up with a phrase from Khalil Gibran: a feeling that "our children are not our children."

So naturally there's anxiety among parents, who grew up in a radically different media environment, about their children being exposed to new unknowns that run counter to their values—and new environments where they have little control. The fears are based on a belief that the internet is separate from our children's real-world lives, wholly apart from the lives in which we are involved and have some influence. And following the faulty logic, we believe that we have no influence in this "alternate reality" of social media, an unknown territory that becomes the focus of our fears.

Finkelhor's "juvenoia" theory is not about technology, of course. Fear of outside influences on our children runs far deeper and is much more long-standing than the digital native–digital immigrant divide so often cited. Adding to that apparent fear of losing control over how their children will turn out is the question of how much of a role digital media and devices are playing in it. Lynn Schofield Clark, professor of journalism and new media at the University of Denver, suggests that the internet is only part of the problem for today's parents. In her book *The Parent App,* she wrote

> As evidenced in the rise of "helicopter parenting" and "over parenting" among especially more advantaged families who seek to manage ever-more minute aspects of young peoples' lives, and the "enmeshed parenting" that occurs as lower income parents attempt to play a large role in their children's emotional lives, western society seems to have developed a discomfort with both the developmental process of growing up and with the roles of parents and of the digital and mobile media within these processes (Schofield Clark, 2012a).

So we need to look at those fears as the iconic excuse they can be for vilifying new media and not allowing their use in school. It may also be helpful to consider the negative effects society's demonization of the social tools our children find so compelling may be having on parent-child communication and child development.

Not Alien Life Forms

In a 2010 talk, Sonia Livingstone, professor of psychology at the London School of Economics, said that the widely used term "digital native" is suggestive of some alien life form which new media somehow "brought into being a whole new species, a youth transformed, qualitatively distinct from anything that has gone before, an alien form whose habits it is our task to understand," when what's being discussed, actually, is our children, who need our support. The term adds humiliation to the intimidation many parents face by suggesting that all children have mastered something adults— "immigrants" from a different media context—can't possibly understand.

"Talking about digital natives and digital immigrants…disempowers adults, encouraging them to feel helpless, and thus justifying their decision not to know and not to care what happens to young people as they move into the online world," wrote media professor Henry Jenkins (2007). Such reasoning increases youths' online risk rather than lessening it. "As long as we divide the world into digital natives and immigrants, we won't be able to talk meaningfully about the kinds of sharing that occur between adults and children," Jenkins added, pointing to a key safeguard for online youth: clear channels of communication with their parents (more on this to come). "And we won't be able to imagine other ways that adults can interact with youth outside of these cultural divides. What once seemed to be a powerful tool for rethinking old assumptions about what kinds of educational experiences or skills were valuable, which was what excited me about [Marc] Prensky's original formulation, now becomes a rhetorical device that short circuits thinking about meaningful collaboration across the generations," Jenkins wrote, detailing a number of other problems with the "rhetorical device." [Jenkins is referring to writer and education consultant Marc Prensky, who coined the term "digital native."]

No Such Generation Gap

David Finkelhor suggests that the generation gap is more perception than reality anyway. "I don't think the cyber revolution shows much evidence of being a big one. If you look back on generation rifts of the past—the feminist movement, flag burning, the antiwar movement—the current generational difference looks small. I think the case can be made that social technology is actually *bridging* generational differences to a degree." He pointed to the "new ways for the generations to connect" afforded by new media. And this technological revolution "does not involve a fundamental change in values the way other generational rifts did."

Findings by the Pew Internet & American Life Project in 2011 certainly confirm that whatever generational divide there is today is no worse than in previous generations—and even suggest that the advent of social media may have had a positive effect on parent-child communication. Both teens and parents told the researchers that "parents are the most often cited source of advice and the biggest influence on teens' understanding of appropriate and inappropriate digital behavior" (Lenhart et al., 2011). Pew added that "the vast majority of parents of online teenagers have had serious conversations with their kids about the do's and don'ts of online behavior," and "overwhelmingly, both groups said that parents are talking to teens about these issues." For example 94% of parents and 88% of teens "report discussing what kinds of things should and should not be shared online."

Clearly, parents of kids growing up in the early 21st century found themselves in a challenging transitional period: not only had research not caught up with speculation about young people's media use in the Web's first decade, but—as social media took off in the second half of the last decade—there was high-profile resistance even to believing the research that had slowly emerged. After the Internet Safety Technical Task Force of 2008 announced the findings of its comprehensive review of the research about youth online risk in January 2009, in a report entitled "Enhancing child Safety & Online Technologies" (http://cyber.law.harvard.edu/pubrelease/isttf/) several of the state attorneys general who formed the task force set an unfortunate example in speaking out against the findings of the peer-reviewed research, including Richard Blumenthal in Connecticut, Roy Cooper in North Carolina (Steel, 2009), Tom Corbett in Pennsylvania (Magid, 2009), and Henry McMaster in South Carolina (CarolinaLive.com, 2009). Before there was a "diagnosis" of the problem of youth risk in social networking sites, the attorneys general had "prescribed" age verification technology as the solution. So in an effort to approach that diagnosis, the task force conducted a comprehensive review of the research about youth online risk through 2008–as well as of some 40 technologies in the general category of user identification. But the attorneys general basically denounced the report's conclusions as "disappointing" and the peer-reviewed research as "outdated or unrealistic." [Disclosure: I served on this task force and co-chaired the next national task force on the subject, the Online Safety & Technology Working Group (OSTWG), which sent its report, "Youth Safety on a Living Internet," to Congress in June 2010 (about which I wrote and to which I linked here http://www.netfamilynews.org/?p=29092).]

A Turning Point for U.S. Internet Safety

However, the report represented a turning point for the national discussion about child safety online, presenting the public with definitive findings from the new body of research about youth online risk, and presenting parents, educators, and policymakers for the first time with a stark choice: be fear-based or fact-based in working with our online children. And the key findings of this study that looked at the full spectrum of online risk offered important guidance, including the following:

- Peer harassment and bullying online—not grooming, predation, and other crimes, which were the focus of the state attorneys general—are the most salient online risk. Ybarra and Mitchell (2007) present a related key finding: that aggressive behavior online more than doubles the aggressor's risk online, ranging from harassment to sexual solicitation..
- Not all youth are equally at risk online and those most at risk online are those most at risk offline.
- A child's psychosocial makeup and home and school environments are better predictors of online risk than any technology the child uses.
- No single technological development can end children's online risk.

Although more insights from the newer body of social media research had yet to emerge, these findings gave us a much better handle on the problem. For one thing, the prescription of the attorneys general before the task force convened—age verification, aimed at keeping adults out of young people's online experiences—was the exact opposite of what children need, online or offline. The removal of adults' presence—and therefore guidance—is actually what fear-based messaging in general has led to, right in the middle of this transitional time when parents feel like digital novices and guidance is greatly needed (and sought after by children, as the Pew study showed). That was the message of Henry Jenkins when he spoke to the Online Safety & Technology Working Group (OSTWG) in September 2009—that we have left young people largely on their own on social media sites.

"Most young people are trying to make the right choices in a world that most of us don't fully understand yet," Jenkins said, "a world where they can't get good advice from the adults around them, where they are moving into new activities that were not part of the life of their parents growing up—very capable young people who are doing responsible things, taking advantage of the technologies that are around them." Jenkins was speaking to the OSTWG, in what would be the first representation of social media scholarship in a national child online safety task force report in the United States.

He said teens are engaged in four activities "central to the life of young people in participatory culture: circulating media, connecting with each other, creating media, and collaborating with each other." It is crucial, he said, to bring these activities into classrooms nationwide so that all young people have equal opportunity to participate. This is crucial, too, because young people "are looking for guidance often [in their use of new media] but don't know where to turn," Jenkins told the OSTWG, which was the next national task force on youth online safety.

Lynn Schofield Clark makes a similar point about families in her book *The Parent App*: "To exist in digital space is to exist in peer culture, especially for teens, and the role of parents is to understand and to act as sympathetic guides as their children navigate this environment as it expands into digital spaces" (Schofield Clark, 2012b). This was a message that, as co-chair, I felt needed to be sent to lawmakers and to be prominent in the public discussion about K–12 education as well as internet safety. Making digital literacy and citizenship instruction part of teaching core subjects throughout the school day, would not only prepare a broad socioeconomic spectrum of American youth for their futures, it would also support their academic and social success. It's a message that we felt would help parents as well, as they worked past fears of new media and worked with their kids in learning to navigate this networked world.

By giving the OSTWG report the title "Youth Safety on a Living Internet," we hoped, with a few words, to encourage people of our generation to entertain the possibility that the internet represented something different to our children (and all of us) than what it had been represented to be in the public discussion for nearly 15 years. We hoped to suggest that it was (1) not a threatening new addition to life and media from which we had to protect youth and (2) not inconsequential or a waste of people's time, but rather something more familiar to us than unfamiliar, embedded in and expressive of our own children's lives, as well as a powerful learning tool. As a user-driven medium of expression, sociality, production, research, entertainment, and so on, social media is the most versatile, customizable, personal tool humanity has seen yet, so its use—whether positive, neutral, or negative—is highly individual. Extrapolating our children's experiences in and with social media from news headlines, or from the views of law enforcement people who spend their days addressing crime is, at best, not productive.

In a 2010 presentation of her research on youth and digital ethics, Carrie James, research director at the Harvard School of Education said, "If youth are to leverage new media for civic participation, they will need to start seeing online life as consequential and meaningful –and not simply as a joke, for fun or something that helps them pursue only their individual interests" (Stepanek, 2010). That won't happen until the adults in their homes and schools treat young people's media use as consequential and meaningful rather than a waste of time or even destructive to their future success and well-being.

Implications of a "Living Internet"

What may help us with that—and with more effectively incorporating digital media and technologies into our parenting—is to understand how our children's media are different from the media with which we grew up. For one thing, the content of today's media is increasingly the content of our lives—as well as our entertainment, research, communications, and so on. We and especially our children are no longer mere media consumers. We can't approach new media intelligently if we view or treat them the way our parents treated our TV-viewing when we were growing up.

New Meaning of "Content" The meaning of "content" has evolved as the Web has become more social—as its use has increasingly meant people using text and other media to interact with each other as much as with content on a screen. Content is now as behavioral as it is informational, and—in the context of children's online safety—it's impossible to block behavior happening in real time the way filtering software blocks content, much less have technology detect what is reliably negative from outside the context of either a conversation or a social circle. It's difficult enough for humans to isolate a single behavior from a chain of action and reaction. Technology can't be a reliable blanket protection for kids. It can serve as a useful, somewhat effective tool for some specific concerns, such as blocking adult content for kids not actively seeking out workarounds or monitoring some of a child's Facebook activities, but it can't resolve issues in human relationships, which is where most online problems are rooted. Parenting and other guidance is what does that.

EMBEDDED IN REAL LIFE

Young people's social lives are expressed both online and offline. Most adults now understand that "online" —which now means on the Web, on cell phones, in gaming communities, and so on—is just another place where life is lived. So the content we see in social media is a freeze frame of relational behavior played out over time in the social context of two or more participants. What this means for parental control tools is that getting a Web or mobile service to block or delete something posted can't solve whatever's going on among the people involved—and in the case of young people's case, this often means what's going on at school.

SAFETY IS COLLABORATIVE

Because media are social and behavioral, now by definition safety, privacy, and reputation management are shared propositions for the participants. Each is a stakeholder in how positive or negative his or her and everybody's experiences are. And, just as in physical environments—such as homes, schools, and workplaces—protective social norms naturally develop in digital media environments, too. Those who maintain those environments, including providers of social networking sites, gaming communities, and virtual worlds can't feasibly be held solely responsible for the culture that develops, but they too are stakeholders and should act as such.

RISK SPECTRUM MATCHES REAL LIFE

Because the internet mirrors and serves as a platform for virtually all of human life, it mirrors the full spectrum of offline risks, not just the few featured in popular TV shows or covered in news reports focused on the most extreme outcomes. Consider cyberbullying, the online risk identified by the 2009 Berkman task force report as the one that affects the most youth (with about 20% of U.S. 10- to 18-year-olds reporting that they've experienced it in their lifetimes, according to more recent data from the Cyberbullying Research Center (Patching & Hinduja, 2010)). Cyberbullying isn't a single identifiable behavior, and what happens online sometimes starts offline and is often only part of a chain of communication and behavior online and offline. Whoever appears to be the "bully" online could well have been reacting to another child's aggression offline. The advent of cyberbullying has renewed national discussions about bullying in many countries, including new multidisciplinary social movements to address it, for example, Lady Gaga's Born This Way Foundation's collaboration with Harvard University's Berkman Center for Internet & Society.

THE INTERNET'S EVERYWHERE

That the internet is everywhere is true in a literal sense, of course—especially as people around the world increasingly see themselves as participants in a global culture (Collier, 2012)—and it's true in terms of devices, with all their fixed and mobile platforms. So the notion of "parental control" is increasingly challenged by multiplying workarounds and hotspots, including the homes of friends, who are subject to different levels and notions of control. The same goes for school, where there may be strict control of internet access on computers, while at least three-quarters of the student body are carrying around in their pockets full-blown internet-connected computers in the form of cell phones (Lenhart, 2012) and where students have a much better handle on filter workarounds than their teachers do (Reich, 2009). So, given the research showing that aggressive behavior online increases online risk, a school culture of respect and civility goes much further toward counteracting social cruelty and protecting students than any filter could.

CONSTANTLY CHANGING

Like the changing relationships and lives expressed in real time in the medium (the internet), the medium itself is dynamic too. That means (1) one-size-fits-all solutions don't exist; (2) laws are a clumsy, blunt-instrument treatment for risk; and therefore (3) a diverse array of tools for supporting users and addressing risk is needed. Those tools include education; ongoing two-way communication;

parental supports such as content ratings and a variety of parental control software products; family and school policies; and privacy and safety features on websites and devices.

THE NET EFFECT

Parenting hasn't changed all that much since the advent of the Web, but there are some new and challenging ways that social media do change the equation—factors that parents and kids could discuss, ideally, before a child goes online and revisit every now and then. Many internet users are familiar with some of them, but they were pulled together and explained by social media scholar danah boyd in her 2008 PhD dissertation. For the purposes of family discussions, boyd's factors might be described this way:

- Online socializers and media sharers need to be aware that there are often "invisible audiences" for what they post.
- Those audiences could be small or huge, or they could start small and grow (and it's difficult to tell in advance if they will).
- Those readers, viewers, friends, acquaintances, potential ex-friends, and employers can copy and paste what you post somewhere else, including places you're not even aware of.
- Once we post things, they're "out there" pretty much forever and can probably be found with a search engine.
- No matter how you've set your privacy settings, you can never really be sure of how private your information is or will be. For example, if they're set so only your friends can see what you post, friends can share with other people, and sometimes friends act out of anger or become ex-friends.

boyd calls these factors "four properties—persistence, searchability, replicability, and scalability—and three dynamics: invisible audiences, collapsed contexts, and the blurring of public and private" (Boyd, 2008, p. 2). The change they represent is due to the fact that the different contexts in which we've always conducted parts of our lives—home, school parking lot, Xbox Live, classroom, Thanksgiving Dinner—with people who also represent various parts of our lives (school friends, relatives, acquaintances, etc.)—are now collapsed into a single context online, such as in a social networking site. But even these conditions are changing, as young people diversify their online social tools and move more and more of their socializing onto the mobile platform (i.e., using apps on cell phones) in an effort to maintain their own social spaces away from the unprecedented surveillance of the adults in their lives, which new media afford (see Steeves, 2012).

No Better Tool Than Communication

This brings us back to the key role of parent-child communication under these media environmental conditions. As always, nonreactive, open communication seems both to help parents keep up with their kids' developing media interests and help children accept whatever safety strategies their parents devise for them. Sahara Byrne and Theodore Lee at Cornell University surveyed "a United States national sample of 456 parents" and "children aged 10–16," looking at "a wide range of [household] Internet risk prevention strategies" and the young people's attitudes toward each strategy. They found that "the more children reported it being hard to talk to their parents [about online issues], the more the disagreement over household strategies" (such as parental control technology, rules, monitoring, etc.) (Byrne & Lee, 2011). The children who said they had good communication with their parents "tend to put up with" whatever online safety measures their parents impose—interestingly, even when parents use a more authoritarian parenting style, Byrne and Lee wrote. "While a lofty goal, parents should aim to reduce their children's perceived difficulty of talking honestly with their parents about problems they might encounter online."

Communication Works Better Than Control Now

Parenting is informed by a lot more than changes in the media environment and their children's practices. Parents also face socioeconomic and societal pressures, as Lynn Clark points out in *The Parent App*. These are having an impact on traditional views of parenting styles:

> U.S. society has tended to view young people either as vulnerable and in need of protection or as a potential menace to be controlled and contained. When we think of children as vulnerable and in need of protection, we want to offer them warmth and support. In contrast, when we think of children in relation to problem behaviors, we consider the benefits of regulation and control. These two components—warmth/support and regulation/control—guide parenting behaviors, and research suggests that the best parenting practices involve finding a balance between responsiveness (warm and supportive parenting) and demandingness (regulating behaviors). This balanced style is termed authoritative parenting, and it contrasts with the less desirable styles of authoritarian (demanding but not warm), permissive (warm but not demanding), and neglectful (neither demanding nor warm) parenting. (Schofield Clark, 2012b, p. 49)

A strictly regulatory approach will probably be even less effective if based on the belief that parents can have complete control over the internet users in their charge. Now that the user-driven highly mobile media now in use afford children unprecedented agency—opportunities to produce, share, participate, and easily find workarounds to restrictions (such as proxy servers that help circumvent school filters)—parents will increasingly find they need to factor that affordance into their parenting. In other words, because of the ease with which teens and technically astute younger children can circumvent control of their online activities, the use of persuasion and communication is more in sync with the conditions of our media environment and its affordances than efforts to control. It seems that, where media's concerned, whether at the household, school or government level, regulatory power is more distributed than ever and self-regulation, both individual and collective (or corporate), more needed than ever.

BREATHERS

Breaks from the drama of school life in the form of quiet conversations, hugs, and support in dealing with social-scene overload are better and more positive than a negative approach of taking away technology or media. Tech and media don't create drama—people do; rather, tech and media are drama-enhancers, -extenders, and -perpetuators. Restricting the latter can help sometimes, if the goal is helping kids get perspective, but it can also cut them off from friends and situations, when being plugged in has become a social norm for most youth. Restricting or banning media can also send the message that escaping social problems is the solution rather than working them out.

REALITY CHECKS

In occasional conversations about social situations, parents can help their children remember that the seeming tsunami of school life they face everyday and then bring home on their phones and other screens does not represent the sum total of reality: there is much more to life and much more to them than the role they play at school, where it's not always easy for them totally to be themselves.

BALANCE

This comes up often with parents in this digital age: the need to help kids balance the social, academic, athletic, onscreen, and offscreen activities in their lives. But go deeper. With constant exposure to friends' thinking, do kids have enough chances for the reflection and independent thought that help them figure out who they are—not just who they are relative to the social network that's always in their pocket? "The anxiety that teens report when they are without their cell-phones ... may not speak so much to missing the easy sociability with others but of missing the self that is constituted in these relationships," writes MIT professor of sociology Sherry Turkle. It's not just a balance of activities, on screen or otherwise, that children need but also of activity and reflection and independent thought (Turkle, 2006).

GUIDANCE

That children need guidance is intuitive, but as the Online Safety & Technology Working Group heard from Professor Jenkins (above), guidance from parents *in and with social media* has been in short supply. Restriction has been the default tendency. Command-and-control seems to work less in this user-driven media environment than ever. With all the workarounds kids have to restrictions on their digital social tools, it's way too easy for them to break the rules and hack the parental controls. And the research backs me up (see Byrne, 2009).

Participatory Media, Participatory Parenting

Because social media use is almost as individual as the way we live our lives, it's problematic for parents to extrapolate family policies about it from the news. Social media research can explain the nature of the media environments and report trends in people's use, but the only way we can understand our children's experiences in social media is to talk with them. Even friending them on Facebook and checking in on their timelines every now and then hardly tells us how positive or negative their experiences are overall—even if they aren't branching out beyond Facebook. Checking in on them is just a freeze frame of the ongoing social interactions of their peer group. It doesn't tell the whole story in another way too: we're seeing whatever's on the page out of context—the context of their peer group's experience. We can't fully understand what we see there without asking them.

Social media researcher danah boyd explains this with the term "social steganography," describing a smart tactic some teens have to spare their parents unwarranted concern about what they see in social media. Here's an example:

> Carmen and her mother are close. As far as Carmen's concerned, she has nothing to hide from her mother so she's happy to have her mom as her "friend" on Facebook. Of course, Carmen's mom doesn't always understand the social protocols on Facebook, and Carmen sometimes gets frustrated. She hates that her mom comments on nearly every post,

because it "scares everyone away.... Everyone kind of disappears after the mom post.... It's just uncool having your mom all over your wall. That's just lame." Still, she knows that her mom means well and she sometimes uses this pattern to her advantage. While Carmen welcomes her mother's presence, she also knows her mother overreacts. In order to avoid a freak out, Carmen will avoid posting things that have a high likelihood of mother misinterpretation. This can make communication tricky at times and Carmen must work to write in ways that are interpreted differently by different people.

When Carmen broke up with her boyfriend, she "wasn't in the happiest state." The breakup happened while she was on a school trip and her mother was already nervous. Initially, Carmen was going to mark the breakup with lyrics from a song that she had been listening to, but then she realized that the lyrics were quite depressing and worried that if her mom read them, she'd "have a heart attack and think that something is wrong." She decided not to post the lyrics. Instead, she posted lyrics from Monty Python's "Always Look on the Bright Side of Life." This strategy was effective. Her mother wrote her a note saying that she seemed happy which made her laugh. But her closest friends knew that this song appears in the movie when the characters are about to be killed. They reached out to her immediately to see how she was really feeling. (boyd, 2010b)

Even so, becoming familiar with the social media our children use—through following them on Instagram, playing online games, texting with them on cell phones, or whatever's appropriate for one's own family—is a good idea, for several reasons. It means we're using social media enough to have informed conversations with our children, informed as much about the media as our kids (hopefully with in-person communication as well). Understanding how social media works increases communication opportunities and makes our guidance more relevant and thus credible to our children. Though using technology with our kids shouldn't become a tool for constant surveillance or provide a false sense of security—it will not (and should not) show us all that they're up to—it does remove a lot of the mystery from their online and on-phone experiences, which reduces anxiety and the chance of overreacting and jeopardizing the routine communication that's protective and increases mutual trust and understanding. Another reason is that it shifts the focus of our parenting from technology back to where it still needs to be: the child and his or her personal development and social literacy.

"In the same way that parents dictate children's sleeping, eating, and playing patterns, there is a need for deep guidance of technology use," wrote Sarita Yardi and Amy Bruckman (2011). "For children, we want to support parents' desire to monitor and manage their children's social media use. For teens, we want to support authoritative parenting practices while respecting teens' growing personal domains."

Parenting from the Inside Out

Parenting has never been easy, but technology doesn't make it exponentially harder. What we see of young people's behavior in social media is, generally, the sometimes posed, sometimes exaggerated, and sometimes confused outward expression of their own experience of life and relationships that's sometimes hard to understand from the outside.

If parents really want to understand a cyberbullying incident, for example, they need the essential perspective of their children, because each case is as unique as the children and their social dynamic at the time. Just like bullying, cyberbullying can only be understood from the inside out, rather than from the perspective of adults on the outside looking in. One motivation for a spike in school drama or some bullying behavior can be attention-seeking. Think about how little children get approval and reality checks from their parents with "Mom, watch me!" or "Dad, look at this!" As they grow, the attention-seeking gradually shifts more to peers—part of the bedrock of school social drama.

"Here's where we run into a major component of bullying," wrote danah boyd (2010a) after weeks of on-location qualitative research.

> In a world of brands and marketing, there's a sentiment that there is no such thing as bad attention. Countless teens are desperately seeking attention. And there's nothing like 'starting drama' to guarantee both attention and entertainment. So teens jump in, adding fuel to the flame because it's fun. They know that it hurts, but it also feels good sometimes too. And this is what makes music videos like Eminem & Rihanna's 'Love the Way You Lie' resonate with both adults and teens. The drama is half the fun, even when it hurts like hell.

So those are some of the conditions leading to what we call cyberbullying. Teens certainly hear us using the term more and more, and so they'll tell you that it's bad because that's the way we present it to them, but it doesn't mean a whole lot to them. They have a really hard time identifying just the negative parts of the chaotic, complex, shape-shifting genie of school life and stuffing that into adults' neat little bottle labeled Cyberbullying. If that whole amorphous genie were completely bad, it might be a little easier, but not much. Plus, relationships also have histories or backgrounds, so history is part of the social-drama genie too, and—when identifying what went wrong between two people or with a group—we often have to ask the individuals to add in history to deconstruct and get to the bottom of what's behind a particular incident. As boyd (2010a) puts it, "combating bullying is not going to be easy, but it's definitely not going to happen if we don't dive deep in the mess that underpins it and surrounds it." Because, depending on the day, the child, the context, the backstory, and so on, the drama is fun, painful, empowering, cruel, humorous, exhausting, entertaining, a joke, a crime—or no big deal.

Where All Participants Learn

Not just for "all participants" in a game, virtual world, social networking site, or classroom but in a home, too, trust and respect grow when all parties are learning, and learning happens when participants are communicating about their experiences. Experiential learning results from the experience itself, but that's not enough. It also requires reflection on or articulation of what happened in the experience. So it helps kids to learn from and make the most of their experiences in social media when their parents talk with them about what was going on. Friending their kids and checking in on them every now and then on Facebook, which can provide talking points; the same is true with video games. If parents can't play with their kids in console, social, or multiplayer online games, they can take an interest in their children's play and occasionally ask them about what they're observing—not to the point of extreme annoyance but with an open mind or curiosity.

Stephne Heppell (2012) has said, "Children are a tight little cycle of iteration" when they're playing video games. They'll see something happen to their avatar on the screen, and they'll form a hypothesis about what will happen next. But something happens that proves their hypothesis wrong and they're on to another one. "In that cycle of observe, question, hypothesize, test, they're problem-solving a lot in games," he says. "Solving problems is important—coping with surprises is important. Talking about how you did it is fundamental. So you have to have those. That's a key role for parents in all this."

Conclusion

Now that we have two healthy, growing bodies of research around youth online—social media and youth online risk—we can now parent young media users more calmly and intelligently, more like the way we've guided them in their offline lives, than in the Web's first two decades. Thankfully, we are less subject to alarmist online-safety messaging and less binary in our thinking about what happens with digital media (e.g., online *or* offline, bully *or* victim, private *or* public), realizing that new media and technologies are not really the context of the expression and actions that appear in them. The contexts are still for the most part home and school.

References

boyd, d. (2008). Taken out of context: American teen sociality in networked publics. Retrieved from http://www.danah.org/papers/TakenOutOfContext.pdf

boyd, d. (2010a). Bullying has little resonance with teenagers. Retrieved from http://dmlcentral. net/blog/danah-boyd/bullying-has-little-resonance-teenagers

boyd, d. (2010b). Social steganography: learning to hide in plain sight. Retrieved from http:// dmlcentral.net/blog/danah-boyd/social-steganography-learning-hide-plain-sight

Byrne, S. (2009). Sahara Byrne on parent vs. child reports of internet behaviors. Retrieved from http://cyber.law.harvard.edu/interactive/events/luncheons/2009/12/byrne

Byrne, S., & Lee, T. (2011). Toward predicting youth resistance to internet risk prevention Strategies. *Journal of Broadcasting & Electronic Media*, 55(1), 90–113. doi:10.1080/08838 151.2011.546255

CarolinaLive.com. (2009). McMaster criticizes internet safety report. Retrieved from http:// www.carolinalive.com/news/news_story.aspx?id=246693#.UciVEdjm_Tp

Collier, A. (2012). Global collective of information: student. Retrieved from http://www.net-familynews.org/global-collective-of-information-student

Frontline. (2009). Video Games 101. Retrieved from http://www.pbs.org/wgbh/pages/front-line/digitalnation/learning/games-that-teach/video-games-101.html

Heppell, S. (2012). The key role of parents. Retrieved from http://www.youtube.com/watch?v= 5lHELWM2TEQ&feature=share

Jenkins, H. (2007). Reconsidering digital immigrants. Retrieved from http://henryjenkins. org/2007/12/reconsidering_digital_immigran.html

Jenkins, H. (2010). Raising the digital generation: what parents need to know about digital media & learning. Retrieved from http://henryjenkins.org/2010/10/raising_the_digital_genera-tion.html

Lenhart, A. (2012). Teens, smartphones & texting. *Pew Internet and American Life Project*. Retrieved from http://pewinternet.org/Reports/2012/Teens-and-smartphones/Summary-of-findings. aspx

Lenhart, A., et al. (2011). Teens, kindness and cruelty on social network sites. *Pew Internet and American Life Project*. Retrieved fromhttp://pewinternet.org/Reports/2011/ Teens-and-social-media/Part-4/Dos-and-donts-of-online-behavior.aspx

Magid, L. (2009). Study challenges AGs on predator danger. Retrieved from http://news.cnet. com/8301-19518_3-10151959-238.html

Marwick, A. (2008). To catch a predator? The MySpace Moral Panic. Retrieved from http://first-monday.org/ojs/index.php/fm/article/viewArticle/2152/1966#p2

Patching J., & Hinduja, S. of the Cyberbullying Research Center (2010). Cyberbullying: Identification, Prevention and Response. Retrieved from http://www.cyberbullying.us/ Cyberbullying_Identification_Prevention_Response_Fact_Sheet.pdf

Ray, B. (2011). Q&A: Cathy Davidson on the brain science of attention and transforming schools and workplaces in the digital age. Retrieved from http://spotlight.macfound.org/ featured-stories/entry/qa-cathy-davidson-on/

Reich, J. (2009). Better strategies needed for school internet access. *The Washington Post.* Retrieved from http://www.washingtonpost.com/wpdyn/content/article/2009/07/10/AR2009071003459.html

Schofield Clark, L. (2012a). The Parent App: Understanding Families in a Digital Age. Retrieved from http://digitalparenting.wordpress.com/2012/06/11/the-parent-app-understanding-families-in-a-digital-age/

Schofield Clark, L. (2012b). *The Parent App: Understanding Families in the Digital Age.* New York, NY: Oxford University Press.

Steel, E. (2009). The case for age verification [interview]. Retrieved from http://blogs.wsj.com/digits/2009/01/13/the-case-for-age-verification/

Steeves, V. (2012). Young Canadians in a wired world phase III: talking to youth and parents about life online. Retrieved from http://mediasmarts.ca/research-policy

Stepanek, M. (2010). Ethically challenged? Retrieved from http://www.ssireview.org/blog/entry/ethically_challenged

Turkle, S. Always-on/always-on-you: the tethered self. Retrieved from http://sodacity.net/system/files/Sherry-Turkle_The-Tethered-Self.pdf

Yardi, S., & Bruckman, A. (2011). Social and technical challenges in parenting teens' social media use. In *Proceedings of the SIGCHI Conference on Human Factors in Computing Systems,* (pp. 3237–3246).

Ybarra, M., & Mitchell, K. (2007). Internet prevention messages: targeting the right online behaviors. *Archives of Pediatrics and Adolescent Medicine, 161*(2), 138–145. doi:10.1001/archpedi.161.2.138D

CHAPTER 16

Conclusion

Amy B. Jordan, Daniel Romer, and Michael Rich

Media and the Well-Being of Children and Adolescents traverses the plethora of roles that media have assumed in the modern experience of "growing up." Many observers argue that children's greater access to media and the often age-inappropriate content to which they are exposed have hastened the transition into adulthood (American Psychological Association, 2010) and have increased young people's participation in risky behaviors (Escobar-Chaves & Anderson, 2008). Others worry that parents and other caregiving adults have been pushed aside by media technology and the impenetrable bubble of youth culture (Buckingham, 2000). But it is also clear that media have opened up new avenues for learning and opportunities for connecting that have enriched the lives of young audiences. A recent study by Grunwald and Associates (2013) of a national sample of nearly 1,000 U.S. parents found that a majority of parents believe that mobile devices and applications "offer fun, engaging ways of learning, connecting, and communicating" and that many parents believe that these technologies "teach academic skills and content" (p. 2). Additionally, observers like Marwick and boyd (2010) and McGonigal (2011) have shown that media technology, when harnessed to its fullest potential, can foster more positive self-concepts and self-identities, and can develop new social, cognitive, and physical skills.

The study of children, adolescents, and media is vast and growing. Understanding the role of media in modern childhood requires a truly interdisciplinary perspective, as media influences children's cognition, social relationships, and physical health. The media we use and the ways that we use them shape the contexts of the home, the school, the neighborhood, and the culture. To this end, we have brought together experts who represent the fields of communication, psychology, education, sociology, business, and medicine. Since so much of our research is relegated to the individual silos of our academic disciplines, this book provides a unique opportunity to think broadly about how media shape the experience of growing up. The authors who have contributed to this book offer diverse perspectives on media, and they provide compelling insights into the challenges and benefits facing today's "digital natives." The authors suggest that the effects of media on children are variable, providing potential for enhancing their lives and expanding their experience, as well as risks for harm to their physical, mental, and social health. What matters most is not the media, per se, but rather the content of the media, the context of media use, and the characteristics of the child.

As the book opens, Bleakley and colleagues (chapter 1) provide a picture of the ubiquity of media in American homes. Virtually all families with children own a television set (usually, multiple sets), and the vast majority now subscribe to cable or satellite and have access to the internet. Adolescents, in particular, own many personal media devices, from smartphones to MP3 players to hand-held game devices. Young people's media-saturated environment offers, sometimes quite aggressively, a multitude of options for obtaining entertainment and information of all kinds. And while traditional broadcast of media content continues to dominate the media landscape, audiences are now communicating directly with each other without intermediation by traditional media producers. This is especially true for adolescents and young adults who now can control YouTube channels (O'Leary, 2013), blogs, Twitter accounts, and Facebook pages. This development promises to dramatically change the way adolescents express themselves and view each other. The rise of an adolescent subculture in the post–World War II period was driven by the music business and advertisers who quickly recognized that an affluent market of baby boomers was ready to purchase music, clothes, and other products (see Jamieson & Romer, 2008). With the development of the internet, today's young people are increasingly able to create their own content and draw wide audiences in the process.

Strategies to Shield Youth from Harmful Media Influences

It will be interesting to see how the rise in young people's control over media content changes the way they use media and the ways media influence them. Many of the concerns about media influences on youth derive from content created by adults. Indeed, adults tend to be somewhat hypocritical about the influence of media, since it is adults who have traditionally controlled what young people see and hear. For example, adults prohibit alcohol sales to youth under the age of 21 and direct media campaigns to discourage underage drinking (www.samhsa.gov/underagedrinking), yet we allow alcohol to be advertised in youth magazines and alcohol products to be placed in television programming that targets youth (The Center on Alcohol Marketing and Youth, 2012; King, et al., 2009; see also chapter 5 by Strasburger). In addition, we allow advertisers to promote foods high in calories and low in nutritional value to families with children. Borzekowski (chapter 3) lays out the many ways in which media contribute to eating disorders, while Harris (chapter 4) argues that food and beverage marketing practices have shaped the way children think about food and have played a key role in the epidemic of childhood obesity facing the United States today.

It is encouraging that media advocacy groups such as the National Campaign to Prevent Teen and Unwanted Pregnancy harness the power of entertainment media by working with Hollywood writers and producers to include safer-sex messages in television dramas and comedies popular with teens (see Nightingale, chapter 13). These efforts can work to counteract the potentially adverse effects of widespread sexual content available on television and in films. Brown and colleagues (chapter 6) examine the evidence for the effects of exposure to sexual media content and early sexual initiation, sexual risk taking, and teen pregnancy. We encourage other advocacy groups to develop similar strategies to help young people make healthy decisions about life-changing behaviors, such as unprotected sex and drug abuse.

The fragmented rating system in place in the United States makes it challenging for parents to follow through on their media content concerns. As the survey of parents described by Bleakley and colleagues confirmed (Chapter 1), most parents find our rating systems unhelpful. Ratings of motion pictures were developed to free media producers from censorship by providing information directly to parents about the acceptability of movie content. The ratings are values-based and, since social values change over time (in part due to media exposure), ratings change with them. Analysis of the movie rating system, for example, finds that violence is increasingly condoned in films rated acceptable for children older than 12 (the PG-13 category) (Leone & Barowski, 2011; Nalkur, Jamieson, & Romer, 2010), even though research consistently finds that exposure to such content teaches youth to use aggressive solutions to conflict (Anderson & Bushman, 2002). Prot and colleagues (chapter 7) lay out the evidence for the effects of violent video games on aggressive behavior, another category of media content that is subject to an uninformative rating system (Haninger & Thompson, 2004). Despite come controversy about the effects of violent video games, like that around violent movies and television before it, what cannot be ignored is the growing body of rigorous scientific evidence associating desensitization, anxiety, and increased aggressive thoughts and behaviors with violent game play. In the wake continuing rampage shootings involving young perpetrators of violence, research is clearly needed to create an evidence-based system of ratings that recognizes the potentially harmful consequences of violent portrayals in the media (see Bushman & Newman, 2013). One helpful approach would be to adopt a system that can be used across all media and that is more age-graded and sensitive to violence.

With the ever-increasing availability of media content, it will be impossible to shield youth from all unhealthy influences. Indeed, some harmful content, such as cyberbullying and sexting, derives from youth themselves. Livingstone (chapter 8) considers the risks and harm of internet use, drawing from a large-scale study of 25 countries involved in the EU Kids Online network. She writes, however, that children must learn to "face the unexpected, to take calculated risks, and, within reason, cope when things go wrong…." She notes that "developmental psychologists are clear—without facing some degree of adversity, children do not become resilient" (p. 143). Collier (chapter 15) also points out that the popular press often exaggerates the online harm to which youth are subject, whether from predators, adult victimizers, or each other. She also encourages parents to realize the benefits of online expression by youth, to stay informed about their children's use of the internet, and to recognize that most of the harmful interaction that occurs online often mirrors what happens offline. Thus, the online world is not too different from what children have always faced in the offline world.

Beneficial Uses of Media

Several authors consider the beneficial effects of media for the social and educational development of both younger and older children. In chapter 2, Takeuchi and Levine lay out the many contexts that shape how young people think about and use media—from the microsystems of the family and the peer group to the macrosystem of cultural values. Using Bronfenbrenner's ecological systems theory to guide their understanding, they argue that media use both reflects and shapes many systems in which children grow and learn. In chapter 9, Ybarra discusses how new media technologies have been successful in the fight against the spread of AIDS in Africa and in encouraging smoking cessation in Turkey. In chapter 10, Lemish describes how media have been used to help vulnerable children struggling with very difficult circumstances, including natural disasters and war. Chapters 11 and 12 focus on the educational opportunities presented by media used by very young children. Wartella and Lauricella (chapter 11) review studies on the new field of digital media use by babies and toddlers, while Calvert and Richards (chapter 12) discuss young children's parasocial relationships with media characters and the unique learning advantages provided by their TV "friendships." Finally, Cohen and colleagues from Sesame Workshop (chapter 14) provide a unique look at the development of an educational program directed at preschoolers and their military families. All of these authors emphasize the beneficial effects of media and the opportunities that media programming provides to enrich and enliven the development of children and adolescents.

As we consider all the many ways in which media can be used in today's world, it will be increasingly important to consider how we manage the wealth of information that is continuously available on all manner of screens (e.g., Giedd, 2012). One result of this information glut is the rise of multitasking, that is, attending to more than one source of content at once and, as some would argue, not spending quality time with any one source (Ophir, Nass, & Wagner, 2009). This behavior is facilitated by the internet, which allows users to view multiple sites while also keeping track of incoming messages via chats, email, and various other feeds. Some have argued that this type of processing encourages short attention spans and difficulties synthesizing longer forms of written content, such as books and essays (e.g., Carr, 2010). This may be a source of concern for education, since reading complex content and completing intricate tasks are important skills to master, especially for the STEM (science, technology, engineering, mathematics) subjects so essential to our future. A recent study of adolescents and young adults found that book reading is associated with better school performance, and it doesn't tend to detract from civic and athletic activity (Romer, Bagdasarov, & More, 2013). Young book readers were found to use the internet at moderate levels without suffering from ill effects and to be among the most well-adjusted of youth in both mental and physical health.

Youth who adjust well to information overload appear to do so by using media primarily to learn about the world rather than simply being entertained by it (Romer et al., 2013). Media researchers are still trying to understand the mechanisms by which overuse of certain entertainment media contributes to negative outcomes. For example, heavy use of television by young people has long been associated with adverse outcomes, such as poor school performance (Sharif & Sargent, 2006), symptoms of depression (Potts & Sanchez, 1994), and obesity (Gortmaker & Dietz, 1993), leading health professionals to recommend limitations on screen media use (American Academy of Pediatrics, 2001). Yet, when examined more closely, using methods that are sensitive to multitasking and complex media environments, associations were not found between reported total screen time and obesity risk. It was the proportion of time that youth paid attention to television, but not video games or computers, that was strongly associated with increased body mass index (BMI) (Bickham, Blood, Walls, Shrier, & Rich, 2013). More recently, there are concerns that heavy internet communication (Ybarra, Alexander, & Mitchell, 2005) and video game playing are linked to poor mental health (Mentzoni et al., 2011). Despite established criteria and psychiatric treatment of internet addiction disorder (IAD) in Korea, China, and other countries, the question of whether one can be addicted to interactive media like video games or the internet has been debated by the American medical community, who have been reporting increasing concerns from patients and families over the past two decades. Because of limited research evidence on this condition in the United States, the recently published fifth edition of the *Diagnostic and Statistical Manual of Mental Disorders* (DSM-5) has included IAD only in the appendix as requiring further study. Given the complexity of rapidly evolving media technologies and applications, particularly by youth who are "early adopters," ongoing study using focused methods is required to determine which uses of which media are associated with adverse outcomes, and whether media use directly contributes to these outcomes or whether it displaces healthier, more adaptive engagement with the world. Clearly, better understanding of these "media effects" will enable parents and caregivers to direct their efforts to the sources of the adverse outcomes rather than to their symptoms.

Promising Uses of Media

It is our hope and expectation that this volume presents the most salient and cutting-edge research of the field. But we are also well aware that new issues and opportunities emerge each day. One understudied area (at least in the academic realm) has been the role of new media technologies in assisting those who are differently abled. Most of what is known in this arena has been based on case studies and published in specialty journals. It is critical to carry discussions of media and disabilities into mainstream social science research in order to bring together experts in media with experts in learning to broaden both the knowledge base and the audience for such research. For example, anecdotal evidence and small sample studies have shown that nonverbal autistic children seem to benefit tremendously from iPad and smartphone apps that are customized to autistic children's unique communication needs (see http://www.autismspeaks.org/family-services/community-connections/technology-and-autism for examples). Even traditional media like television have provided a valuable resource to immigrants learning the language and customs of their adopted country (Katz, 2010); interactive media can support and supplement the needs of young people facing a wider array of physical, mental, and social challenges (e.g., Mechling & Bishop, 2011).

New media technologies can provide children with valuable resources and information when the adults in their world feel dangerous or judgmental. In the Netherlands, researchers are testing the efficacy of a website for adolescents and young adults who have been exposed to family violence, where the primary goal is to provide peer support and information to address mental health and behavioral problems and to end the cycle of violence (van Rosmalen-Nooijens, Prins, Vergeer, Wong, & Lagro-Janssen, 2013). In another example, the Anar Foundation in Spain has created a billboard with a message and a hotline number that can only be seen by people shorter than 4'5" (generally age 10 and younger). The secret, according to their video describing the process, is a precisely serrated surface that reflects light differently to those looking from above and below a specified height (http://www.youtube.com/watch?v=6zoCDyQSH0o). The ad is especially designed for children who may be traveling with their abuser, as the child receives one message while the adult receives another.

The authors who have contributed to this book have suggested many opportunities for future research, interventions, and policy initiatives. For many, media literacy and media education are seen as the answer to the thorny problem of how to protect children while also protecting the free speech rights of media makers. A recent report from the National Academies Keck Futures Initiative (2012) asks the important question of what it means to provide media literacy to youth who have literally grown up consuming and creating media on every imaginable platform. The answer will lie in helping young people navigate safely, but also in helping them cope with the multiple and ubiquitous demands on their attention and the information overload that comes from having the world at their fingertips.

In addition to teaching youth how to deal with media, we have much to learn about how children use media to deal with the world around them. As we enter into an era in which higher education is migrating from physical campuses to online websites through massive open online course (MOOC) structures, it is clear that digital media experience in childhood can provide an important foundation for learning in the young adult years. We need to ask ourselves, what are the skills that learners will need? How can we integrate the media technologies that young people have learned to love into educational settings in which they love to learn?

As we continue on the path to understanding how media can contribute to the well-being of children and adolescents, we must recognize the hurdles to be surmounted. First, the ways in which we measure the amount, content, and context of media use must develop to keep pace with the rapidly evolving technologies that youth use. Rich and colleagues at the Center on Media and Child Health have developed a protocol which they call MYME (Measuring Youth Media Exposure) (Rich et al., 2007). MYME uses smartphone technology and video recording devices to capture media use in real time and in real-life contexts.

Second, it is essential that we place greater emphasis on bringing our research to those who would benefit from it the most. Parents have many questions about whether and when to introduce media to their children, and how to monitor it. Our research speaks to their concerns, but it doesn't always reach them in ways that are accessible or understandable. Additionally, while producers of youth-oriented media are quite skilled at creating innovative and attention-grabbing content, they rarely have training in child development. We should help. Policymakers, too, need access to information that can guide sound, empirically driven policies that speak to the needs of parents, respect the rights of producers, and value the health and well-being of children. In this spirit, we look forward to continued cooperation among researchers, child development experts, media producers, and policymakers as the exciting new hyperconnected media world unfolds and advances.

References

American Academy of Pediatrics Committee on Public Education. (2001). Children, adolescents, and television. *Pediatrics, 107*, 423–426.

American Psychological Association. (2010). Report of the APA task force on the sexualization of girls. Retrieved from http://www.apa.org/pi/women/programs/girls/report-full.pdf

Anderson, C. A., & Bushman, B. J. (2002). The effects of media violence on society. *Science, 295*, 2377–2378.

Bickham, D. S., Blood, E. A., Walls, C. E., Shrier, L. A., & Rich, M. (2013). Characteristics of screen media use associated with higher BMI in young adolescents. *Pediatrics, 131*, 935–941.

Bushman, B., & Newman, K. (Eds.). (2013). *Youth violence: What we need to know. A report to Congress.* Arlington, VA: National Science Foundation.

Carr, N. (2010). *The shallows: What the Internet is doing to our brains.* New York, NY: W. W. Norton.

Center on Alcohol Marketing and Youth. (2012). Youth exposure to alcohol advertising on television, 2001–2009. Retrieved from http://www.camy.org/research/Youth_Exposure_to_Alcohol_Ads_on_TV_Growing_Faster_Than_Adults/index.html.

Escobar-Chaves, S. L., & Anderson, C. A. (2008). Media and risky behaviors. *The Future of Children, 18*, 147–180.

Giedd, J. M. (2012). The digital revolution and adolescent brain evolution. *Journal of Adolescent Health, 51*, 101–105.

Gortmaker, S., & Dietz, W. (1993). TV or not TV: Fat is the question. *Pediatrics, 91*, 499–501.

Grunwald and Associates, LLC. (2013). Living and learning with mobile devices: What parents think about mobile devices for early childhood and K–12 learning. Retrieved from http://www.grunwald.com/pdfs/Grunwald%20Mobile%20Study%20public%20report.pdf

Haninger, K., & Thompson, K. M. (2004). Content and ratings of teen-rated video games. *JAMA, 291*, 856–865.

Jamieson, P. E., & Romer, D. (Eds.) (2008). *The changing portrayal of adolescents in the media since 1950.* New York, NY: Oxford University Press.

Katz, V. S. (2010). How children of immigrants use media to connect their families to the community. *Journal of Children and Media, 4*, 298–315.

Keck Futures Initiative (2012). The informed brain in a digital world. Retrieved from http://www.keckfutures.org/conferences/informed-brain.html

King, C., Siegel, M., Jernigan, D. H., Wulach, L., Ross, C., Dixon, K., & Ostroff, J. (2009). Adolescent exposure to alcohol advertising in magazines: An evaluation of advertising placement in relation to underage youth readership. *Journal of Adolescent Health, 45*, 626–633.

Leone, R., & Barowski, L. (2011). MPAA ratings creep. *Journal of Children and Media, 5*(1), 53–68.

Marwick, A., & boyd, D. (2011). I tweet honestly, I tweet passionately: Twitter users, context collapse, and the imagined audience. *New Media and Society, 13*, 96–113.

McGonigal, J. (2011). *Reality is broken: Why games make us better and how they can change the world.* New York, NY: Penguin Press.

Mentzoni, R. A., Brunborg, G. S., Molde, H., Myrseth, H., Skouverøe, K. J., Hetland, J., & Pallesen, S. (2011). Problematic video game use: Estimated prevalence and associations with mental and physical health. *Cyberpsychology, Behavior, and Social Networking, 14*, 591–596.

Nalkur, P., Jamieson, P. E., & Romer, D. (2010). The effectiveness of the Motion Picture Association of America's rating system in screening explicit violence and sex in top-ranked movies from 1950 to 2006. *Journal of Adolescent Health, 47*, 440–447. doi:10.1016/j. jadohealth.2010.01.09.

O'Leary, A. (April 12, 2013). The woman with 1 billion clicks, Jenna Marbles. *New York Times.* Retrieved from http·//www.nytimes.com/2013/04/14/fashion/jenna-marbles.html?_r=0

Ophir, E., Nass, C., & Wagner, A. D. (2009). Cognitive control in media multitaskers. *Proceedings of the National Academy of Science, 106*, 15583–15587.

Potts, R., & Sanchez, D. (1994). Television viewing and depression: No news is good news. *Journal of Broadcasting and Electronic Media, 38*, 79–90.

Rich, M., Bickham, D., Koren, S., Aneja, P., de Moor, C., & Shrier, L. (2007). Measuring youth media exposure (MYME): A pilot study. *Journal of Adolescent Health, 40*(2): S5–S6.

Romer, D., Bagdasarov, Z., & More, E. (2013). Older vs. newer media and the well-being of United States youth: Results from a national longitudinal panel. *Journal of Adolescent Health, 52*, 613–619.

Sharif, I., & Sargent, J. D. (2006). Association between television, movie, and video game exposure and school performance. *Pediatrics, 118*, e1061–e1070.

Van Rosmalen-Nooijens, K, Prins, J. B., Vergeer, M., Wong, S. H. L., & Lagro-Janssen, A.L.M. (2013). Young people, adult worries: RCT of an internet-based self-support method "Feel the ViBe" for children, adolescents and young adults exposed to family violence, a study protocol. *BMC Public Health, 13*, 1–11.

Ybarra, M., Alexander, C., & Mitchell, K. J. (2005). Depressive symptomatology, youth internet use, and online interactions: A national survey. *Journal of Adolescent Health, 36*, 9–18.

INDEX

Page numbers followed by *f* or *t* indicate figures or tables, respectively. Numbers followed by n indicate notes.